ID0873888

Reflections on Jesus and Socrates

Reflections on Jesus and Socrates

Word and Silence

PAUL W. GOOCH

Yale University Press New Haven and London

To my family

Designed by James J. Johnson and set in
Stempel Garamond types by Northeastern
Graphic Services.
Printed in the United States of America by
BookCrafters, Inc. Chelsea, Michigan.

Library of Congress Cataloging-in-Publica-
tion Data

Gooch, Paul W.
Reflections on Jesus and Socrates: word
and silence / Paul W. Gooch.
p.   cm.
Includes index.
ISBN 0-300-06695-3 (alk. paper)

1. Jesus Christ. 2. Socrates. 3. Socrates—Death and burial. 4. Jesus Christ—
Crucifixion. I. Title.
B317.G66 1996
128—dc20   96-15792

A catalogue record for this book is available from the British Library.

The paper in this book meets the guide-
lines for permanence and durability of the
Committee on Production Guidelines for
Book Longevity of the Council on Library
Resources.

10 9 8 7 6 5 4 3 2 1

Contents

Preface

Rarely do our creations realize completely our original intentions. This book on Jesus and Socrates is no exception: indeed, when I first thought of what was to be my next project I never would have predicted this outcome. Instead, I planned to write about the philosophical problem of evil, picking up a theme from an earlier book. Dissatisfied with analyses that structured the problem simply as a conversation between skeptic and believer, I wanted to devote some attention to literary presentations of the problem. If novelists, playwrights, and poets do not generate watertight arguments about the compatibility of divine goodness with human misery, they nevertheless uncover layers of perplexity over human suffering. They hold up for our inspection a variety of stances toward evil, sometimes hinting at resolutions that seem forever to lie beyond the wit of our kind. Hoping that philosophical reflection might profit more from listening to the poets than from banishing them, I got to thinking at odd times and places about narrative genres. Soon I found myself wondering whether the stories I knew best—about Jesus and about Socrates—would yield anything of philosophical interest for my project.

And then I sat down to write. It was a deliberate early decision that, against all my training, I would not write about the thoughts of other thinkers who had themselves thought about earlier thinkers on the subjects of my interest. Partly that was a pragmatic matter: the literature of commentary and criticism on Jesus and Socrates is measureless. If I glanced favorably upon one school of thought, scholarly etiquette would require nods or shakes of the head about others. I cannot pretend, of course, that I have written in a vacuum; but I knew that yielding to the temptation of writing the first footnote would commit me to a prolonged countertextual conversation with innumerable authors demanding each their equal time. I lacked, frankly, both the heart and the mind for such a venture. But there was in the end more to it than that. For what took my interest, indeed seized and shook that interest, were Jesus and Socrates themselves—or, more precisely, these two characters as they are presented in gospel and dialogue. Their hearts and minds pulled mine into a reflective space where I had to encounter not just my anticipated themes of suffering and injustice and divine goodness but whatever it was that lay in the centers of these characters.

So I read gospel and dialogue, dialogue and gospel. Initially intrigued by the contrast between defensive strategies in the silence of Jesus and the arguments of Socrates, I started with Matthew. It was in his Jesus that I began to learn of the poignant interplay between not knowing and not speaking: I also found myself beginning to suspect that I could not avoid the awkward category of obedience if ever I were to write adequately about this character. But I put that off, for prayer was also an essential category. It was to this theme in Luke that I next turned my attention, writing a chapter that I soon saw could be framed by a discussion of the problem of evil, the perplexity that got me started in the first place. Socrates kept finding his place alongside Jesus as I turned over these themes. When I considered love in the Gospel of John, the connection with the *Symposium* and *Phaedrus* was natural; I did not, however, expect the vulnerabilities of Johannine love to contrast so sharply with the divine nature of Socratic love. Naturally again, the *Apology* and *Crito* were in my mind as I dealt with trial, defense, and death; but those two dialogues raised once more the issue of obedience. Given that I had to confront that issue in Jesus, and that there was only one gospel about which I had not yet written, I read Mark for that theme—and discovered that I had to begin with authority. Near the end of my writing I needed to complete my third chapter by contrasting Socrates' apologia with the silence of Jesus, but in working through that defense I came to see that these differences arose in each of them from a like place of obedience. With discoveries like this from the beginning of my writing to the end, the product of these philosophical reflections on Jesus and Socrates differed from anything I might have foreseen.

PREFACE

If reflective results cannot be quite predicted, neither can they be programmed with precision. Time is what's required, and I wish here to thank the University of Toronto for its enlightened leave policy. In the winter of 1992 I left the School of Graduate Studies to write for six months, then took a second six months in the summer of 1993 after a year as acting dean of the school. Returning in January 1994 as vice-dean, I drew from time to time upon the goodwill of my obliging colleagues and completed the book by the end of summer 1994. For my place of quiet refuge for reflection and writing, I thank University College in the University of Toronto.

To colleagues and friends who upon learning of this project added their encouragement in word and gesture, my thanks. Sometimes an expression of genuine interest meant more than could be known. And I owe some special debts: to Kem Luther, who read with the sensitivity of a careful stylist some early parts of the manuscript; and to Ansley Tucker, priest and wise listener, for her acuity, which helped much to shape my responses to these ancient stories. Finally, thanks to Judith Calvert and Dan Heaton at Yale University Press, best of editors.

I dedicate the book to my family, first and always to Pauline, Jennifer, and Alison, but to all who share as family in my life as well.

Acknowledgments

Scripture quotations identified as REB are from the Revised English Bible, copyright Oxford University Press and Cambridge University Press, 1989.

Scripture quotations identified as NRSV are from the New Revised Standard Version of the Bible, copyright Division of Christian Education of the National Council of the Churches of Christ in the USA. Used by permission. All rights reserved.

The translation of Psalm 38.12–15 at the end of Chapter 3 is from *The Book of Common Prayer* (1979) of the Episcopal Church of the United States of America. The Liturgy of the Palms in Chapter 5 and the funeral prayers in Chapter 6 are from *The Book of Alternative Services* of the Anglican Church of Canada, copyright 1985; the prayers for deliverance quoted in Chapter 6 are from the Litany in *The Book of Common Prayer* of the Anglican Church of Canada, copyright 1962; both copyrights by the General Synod of the Anglican Church of Canada; used with permission.

Acknowledgment is hereby made for translations of the following passages in Plato:

The *Symposium* 216 quotation at the beginning of Chapter 1 is from *Symposium of Plato* (trans. Tom Griffith), Collins Harvill, 1989. The *Phaedrus* 279bc prayer in Chapter 4 is from *Plato: Phaedrus* (trans. Christopher Rowe), Aris & Phillips, 1986. Diotima's words at *Sympo-*

sium 209bc in Chapter 6 are from *The Symposium of Plato* (trans. Suzy Q. Groden), University of Massachusetts Press, 1970.

The quotations in Chapter 2 from Robert Bolt's *A Man for All Seasons* and from Bolt's preface to that play are used by permission of Random House, copyright 1960, 1962.

The quotation in Chapter 2 from Helen Gardner is found in *The Art of T. S. Eliot*, Faber and Faber, 1949, p. 133. Used by permission.

In Chapter 2, excerpts from *Murder in the Cathedral* by T. S. Eliot, copyright 1935 by Harcourt Brace & Company, renewed 1963 by T. S. Eliot, are reprinted by permission of the publisher, and outside the United States by permission of Faber and Faber Ltd.

The indictment of Socrates quoted in Chapter 3 is a translation of Xenophon, *Memorabilia* I.I.1, from W. K. C. Guthrie, *History of Greek Philosophy,* vol. III, Cambridge University Press, 1969, p. 382.

The Kierkegaard quotation at the beginning of Chapter 4 is taken from Alexander Dru, ed., *The Journals of Søren Kierkegaard,* 1938, p. 572, by permission of Oxford University Press.

At the end of Chapter 5, the excerpt from "The Dry Salvages," which appeared in *Four Quartets,* copyright 1941 by T. S. Eliot, renewed 1969 by Esme Valerie Eliot, is reprinted by permission of Harcourt Brace & Company, and outside the United States by permission of Faber and Faber Ltd.

The quotations from Edith Hamilton in Chapter 6 are from her introductions to the *Phaedo, Gorgias,* and *Phaedrus* in the *Collected Dialogues of Plato,* pages 40, 230, and 475. By permission of Princeton University Press.

Some of the material on Socratic love in Chapter 6 first appeared in a section of my chapter, "A Mind to Love: Friends and Lovers in Greek Philosophy," in *The Nature and Pursuit of Love* (ed. David Goicoechea), Prometheus Books 1995, on pages 90–95; it is presented here with permission in a somewhat revised form.

ONE

Jesus and Socrates

When he's serious, when he opens up and you see the real Socrates—I don't know if any of you has ever seen the figure inside. I saw it once, and it struck me as utterly godlike & golden and beautiful & wonderful.

—ALCIBIADES, *Symposium* 216 (T. Griffin, trans.)

Where does he get it from? What's the wisdom given to him? Isn't this the carpenter, Mary's son?

—TOWNSFOLK OF NAZARETH, in Mark 6

I START WITH TWO STORIES. The first is called Socrates at the Metropolitan Museum of Art. It takes place, as the title requires, in New York City; the time is late one Saturday afternoon. We are visiting friends whose children are of an age with our two daughters, and the day's tour has included the Met. There is too much to absorb; the competition for our attention—one gallery vying with the next, children vying with art and with each other—has become tiring. And closing time is upon us. The bell sounds, we thread our way back toward the entrance through room and corridor, one eye on our charges, the other on the walls. Suddenly the children stop, falling silent, all four looking up. We are in the presence of Jacques Louis David's large painting of the Death of Socrates.

There sits the unshackled Socrates, eternally poised on the brink of death. While one hand reaches for the cup the other confidently points heavenward; the light pours endlessly over his straight, resolute figure. His friends, bowed and bent, cover faces from their loss, raise hands of despair, weep out forever their inaudible grief. In the dark distance Xanthippe makes one last gesture of farewell. The bell rings again. Socrates continues to point to heaven; again the bell rings.

In the car's back seat on the way home, I tell the story of the death of Socrates to four uncharacteristically quiet children. Finished, I wait for questions about hemlock, or about how long it will take to get back to the house. Instead our older one says simply, "What a wonderful way to die."

[1]

It's a gray morning for the second story, Jesus at the University of Toronto. Too cold for an Ontario October, the air is still damp from yesterday's heavy rain. Around the large circle forming the center of the university's campus are stations for performances of the series of biblical plays in a medieval English drama, the York Cycle. At least the plays will take place outside today; yesterday the rain forced them onto the stage inside Convocation Hall. Our daughters had watched some Old Testament stories there, ending their day with the Slaughter of the Innocents, done vigorously with plastic dolls and swords. One zealous soldier (it may have been a colleague of mine) had hit too hard, decapitating one of the dolls, whose head bounced down an aisle. Perched high in a gallery, the girls found the scene hilarious. Can we come back tomorrow, asked the younger, and see the Crucifixion?

We are back today. Jesus has been arrested and arraigned, and it is time to crucify him. But today there is no balcony, no demarcated stage. We are together with the soldiers on the grass, and right here—here—is Jesus. We, with the children sitting on their raincoats on the ground— we are the mob. We cannot close our ears as hammer hits nails; we cannot avert our eyes as the cross is raised, then dropped into its prefashioned holder. We feel the cold on the unprotected body, the strain on bound arms; we notice the bare feet balanced tentatively on a small wedge of wood. And in all this, most strikingly, we feel complicitous. We do not jeer or mock along with the soldiers; but none of us protests, no one cries shame, no one gives comfort. Neither daughter says a word. Nor could we, driving home, quite say that it was only a play.

It may help to reveal a little of my purpose in beginning this book about Jesus and Socrates with these stories. They are my accounts, not some other family's stories; they are not about Jesus and Socrates themselves but about presentations of both of these figures; they expose different reactions to Socrates and Jesus, involving explanation and reflection, word and silence; they are about a knowledge and experience of both these deaths accessible to the unlearned and the learned alike.

In this book I will continue to tell, and retell, the deaths of Socrates and of Jesus. You know the stories, of course, and I will not repeat the narratives the way parents repeat tales at bedtime, with familiar phrases and responses, reminders that there is memory, and order, and a proper resolution for every difficulty. I will often return to episodes and details, in that way going over familiar territory; but it will be a search for yet more understanding of events that we thought we already knew. The telling is very much my own. It is not personal in the sense that it displays my own feelings directly; but it does reflect upon experience, the experience that readers of the stories of Socrates or Jesus have, or may have if they position themselves to see and understand. In that the focus of these studies is on experience, I attempt to make it clear that I do not speak of the historical Socrates as he might have lived apart from Plato's writings, or of the historical Jesus whose existence is independent of the Gospels. Those realities remain problematic. More accessible to us are presentations and representations of their lives, trials, and deaths; that narrative store is what informs our experience, and that is what we shall explore. It is no part of my design to deny the importance of more distanced and impersonal scholarly investigation into these matters. The aim, rather, is to hold up for inspection the standard accounts, available to all readers, of these two compelling figures, and to allow the inspection to be guided by what we find of life-and-death matters in our own experience. One need not be a specialist in any one branch of knowledge to enter the discussion. I take it as given that those who will join me in this exercise have all been shaped by a culture deeply influenced by accounts of the teachings and examples of Socrates and Jesus. In this way our own lives have become the meeting place for two men whose historical times did not intersect. By thinking of their interests and commitments, we will be able to draw parallels and strike contrasts that reflect back upon us more than they throw light upon either of our subjects.

Now that's been a long, tightly packed paragraph; it needs its many claims and assumptions pulled out into some wider space. I'll do that in the remainder of this introductory chapter. This introductory explanation might be skimmed over by those who enjoy eating the meal without having studied the menu, but it's best, I think, for readers to have some sense of the progression of courses before sitting down to dinner. They may have strong likes and dislikes; they may even have allergies to what will be set before them.

Part of what follows is an attempt to provide some basic information. In so doing I hope not to distort the main shape of scholarship on such matters; although a few of my comments may be provocative, this is not a book disclosing some brave new theory about Jesus or Socrates. In this ever-contentious world, of course, anything that one person thinks uncontroversial will be dismissed as wrongheaded by another informed critic. And because everyone has opinions on the figures and topics under scrutiny here, I won't succeed in putting even simple things quite the way others might.

That's a small warning. It may be worth entering a larger one, about my efforts to describe what is and what is not the approach these studies take. Because I have not consciously adopted any particular scholarly method, I cannot situate the reader to believe my work an example of one or other school of criticism. Undoubtedly different readers will discern different flavors; if I am not able to give a detailed recipe, I trust nonetheless that the work will be sampled and enjoyed for what it has turned out to be.

Our Knowledge of Jesus and Socrates

What are the sources of our knowledge of Jesus and Socrates? The answer seems straightforward. We know about Jesus not from his own writing, because he left nothing, but instead from four sources, called Gospels, all written after his death. The first three—Matthew, Mark, and Luke—get classed together as the Synoptics because they have a fair degree of commonality in their accounts of the ministry of Jesus; the fourth, John, is curiously different in detail, focus, and approach. There are other writings or reports of writings—some scraps and some more complete—that go by the name of gospels because they provide stories and sayings around the life and teaching of Jesus. None of them, however, has received the level of acceptance, either official or informal, across widely diverse communities of readers, that the Four Gospels have enjoyed from the earliest period.

The case of Socrates is not much different. He, too, left nothing from his own hand. His followers Plato and Xenophon give us postmortem accounts of his life, teaching, and death. While Socrates was alive, the playwright Aristophanes created a character bearing his name in *The Clouds,* though against our other evidence the portrait is comically exaggerated, even distorted. A few other followers pass on conversations as Socratic: Aeschines is said to have written seven dialogues, from which some quotations and passages survive. Plato's pupil Aristotle refers on several occasions to Socrates, often to comment on the relation between Socratic and Platonic beliefs.

So it seems that we should go to a quartet of writers for Jesus and rely on two or three authors for Socrates to learn of their lives and deaths. But of course it's not that straightforward. Any New Testament scholar or classicist would recognize what I've said as the start of a lecture that would go on to problematize each source of our knowledge of Socrates or of Jesus. For Socrates our fullest accounts come from Plato and Xenophon, but their portraits are very different in tone and purpose. They both wrote Defenses, speeches that Socrates makes at his trial; but the character and commitments revealed in those two speeches couldn't belong to the same personality. Even if we stay only with Plato's writings, it is difficult to generate a consistent reading of Socrates. He is very much the dominant speaker in Plato's dialogues, curiously absent in only a few later works; but over the course of the dialogues this Socrates espouses a series of beliefs and theories that don't always sit well together. Against the earlier Socratic profession of ignorance we find a grand metaphysical vision of Forms. Theories of the nature of the soul change: arguments for its immortality on grounds of its indivisibility must coexist with arguments that it is tripartite. In some places this Socrates says practically nothing good about pleasure; elsewhere he praises some pleasures as pure. And so on. The Socratic problem remains a puzzle whether we try to assemble pieces from different authors, or from different works by the same author, into the contours of a recognizable portrait.

In Jesus' case we don't have the challenge that Plato's Socrates gives us, of trying to reconcile a series of accounts across time from the same author. But New Testament scholars have much graver perplexities over authorship for their sources than do classicists for Socrates. None of the first three Gospels is signed, so to speak, by its author or authors. The fourth Gospel is signed by the "disciple Jesus loved," but that disciple refrains from revealing a name. So only ancient tradition assigns Matthew to the first Gospel, and Mark, Luke, and John respectively to theirs. True, authorship of many ancient works is known only through traditional attribution. But New Testament scholarship has developed a significant multinational industry whose products are theories, some minutely intricate, some highly speculative, about the composition of the Gospels. It is far too simple to assume Luke, say, as a source for our knowledge of Jesus; we must go on immediately to ask how Luke (the book, not the author) reflects its own sources for this knowledge. Its prologue refers to many authors and to original eyewitnesses. But we have only two other Synoptics. Does Luke contain events or teachings that appear in one or both of the other two? Does the language suggest a written account the author drew upon, and might that account be common to the others? Is there more than one such written source for Luke? There must have been popular oral traditions about Jesus: how do they figure in the writing? Or in the author's claim to have developed an orderly narrative? How does the audience influence the weaving together of sources—does Luke work his cloth to fit a Gentile body of readers? What is it to be called an author for such a weaving?

This is in itself but the most elementary reminder of the complexity of scholarly concerns surrounding authorship and source for the Gospels. The result is an uncertainty among nonprofessionals about what they should be doing when they read the Gospels. It has become embarrassingly unsophisticated just to read Matthew as Matthew. But coming up with a series of texts that would act as source for a more authentic or less filtered Jesus would be difficult, for that's a product about which there is no scholarly consensus (even though one group of scholars has developed formal procedures for deciding such things).

Into this entirely proper problematizing of the sources of our knowledge for Jesus and Socrates, I want to inject an entirely different consideration, not about the origins of our standard sources, but about their very function for us. It's a small observation: *The texts we've been worried about are a remote source for our knowledge of these two figures.* I don't mean remote in time because of their antiquity, but remote in their sovereignty over our consciousness. Most of us have heard, seen, and believed from all manner of sources long before we ever sat down with these books.

It would be tiresome to load example upon example of this point, so let me select only a few. Those who grow up in church families learn about Jesus from songs, prayers, oral stories, and picture books; for the rest, even in multicultural societies, Christmas still puts the Baby in the manger. It is barely possible anywhere within the reach of Western culture to escape the multifarious images of Christ: crucifixes in cathedrals and on necklaces, paintings by Holman Hunt or Chagall, Michelangelo's sculpture, African masses and Bach Passions, Andrew Lloyd Webber's *Jesus Christ Superstar,* the poetry of Milton and Christina Rossetti and W. H. Auden, Flannery O'Connor's fiction or John Irving's *A Prayer for Owen Meany* or the film *Babette's Feast*—but I promised to be brief. The sources for our knowledge of Jesus cannot be numbered; they form the large part of the root and flower of our culture. If we are going to be serious, not about Knowledge-in-General about Jesus but about our own impressions, beliefs, and evaluation of Jesus, then we cannot leave all the answers to the experts. We have to look to ourselves and the shaping of our own experience; or as Socrates would have it, we must engage in some self-examination, for the unexamined life isn't worth living.

Most of us could identify Socrates as author of that memorable dictum, even if we had to resort to a book of quotations to locate its written record. We've heard of the Socratic method from schoolteachers who themselves couldn't guide us to a good example of Socrates' use of that method. It is true that, because philosophy enjoys much less popular interest than religion, Socrates' name is not sung by little children. Nor, since philosophy has no rituals, does Socrates appear seasonally. His iconography is more limited, typically in painting and reproductions of statuary. Nonetheless, it is practically inconceivable that among those who have heard of philosophy there are any who do not know the name of Socrates. And, although many who know him might not be able to define Socratic irony or describe a Socratic paradox, all can speak of his commitment to inquiry and the manner of his death.

My point again is that, for all the ultimate dependence of this knowledge of Jesus and Socrates upon their source texts, we achieve our own acquaintance with them apart from reading those texts. Even when we get to the books themselves, whatever reading around in them we manage may be spotty or limited. Most Christians have read or heard the Gospels only in small chunks, with special attention to the "good parts"; and students introduced to Plato's writings usually have space in their curricula for no more than one or two dialogues.

I propose in this book to sit down with those source texts so that we may bring our attention to bear upon *their own* presentations of Jesus or Socrates. We will attempt to put to one side popular opinions, dim recollections, beliefs snatched on the run; and also to bracket a range of questions that expert opinion raises about our two figures.

I've said source texts, but that characterization needs further explanation in the light of the genuine problems that scholarship has uncovered. Plato is my choice for Socrates, because there is consensus that his Socrates is more philosophically interesting than Xenophon's, and because it is predominantly the weight of this Socrates that has made itself felt throughout the centuries. The same justification—about the incalculable weight of influence upon culture and thought—will work for my decision to read the received texts of Matthew, Mark, Luke, and John. Their presentations of Jesus are the ones we may explore just because they have such authority within our consciousness. To proceed otherwise would require us to rewrite those texts in accordance with some or other theory of production. As I have noted, we wouldn't be at a loss for options, but no one has yet come up with a product that will sell itself widely. It counts for something that, whatever editorial spins, additions, and adaptations the four Evangelists (or their proxies) made, their products have continued to be purchased—by a community of readers whose countless numbers even Saint John the Divine might not have imagined. When ecclesiastical language refers to these Gospels as *canonical,* that reception and acknowledgment on the part of the community is part of its meaning. My point accommodates such a view, but differs from it in two respects. First, these presentations of Jesus spread their influence beyond the community of faith, so their readership is wider than just the faithful. And second, my approach may be accepted at one level as simply pragmatic: were some other version of the life and Passion of Jesus to achieve status for those who care about such things, we would then position ourselves to listen to its concerns in presenting Jesus to its readers.

At this point, I should add some necessary details about the texts that we will read in these studies. I am conscious of the possibility that, for all we do know of Socrates and Jesus, some readers will not have spent as much time with one set of texts as with the other. For Socrates, the dialogues most familiar will probably be the *Apology,* in which Plato presents the defense before the jury, and the death scene in the closing pages of the *Phaedo.* They are important sources for these studies. In addition, Chapter 5, on obedience, looks at the *Crito,* and Chapter 6, on love, draws upon the *Symposium.* In connection with Socrates' trial I look at some of the *Gorgias;* there are some references to the *Phaedrus* and to the *Euthyphro.* In the case of most other passages cited, little is lost if their context in a particular dialogue is unfamiliar. None of the material requires a deep memory of Plato's philosophy, and the texts are not difficult to comprehend. For the reader who finds it useful to have it all between two covers, the standard book is *The Collected Dialogues of Plato,* edited by Edith Hamilton and Huntington Cairns. Recent translations of individual dialogues are available, some better than the ones collected there, but that edition has the advantage of including in the margins the accepted system of reference to Plato's text, the Stephanus pages divided into five sections (a number followed by a, b, c, d, or e). I usually give that number for ease of reference (for example,

Apology 38a). I do not always quote from the translations in Hamilton and Cairns, however, sometimes preferring another (noted at the time) or paraphrasing from the Greek text.

As for the New Testament, I work almost exclusively with the Gospels, with only an occasional nod to another text and a few pages on inarticulate prayer in Paul's letter to the Romans. Because I am after presentations of Jesus, each chapter after the next is devoted to one Gospel alone, rather than trying to collect themes and ideas across three or four. Sometimes I will draw comparisons—most extensively in the last chapter, on John—but only for the sake of getting the presentation of this particular author more clearly in focus. The translation I most commonly consult is the Revised English Bible (REB), with occasional reference to the New Revised Standard Version (NRSV); but often my choice of words will reflect my reading of the Greek. No one needs to know Greek to read the book, though. Where I do employ the vocabulary of *erôs* or *agapê*, the terms are themselves sufficiently anglicized to be understood in context. The system of reference for the New Testament is as usual by chapter and verse.

Enough of such small detail. It's still worrying that we are supposed to suspend some perfectly good intellectual questions in reflecting on the presentations of Jesus and Socrates in the chapters ahead. What kind of objects are we intended to study?

Jesus and Socrates as Objects of Study

A presentation or representation is so called to distinguish it from that which it is about. We could speak of this distinction in ontological language that Plato would approve by labeling the former an appearance and the latter the reality. That would have the advantage of reminding us that there may be several perspectives on one thing, but would bring with it the disadvantage of causing us to dismiss as unimportant mere appearances. The appearances we investigate here are not in the least "mere."

Nevertheless, our subjects are not the historical Socrates or Jesus. I myself am not beset by any doubts that there were two such men, one in ancient Athens and one four centuries or so later in Jerusalem. But they remain beyond our present reach, because we have available none of their words that have been directly authorized by them. Nor do our sources intend to deposit with us a series of neutral facts; they rather give us thoughtful and perspectival presentations of their subjects' lives and beliefs.

Now from this we might claim that *we should stick to the appearances, for they're all we have.* Though there's a certain prudence in the advice to spend effort where it will be repaid, we need not abandon history so quickly. For we do have other kinds of knowledge about the context in which these presentations were developed. We know something of Athenian law and religion in the fifth century; we have sources for intertestamental Judaism and for political movements in Jesus' day. So even where we have concluded that we cannot construct a historical Socrates or Jesus, we still have material by which to develop critiques of their presentations. Our source texts continue to be the objects of historical study, including, in the case of the New Testament especially, investigation with tools from such disciplines as social anthropology.

Those are not the only types of questions we bring to our texts. Philosophers have collectively spent a good deal of time reading Plato. Their interest is attracted by the way his Socrates reasons. He is not satisfied with certain kinds of answers to his questions: he finds problems with those who respond with examples instead of definitions. He uncovers inconsistencies in the beliefs of his interlocutors or tries to demonstrate why a particular train of thought leads to absurd conclusions. In such ways Plato's Socrates provokes philosophical thinking in his readers. They are less concerned with the historical background of Socrates' ideas than with the validity of his arguments and the adequacy of his views for their own understanding of issues that persist in their own studies. Moral weakness, for example, is a perennial puzzle in ethics and moral psychology, and one on which Socrates held a distinctive view in claiming that nobody does wrong voluntarily.

Especially among postwar English-speaking philosophers, Plato's Socrates has been scrutinized for the quality of his arguments. Recent scholars have increasingly recognized that those arguments aren't neatly extractable from the context in which they were delivered, a context of interpersonal space created by Plato's dialogue form. Socrates is the name not of a set of timeless propositions but of a character in a series of philosophical dramas. He has intentions, motives, attitudes, and relationships as well as articulated beliefs. And the same holds for those others he encounters in conversation. What passes between them in philosophical discussion must be read with one eye on its logic, to be sure; but the other eye must watch for all those signs that create context and thereby color meaning.

And now note that our language about our reading of Plato has shifted from argument to characterization—from philosophical issues to literary concerns. The literary approach to our texts for Socrates cannot be severed from philosophical questions, precisely because of the kind of writing that Plato does in his dialogues. Nor need philosophical and literary concerns ignore the fruits of inquiry into the historical context of a dialogue and its intersections with independent aspects of our knowledge. Yet there does seem to be a place for reflection upon Plato's Socrates, neither as disembodied utterer of argument nor as stand-in for the historical figure, but instead as a *philosophical character* in Platonic drama, a character presented for our viewing. That viewing, because it is from our particular time and place and not another's, is informed by our concerns and interests. It may have tighter or looser connections with Plato's authorial intentions, because we may see what he could not have guessed. The place of our viewing, although our own, does not have to be private; it may accommodate a community of viewers who discuss what it is they see and thereby enlarge each other's perceptions.

So some do read our texts about Socrates in order to explore the meaning and implications of Plato's construction of his philosophically rich persona. And in similar fashion there are readers of the Gospels— large numbers of them—who are after the meaning and implication of their presentations of Jesus. The interest of such readers is attracted by the good news he announces. They want to know how his teaching impinges upon their own practice and understanding. This Jesus provokes faith in some who read, and they want to know less about historical background than about how the meaning of his life and death may be worked out in their own. They read because they need to learn how to pray or to forgive or to situate their living in the care of God.

Now there's a parallel between the reading-for-argument of Socrates that philosophers have sometimes done and the reading of Jesus by thinkers who are interested in bringing order into their beliefs. Philosophers have extracted from Plato's Socrates a series of statements or beliefs and attempted to assess them as though they were impersonal. Moreover, they have often tried to arrange these beliefs into a system of thought called Platonism. Philosophical systems are most attractive when they are consistent, clear, and sufficiently developed to hold out the hope of comprehensiveness. They are in these ways not merely impersonal; they are quite unlike human beings at all. The parallel with some readings of the Gospels lies, of course, in the development of *theological* thinking. Statements and beliefs are extracted from the texts and arranged into a system that is meant to be clear and comprehensive in explaining all manner of metaphysical and ethical puzzles that face thoughtful believers.

Immediately I must temper my assessment of systematic thought. If my tone suggests a certain distancing from such enterprises, regard that simply as personal preference for the time being; there's nothing wrong with other thinkers carrying out tasks they enjoy and are good at. My purpose is only to propose another approach, a modest one they could regard as prologue to their own work. In the same way as we approach Plato's Socrates as a character in philosophical drama called dialogue, so we may read, say, Matthew's Jesus as a presentation of this character in the story of faith called Gospel. To read in this way would be to bracket perplexities about layers of sources, or about getting the best historical grasp on the material. It would also, however, leave unanswered a host of refined theological questions, chiefly about christology. We would not be able to bring fully articulated opinions about the identity of Jesus to the Gospels. We'd be reading to find out about this character, much as we reflect upon fictive personalities in order to discern their commitments and motivations. We would be trying to learn what makes Mark's Jesus, or Luke's, a persona of such compelling interest, so rich for faith.

To come to Plato's Socrates or the Jesus of one of the Gospels with these more literary sensitivities does not—I must repeat, does not—demand that one believe the authors simply to have made up these creations out of their own fantasies. It is only an acknowledgment that the forms of presentation in dialogue and Gospel are, broadly speaking, literary. They give us insight into character rather than impersonal philosophy or theology. And among the responses that they invite is reflection upon our own thinking and living in the light of the values and commitments we discover in those characters.

In other words, when Socrates and Jesus are made objects of this kind of study, we may find ourselves opened up for self-examination.

Socrates and Jesus Compared

Comparisons, it is said, are odious—not in the least because we make them in order to choose what will best serve our needs, and all of us would prefer to be valued just for our own unique selves. This explanation suggests, though, that what's odious is the business of *being compared*. The *making* of comparisons is something we can hardly avoid, and in fact may be an exercise in discovery that enlarges our understanding. Not only do we compare relative usefulness and value; we may also be struck with similarities and differences between objects that intrigue us, and in drawing comparisons between them come to a fuller appreciation of both.

Almost anything may be compared to some other thing. That's apples and oranges, we protest, when two measures don't map onto each other: naturally enough, for one can't think that this apple has more segments or pith than that orange. Yet we can inquire about their relative vitamin C content in relation to their respective costs at the market. It all depends on what we're after. Likewise, in spite of all the differences between the Greek-speaking Athenian Socrates and the Aramaic-speaking Jesus of Galilee and Jerusalem, we can compare these two men. But it does depend on what we're after.

If it's primarily to understand them in their own contexts through the clash of contrasts and the heightening of similarities, then we would more profitably look for comparisons within their own cultures and traditions. The Gospels compare Jesus with John the Baptist, for instance, or with Moses. He comes eating and drinking, the friend of sinners; he promulgates new law and commandments. Plato gives us a Socrates often compared to sophists and rhetoricians—thought to be one of that crowd by the Athenians, but distinguished firmly by Plato from a Protagoras or a Gorgias in his philosophical commitment and dialectical skill. Such comparisons work partly because they offer plausible commentary on the self-understanding of Jesus or Socrates. But to compare them with each other in those terms—to think how they might have regarded each other—that would require powers of imagination you will not discover in this book. I don't try to construct a Socrates teleported to Jerusalem to become a contemporary of Jesus, or Jesus sent back in time to Socrates' circle in Athens.

The place from which comparison is made, therefore, is our own place and neither of theirs. And what motivates us to put Jesus and Socrates together is, at one level, simply our curiosity. For when we have learned something of their stories, we find ourselves intrigued with parallels, as we might be struck by resemblances between two members of widely separated branches of a family tree. Their fathers worked with their hands, the one a sculptor and the other a carpenter. They themselves spent their time among the tradespeople and common folk, but were known more for talk than manual work. Neither had any visible means of income; both seemed to hold money of little importance. Their teaching challenged received wisdom and upset religious authorities. Both argued against doing harm to one's enemies and emphasized the value of the soul above the body. Their manner of teaching, in paradoxes and aphorisms and parables, was similarly memorable. Disciples followed them, but they also made determined enemies who set about to bring them down. Though innocent, they were both convicted and died a death of witness to the truth.

Mere curiosity at parallels must be balanced by a recognition of significant differences between Jesus and Socrates. We have physical descriptions of Socrates from which we garner impressions of an unhandsome, snub-nosed man; but of Jesus' appearance we know not a word. The circumstances of their deaths distinguishes them further. One dies, betrayed for silver and deserted by followers, in his prime; the other, with friends, in old and fulfilled age. But it is especially important to appreciate the contrasts between the beliefs or commitments shaping their lives. Socrates lives and dies for philosophy, a pursuit of wisdom that Jesus could not comprehend outside the context of what we'd call his religious existence. The Hebrew Scriptures, Temple, synagogue, and preeminently his relationship as Son to the Father—all that must be included in the existence of Jesus, and all that is foreign to Socrates. Socrates read Homer and Hesiod, not Isaiah. Unlike Jesus' relation to Scripture, Socrates' stance toward the texts of Olympian religion was critical. In our studies of Jesus and Socrates we must respect the fact that they inhabit their separate religious and cultural spaces, and we must refrain from assimilating one to the other.

That caution is necessary because the comparison between Jesus and Socrates arose originally not from some place equally distant from each, but as Christians attempted to interpret Socrates in the light of Jesus. And certainly, in spite of their chronological sequence, the development of the character Socrates has been influenced by Jesus much more than Jesus' reputation has been influenced by Socrates. The tendency to see Socrates' death as martyrlike may have been colored by the death of Jesus, and he has been appropriated by Christian readers in the language of sainthood. Perhaps the odd tradition that Socrates was silent at his trial was somehow influenced by the Gospel accounts of the Passion, for it doesn't appear until a couple of centuries after Jesus. But we ourselves should recognize the difficulties in discussing Socratic religion in the vocabulary of Hebrew or Christian faith.

For that reason I will always make distinct the theistic references of Socrates by writing of "the god" in lower case. The capital-G God is the God of Abraham, Isaac, and Jacob, the Father of Jesus who is the Son. Because capitalization implies greater significance than lower case in our orthographic conventions, this strategy has the effect of demoting the object of Socrates' religious commitment. I intend no disrespect, but I must signal the difference between the content of belief and commitment for Jesus and Socrates—and, I add, since I am not indifferent, for Socrates and me.

So we must exercise discretion in bringing together Socrates and Jesus from their own places into ours. Nevertheless, we still want to reflect on their likenesses and differences, and not only for intellectual recreation. Although parallels and contrasts in their basic stories are readily stated, it's their *experience* we want to compare in these studies. We want to know how they themselves construct the meaning of their deaths; what are their fundamental commitments and motivations; how they relate to authority, temporal and divine; why they use, or refuse, words in order to defend themselves; what it is that they do when they pray; what or who counts among the objects of their loving. As perennially human issues, these sorts of concerns inhabit our own living. It is out of our philosophical and religious questioning that we continue to find Jesus and Socrates compelling figures.

In comparing the respective experiences of Jesus and Socrates, we will have to pay attention not only to what they say as characters in their stories but to the ways in which our source texts present them to us. We are positioned by the narrative choices and characterizations of our authors to experience Socrates or Jesus as obedient or as loving. Our comparisons will sometimes lie, then, in how the texts construct our relations and attitudes to these two lives and deaths. Perhaps a brief example is in order. By the end of the book we will have come to appreciate a contrast between our two: death matters much more for Jesus than for Socrates. Why we believe this arises from the centrality of death in the story of Jesus; the Evangelists all build their narratives up to this event as shaping the meaning of Jesus' life and mission. By contrast, the meaning of Socrates' life and mission lies not in his death but in his devotion to philosophy. This commitment does grow out of his obedience to the god, and indeed his acceptance of death is characterized by that very obedience as well. All the same, we can appreciate Socratic philosophizing on its own, without the hues of death upon it, perhaps because he was able to fulfill his mission during a long life.

Two other features of Plato's writing make their contribution to the contrast between Jesus and Socrates. For one thing, Plato never wrote a work that was dedicated solely to the life and times of Socrates. Without that kind of source, we don't structure his life in the usual narrative line that starts with birth, gives time and place and significance of definitive events, and ends with death. Instead, Plato's dialogues give us philosophical episodes in the life of Socrates, almost achronological, motivated by some philosophical perplexity or other rather than by their position on his biographical line. Even the *Phaedo* places at its center a series of arguments about the immortality of the soul, relegating the account of Socrates' last day on earth to a narrative frame.

A second element of Plato's works—though not of his own design—contributes to the deemphasis of death for Socrates. For at least twenty-one centuries the dialogues have been arranged in nine tetralogies, with the first grouping containing the *Euthyphro,* the *Apology,* the *Crito,* and the *Phaedo.* Because of their dramatic interest and accessibility, these four dialogues usually form the reader's introduction to Socrates—witness the popular Penguin translation titled *The Last Days of Socrates.* The first tetralogy ends with Socrates' death—but there is much more to read. Though Socrates has drunk the hemlock, he has not ceased to philosophize. The trial and death dialogues are early, getting us started with Socrates. In the rest of his timeless philosophical life, we encounter him again and again, tirelessly, agelessly going about his questioning.

That's only a hint about how a contrast takes shape between Jesus and Socrates—and a contrast that will surface on several occasions throughout the book. For although I promised no brave new theories about either of them, I have found that, by throwing their presentations into relief, the mortal and humanly fragile Jesus stands out against the immortal and divinized Socrates. There are implications in that for our own understanding of love and of death, to be explored in the final chapter. But we won't arrive there without getting started, so let me finish this introduction with two or three more comments.

This Reading of Their Lives and Deaths

We read in these studies Matthew as Matthew, John as John, unapologetically because of what we are after. It's the presentation of Jesus' motives, intentions, commitments, relationships—all those ingredients in the literary construction of character—that we want to reflect upon. We're interested as well in the persona of Plato's Socrates, and we read the dialogues for insight into his character. But our reflections are themselves guided by the importance, within our experience, of the questions of philosophy and of faith.

The themes and topics in the following chapters are, broadly speaking, philosophical; they also arise within the life of religious faith. Take the issue discussed in Chapter 5, obedience and authority. The question of when we ought to obey an authority belongs to moral and political philosophy, but also to faith. Given our moral autonomy, there must be limitations on obedience; but in our relation to God, obedience doesn't seem optional. Socrates and Jesus both display commitments that turn out to assist us in developing an understanding how obedience can be exemplary. The topic of Chapter 4, prayer, is likewise of philosophical interest because of the peculiarities of its speaking; but it is a practice that belongs to faith. Throughout the studies the theme of language and its limits threads itself: in the trials of Jesus and Socrates, in prayer, in obedience, and in love as well as death, we discover Word and Silence.

Even though philosophical questions propel these studies, they don't work toward an end that belongs neatly to philosophy as a discipline. At least not if one believes that philosophy should concern itself with rational analysis and argument, proceeding from premises to conclusions. I do some analysis here and engage in argument. I do not intend, however, to argue readers into accepting the truth of beliefs here discussed. That would require much more work than I am willing to undertake here in defending assumptions and ferreting out weaknesses in opposing views. Much of contemporary philosophy of religion does that. But the source texts I have reflected on—particularly the Gospels—are not amenable to that kind of analysis. I've found that the kind of reading done for these studies requires me to expose the structure of experience, to hold it up for inspection. So my approach is to place the thinking done here in the service of what I'll call *witness*. Philosophy can be persuasive by arguing one's opponents out of their convictions into one's own beliefs; it can also convince by witness. Although Socrates did much of the first type of philosophizing, I'll argue in the next two chapters that his Defense is an example of philosophy as witness, because his primary aim was not success but truthful speaking. And I tend to regard the argument of this book not as philosophical apologetic against all comers, but as an *apologia* in the Socratic sense.

What's witnessed to is *faith*. That's why these studies are not even-handed, giving Socrates equal time or prominence with Jesus. I find in Socrates not Christian faith but a stance toward the god that shares a recognizable architecture with the experience of Christian faith. So Socrates illumines, by similarity and difference, what I discern in Jesus. That said, however, it remains true that these studies are only a preface for theology. The faith set out here requires further articulation if it is to become theology, just as the underlying concerns animating reflection need additional philosophical argument to become more than witness.

Before starting upon Matthew's Gospel and Plato's *Apology*, we consider in the next chapter the character of the deaths of Jesus and Socrates as witness, developing, as it were, a philosophy of martyrdom. Chapter 3 reads Matthew on the silence of Jesus, Chapter 4 goes to Luke for Prayer, Chapter 5 to Mark for obedience and authority, and Chapter 6 to John for love and death. Socrates appears and reappears, speaking at his trial, silent in his trances, obedient to the laws of Athens and to the god, loving only the eternal and unchanging, more secure in his dying than Jesus. And we reflect upon ourselves—the limits of our speaking, the meaning of silence, the demands of obedience and the paradox of dying to self that love requires.

So this reading of two lives and deaths is a little like stopping in the presence of the Death of Socrates, or sitting down among the crowd at the Crucifixion in a Passion play. We look, and look again—for we want to discuss not those good questions about technique and materials but the meaning for Socrates, for Jesus, and for us about what's going on in these stories. After the bell has rung and the performance has ended, there remains on the way home much to talk about; and I hope, with these words, to have made a place as well for silence.

TWO

Death and Witness

Consider first the silence of a man when he is dead. . . . What does it betoken, this silence? Nothing. This is silence pure and simple.
—Thomas Cromwell in Robert Bolt's *A Man for All Seasons*

We are not to think of a martyr as primarily one who suffers for a cause, or who gives up his life for truth, but as a witness to the awful reality of the supernatural.
—Helen Gardner, *The Art of T. S. Eliot*

Twenty-four hundred years ago a seventy-year-old Athenian prisoner took poison and died in the presence of a few friends. Four hundred and thirty years later, a young man, half the other's age, died abandoned by most of his followers on a hill outside Jerusalem in the asphyxiating pain of crucifixion. Neither had to die when he did, or as he did. In some important fashion, their deaths came about as the result of their own choosing, and for their own reasons. Their deaths have had monumental consequences for philosophy and for faith; but we must come in this chapter to view the dying of Socrates and of Jesus not by the light of those consequences but in terms of their own understanding. A simple and fundamental notion best illumines the character of both their deaths: the idea of *witness*.

Talk of death as witness immediately calls martyrdom to mind: the martyr dies as a testimony to the overriding importance of some belief or commitment greater than life itself. So a natural reading of my invocation of witness would be that we treat both Socrates and Jesus as martyrs to something or other, then attempt to find out the construction they place upon their respective martyrdoms. We will in fact proceed in that fashion, exploring the character of the martyr and the nature of martyrdom; but we will discover some difficulties in classifying the stories of Jesus and Socrates without qualification as martyrological literature. The simple question "What kind of martyr" was Jesus or Socrates has no obvious answer. Jesus wasn't quite a *Jewish* martyr or a

Christian one; and if we call Socrates a *philosophical* martyr, then exactly what does that mean?

So these two deaths-as-witness require investigation if we are to continue to associate them with martyrdom, as we think we should. First, however, we must raise a different issue. It sits in our very language. Contemporary users of English speak out of two sides of their mouths when they employ the language of martyrdom. In its standard descriptive sense, the word *martyr* belongs to a wider family like *saint, prophet, apostle, priest*—terms all classifying groups of people on religious criteria. Whereas some of those labels refer to a particular social role or function, *saint* and *martyr* are more general: the former designates believers with a particularly holy quality of life, and the latter a group of the faithful whose deaths have certain features in common. Once it is agreed that someone's death shares in those features, that person may be called a martyr. Whether the user of this term shares in the deep religious convictions of the martyr is irrelevant to the application of the term— just as classifying someone else's death as suicide is independent of personal attitudes about the courage or tragedy of taking one's own life.

That's the word from the side of the mouth that articulates the vocabulary of religious social meaning. From the other side, however, comes a much more strongly flavored, even pejorative, articulation of the language of martyrdom. Think of a phrase like "a martyred look" or the expression "making a martyr of yourself"—these are not meant as words of praise or approval. Perhaps there is a little more ambiguity in calling someone "martyrlike" or a "martyr to a cause." But, in that none of the objects of this discourse has actually died, this kind of talk about martyrs is derivative, revealing the speaker's attitude and evaluation. So it's important to clear the air by facing up to the problems of negating yourself for the sake of something you hold to be of much greater worth.

On Being a Martyr

We are after an understanding of the phrase "being a martyr" that will capture both kinds of speaking about martyrdom. For on the one hand we can have in mind what it is for a Stephen or Thomas à Becket to be a martyr; and on the other we can think of the disapproving injunction spoken to a relative who wears an injured look: "Don't be a martyr!"

Because we need then to understand how this language works, we should act as we often do when some concept or other puzzles us: send for the lexicographer. The standard dictionaries reflect the derivative as well as the religious use of the term, but not, perhaps, as prominently as we might like. For good reasons having to do with the original home and historical development of the concept, *martyr* is defined primarily in the context of religious faith. For the *Oxford English Dictionary*, the essential elements are voluntary acceptance of the penalty of death for refusing to renounce the Christian faith; that is widened to other religions or beliefs only secondarily. *Webster's Third International* begins with that wider sense, adding the notion of witness as well as refusal to renounce. Both dictionaries, however, postpone until the second half of their third sense what I have been calling the derivative and negative meaning. So the *OED* reads under sense 3(b): "now often jocularly *to make a martyr of oneself:* to make a real or pretended sacrifice of one's inclinations for the sake of gaining credit for it"; and Webster's 3(b) is "one who adopts a specious air of suffering or deprivation, especially as a means of attracting sympathy or attention."

Self-Appointed Martyrs

Now I should think—though this is confessedly but a suspicion— that outside an occasional newspaper report or a service of worship, most of the talk of martyrs we encounter or employ does belong in negative contexts. We regard the state of mind of the "martyr" as a "complex": something to be inspected, taken apart, fixed, and avoided. There's a falseness and disguise in this behavior that we cannot approve, a preoccupation with the self that masquerades distastefully as its opposite. Hence it seems inappropriate for the *OED* to privilege the contexts in which we *joke* about somebody's making a martyr of himself or herself. We do, sometimes, intend to treat with humor the self-consciousness of the "martyred" look or behavior; but the charge of "being" or "making oneself" a martyr might also express a host of negative attitudes, from cynicism to moral outrage.

It's important to pay attention to the *motivation* of the person who acts in derivatively martyrlike ways. It's not the deprivation or suffering per se that's the problem; rather it's the construction of the hardship as (the *OED* has the right term) "a sacrifice"—and a sacrifice of a doubly contradictory nature. First, there should be in sacrifice a voluntary rather than enforced offering—which is why the true religious martyr cannot be dragged unwillingly to death. In drawing attention to the suffering self, the person who "acts the martyr" communicates a reluctance about making the sacrifice. Second, sacrifice is denial *for the sake of the other;* but in "being a martyr" one communicates the denial so self-consciously that the suffering self cancels out the interest in the other. The martyred look, the martyred sigh, the martyred stoop—all cry in whispers: *I shouldn't have to be enduring this on your behalf; but I am. And look at me: I'm not complaining about it or refusing it. A little expression of gratitude on your part, though not of course necessary or expected, would be appreciated.*

So the psychology of the self-appointed martyr contains a motive without which the concept would not be applicable. The *OED* expresses it as sacrifice "for the sake of gaining credit" (or as the revised *Shorter OED* has it, "in order to be more highly thought of"); *Webster's* looks to "sympathy or attention" as the end in mind. Now this sort of martyred consciousness often will not want the burden lifted, and will deny that it desires sympathy or reputation, perhaps even taking its satisfaction from such denial. So I propose that at root what's wanted is this simple attention and recognition. Thus the word and gesture of "being a martyr" in the derivative and negative sense becomes *a witness to the presence of the self,* fraudulently proclaimed in self-negation.

This is a degenerate form of martyrdom, a parody of the sacrificial death of the true religious martyr. Worse, it is parasitic, morally as well as semantically, upon the original meaning of the martyr's death.

And this parody has a potentially destructive backwash upon the original. So suspicious are we of the martyred personality that we may well begin to wonder what lies behind the words and actions of religious sacrifice-to-the-death. The standard dictionary definitions of martyrdom as death for the faith do not, after all, make much of the mind of the martyr. What would be a sufficiently powerful motive for this voluntary surrender of one's life in the midst of determined hostility toward one's being and identity? It's true that Christian martyrs die in the hope of resurrection and the rewards of heaven, and that the Church has promised unique honor for them. Holy Scripture itself holds out the promise, spoken by the Spirit's voice to John the Divine, in words from the risen Christ: "Be faithful till death, and I will give you the crown of life" (Revelation 2.10). White robes are granted to those murdered for God's word and their witness (Revelation 6.11). Are faithful martyrs then best thought of as those who catch such confident sight of their own future glory on the other side of Death's wall that they can squeeze themselves through the narrow gate of mortal persecution?

Or, more darkly, does the "complex" to which they give their name infect the deep motives of even these religious martyrs? We know of people bent on their own destruction; we have heard of the illness of mind that discovers its pleasures in being the object of hatred; we may have tasted ourselves something of the sweetness of self-righteousness. Is the mind of the martyr, we ask ourselves, a troubled mind in need of healing ministrations?

Having given voice to these suspicions, I must leave them unheeded for the present. It would be too easy to answer by parading a series of stories about martyrs. The evidence available from the history of the Christian Church includes an ample number of cases of peculiar motivation or abnormal psychology in our martyrologies. Under certain conditions we might think our sampling secure enough to dismiss martyrdom as unworthy of our serious moral attention. But think: it would be as easy to generate a host of stories about the peculiarities and abnormalities of philosophers. For some detractors, Thales' falling into a well while looking at the heavens says everything worth knowing about philosophy. Others, though, understand that the philosophical enterprise has a human significance apart from, indeed in spite of, some strange habits of its practitioners. We need to look not at a series of randomly selected examples but at *exemplary practice*, commonly acknowledged by those familiar with the enterprise to be admirable and worthy instances of how it should be done.

So we will come soon to reflect upon what I call *exemplary martyrdoms*—as indeed we'll investigate exemplary prayer, exemplary obedience, and exemplary dying in the course of the book. In each case Jesus and Socrates will stand as exemplars, though never in any nonproblematic way. But we are still at some distance from them here; and even before moving to exemplary martyrdom we must say a little more about the elements we have already discerned in faithful, nondegenerate, religious martyrdom.

Elements of Religious Martyrdom

It will be useful to distinguish two types of question in sorting out the basic features of martyrdom. The first, already proposed, concerns the inner life of the martyr, especially such issues as motivation, justification, and related matters of moral psychology. The second is equally important. Martyrdom takes place in a social context, in a complex of competing beliefs and authorities. It is accorded different meanings by different communities. Although we can't even begin upon a sociology of martyrdom here, nonetheless we must make sure that we've got some appreciation of the main elements that such a study would address.

Come back to the psychological briefly. I will continue to leave suspended the worry about the moral and mental states behind the martyr's motivations. Instead let us simply recall that the lexicography of martyrdom stresses its *voluntary* nature. So we can propose this element as essential: that the martyr's mind must be present and must consent to the penalty of death. I've said "mind," but naturally we find voluntariness expressed in bodily stance and gesture. Whatever the somatics of martyrdom, the martyr remains, in some important sense, a participating agent in the proceedings. She moves of her own accord to the stake; he does not cry out in protest or struggle while being dragged to the gallows.

There's another vital feature of the martyr's mind, this time epistemic. Martyrs *believe.* The content of their beliefs they hold to be of the highest importance, and their grasping onto those beliefs of more value than their hold upon life. If we call this a tenacity of mind, we must see it as one that survives the strongest challenge. Not even being cut down themselves can cause martyrs to loosen the grip of their own accord. And that resolve becomes part of the voluntary character of their dying.

That martyrs believe, and that they willingly accept death, demands further qualification, but first we should return to the question of the social context of martyrdom.

It is part of Catholic teaching that, in order to classify a death as martyrdom, the believer must not only die voluntarily but must be a victim of *odium fidei,* a hatred of the Faith. For there to be such a thing, we need two discernible social groups, one defined by its adherence to a set of beliefs, practices, and so on, and the other by its opposition to those beliefs. In labeling them Believers and Persecutors, we must acknowledge that the opposition is persecution from the subjective standpoint of the believer; the opposing party would use different language, such as *retribution* or *cleansing* to characterize its behavior. Still, the

Persecutor label will suffice for our purposes as well as for the martyr's. Within these two groups, the two parties in any martyrdom must be identified *as* members of their respective groups, and their actions interpreted *in light of* that identification. It wouldn't be a Christian martyrdom if, for instance, the person killed were not acknowledged by her group to be a faithful Christian; or if some Christian were executed because he was guilty of a nonreligious capital crime in a regime otherwise thought to be persecutory.

Another societal feature associated with martyrdom by its dictionary definition is judicial: death is a penalty suffered for refusing to deny one's faith. That strongly implies an institutional opposition to the martyr: law and authority are invoked, with some set of procedures followed in order to establish the refusal to recant, and to legitimate the death penalty.

Of course, once the social conditions of martyrdom receive this kind of specification, we wonder about unusual cases. So while we can think of examples of martyrs tried and executed in accordance with judicial practice, we nevertheless would be reluctant to deny martyr status to someone murdered for faith by agents unsanctioned by duly constituted civil or religious authorities. That, however, introduces a further category—death by assassination, as in the case of Archbishop Oscar Romero of El Salvador. For such sudden death not only violates judicial procedure, it also undercuts the voluntary nature of the victim's acceptance of death. Without an opportunity to recant or to affirm the faith, the believer has no choice in the matter. How then can such dying be martyrdom when such an essential feature of the martyr's mind cannot be present? And yet we do think it possible that believers may be killed for their faith even when struck down unawares.

What of a reverse situation, in which the believer is fully voluntary in death but without that death being imposed by an external power, legitimate or otherwise? One may certainly die for one's beliefs by one's own hand. Suicide in some circumstances is freely and willingly embraced as a potent sign of commitment to some cause. But is it martyrdom?

And while we puzzle over the application of the features we think important to faithful martyrdom, we should return to the need for Believers and Persecutors. We might imagine scenarios in which a believer dies intending to witness to the faith, but where the persecutor seriously misunderstands the witness. Is it possible to die for the faith when the murderers may not possess enough understanding of that faith to permit their opposition to be called *odium fidei?* The question arises over contacts between cultures that have no developed understanding of each other—in missionary contexts, say. But it leads to a related and embarrassing issue. For it is also possible for the persecutor to understand very well, and indeed share, much of the faith of the believer. Hatred does not have to extend to all of the contents of the believer's mind; indeed, our history makes it painfully clear that many have died not so much for The Faith as for one or two items of belief they consider essential to that Faith. Someone outside the Christian tradition compiling a list of Christian martyrs would have to include believers put to death by other believers, all of whom identified themselves as Christian. We have been Believers and Persecutors together, of each other. So it is often insufficient to speak of Christian martyrs; instead we must refer to Roman Catholic or Anabaptist or Huguenot martyrs, each defined by the piece of the Faith for which they died. If that fact about the language of Christian martyrdom does not in itself raise embarrassment, one has only to read the entries under *Martyr* in a few encyclopedias sponsored by different Christian communities.

Because we have discovered difficulties in applying the features we thought definitive of martyrdom, it is time to turn our attention to some exemplary cases. Perhaps in a more concrete and specific examination we will arrive at a better appreciation of the meaning of voluntary dying for faith—and thereby better understand the deaths of Jesus and Socrates.

Exemplary Martyrs: Death as Witness

Before addressing the concern over the motivation of the religious martyr, let us deal with our questions about assassination and suicide as possible means of martyrdom. And let us begin that endeavor with a technical anachronism: Biblical martyrs.

Biblical Martyrs The reason we must call our heading anachronistic is simply this: the Bible contains no term that readily corresponds to our English *martyr.* That may come as news to those whose memory of the King James Version extends to verses like Acts 22.20, and Revelation 2.13 and 17.6 (and not just the KJV; J. B. Phillips' translation uses "martyr" in the Acts reference, and the Revised Standard Version, though not the NRSV, does so in the last reference). But the Greek that our English translates, *martus* (genitive *marturos*), simply means *witness*, one who bears testimony to something. It is used in a variety of contexts, some of which have nothing to do with death or religious fidelity: as in the requirement of "two or three witnesses" to establish the facts (Matthew 18.16). All the same, though the concept is missing in the text, we do find deaths in Scripture that we readily call martyrdoms.

I propose that the clearest case for Christians must be the death of Stephen. In beginning with him, I am conscious of the view that Christians must regard as the first and preeminent martyr Jesus himself. It is admittedly strange to hold up another's death as exemplary for Christian saints who die for their faith. All the same, for my original reasons I will postpone until the next section any consideration of martyrdom in the death of Jesus. Stephen was, after all, the first to die as a believer in Jesus and must hold the place of protomartyr in that sense. So it is appropriate to examine the features of his death for whatever standards they set.

The account of Stephen's trial and execution occupies a significant piece of text in Acts 6 and 7. Noticeable immediately is the large amount of speaking Stephen does: his defense to the Council is about twice as long as Peter's Pentecost sermon. It also precipitates his death. Stephen had been arraigned on charges by false witnesses (6.13) like those brought against Jesus, that "this holy place" would be destroyed and that the customs of Moses would be changed (6.14). There is no sense initially that these are capital offenses. But by accusing his contemporaries of betraying the Righteous One, and by announcing his vision of the Son of Man standing at the right hand of God, Stephen enrages the Council. They rise up, drag him outside the city, and stone him to death, the witnesses laying their coats at the feet of Saul of Tarsus. That Saul, become Paul the apostle, recounts this incident much later in his life, confessing that he stood by approvingly while the blood of the Lord's *martus* Stephen was shed (Acts 22.20). Since we have no evidence that Paul had a developed concept of martyrdom in the sense that we have been considering, we should understand that by *martus* Paul simply means that Stephen was witness to the Lord on that occasion.

So we have three types of witnesses in the accounts of the death of Stephen. Witnesses accuse Stephen of blasphemy; witnesses preside at his death; and Stephen himself is witness. Legal procedures require the first two types (the presiding witnesses are the first to throw stones:

Deut. 17.6–7). Stephen's own role, though, is odd: he is witness as well as accused. What in his speech makes that role appropriate? It is, I think, that he gives testimony of his own experience of the risen Christ, the Son of Man, standing at the right hand of God.

The first witnesses are false, and the second set put Stephen to death unjustly—at least from the perspective of the Acts account and his own faith. Had Stephen properly deserved death, this would not be the story of the first Christian to die for his faith. In order that his death be seen *as for* faith, the witness of his speech is required. But one other feature of the account deserves notice: the manner of Stephen's dying. He prays, while still standing, "Lord Jesus, receive my spirit." He then kneels down, praying that the Lord not hold this sin against his persecutors. These somatic gestures are significant. Although dragged out of the city under the power of others, he is not unwilling. By his words Stephen follows the example of his Lord in forgiving his executioners (Luke 23.34); and by his gestures he imitates Jesus in actively accepting death.

In summary, then, the death of Stephen has several elements important to this study. First come accusations denying the legitimacy of his faith and an active opposition to it (easily characterized here as *odium*); then his own explanation of faith and his witness to it; an ensuing death that is undeserved within the context of his beliefs; and a death that models the death of Jesus by being freely embraced.

While Stephen functions as protomartyr for Christianity, his is not the only martyrlike biblical death, nor does it contain every element in martyrdom. An earlier Jewish example is instructive: the death of Eleazer in 2 Maccabees 6. He is made to do something repugnant to his faith and way of life, to eat pork. His tormenters, respecting his age and character, offer to strike a deal: they will allow him to bring his own meat to the trial so that he can appear to pass the test yet save his life with a clear conscience. Eleazer will have none of it. He points out that observers will believe he has "gone over to an alien religion" (v. 24 NRSV) and would be led astray by what they took to be his example. His life, advanced as it is, is not worth preserving in such circumstances: so he deliberately goes to the rack, enduring great suffering for the sake of the holy laws and the fear of God.

Features essential to the martyr's death are to be found here. The meaning of eating and refusing to eat is crucial to Eleazer: he needs to offer an explanation of eating in terms of his faith and respect for God's holy law. Though the word *witness* is absent from the account, nevertheless the concept is entirely appropriate. Eleazer's tormenters deny the legitimacy of his belief and put him to a death entirely undeserved—but a death to which he goes willingly. "It is clear to the Lord in his holy knowledge," he says, "that though I might have been saved from death, I am enduring terrible sufferings in my body under this beating, but in my soul I am glad to suffer these things because I fear him" (6.30 NRSV).

But Eleazer's story contains an element not present in Stephen's, one that heightens the voluntary nature of his death. Eleazer is offered a clear and deliberate choice: he is put to the test, and given a way of escape, which he refuses. Further, whereas Stephen's executioners think his claims offensive, Eleazer's test is not something that his tormenters find repugnant or wrong themselves. The point of the trial lies in its deep offense to Jews, not to their persecutors. Their action is simply for the sake of doing violence to another's conscience. It is the expression of a radical *odium* and a perverse will, one that Eleazer opposes in the name of the holy will of God.

Thomas à Becket Both of our biblical exemplars underwent trial and examination for their faith. We had earlier wondered, however, how central to martyrdom is an institutional opposition that employs some type of judicial practice. The problem lies in the importance of a voluntary death: without an opportunity to give witness or to refuse to deny the faith, the martyr's mind and motive may remain opaque. At the time of raising the matter we recognized that it's possible to be assassinated for one's faith: sudden murder may indeed be martyrlike. We turn now to another instructive example of martyrdom, this time in a twentieth-century dramatization of a twelfth-century murder.

I have in mind T. S. Eliot's *Murder in the Cathedral,* first produced in the Chapter House of Canterbury Cathedral in 1935 and perhaps the most lucid presentation of Christian martyrdom in our time. Thomas à Becket returns to his archbishopric in Canterbury in 1170 amid fears for his safety and easily turns aside temptations to take up his old lives of pleasure, power, and class. The fourth tempter, unexpected, strikes a more telling blow—right at Thomas's pride. He asks him to think "of glory after death," to think of ruling as saint and martyr from the tomb, of winning an enduring crown: "Seek the way of martyrdom, make yourself the lowest / On earth, to be high in heaven." It is the subtle role of this unnamed tempter to speak Thomas's own thoughts aloud, but in the speaking Thomas comes to recognize that this last temptation "is the greatest treason: / To do the right deed for the wrong reason." And he submits himself neither simply to action nor simply to suffering, but to an active embrace of the will of God. As Thomas puts it in his Christmas Day sermon,

> A Christian martyrdom is never an accident, for Saints are not made by accident. Still less is a Christian martyrdom the effect of a man's will to become a Saint, as a man by willing and contriving may become a ruler of men. A martyrdom is always the design of God. . . . It is never the design of man; for the true martyr is he who has become the instrument of God, who has lost his will in the will of God, and who no longer desires anything for himself, not even the glory of martyrdom.

That captures, I think, what we have been uncovering in our understanding of martyrdom, that it is determinedly voluntary. Thomas willingly exposes himself to death: "Unbar the doors! Throw open the doors!" But it has, too, an additional character that we have not yet isolated and named as belonging to the consciousness of the religious martyr: *obedience.* Thomas speaks of his choice as a giving of himself;

> It is out of time that my decision is taken
> If you call that decision
> To which my whole being gives entire consent.

In the first edition of the play Eliot had added to Becket's Christmas Day sermon that the martyr had not lost his will "but had found it, for he has found freedom in submission to God." Martyrdom thus has at its heart the paradox of a willing submission to another will. This is an intolerable contradiction of moral autonomy and worth for some, and we will face the difficulties around the practice of obedience in a later chapter. But we must not be mistaken here about the experience of the martyr: the absolute necessity of obedience is still a freely offered obedience, not an abdication of responsibility; it is a most active embrace as one's own of what is already given.

In locating voluntary obedience at the core of martyrdom, we have moved away from the importance of witness, the etymological root of the concept. But its significance may now be reassessed by a return to the question whether death by suicide may constitute martyrdom.

Witness, Suicide, and Assassination When he attempts to justify the murder of Thomas à Becket, the Fourth Knight explains that Thomas had deliberately courted death and had thus in fact committed suicide. "I think," the Knight continues, "with these facts before you, you will unhesitatingly render a verdict of Suicide while of Unsound Mind. It is the only charitable verdict you can give, upon one who was, after all, a great man." Thomas himself prepares us for this distortion at the end of Part I: most of us will want to read his story as futile, arrogant passion, the "senseless self-slaughter of a lunatic." But just suppose that he had engineered his death in full possession of his senses. If one commits suicide in one's right mind, might that sort of death sometimes constitute martyrdom?

Take the rightness of mind seriously, for unsoundness would prevent us from seeing the agent as fully responsible. A death for a principle or belief knowingly and without coercion and by one's own hand: that is perhaps the clearest example of a fully voluntary death, because no other agent is involved in the doing. The suicide may attract great attention: there is no stronger way to announce that war is immoral than by dousing yourself with gasoline and becoming a sacrifice to peace. And it may be performed in the hope that the sacrifice will contribute to the bringing about of peace in the world. But the suicide-martyr need not justify death by the success of that death in effecting change in other people's beliefs and behaviors. One can bear witness to a supreme truth or value just because it is supreme, greater than the value of one's own life. One hopes that others will notice, and will accept the same value. But the finality of the act as witness is such that it will require no further justification.

So some suicides may share essential features of martyrdom: voluntariness, and witness to a belief or truth of great value. And yet there is something more in Christian martyrdom that is missing in such suicides—something so important that it might become improper to count suicides among Christian martyrs.

I don't mean to argue on the premise that suicide is never right, from which it would follow that no Christian who commits suicide could be elevated to the status of martyr. That admittedly would be a moral argument with some support in the history of Christian ethics. The prohibition of suicide was based on the impropriety of taking into one's own hand a power that belongs only to God. As Bach's Cantata No. 106 (the *Actus Tragicus*) has it, "God's time is the best time"; to decide that time on one's own requires a knowledge of future goods or ills that human beings do not possess. Many Christians have also agreed with the conviction that Socrates expressed in the *Phaedo*: since we are the possessions of the gods, it's not within our moral competence to decide on our own deaths.

Now there are problems in extracting an absolute prohibition of suicide from this kind of thinking. But that is not why suicide is inappropriate as a form of Christian martyrdom. The reason lies rather in the meaning of the witness made by the martyr. The Christian martyr dies in obedience to God: that is fundamental. If death is by one's own hand, how can it be made apparent that this is an act of voluntary obedience to another will? Only where there is a contrary will, a power of life and death that demands disobedience, can the Christian martyr's submission to death be transparently an act of obedient surrender. Only then does it gain the special character of witness to something beyond one's own will.

Two things follow from the impossibility of Christian martyr-suicide. First, in a peculiarly ironic fashion, the martyr co-opts the wrongful actions of the ungodly and turns them into the instrument of the divine will. So those who set themselves in opposition to God, who seek to break God's authority, are made complicitous in the workings of divine purpose. This is the power of martyrdom: if the persecutors do not carry out their ultimate threat, their victim's faithful refusal to recant is vindicated; if the persecutors do kill the innocent, the meaning of their work is transformed by the martyr's commitment to the ultimate authority of God, which thereby vindicates faith.

Second, we can see that the notion of witness has a subtlety in Christian martyrdom that we may have missed until now. For the Christian does not simply die because of a set of beliefs or for a cause. You can be killed for your beliefs by hostile hands without your consent or under protest, bearing witness only to your fear. Or you may accomplish by suicide a death for the sake of a belief held to be more important than your own life. What the Christian martyr witnesses to are not propositional beliefs so much as faithfulness, commitment, loyalty, and obedience to One who stands in judgment over against all powers and authorities, over life itself.

There are two caveats to this. First, though I have been speaking of Christian martyrdom here, the point is not that Christians must be unique in their witness. The principles may be generalized within theistic martyrdom: think of Eleazer, for whom the eating of pork betrays beliefs not about pork but about obedience to God's holy law. Second, in stressing obedience I do not mean to imply that there can be some contentless obedience without propositional beliefs. In order to obey you must believe lots of things—about authority and who holds it, for instance. Still, you may obey out of trust and loyalty without understanding all the reasons why this particular act is right, without having sorted out all the perplexities in your situation. And this means that acting out of obedience need not be the same as acting to proclaim the truth of a set of doctrines about which you have achieved clear understanding.

I conclude, then, that exemplary martyrdom is the voluntary obedient surrender of one's life for faith; but that the faith found in the martyr's mind is primarily loyalty. What's witnessed to is not the self, or the self's hold on some belief or idea, but the absolute authority of God. All of this the second epigraph of the chapter puts with great simplicity: "We are not to think of a martyr as primarily one who suffers for a cause, or who gives up his life for truth, but as a witness to the awful reality of the supernatural."

This conclusion about the nature of martyrdom as witness will help us with the absence of fully conscious choice in death by assassination. It is true that someone like Archbishop Romero or Martin Luther King, gunned down suddenly, had no choice to recant and live, or die. Yet in their whole manner of living and speaking these men bore witness to the doing of God's will. Whether in other respects history will judge King's life saintly, nevertheless the context of his dying turns out to be of great significance. Others have noted parallels with Eliot's Becket in King's last public speech in Memphis, the day before his death, in which he confesses his great uncertainty about the future and also his resignation. "Like anybody, I would like to live a long life. Longevity has its place. But I'm not concerned about that now. I just want to do God's will." King knew the likely cost of continuing his mission; he knew that his actions had to be nonviolent; he knew that he could continue only if he did not care to preserve his own life but instead offered it willingly to God. In the context of his self-understanding, then, his death becomes martyrlike precisely because he saw its possibility as a voluntary witness to obedience regardless of the consequences.

So while being put to the test is a vivid way of marking the obedience of the martyr, it is not the only way for this obedience to be known, and is therefore not always required in the making of martyrs. The witness of obedience is central: that is why death by assassination may be, and why suicide may not be, the death of a martyr.

Jesus and Socrates: The Witness of their Deaths

With this understanding of the elements in exemplary martyrdom now available to us, we must return to the deaths of Jesus and Socrates. I began with the claim that the idea of Witness is the simple notion that best illumines the character of both their deaths; but I had also pointed to a difficulty in classifying those deaths as martyrdoms. The problem raised had to do with what section in a martyrology their stories would fit: what *kind* of martyr is Jesus, or Socrates?

Jesus There is strong reason why the Church should consider the death of Jesus as martyrdom. He is the faithful *martus,* the firstborn from the dead, in Revelation 1.5; in 3.14, the faithful and true witness. And his witness certainly became exemplary for his followers. Stephen, we saw, replicated in his own trial and death aspects of the Passion of his Lord; Eliot's Thomas à Becket faced temptations, overcame them, and shed his blood for the Church. That, of course, is only to be expected: from the first, Christians believed Christ's example of innocent and nonretaliatory suffering to be worthy of imitation (I Peter 2.19–24). But does this mean that Jesus himself died a martyr's death, in the sense of that term as we now use it?

As long as we think of martyrdom in its religious and institutional setting, it remains problematic to think of Christ as martyr. He is not, in the sense that his followers are, a *Christian* martyr. He did not die for a set of beliefs about himself, or to absolutize his own claims against other authorities—there is nothing Christian, in the institutional sense, about the death of Jesus. Nor does Jesus fit into the context of *Jewish* martyrdom. Unlike Eleazer, he died for no distinctively Jewish belief so that members of his community could identify him as one of them. His executioners did not see themselves as the opponents of the God of Israel—there was no *odium fidei*—nor did he perceive himself as defending that faith against the ungodly. That he was charged with blasphemy by the authorities of his own religious group suggests an analogue with the deaths of those regarded as heretics by the dominant religious authority. Yet that's also a difficult comparison. There isn't a well-articulated doctrine or teaching against the establishment with which Jesus could be identified as a member. And more difficult still is the refusal of Jesus to say anything at all in his own defense. He does not bear witness to himself as a believer in this or that truth for which he is prepared to die. In this refusal his trial is completely unlike that of Stephen, so full of explanation and defense; his death in silence differs from all of the martyrdoms of his followers, who die because of words of witness to him.

How can one be a martyr without being a martyr *to* a particular faith? There are no generic martyrs, just as there are no generic and unattached citizens: one's story must belong to some section or other of a martyrology, under a Jewish or Islamic or Christian or Huguenot heading.

Nevertheless, without this silent death of Jesus there would be no Christian martyrdom. I mean more than the obvious, that without Jesus' death there would be no followers who called themselves Christians, and therefore no Christian martyrs. I mean rather that in his death there is something fundamental to martyrdom which all Christians put to the final test are called upon to imitate: an obedience to the will of the Father that transcends all human concerns, even the concern to understand and justify one's own decisions and actions. I cannot go into the evidence for this here; it must suffice to remind you of Jesus' setting his face to go to Jerusalem, his refusal to back away from confrontation, his unwillingness to speak words that could be twisted and misunderstood, his concern that doing the will of the Father consisted in the doing and not the saying, his most active submission, his sovereign abdication of control, his surrender to a death that stripped him as victim yet was at the same time wholly his gift. As we reflect on this story, again and again we find the Passion and death of Jesus to be the voluntary expression of an obedient submission to the will of God, a gift of trust even where he cannot sort out the meaning of all his beliefs. This faithful witness is, as we have argued, exemplary martyrdom. But it is not merely generic, for the witness is to a divine authority and care deeply rooted in the faith of Israel.

Stephen remains the protomartyr of Christian faith; but that is only because the dying of Jesus stands behind and underneath, the archetype of martyrological witness. Our inability to classify his death as a religiously specific martyrdom signals his occupation of his own unique territory between Jewish and Christian faith. In that territory he bears his distinctive and costly witness of obedience to the Father's will. Witness is the word for his death.

Socrates Without much trouble, readers of commentaries on the death of Socrates can discover the language of martyrdom used about him. We might wonder among what sort of martyr he should take his place, and in what sense there could be philosophical martyrdoms. It turns out that Socrates is like Jesus in having a special place for his death, though not for quite the same reasons.

It's best to retrace our steps in order to position Socrates' dying among the martyrs. We had characterized the martyr's death as undeserved, at least in the eyes of the group for whom that death is witness (Jews or Christians in the case of Eleazer or Stephen). The death is voluntary: the martyr must consent to die, not struggle against fate. And in the dying there must be witness to something greater than the life of the martyr; in theistic martyrdom, what is witnessed to is God, alone worthy of obedient love and trust. This demonstration of loyal obedience is more fundamental, I've argued, than providing testimony about the truth of a set of religious beliefs.

Now Socrates' death shares most of these characteristics, except that he does not die within a religious institutional context that had developed a conception of martyrdom or anything like its practice. But can we nevertheless assimilate his death to our general scheme? And if so, what is the relation between martyrs and their religious commitment and identity?

Take the features of martyrdom in order. Is Socrates' death *undeserved?* Certainly both Plato and Xenophon wish us so to regard it. There is reasonable doubt that Socrates was guilty as charged; even if so, it would be very difficult to believe that he deserved death as the penalty. So we think Socrates an innocent victim of malicious schemes and designs, of a popular mood and temperament that cannot be explained in terms of legal guilt.

As for the *voluntary* element so necessary in martyrdom: Socrates does not struggle against his own death, but accepts it and indeed embraces it. There are several aspects to this voluntariness:

1. Refusing to conduct his defense as the Athenians would like to hear it, Socrates deliberately chooses a course of action that will not save his life.
2. He proposes a provocative penalty, showing little regard for its likely effect on the jury.
3. He declares that he will never stop philosophizing even if ordered to do so.
4. He argues that death is not something to be feared but instead probably a good.

In all of these ways, Socrates retains control over events and outcomes, or at least influences them strongly. Had he acted differently in the first three matters, his penalty might well have been different; his argument in the fourth is designed to express his acceptance of his fate.

There is another crucial aspect to the voluntary nature of Socrates' death:

5. He refuses to leave prison, though a surreptitious flight into exile would have been entirely feasible and even expected.

The decision to stay was maintained unwaveringly across an unusually long period of time (Xenophon says it was a month) because no executions were allowed in Athens until the religious expedition to Delos had returned. The *Crito* makes it abundantly clear that Socrates' acceptance of the death penalty is voluntary and principled.

What of the *witness* that lies at the core of the martyr's action? It is possible for someone to be put to death unjustly, and to accept the injustice unprotestingly, without that death bearing witness to any larger value or truth. It depends on the reasons the person has for accepting death. Someone who does not, or cannot, disclose the meaning of his or her innocent death cannot be a martyr. And the reasons for dying may be so centered on the self that there is no witness to something more important than life itself. I have in mind as example the Socrates that Xenophon gives us. Xenophon's Defense has his Socrates explain that he went willingly to death in part because in this way he would avoid the problems of senility: "If my years are prolonged, I know that the frailties of old age will inevitably be realized." Here the belief for which one dies is simply that one's own nonexistence is better than anticipated pain, forgetfulness, and the like. Were this really Socrates' principal motivation, then he might be regarded as an example for believers in the right to end one's own life whenever one wants, but he would scarcely qualify as martyr. The innocence of his death would be irrelevant to his decision to die, as would the fact that death was imposed by others.

That said, there does seem to be more personal control over the events in his trial and death for Socrates than for Jesus. And if Socrates exercises sufficient authority and responsibility in the proceedings that lead to his death, the suspicion of suicide begins to intrude. It may not be accidental that Plato explicitly raises the question of suicide in the *Phaedo*. Even so, we have already agreed that some suicides (though not

Christian martyrdoms) may be martyrlike. Is Socrates' death like them? We can answer only after considering what Plato's Socrates really does witness to in his trial and death.

That may seem a difficult business, given that Socrates is so insistent upon the limitations of his own knowledge. What commitments is he willing to acknowledge, this man who claims to know only that he does not know? Were we to insist that the martyr confidently witness to a body of clearly defined beliefs, Socrates would distance himself from this kind of witness; he would be more interested in probing the meaning of beliefs than in testifying to their truth. But since we've come to a different understanding of the witness of the martyr, Socrates may yet belong to this company.

Think of his fundamental concerns. Most basically Socrates is after *goodness of soul*, something he opposes to wealth, reputation, and bodily health. This goodness is individual, in that no one can achieve it for anyone else. It is not to be got by political involvement, by practicing the crafts or other pursuits that require technical know-how, or through art and literature. This goodness is the object of a search or inquiry in which one examines the limits of one's knowledge, testing opinion against opinion so that false beliefs are exposed. The search has its beginning in the recognition that human knowledge is a paltry thing in comparison with divine knowledge. And the search is conducted in obedience to a divine voice and calling: philosophizing is a duty owed to the god. It takes precedence over every other human concern, even the concern to preserve one's bodily life.

All of this but quickly sketches the contours of our investigations into Socratic motivation and commitment in later chapters. What we'll encounter is a Socrates who witnesses to the demand laid upon him to philosophize as an overriding duty, beyond the duties to state or self. Because he sees this demand as arising from the god—the oracle initiated his search, and he has had the divine sign since youth—his death is obedience to the god.

So it seems that Socrates fits the basic pattern of martyrdom as we have set it out: dying voluntarily an innocent death in order to witness, not so much to a body of truths as to the absolute demands of the divine. Godward obedience unto death is his mark and the mark of all martyrs; for his death again the right word is Witness.

Witness, yes: but may we call him martyr? Our answer for Jesus required us to see him as archetypal martyr, pattern and source for all

Christian martyrdoms. But it remains difficult to find a similar place for Socrates. Two sorts of reservation must be entered, the second more serious than the first.

I claimed above that Socrates exercises more control over the circumstances of his trial and death than does Jesus. Crito makes it clear in his rather frantic discussion three days before Socrates' execution that Socrates did not have to come to court at all, or conduct his defense as he did, or remain in prison. But the more choice and power the subject has, the less ready we are to see an innocent victim; and if the martyr does not willingly embrace a fate imposed, but instead creates that fate, then death resembles the witness of suicide, not obedience to the higher will of God. Now Socrates does in fact reject the idea that he is about to commit suicide; and he unequivocally invokes obedience to the god as his motive and justification. Unfortunately he has a reputation for being sly and slippery, so readers of his story—like some members of his jury—may suspect that he has engineered his own martyrdom. It doesn't help that in the *Crito* Socrates overdetermines his obedience by claiming that his duty to obey the laws of Athens supersedes his other duties toward self, family, and friends. Because we wonder how it's possible to live with two different (and possibly conflicting) absolute allegiances, the god and the laws, we may continue to suspect Socrates of providing handy justifications for his own wish to die.

A Socrates who would make a martyr of himself, of course, would bear false witness in using the words of obedience. Suspicions about his motives are, however, misplaced—or so I shall argue when discussing his Defense and his obedience to the god and the laws in later chapters. I'll claim that the moral integrity in his choices makes his profession of obedience to the divine will genuine, not manipulative. I shall also suggest that Socrates believes the state to be the instrument of the divine will in his death. That is just what martyrs themselves believe: so I find no considerations of Socrates' motives sufficiently strong to deny the appropriateness of viewing his death as martyrdom.

The second kind of reservation about Socrates as martyr reminds us of the problem we had in categorizing the nature of Jesus' martyrdom. Like Jesus, Socrates requires a special place for the witness in his death; but it is, and is not, like the territory Jesus inhabits. Let us clear away straight off one possible misdescription of the difference. We started this chapter wondering whether we might call Socrates a *philosophical* martyr. Without knowing quite what philosophical martyrdom entails, we would guess that Jesus is not *that* kind of martyr. Now, though, we understand more fully the witness of Socrates' death. He doesn't die so that free inquiry may flourish, or because he has latched onto philosophical beliefs he holds to be immutably true. Instead, he witnesses to a commitment to the pursuit of goodness that is carried out obediently, as divine duty. Insofar as the locus of Socratic obedience is in the will of the god, Socrates is appropriately situated among religious martyrs. His witness is thus like the witness of Jesus. Further, that Socrates does not testify as a recognized member of any identifiable religious group or movement—that too brings him close to the fundamental and archetypal testimony to faithfulness in the death of Jesus.

Nonetheless, we cannot call Socrates and Jesus identical archetypes of the martyr. That's not because the content of their religious beliefs is so different—though that is the case. Nor is it because the one witnesses in powerful words and the other in a defenseless silence—though that, too, is strikingly true. Rather, their difference lies in the appropriation of their witness by those who saw and believed. Socrates was not claimed by any form of social organization that revered him as martyr and was willing to imitate his death. Socrates has no Stephen; he isn't even a prototype from which other philosophical martyrs are made. Quite the contrary: when a charge was drawn up against Aristotle in 323 B.C., he left Athens so that, as the ancient story has him say, the Athenians would not "sin twice against philosophy." That's not to diminish Socrates' archetypal role as philosopher, or to ignore the veneration he has attracted. Still, philosophical followers do not die for Socrates, whereas the believing faithful have died for Jesus. That's the nub of the difference. Stephen's death not only bears witness to the same faithfulness as Jesus displayed; it is also testimony *to Jesus,* who, at the right hand of God, becomes himself the divinely worthy object of unconditional loyalty.

I remarked earlier that there are no generic citizens; to be a citizen requires identification with a particular state. We do, however, speak of "citizens of the world," by which we mean those who exemplify the virtues that any citizen of whatever state should exhibit, and whose spheres of concern cross national boundaries. Socrates inhabits if not a stateless martyrdom then one without clearly demarcated borders. The death of Jesus, however, establishes a new kingdom.

Witness and Death

We have met with our exemplary martyrs, and we know better how to regard the witness in the deaths of Jesus and Socrates. What is not yet resolved is our suspicion over the motivation of those who are willing to sacrifice their very lives in martyrological witness. We therefore must conclude with some discussion about the motives of martyrdom, and about the ethical and religious significance of dying for the faith. Those crowns and white robes still glitter in the celestial city. Giving up one's life requires such strength of motive that, we feel, only the promise of eternal rewards could win out over instincts for self-preservation—and then only in a few religious psychologies of extreme, perhaps unsophisticated, devotion. The moral mentality involved in refusing to save one's life would, on this view, be a matter of calculation in the currency of religious hope: great temporal loss for the sake of greater eternal gains. What seems stubbornly senseless to the observer would thus become entirely justifiable from the standpoint of belief, indeed justifiable on the grounds of one's own good.

Motivation and Martyrdom

But that sort of explanation just won't do. We who have listened to words of martyrological witness know that martyrs do not determine the rightness of their action by counting up robes and crowns. They don't even base their decision on the weight of good and bad consequences for people other than themselves. That is not to say that martyrs will reject all forms of consequential reasoning, including assessment of outcomes should they renounce the faith. Eleazer reasons conditionally with his tormentors, pointing out that being thought to eat pork would generate a false belief about his commitment and set a bad example to the young (2 Maccabees 6.24–25); he also reflects on his inability to escape the judgment of the Almighty (v. 26). And he recognizes the power of obedience in teaching the young through his death (v. 28). Nevertheless—we remind ourselves—Eleazer's primary motivation is awe for God and reverence for his holy laws. That precisely is the instructive content of his witness; that is why others would be led astray if they were deceived about his commitment. Moreover, Eleazer is not alone: most martyrs trust for some greater good from their deaths— which good may indeed result, if the faith of others grows stronger.

Even Eliot's Thomas à Becket says, near the end, "For my Lord I am now ready to die, / That his Church may have peace and liberty." In holding up striking examples of supreme commitment, martyrs encourage the aspirations of others to be faithful, uniting them against opposition and solidifying the community. Their blood, as the proverb has it, is the seed of the Church. Faced with the supreme test, a martyr may find comfort from that thought.

Nevertheless, the primary meaning of martyrdom is not instrumental for some temporal end. The martyr sees death as obedience and witness to the One who is to be obeyed unconditionally, whether or not the Church is strengthened by this death. That this is so may be seen by imagining a temptation more insidious than the one offered to Eleazer: Would you gain your life by renouncing the holy laws, or God, or Christ, if you knew for certain that no one else would ever know of your decision? It will not matter to the martyr that others cannot be misled by a betrayal of faith of which they are ignorant. God and the tempter know, and that is enough.

The martyr's decision is thus not taken for the good that it may bring to others, or for self-regarding reasons. It has a purity that is close to deontological—that is, the choice is made simply because it is the right one, consequences apart. But there is a special character of the martyr's opting to die rather than disobey. For in this final act of witness, the martyr—at least the martyr put to the test—is faced with a specially constructed choice: a choice between what is often deliberately set up as a disobedient and disloyal act, and a costly obedience. The structure of such choices is not unique to religious martyrs: Aristotle acknowledges in his *Nicomachean Ethics* that there are some actions so wrong that we should never give in to them, but must suffer instead the most terrible consequences, including death. Think, for example, of incest or the torture of the innocent. But the Christian martyr does not say of the tests and temptations imposed upon faith that they are "just wrong" in themselves, consequences apart; instead, they are seen as breaches of faith with God, as disloyalty and betrayal. This personalizes the commitment to the absolute and supreme, making it possible for the martyr to act out of love, not simply an impersonal respect for law or duty. It follows, then, that the moral justification of martyrdom does not entail that the martyr espouse an entirely deontological system of ethics, or believe that Christian morality consists in an uncomplicated obedience to divine commands in every other sphere of life. For most other situations are not like martyrdom; they are more problematically related to the believer's understanding of the divine will.

The choice between God and one's life is uniquely presented to the martyr. Yet the martyr's *motivation* is not unique to this one occasion; it is exhibited in the final trial only because it has informed the martyr's entire way of life. That, I suggest, becomes an unsettling realization for those who strive to be faithful believers—or indeed anyone who wishes to live in a developed integrity of character. We all find in martyrdom something to intrigue and to disturb our moral sensibilities; and if we reflect just a little on that, we may be able to sort out how this disturbing witness both compels and unsettles us.

The Disturbing Demands of Faithful Witness

Our time is skeptical of supreme sacrifices in the service of others: we are too conscious of ways in which the propaganda of patriotism and altruism may manipulate the unsuspecting into serving the desires of the powerful. We are wary, too, of the psychology of the self-appointed martyr, knowing well how our own needs may be cloaked in professions of interest for the well-being of others. We may not find it easy, then, to accept the purity of motive in the true martyr—which is why, perhaps, the most compelling presentations of martyrdom for our day are in dramatic literature where motivation may be carefully constructed, or in assassinations like Romero's, where death was not deliberately chosen.

And yet such examples do overcome our skepticism. They expose the conflict between our own moral practices and our moral ideals. It is contrary to moral trust that we should betray another for some perceived selfish gain; but we do it nonetheless. And not always in gross ways: what's significant is that our gains are so often meager—the childish pleasures of the snub, the tinny triumph of the put-down. Though we grow adept at providing leaky justifications to ourselves, our self-deceptions are not so successful that we do not recognize integrity and yearn for it. We still find it in our natures to admire those who cannot be bought at any price. Presented with someone who has a soul that cannot be purchased even at the cost of its very life, we step back as from sacred ground. This seems to have been the experience of the playwright Robert Bolt in writing *A Man For All Seasons*. As Bolt explains in his preface, he found in the character of Thomas More "a man with an adamantine sense of his own self. He knew where he began and left off, . . . but at length he was asked to retreat from that final area where he located his self. And there this supple, humorous, unassuming and sophisticated person set like metal, was overtaken by an absolutely primitive rigor, and could no more be budged than a cliff." As for the rest of us, "We feel—indeed we know—the self to be an equivocal commodity. There are fewer and fewer things which, as they say, we 'cannot bring ourselves' to do."

Nevertheless, in spite of all the admiration we feel toward the solidity and centeredness of character in the exemplary martyr, we do remain disturbed by martyrdom. For that, there may be psychological reasons; we can't quite put out of mind the serious abnormalities of the "martyr complex." Here, however, I am more concerned with the moral awkwardness we experience in the midst of our recognition of integrity. We are unsettled because the martyr takes the notion of duty beyond the limits of our comfort and uses the language of unconditional obedience in doing so.

It is commonly assumed that among the duties of the moral life must be counted self-preservation, in no small part because it is the necessary condition of all other virtues and duties. One should voluntarily give up one's life, then, only for very strong reasons. If one's death is necessary to save the lives of others, that could be justification for self-sacrifice. But even then, something within us wants to argue that there is no strict obligation to surrender one's own life, that the disinterested selflessness of the moral point of view does not entail as a duty the death of the self. Instead, those who make that sacrifice go beyond the strict requirements of duty, expressing a supererogatory love. Christians may think of such surrender as a Christlike gift of love, if that is their understanding of Jesus' own self-sacrifice.

But Christian martyrs inhabit a different moral space than do those who sacrifice themselves for others. Their duty to preserve themselves is not overridden by a duty to save others, or even by their love for them; nor do they regard their offering as a work of supererogation. It is instead an unconditional obedience to God. It's that unwavering and self-sacrificial obedience, I think, that we find unsettling. Moral integrity and the refusal to set a price on one's soul—that we admire; but must this be seen as absolute loyalty to another will outside the self?

The answer of the martyr is Yes. Otherwise witness is only *to the self*, and there is no martyrdom. But Yes must also be the answer of all faithful Christians, for themselves and not only for their martyrs. After all, the demand experienced in the trial of faith is not different from the demand laid upon the faithful in their lives. All believers, in life or in death, are to see themselves under obedience to God; martyrs are only the faithful exercising their obedience in stark circumstances, where witness is made in blood as well as word and deed.

It is the reluctant recognition that we should find our own commitment mirrored in the martyr that is disturbing. Most believers can acknowledge that in some things they may find it reasonable to be obedient, given that they need a little assistance now and then to work out what they should do. Yet obedience to God, as Abraham knew, may be costly. He was asked to surrender not just the son of his love but with him the entire meaning of his life, the future blessing promised to him and his offspring forever. Abraham is the father of the faithful, and the Gospel of Christ is no less difficult. The demands of Jesus relativize everything: to stay just with Matthew's account, everything is less important than the kingdom—possessions, clothing, food, drink; even family obligations and relationships. And the demands escalate, past Abraham's love of son, to strike at our embodied selves in the self-inflicted tearing out of eye or cutting off of limb should they be cause of even an intention to sin. There is yet more: the followers of Jesus are to deny their very selves, to take up the cross and become obedient like their Lord, losing their life to death; for those wanting to save their life will lose it. In their daily dying they are to imitate Jesus, for as we have seen, this obedience—and not a calculation about the salvation of the world—seems to have been the motivation for his own voluntary death.

That such language has application beyond literal martyrdom to the way in which one lives is expressed for all Christians in baptism as dying with Christ and in the Eucharist as the remembrance of that death and participation in it. If not the whole Gospel (I have said nothing of resurrection or of finding life having lost it), this is indeed hard good news, not reasonable at all. What can it mean? What notions of self and personal identity can survive this daily dying? Is it all poetry and paradox, designed to deny human worth by undermining the very conditions of our existence?

The questions seem as difficult as the message. It is tempting to ignore the unconditional demand of the Gospel by directing our attention elsewhere; we much prefer to regard the message of Jesus as one of love, acceptance, and affirmation that encourages us to make progress in learning to like ourselves better. And there is indeed acceptance in love; but there is also obedience to the will of God. We deceive ourselves if we think that there can be one without the other. Nevertheless, just as we must not cheapen divine love, neither must we cheapen obedience by mindlessly bowing to demands. The difficult questions persist. We rightly mistrust those who claim privilege in knowing the details of the divine plan; we rightly suspect those who make martyrs of themselves for the sake of the kingdom, ironically attending to the self that they claim to negate. So we must pursue to some conclusion the question of what it is to obey, and the puzzlement of daily dying. That work around obedience, love, and death awaits the last two chapters of the book. In the next we return to the trials and deaths of Jesus and Socrates in order to examine in more detail the character of their witness in word and silence.

As we leave martyrdom, however, we must impress upon our forgetful selves what we have learned. So let this serve as summary. Martyrs witness to a world determined to provoke disloyalty by threat of death. They also witness disturbingly to the Church that their commitment in the final hour cannot be optional for other faithful Christians: the demand is laid on all to be willingly and wholeheartedly obedient, even to the point of losing the self, and in this obedience to witness to the awful reality of God.

THREE

Word and Silence

He was maltreated, yet he was submissive and did not open his mouth; like a sheep led to the slaughter, like a ewe that is dumb before the shearers, he did not open his mouth.   —ISAIAH 53.7 (REB)

You shall hear from me the whole truth.   —SOCRATES, *Apology*

Whereof one cannot speak, thereof one must be silent.   —WITTGENSTEIN, *Tractatus*

AS WE COME NOW IN THIS CHAPTER to consider the Passion of Jesus, we will find ourselves struck by the contrasts between the angry noise of the mob and the silence of the victim, the repeated interrogations of the authorities and the persistent impassivity of the accused. When we move to Athens and the trial of Plato's Socrates, however, we will enter upon a very different linguistic space, one in which the chief speaker is the accused himself. The powerful words of Socrates in his own defense contrast boldly with the silence of Jesus, suggesting that Socrates is no pawn in these proceedings but an eloquent determiner of his own destiny. What that says for the respective personal authorities of Jesus and Socrates, and how both nevertheless construe their lives as obedient to a higher determination, we shall undertake to consider in Chapter 5. Here, though, our interest remains with words—their use and misuse, and especially their limitations.

The very title of this chapter suggests that, as Silence belongs to Jesus, so Word must be the category for Socrates. But we must not overdraw the contrasts, or be seduced by the simplicities of juxtaposition. The Word is the preeminent term for Jesus in the prologue of the Fourth Gospel; Socrates strikingly inhabits Silence in attending to his voice, a theme we shall have occasion to pursue later. Without their words, precious little would remain of either of them. Still, the opposition holds for their trials and deaths. The Jesus who had been so strangely authoritative in his teaching, and so skilled in evading the rhetorical traps of his enemies, sinks into silence. He shuts up, refusing to employ words to save himself. Socrates, unlike Jesus, takes up the weapons of words to explain and defend himself. Words are highly appropriate to Socrates' apologia, since he has devoted his entire life to Word. Or perhaps we should say Logos, the Greek term translated by word, which carries a complex of meanings, including reason and argument as well as the words Socrates so loved to exchange with anyone who would take part in discussion. Curiously, though, in his trial Word makes no more difference than did Silence in Jesus' trial. However skilled a wielder of words, Socrates cannot save himself with argument, reasoning, or language.

We shall learn something of the limits of language, then, in the lives and deaths of our two figures. The first part of the chapter will take us into silence by exploring Matthew's presentation of the Passion of Jesus, looking for clues as to why his Jesus does not speak. In the second half of the chapter we'll consider why Socrates claims to avoid certain kinds of speaking at his trial but nevertheless ends up using language that does not succeed in convincing the jury of his innocence. Our sources will be the *Apology,* of course, but also Plato's *Gorgias.*

Although our interest at present remains the trials and deaths of Jesus and Socrates, the theme of word and silence will persist throughout the rest of the book. Again and again we will discover ourselves up against the limits of language as we reflect upon prayer, obedience, love, and death. By the end we may have glimpsed something of what it might mean ourselves to keep silent—or better, to hand over to God our silence—where we do not know.

The Silence of Jesus

For a death to be martyrdom there must be witness; for witness there must be words. Without a context of shared meaning expressed in language, the commitment of the martyr remains opaque.

Yet silence sometimes speaks.

Take the silence of the martyr Thomas More—Robert Bolt's man for all seasons will do nicely for our purposes, for a dramatic construction can explore character and motivation in ways that strict historical evidence may not license. Bolt's character refuses to speak deliberately and out of principle, thus challenging his enemies so that they attempt to catch him out in some careless bit of talk. Finally he is brought to trial for denying the king his title as supreme head of the Church in England. Though More did not in fact take the oath, his defense lies in his never having uttered words of denial. At the trial Thomas Cromwell, acknowledging the existence of a silence pure and simple without further meaning (of a corpse, say), claims that More's silence is different. To say nothing in the face of imminent danger is to be complicitous; saying nothing when everyone is expected to make an affirmation is not silence at all, but the most eloquent denial.

To this More counters that his refusal must be construed according to the principle of the law, not by a guess about his inner beliefs. *Qui tacet consentire:* silence gives consent, not denial. But when done in by shameless perjury—Rich's false claim that More did deny the title— More speaks at last. His silence was not in fact consent but a resolute unwillingness to recognize a title that was not in the competence of Parliament to bestow, and contrary to both Magna Carta and the king's coronation oath.

More's silence must be broken if he is to die as witness to a loyalty that transcends earthly authorities. But his martyrdom is distinctively shaped by his silence, for it bears its own kind of witness, however incomplete, in two aspects. First, More hides in the law as refuge against the attacks of his enemies. If he will not perform the oath, nevertheless he will not deny the title in the oath; and he hopes that in this silence he will find his protection. His not speaking thus testifies to his trust in law as expressing an order that judges merely human institutions, standing above individual and national particularities. This respect for law is reminiscent of Socrates, who, however, sacrificed life for that respect rather than seeking salvation in it. Second, silence serves to underline what Bolt calls More's adamantine sense of self, an internal territory that could not be violated, the place where his conscience ruled uncompromised by external pressures. The greater the speaking, the more the self consists in words. In silence there is a stubbornness and tenacity of will, a wall around the well of the self. That More's keeping quiet should point to a stubborn confidence in something beyond the accidents of history requires, of course, that he say enough to make this witness possible, even before his final public self-disclosure at the trial. So Bolt has him reveal in the course of the play the meaning of his silence under the law. Given that context, the lack of words speaks eloquently to the reader, not so much of denial of the king's title as of the ground on which More guards his conscience.

For More, then, as for the Preacher, there was a time for silence and a time for speech, words being required to explain the significance of their absence. Unlike Socrates, who defended himself with much speaking, More attempted to find security in what he did not say. That he was ultimately unsuccessful does not mean that all who are silent fail; sometimes silence does afford more protection than speech. In most codes the accused is not required to speak words of self-incrimination, for the good reason that such evidence may be unreliable. Nevertheless this permission to refrain from providing evidence provides minimal protection; silence does not do the work that is usually necessary, the answering of accusations. If charges are to be rebutted, words are required.

Neither Socrates nor More keeps his quiet when accusations become formalized at their trials and they have to render an account of their behavior. Jesus, on the contrary, says practically nothing at his trial.

How shall we account for this silence of Jesus?

As Philip put it to the Ethiopian in Acts 8, Jesus went to his trial mute as a ewe before her shearers, to his death like a lamb to the slaughter; he did not open his mouth. The explanations of dumb terror or lack of comprehension must not be squeezed out of the similes, which are rather meant to express innocent submission. Jesus knows full well what is happening, and seems in ways we will examine to remain self-possessed. Why not, then, take the opportunity to speak, to make apparent the meaning of his conviction and death?

Jesus' refusal to speak does not inhabit the same kind of context as More's, where one hopes to gain protection from prosecution by not saying anything that might be construed as constituting an offense. When his enemies had attempted to trap him into saying the wrong thing, Jesus defended himself with effective language and strategies. His silence may be regarded simply as a strategy deployed against self-incrimination, so that not speaking became his best protection given the nature of the evidence marshaled against him. But as More's silence bears witness to something deeper within him, so there are dimensions to the silence of Jesus that make inadequate a reading of his speechlessness as a simple legal expediency.

To open up these dimensions will take some time. We will have first to set out the pattern of speaking and not speaking in the arrest, trial, and death of Jesus, an exercise that will suggest a couple of themes illuminating his silence. But we shall find ourselves drawn before long to the difficult question of his internal life, his sense of self, in order to appreciate something more of the silence of his Passion. After looking at the narrative, then, we will think of innocence and of false words, then of the motives and intentions of Jesus, before concluding what we can about his silence.

That one even suggests the possibility of investigating the inner life of Jesus will raise eyebrows—and from very different perspectives. The critical eye of the historian widens a little, as scholarship wonders how I plan to substantiate claims about a remote individual when we have nothing he himself wrote, and when the sources for his life are so complex and controversial. From another direction, some religious eyes regard with suspicion such a venture, for piety thinks it borderline blasphemy to intrude with audacious speculation into the life divine. So perhaps I must hark back to my introductory remarks in Chapter 1 and repeat that my aims are modest in comparison with fully developed historical or theological projects. In what follows I restrict myself to one piece of writing, Matthew's Gospel. And I reflect on the received text that all readers—a vast number, across centuries—have available to them, rather than upon a text reconstructed according to one or another theory of composition. Instead of bringing to that text a set of highly articulated christological beliefs, insofar as possible I attempt to listen to its presentation of the character of Jesus. And I have discovered that Matthew's account of the events of the last days of Jesus' life encourages us toward beliefs about the interests, concerns, and commitments that characterize his Jesus during those days. This tentative discernment of something of the inner life of Matthew's Jesus is like the exercise of developing the glimmers and insights we have into other people's lives in literature—where certainty eludes us and our accounts are revisable, even reversible, but where we may learn something true and valuable about them and about ourselves.

What follows, then, is to be understood as reflecting *Matthew's Jesus*. If occasionally I make some reference to another Gospel, nevertheless the question of the meaning of the silence of Jesus for the other evangelists is not addressed directly here. Nor are all those vexed historical questions about the arrest, the trials, and the crucifixion. It is the meaning of Matthew's story that we are after.

Speaking and Not Speaking in the Passion

Though the use of the word *passion* for the last events of Jesus' life is familiar, it may be of help to remember that its meaning lags behind current English usage. It is not intensity or depth of emotion (or another choice from one's thesaurus) that is to be understood in the term; rather the contrast is between action and passion, between doing and being done to, between being the subject and the object of verbs. In the closing scenes of Jesus' life, other people are constantly doing things to or with him; he is the object rather than the source of action. This is in contrast to his earlier activity, as may be seen especially in Mark's Gospel, which switches from the constantly active Jesus to a passive figure once Judas and the crowd come to arrest him in the garden called Gethsemane. One writer has counted up Mark's verbs: after the arrest, Jesus is the object of fifty-six verbs of action, but the subject of only nine verbs—four of which are negative; four are verbs of speaking, and one is the act of dying. Thus Jesus appears to do practically nothing in his arrest, his ecclesiastical and civil trials, and his death. These events constitute his Passion.

That said, it remains true that the Gospel accounts of the Passion are not narratives of a passivity so complete that all presence has been emptied out of Jesus. He occupies the center of the action, not just because things are done to him, but also because of what he says and does not say. That *saying* is its own form of *doing*. This principle may best be seen in Matthew's account, where Jesus speaks seven times: three times at his arrest, twice in the trials, and twice at the end of his life. In the rest of this section we will deal with speaking and not speaking in the arrest, the two trials, and the crucifixion.

The Arrest (26.47–56) Jesus has finished speaking words of prayer in the garden. As he is rousing his disciples, a great armed crowd arrives to arrest him. Matthew reports several lines of speech, to three audiences: to Judas, to the follower who cut off the servant's ear (whom John identifies as Peter: 18.10, 26), and to the crowd.

In Jesus' words of arousal, Judas had just been named betrayer: "The traitor is upon us!" (26.46); yet to his face Jesus calls him friend, adding a sentence fragment: "What you're here to do" (v. 50). Although some translators see this as a question ("What are you here for?"), the words may be a simple acknowledgment that Jesus knows Judas' purpose and in this speaking permits him to get on with it ("Do what you are here to do" NRSV). The words on his lips say the same thing as the offering of his cheek for the kiss: in both Jesus underscores the subversion of the conventional meaning of word and gesture in this scene by submitting himself without resistance to the decidedly unfriendly designs of Judas.

One follower does resist, blade slashing a servant's ear. He is rebuked for this violence: "Put up your sword." That cessation of hostility may be regarded as an act of surrender; but this is not weakness. Instead, Jesus' rhetorical question ("Do you think I cannot appeal to my Father, who would at once send more than twelve legions of angels to my aid?") proclaims his ability to secure effective help from his Father upon request. His order, and his refusal to invoke this power, repeat the message to Judas, that he does not resist the arrest. But he adds something else: this acceptance is in order that the Scriptures be fulfilled, which say that "this must happen."

Addressing now the entire crowd, Jesus questions their assumptions about him. By arming themselves they assume that he will resist like a lawbreaker escaping justice; in fact, he had not hidden himself but rather had been available publicly in the Temple to be taken. Again he adds that the whole thing has come about to fulfill the prophets' writings.

Jesus is not silent in his arrest, then; rather his questions and statements make it plain to all participants in the drama—followers, betrayer, arresters—that he does not struggle against the stream of events. Having been stripped of his liberty, he offers no resistance, and in a few hours will practice what he had said about turning the other cheek. In the words and gestures of nonresistance, some sense of dignity is preserved for an agent-turned-captive because that agent retains a genuine self-control. So for Jesus there is a difference between *being overpowered* and *handing himself over*. But that difference is emphasized in two further ways, by his assertion of superior power at the hand of his Father, and by his placing his arrest and what follows within the context of Scripture and the prophets. In some unexplicated fashion, what is about to take place will fill out these writings. That claim dislocates the initiative from the arresting mob and its leaders, implicating them in the unfolding of a wider scheme and purpose.

The words at the arrest thus reinforce the foundation and framework of the Passion and disclose a deliberate relinquishing of control. From now on Jesus will say very little. Unless asked, he will volunteer nothing until the closing moments of his crucifixion.

The Trial at Caiaphas' House (26.57–68) Matthew makes his perspective quite clear: the trial is based on false evidence, a false speaking that was not persuasive even to the court at first. Then two men allege that Jesus claimed that he would destroy the Temple and rebuild it in three days. The high priest rises and tries to provoke words from Jesus: Aren't you answering these charges? Nothing: Matthew expects us to know that this report is a distortion (see 24.1), but Jesus remains silent. Why? Did he wait in hope that this claim would also be discredited by another witness? Or perhaps he was remembering his earlier advice to the disciples: When you are dragged up before governors do not worry what to say; when the time comes, the words you need will be given you; it will not be you speaking but the Spirit of your Father speaking in you (10.17–20).

The high priest next uses words of solemn power: *I demand of you on oath by the Living God that you tell us:* are you the messiah, the Son of God? To this Jesus might again have said nothing, but something finally pushes him into speech. Though the high priest forces the oath upon him, it is not clear that Jesus accepts this condition of utterance; and it is far from clear that he answers the direct question, to which he might simply have replied according to his own teaching: Do not swear oaths; plain yes or no is all you need say (5.33–37). Instead, he utters those ambiguous words, "you say"—not "*it is as* you say," but "yours are the words." And he then adds, as though his own words ("but I am telling you"), what is but a conflation of two bits of Scripture: Psalm 110.1, where the Lord is seated at the right hand of his Lord, and Daniel 7.13, where the son of man comes on clouds of heaven: *From now on you will see the Son of Man seated at the right hand of the Almighty and coming on the clouds of heaven.* In these words we are given some Scriptures under the meaning of which Jesus might see his Passion, and they will become significant later when we attempt to consider his self-understanding. For now it is sufficient to note that even though these were (in a rhetorical sense) largely words with quotation marks around them rather than his own speech, everyone on the council took this to be evidence of blasphemy, out of Jesus' own mouth, so that no further witnesses were required to convict him. That Jesus intended this result is unlikely. Nevertheless it is a provocative assertion, privileging Jesus in his knowledge of what will happen and demoting the high priest's own authority.

After the guilty verdict, some begin to abuse Jesus, spitting at him, beating him—and taunting him to speak again, this time to provide proof of his prophetic powers by identifying the author of the blows (he had been blindfolded, says Mark). Matthew finds it unnecessary to add that Jesus remained silent.

Before Pilate (27.2–31) Pilate now questions Jesus, this time about his political role: Are you the king of the Jews? Again the reply that is no reply—*You are the one saying that*—and absolutely nothing in response to the repeated charges levied against him. Pilate is so astonished at this that he pointedly asks whether Jesus doesn't hear how many accusations are brought against him; but Jesus answers (Matthew spells it out) not one word.

Words follow upon words: questions from Pilate, warnings from his wife, much shouting with one voice from scores of angry mouths, disavowals of responsibility, more clamoring, terms of mockery, and jeering. Throughout it Jesus remains silent.

The Crucifixion (27.32–54) Led out to Golgotha, Jesus says nothing. Whether he made verbal complaint about the weight of the cross or protested in words the bitter wine, whether nails drove words from his lips, we are not told. Matthew moves Jesus silently out of the city and onto the cross, where he is made the target of taunting speech yet again. Much of the narrative looks as though it were written over snatches of the Psalms, especially Psalm 22, as Scripture is filled out in the death of Jesus. At last, near the end, Jesus breaks the long silence with a loud cry from the start of that Psalm: *My God—my God—why have you forsaken me?* There is no answer. Jesus' last vocal act is another loud cry, the words unrecorded, perhaps not speech at all if there was nothing left to say.

We can summarize now the pattern of word and silence in the Passion of Jesus. It turns out to be straightforward. The threefold speaking at the arrest throws light ahead onto what is said and not said in the trial and crucifixion. Jesus asserts the authority of the Father and of Scripture over what is about to happen, but relinquishes in an explicit way his own initiative by handing himself over. Once that is done, his words seem to contribute little of his own voice. Either he observes without any necessary commitment, "you put it that way," or else he utters phrases that are the psalmist's or the prophet's. Where is *he* in this speaking? Why does he say nothing, or only draw attention to the words of others?

Reasons for Silence: Innocence and False Words

Having suggested that there is more to Jesus' saying nothing than the desire not to incriminate oneself, I want to probe his silence a little further. In the course of the last section I hazarded two more possibilities, the first of which may now be rejected. If Jesus did not speak because he was stalling, waiting for another contradictory witness to come forward, he would have nevertheless been able to answer in his own defense eventually. He did not. As for the second suggestion, harking back to the saying about the arrested follower's dependence for words on the Spirit of the Father: on that view Jesus must have thought God to have given him very little to say, and nothing effective in the end.

There may be other reasons. Perhaps he doesn't speak because he will not be heard. Given a certain kind of determined opposition there is no point to trying to influence actions or attitudes through more talking, as anyone who has been child or parent knows. Or again, sometimes speaking will insinuate too much of the self into a situation. As further reflection will shortly confirm, Jesus believes that he must die. To mount a defense might constitute a retrieval of what he has handed over; speaking words is dangerous because their skillful use could erode the grounds for prosecution, contrary to purpose. At the same time, because there is strong emphasis on Jesus' own innocence, he must not attract by his speaking a guilty measure of responsibility for his death. Socrates, remember, did use words to push the jurors further than they might have gone in sentencing him.

Guilt and Innocence Lambs to the slaughter: the image is an archetype of innocence. It relates to ancient sacrificial practice, the helpless and unblemished put to the knife because of guilt that does not belong to them. Applied by the psalmist (Psalm 44.22) to the suffering of the faithful and echoed by Paul (Romans 8.36) in the context of persecution, the image survives in our time in the metaphors of war, where the undeserving are sacrificed in some useless cause.

Though the early Christian assignment of the term *lamb of God* to Jesus does not appear in Matthew, nevertheless this gospel does portray Jesus as guiltless. He does not open his mouth. How does his silence relate to that most crucial feature of his death, its innocence?

A quick reminder of Matthew's construction of the life and Passion will serve to establish his presentation of the innocence of Jesus. From the very beginning, in chapter 2, Jesus' life is in danger as Herod slaughters those other innocents. By chapter 12 the Pharisees are plotting to get him, and the net tightens during the final week in Jerusalem. The chief priests and Pharisees, wanting to arrest him (21.46), attempt to trap him in argument (22.15, 35) as do the Sadducees (22.23). The elders join to hatch a scheme (26.3) in which Judas participates (26.15). There is much emphasis on handing over and betrayal, reinforcing the conviction that his enemies were determined to do Jesus in regardless of his legal position. That his betrayer should repent his action after the arrest, saying he has betrayed innocent (*athphon*) blood (27.4), only strengthens that conviction.

At the trial before Caiaphas, we are told that the witnesses are false (26.59–61). Pilate's wife is brought in to call Jesus an innocent (*dikaion*) man (27.19); and Pilate himself, not convinced of Jesus' guilt, washes his hands in an attempt to make himself as innocent as Jesus must be ("I am *athphos* of his blood" [27.24]). Given all this, the imposition of death by crucifixion seems the outcome of mob psychology rather than fair judicial process.

In general terms one can distinguish between legal guilt and victimization: it's possible to be guilty of an offense without being victimized in the punishment assigned, if the treatment is indeed deserved and sanctioned by law. But to be maltreated, made the object of gratuitous hatred, when one is innocent—that is to be doubly victimized. In Jesus' case, Matthew writes his Passion narrative with verbs of spitting, striking, beating, flogging, stripping, dressing up, jeering, mocking, taunting. Such language conveys a sense of unwarranted abuse and sheer brutality against which the innocence and victimization of Jesus stand out with tragic and ironic force.

One function of silence is to heighten this innocence. This is especially so with physical abuse, which so often provokes words of protest that their absence increases the sense of victimization. When the intention of humiliating abuse is to break the victim, words often signify the breaking; if they do not come, the wrongness but also the senselessness of the very attempt is potently exposed. Imagine the lash on the back of someone gagged to prevent speaking, then on someone's back who *will* not speak. Matthew's silent Jesus proclaims by silence his innocence. And in handing his body over to malice without speaking, he also hides his inner self in that silence.

Within the trial procedures themselves, silence contributes to our sense of Jesus' innocence. Partly because his lack of defense sits so squarely in the midst of evil designs and false witness, his refusal to speak is accusatory in itself. Moreover, the limited speaking Jesus does engage in does not exactly break his silence about himself. Counteraccusation may be one reading of those terse the-words-are-yours retorts: "Those are your charges; I am saying nothing"—which is, of course, an ironic maintenance of silence even in speaking. That his speaking at the trial is not in his own voice contributes to the sense of a subverted justice. Why should merely repeating words in the public domain constitute compelling evidence for conviction? In refusing to answer and in disclaiming ownership for what he does say, Jesus keeps himself from being implicated in guilt. Yet he does not withhold himself completely from the action: Matthew makes sure that we understand him to perform something by his speaking to the high priest. *But I myself tell you: from now on you shall see*—these words preface the repetition of Scripture. In the I/you dichotomy comes a flash of assertion, undercutting the high priest's authority. So this pattern of word and silence, though it locates blame outside of Jesus and enhances his innocence, also reinforces his presence in the narrative.

False Words Return now to the theme of false speech that plays in the mouths of all those around Jesus in the Passion story. Matthew uses the word *false* explicitly of the trial witnesses; because of its falsity their testimony is powerless to bring about Jesus' conviction. But other false speech is damaging. Some of it manifests an immediate irony of word and gesture: Judas' salutation "Master" with its kiss, handwashing Pilate's proclamation of his own guiltlessness. Had their words been true, neither would have acted as he did.

But what holds for Judas holds for the rest of Jesus' followers—they, too, speak falsely, though it is only later that their deeds belie their words. Each of them implies in his "Surely you do not mean me" (26.22) that his own loyalty is firm; all of them echo Peter's "Even if I have to die with you I will not disown you" (26.35). Unlike the betrayer, they intend well at the time. And three of them are singled out for special treatment because of the strength of their intentions. In the garden Jesus takes Peter, whose profession of allegiance is so explicit (Everyone else may lose faith, but not me), and the two sons of Zebedee (who a few days earlier had no hesitation about their ability to share his cup with him [20.22]), and gives them a simple request as an expression of commitment: to stay awake with him. They fail—three times over. Then all the disciples desert him and run away at the arrest. The taunts of his enemies are matched by the broken promises of his friends; those who will watch his death are women who said nothing but followed him anyway, including the mother of those sons of Zebedee.

Peter's false speaking—his capacity for disloyalty—deserves special attention. Three times he lies baldly, breaking his association with Jesus and his very knowledge of him, with the verbal violence of curses directed perhaps at Jesus himself. Unlike the betrayal by Judas, Peter's denial serves no purpose in the unfolding of the Passion. Peter doesn't even do it for money. He becomes the antitype of the martyr: he will do anything, say anything, to save his own skin. Of all the untruth in this story, Peter's words are the worst. At least Judas returned to the place where he went wrong and gave back the blood money with words of repentance. When Peter came to himself, he went out into the dark; and the only noise Matthew lets us hear is the sound of weeping.

Amid this disloyal and ironic discourse, this lying and promise breaking, what is Jesus to say? Who will hear him? Not his friends, whose professions mean nothing. Not his accusers, for whom words are only tools to accomplish their designs; not the mob, who hearken to nothing but their own rage.

The silence of Jesus stands, I suggest, not only as an assertion of innocence but also as a rebuke to false words. In the resolute saying of nothing, he shows that loyalty and obedience consist not in the word but the deed. But in that claim I have run ahead of myself, because there is more evidence for this than I have yet adduced. There is much in Matthew to point to this conclusion, however, and it is time to enter upon that material. In the next long section, then, we will ask what, for Jesus, is involved in obedience—which of course for him means obedience to the will of the Father.

The Interrogation of Motive in Matthew

It is only fair to be warned: this section will shortly move into a fairly close reading of five and a half chapters of Matthew's Gospel, setting out block after block of text only loosely arranged around the themes at which we have arrived—silence, motivation, and action. If the events, parables, and discourses of this part of the Gospel are unfamiliar, the reader may wish to glance at chapters 20 through 25 or to keep a copy at hand for consultation. In the end, though, the assembled material will disclose a consistent and (for me at least) compelling architecture of the inner life of Matthew's Jesus during his final days. Occasionally the motif of silence will appear, and we will not forget to retrace that in our conclusions. Our beginning is a long way from that, however; we start with more words.

What Do You Want? Matthew's choice of vocabulary suggests an interest in the wanting that we engage in, the objects of our wishes and desires. He uses the verb *thelein* and the noun *thelêma* a total of forty-eight times (compared with Mark's twenty-six, Luke's thirty-three, and John's thirty-four). The verb has a range of meanings involving what we might call inclinations or affective attitudes, as well as our will. It can be translated, depending on the context, as *to want, to desire, to wish, to will;* its negative is often simply *to refuse.* (Before the crucifixion Jesus *would not drink* the wine with gall, 27.34.) In the Septuagint the verb sometimes picks up the desiring side of the term and so can mean *to delight or take pleasure in* (as at Psalm 18.19, 41.11). The noun is usually translated by *will,* as in *the will of the Father.*

A term with this range of meanings begs for some exploration. Our psychology is such that what we find ourselves desiring may or may not be the object of our willing (in the sense of deciding in favor of that object or action). This is clearest in the case of some appetites, when we find in ourselves a desire for a pleasure that we know is not good for us; so (if we are wise) we reject—do not will—what we were wanting. The experience is familiar: we all know what it is to be caught up in a tangle of conflicting desires and wants. At such times we often resort to asking what we *really* want, and in this interrogation of desires and wants we hope to discern our true will.

Were we to continue this exploration we would have to relate the terms just introduced to other concepts in the same family, like choice, intention, and motivation. Philosophers have spent a good deal of time trying to sort out relations among these concepts in the philosophy of action, with results that are not without interest. Nevertheless, our text here does not lend itself to careful analysis, for Matthew has no concern with questions of motivation and action for their own sake. His language does, however, permit us to focus on what I call the interrogation of motivation, for on several occasions his use of *thelein* and *thelêma* raises the issue of conflicting desires and true wants. To help us focus on those occasions, in what follows the italicized words are translations of these terms. But the translations and vocabulary are not philosophically rigorous: I will tend to speak about the wider family of these related concepts rather than their individual members, of motivation but also of wants and intentions. We can do this because the issue before us is the uncovering of the inner life in its conflicts and its relation to speech and action. And so to the text of Matthew's Gospel.

For Matthew, the *will* of the Father is ultimate, though it is not automatically fulfilled—which is why we must pray that his *will* come about on earth as well as in heaven (6.10). It is the doing of this *will* of the Father in heaven that is important, not simply using the words "Lord, Lord" of Jesus (7.21); it is that which makes one brother, sister, mother to Jesus (12.50). These oppositions between earth and heaven, words and deeds, indicate immediately that there is a difference between our inclinations to action or speech and the *will* that we need to make our own and follow. Indeed, if one does *wish* to follow Jesus (16.24), one must deny self; who *wishes* (16.25) to save life will lose it. So we must be on guard against the wantings and desirings that we find within ourselves: they may deceive us and lead us astray. A clear example of that comes in chapter 19, when someone asks Jesus what he must do to gain eternal life. If you *want* (19.17) to enter into life, Jesus replies, keep the commandments; if you *want* (19.21) to be perfect, give your possessions to the poor and follow me. The young man's disappointed departure reveals his true heart: the desire to hang onto secure wealth wins out over what he had presented as the object of his interest. Though good, his intentions lacked proper motivation.

Sometimes Matthew's language is straightforward, as when Judas questions the chief priests (26.25): what *do you want* to give me to hand him over to you? Or the choice between two objects, though in conflict, may be so obvious that the question becomes rhetorical (for the reader if not for the asker), as in Pilate's interrogation of the mob (27.12, 17): Which one *do you want* me to release, Barabbas or Jesus? But even if uncomplicated, such questioning peels away behavior to expose intentions. Sometimes the result is revealing, as when the disciples ask Jesus about a location (26.17): not simply "where should we . . . ," but "where *do you want* us to prepare the Passover for you to eat?" The answer reveals that the location is not the true object of his attention. Instead of announcing a place, Jesus replies that they should tell the unidentified host that the teacher's appointed time *(kairos)* is near: that is what is foremost in Jesus' mind, casting its shadow on the meal to be made ready.

Self-Questioning in the Questioning of Jesus The themes of attention and intention in Jesus' own mind may be approached more and less directly. Matthew is sometimes explicit about Jesus' desires and will. That will can be dominant beyond the ordinary: the leper in chapter 8 says to him, Lord if *you want to,* you can cleanse me. Jesus' answer is: *I do want to;* be clean. In spite of that authority, by the time of the imminent arrest in the garden, Jesus is praying, *Not as I will, but you* (26.40); it is *your will* that is to be done (26.32). How it can be God's will that Jesus should die is a perplexity brought out with taunting cruelty during the crucifixion by his enemies: "He trusted in God, did he? Let God rescue him if *he wants* him" (27.43). The words recall Psalm 22.9: "He threw himself on the Lord for rescue; let the Lord deliver him, for he *holds him dear.*" The Septuagint's use of the same verb for both wanting and delighting underscores the taunt: if God delights in Jesus, how then can it be God's will that he die this death?

Matthew does not answer this question by a direct presentation of Jesus' self-understanding. That does not mean, however, that we have no material to aid our appreciation of his intentions and desires. For in the interrogation of motivation of others undertaken by Jesus in narrative, parable, and discourse, we can glimpse indirectly the objects of his own attention and will during the final days of his life. Remember that we are not thinking to uncover in the reading that follows the inner consciousness of the historical Jesus himself any more than we get at the "real Socrates" in Plato. Instead the question is: if one listens to Matthew for clues, what may reasonably be believed about his Jesus' own self-interrogation? Instead of looking directly through his questions to their audiences, we may tilt them so as to reflect a little of his own mind.

Start with the last trip to Jerusalem, in chapter 20. The mother of Zebedee's sons approaches Jesus to beg the favor we considered in the previous section. Jesus' question is the simple, *what do you wish?*— significant because the brothers did not comprehend what they were putting their mother up to in asking for their honored places in the kingdom (cf. 19.28). All Jesus can offer is a share in the cup he has to drink. In this incident Jesus must have reflected on his own reasons for acting, for as he goes on to explain to the others, he himself did not come to be waited on, but to be slave, servant, ransom for others. He puts it this way: who *wishes* to be great or first must *be* servant or slave. Nothing here about *wishing* to be: the emphasis is on the doing, and Jesus deliberately removes himself from the kind of wishing the brothers were engaging in.

It's otherwise, however, in the event immediately following this story. For by the side of the road out of Jericho are two blind men, shouting out their *kyrie eleêson* until Jesus asks them, *what do you wish me to do?* Their response is direct and simple: open our eyes, sir. Jesus, stirred deep down inside (the verb's root refers to the viscera), touches their eyes. Why is he so moved by this request, so distanced from the other? Because the blind know deeply what they want, and what they want is what Jesus can give. But their desire also relates to what he himself feels about his coming ordeal—the need for clarity of vision, simplicity of motive. What darkness will he encounter in that trial? Is he about to submit to the suffering of obedience only because what he really wants is that center throne in the kingdom?

I do not claim that Matthew's Jesus stops to put this question to himself, that he remembers just now the third Satanic temptation, to gain the kingdom (though the kingdoms of this world and their kind of glory) by a simple act of painless obedience to the devil (4.8–10). But Matthew does permit us to put the question for him, especially because in chapter 16 Peter, when he rejects for Jesus the way of great suffering and death, is dismissed with the same words as the tempter. What we may reasonably believe is this: if there is any force in these temptations for Jesus himself, then he must be struggling with his own wishes and desires; and the way he deals with others may be clues to those unvoiced struggles.

Or so I propose. The test of my proposal is the reading we may give the words and events of the next chapters in Matthew, up to the evening of that last Passover meal and Jesus' arrest. The structure of this section of the Gospel I see as follows:

Jesus enters Jerusalem in tumultuous triumph on what we now call Passion Sunday (the first part of chapter 21); he encounters adulation and opposition for the next few days but is determined to stay his course without giving in to either. There come four distinct challenges: questions about his authority, answered in three parables (21.23–22.14); then questions about taxes (22.15–23); about resurrection (22.24–33); and about priorities for obedience (22.34–40). Having turned back these challenges, Jesus puts a question of his own (22.41–46). He then counterattacks with a full chapter (23) of public denunciation of hypocrisy and follows that with a long private conversation about the end of the world, occupying two chapters (24, 25). By chapter 26 the plot to kill him comes to the fore as the leaders plot in Caiaphas's house, Jesus is anointed in Simon's house, and Judas sells him out for silver. But in the words and events leading up to that betrayal, we may see something of Jesus' attitude toward his own death—which will explain why he answers as he does, why he introduces parables, why he deals with hypocrisy, why he speaks of the end of all things.

Before we come to the challenges, note three things about the events in the first half of chapter 21. First, amid the clamor of the triumphal entry Jesus remains—according to the narrative at least—silent. The contrast between shouting crowd and silence prefigures the same contrast at his trial; here as there we know little of Jesus' own construction of this event. If we ask why he takes the donkey, the only answer will be, "the master has a need"; what need we don't know. But we may expect him to experience some small gratification that his mission has attracted such attention, some positive feeling toward this turn of events. Instead—this is second—the only clue reveals anger: Matthew has Jesus going straight to the Temple to overthrow tables and cast commerce out of the place of prayer. Even the next morning he is still sufficiently peeved to curse a fig tree. Of course—this is the third thing—there is another purpose in the fig tree story. The point, says Jesus, is to demonstrate the power of prayer in faith: any of the disciples could do what he did, and, more impressively (but also more destructively), hurl mountains into the sea. We are to understand that there are reserves of power available to Jesus: if he is about to pray faithfully without being answered, about to bear himself the curse of the tree, it must be because in some sense he wills that to happen. His later words relinquishing control at his arrest, we now see, pick up a theme present in this peculiar story, contrasting the power of his speech here with that relinquishment.

So we begin the last round of conflict with the city's leaders, tightening the circle to entrap Jesus. He has distanced himself from rule and power, emphasized obedient service, questioned motive, ignored in silence popular acclaim, experienced frustration and anger. Now comes the battle of wits.

The Questioning of Authority: 21.23–22.14 First question: on what authority does Jesus act? His answer is to ask the questioners whether they are able to tell whether or not John's baptism was God's work. In dealing with that parry, the leaders worry not about the truth of the matter but only about what their possible answers would entail. (Would they commit themselves to belief with a positive answer? Incur popular disapproval with a negative one?) The trappers are themselves snared and plead ignorance as their escape. Jesus does not plead ignorance of the source of his authority; he uses their professed ignorance as reason for his silence. But behind that silence lies his own choice, doing the wishes of the crowd or the will of the Father.

The three parables he tells to those who profess ignorance of God's work may be read on two levels, directly exposing his adversaries and tilted in order to uncover his own mind. All three parables concern sons and fathers.

In the first, one son tells his father that he will work in the vineyard but does nothing; the other, when asked, replies, *I don't want to*, but goes anyway. Which did the *will* of his father? In the second parable, the landowner sends servant after servant to collect what is his own, but they are killed; finally he sends his son, whose authority should be respected. But the son is killed too, and justice falls swiftly upon the tenants. The chief priests and Pharisees, says Matthew, saw themselves in these two stories—not surprisingly, for Jesus does not let them miss the message. Because they did not heed John the Baptist, they did not do the will of the Father (though sinners did); they killed the servant prophets and refused to give God proper fruit. That, though, is only one level. For the parables apply also to Jesus as son: to do the Father's will is not—emphatically not—to *say* that one will do it; it is instead simply *to do* it, even if one has said that one does not want to. That links directly the second parable with the first, and both to the question of authority: for it is the father's will to send the son to the murderous tenants, even though his authority will be rejected. It matters not what the son says; it matters only that he obey.

The son in the third parable plays no role other than being the reason for a wedding feast. The attention is rather on guests and the king who is host. The invited guests *don't wish* to come, but this is no polite refusal. Instead they reject the whole business, some even murdering the messengers. So the king retaliates with fire, and ends up bringing in people off the streets for the feast. So far so good: the point is like the previous one. As the first shall be last, so those "in" may find themselves "out," and those out may find themselves in. But there is a disturbing coda. The king finds some unfortunate who took up the invitation but without wedding clothes. When challenged the guest has nothing to say (the root of the verb is "muzzle"), and he is thrown heartlessly into the night. Did he not do the father's will in coming to the son's wedding? But how so, if he did not come dressed *for* a wedding? If the saying is not the decisive thing, nevertheless there must be the right purpose in the doing. The silence cannot be the inability to open a mouth muzzled by mindlessness about one's actions.

It would be useless to ignore the violence in the second and third stories: seizing, thrashing, brutal attacking, stoning, and murder are essential to their plots. So is retributive justice and the greater purpose of God in reversing positions and elevating the rejected stone to the final key place of honor. If the language of Matthew mirrors Jesus' anticipation of violence and death, it also suggests the possibility of a final vindication.

Three More Challenges and a Counterquestion: 22.15–46 Halfway through chapter 22 we come to a succession of three encounters, one about competing allegiances, one about a belief, and one about priorities for obedience. The point of these challenges is to use language to lay a trap or snare for Jesus.

God and Caesar first. The introductory comments are saccharine: we know you are honest, sincere, true, without regard for anybody's favor—so you won't be afraid of the Romans or hesitate to tell us what's right. Should we pay taxes to Caesar or not? If yes you advise support of our enemies; if no you counsel civil disobedience. The answer, prefaced by the charge of hypocrisy for the sake of entrapment, is successful in its simplicity. That simplicity does not, however, answer all questions about the things of Caesar and the things of God. Caesar will require of Jesus his life, which requirement he will not resist; yet he will render that life not to Caesar but to God.

Next come the Sadducees, to try Jesus out on a question of belief. This is not exactly a legal trap, because there would be no charge of heresy on which Jesus could be convicted if he got the answer wrong. It is instead an attempt to play around with him. By picking a tough question, they hope not only to embarrass him but to bring into disrepute a belief held by others, chiefly their rivals the Pharisees. If his defense is inadequate, the others will be let down, which will increase their hostility toward him. The Sadducean maneuver is thus malicious, a verbal counterpart to the purple robe that mockery will later put on Jesus, a strategy whose only point is diminishment.

The question is one of the logical coherence of belief: how can a resurrection world be coherent if in collapsing a series of temporal relationships those relationships become incompatible? Jesus might well have commented on the malice behind the question, as in the first case. He doesn't. For some reason he is not content to silence the attackers; he wants rather to speak the truth. The Sadducees have strayed far away, ignorant of scripture and God's power: their assumption about what relationships will obtain in the resurrection world is mistaken. There is no incompatibility, no incoherence of belief about that world.

That would do it: one succeeds in rebutting an attack on consistency by such a defense. Jesus is unable to leave it there, though. About the resurrection itself, he continues: the God of Abraham, Isaac, Jacob is the God not of the dead but the living. The assertion rests on the assumption that the fathers are indeed living, so that cannot itself constitute a proof. But forget the logic, which isn't the point; ask instead why Jesus bothered. What was going on in his mind that he should speak so? A concern that obedience to death would not leave him among the Sadducean dead but with the God of the living?

Though the answer perhaps reveals more about Jesus than about his opponents, it, too, is effective: the Sadducees are silenced, shut up—muzzled, like the poor wretch at the wedding. The Pharisees move in for one last try. What sort of commandment in the law is the greatest? This is the sort of question philosophical types love: claim there is no ranking and you cannot act when two commands clash, as they well might; but it's hard to spell out criteria of importance, and any particular commandment will always be open to challenge from its near rivals in importance. The answer again is more direct than clever. Quoting from Deuteronomy, Jesus places loving God with all one's powers as the first commandment; adding love of neighbor from Leviticus, he makes all the law and the prophets hinge on two fundamentals. If not entirely unique as rabbinical teaching, the answer is nevertheless memorable. It has two features not often noticed, the significance of which is perhaps too easily exaggerated. The Shema in Deuteronomy enjoins Israel to love God with all one's heart, soul, and strength. In Mark and Luke "mind" appears as an addition to "heart" (curiously, for the Septuagint manuscript traditions have either "heart" or "mind," but not both). Matthew's Jesus gives us the same addition, emphasizing that love for God must employ the understanding *(dianoia)*. If one looks for significance, the message may be that the setting of wit against wit in verbal traps is not an expression of the mind's love for God. But Matthew (and he alone) makes another change: his Jesus omits the phrase about loving *with all one's strength.* Contemplating his own obedience in love to the Father, Jesus knows that his entire being is to express that love which fulfills the first commandment. But what is it to love obediently with the whole of one's understanding? Neither the doing nor the loving must be mindless—but how much understanding is present, or absent, in the silence of the doing? How much strength will be available in that silence if the understanding fails?

The chapter ends with the tables turned on the pursuers. They are given a question about a son: whose son is messiah? David's. "How then . . . " and Jesus puts a text to them which makes the same person both son of David and Lord over David. The resolution of the paradox involved continuing a discussion they did not want to have. So from that day the opposition was silenced. Words would no longer do.

Speaking Out in Public: Chapter 23 The Jesus who had been silent among the noise of Passion Sunday now speaks out publicly, probably in the Temple (cf. 24.1). He addresses the crowds and his disciples (23.1–12), pronounces seven woes upon scribes and Pharisees with increasing anger (vv. 13–36), and ends up lamenting over the entire city in an image of surprising tenderness (vv. 37–39) that openly discloses his own mind.

The subject of the initial address is a return to saying vs. doing (do what the scribes and Pharisees say on the authority of Moses; do not imitate their behavior). It moves quickly to the intention behind the doing (what they do is done only with an eye to self-exaltation), and the rest of the chapter stays on that topic. These striking and passionate woes all have to do with the failure of intentions in one way or other. Not only do they increase in the intensity of emotion with which they are uttered, culminating in the "Snakes! vipers' brood!" of v. 33; they also move from failure to intend or to intend rightly, to failure to perform what one intends, to failure to understand how one's actions relate to intentions.

The first two woes involve fairly straightforward failures. The scribes and Pharisees succeed in their desire to keep others out of the kingdom, but they do not themselves enter that kingdom. Perhaps the reason is that, wanting no part of that kingdom, they fail to form the right intention to enter; or possibly they are so busy keeping others out that they fail to act on an intention to enter. Either way, their distraction by an improper motive to exclude others trips them up. In the second woe the intention is correct, and pursued with vigor: they cross sea and land to win one convert. Nevertheless they do not succeed in proper conversion because they make the victim like themselves and worse. That suggests they do not know what they are doing; and indeed this is the theme of the next three woes, with their fivefold repetition of the language of blindness—a metaphor recalling, of course, the literal blindness cured three chapters back.

The difficulty is that one may claim to form the right intentions, and even be half taken in by one's own claim, but then act in ways that do not express those intentions. It's also possible to engage in certain actions in the hope that they will be interpreted as expressing the right intentions, when in fact one's real intentions are otherwise. Two little examples. You say to yourself that you are only acting for her own good when you deprive your daughter of something she wants—when it is really your laziness or stinginess that impedes your action. Or you give someone a good recommendation, implying your positive appraisal of his ability and performance, when your real motive is to get the person out of your hair and into someone else's.

Such gaps between act and intention lie behind Jesus' accusations. You swear an oath with a certain intention—to make a solemn commitment in the name of what is holy. Oath swearing is so regarded by those to whom the commitment is made. If you then try to get out of the promise by claiming not to have used the right verbal formula, you are trading on an ambiguity over whether you have in fact intended the commitment: you try to tell yourself that you didn't really intend, though you wouldn't have used *almost* the right words unless you'd wanted others to think you had intended. Such duplicity is indeed a kind of blindness to the object of intention. Likewise with tithes on herbs, a kind of gnat straining that you hope proclaims your careful attention to keeping the law. If, however, you forget justice and mercy you can have no deep intention to fulfill the law. Sometimes your law-abidingness in the little things belongs to a story you tell yourself so that you don't have to face up to full implications of camel swallowing; if so, the metaphor of blindness to your own condition is apt indeed. That Jesus continues the language of blindness in the fifth woe, about cleaning the outside of the dish, suggests that he is continuing to deal with half-formed intentions that aren't expressed in action. There are the motions, not entirely pretended, of cleaning the cup, for the outside gets washed off. Inattentiveness to the reason for washing—to remove the grease and leftovers—means that the inside is still dirty, so the motions have a mechanical quality, a lack of full intention. The eye is elsewhere, the heart not in it. Now the kind of half-heard dissonance between action and intention that I've been pointing to here need not be full-blown *hypocrisy.* The proper diagnosis of that condition requires that the agent understand the gap and exploit it with some degree of awareness. The epithet *hupokritai!* on Jesus' lips need not be translated by our "hypocrites!" for the word may mean more generally evildoers, false players. All the same, the ingredients for developed hypocrisy are here, and they emerge in the sixth and seventh woes. The outside/inside contrast of whitewashed tombs and the decay they contain is applied to the appearance of justice that masks inner lawlessness—without any hint of blindness or ignorance. Where the exterior is carefully constructed to hide and represent the content in opposites, there must be full intention to cover up. So there is not just a gap between action and intention, but misrepresentation of the latter in the former.

The final woe brings together deeds and words in this opposition to true intention. Given the chance, these hypocrites will kill the prophets as quickly as their ancestors have done. Yet they proclaim that they never would have acted that way; and indeed they construct, and no doubt whitewash, tombs and monuments to those whom their forebears murdered. This woe thus looks back in imagery to the previous one, and in theme to the last apostrophe of the chapter, in which Jesus proclaims his own intentions.

For after the venting of this anger against subtle and gross hypocrisy, Jesus slips into prophetic denunciation as he predicts the continued persecution of messengers and teachers and lays out blame for innocent death. The verbs are all violent: flogging, hounding, stoning, blood spilling, murdering, killing, even crucifying. Recalling the violence in the parables of the preceding passages, Matthew wants us to anticipate Jesus' own fate; but he also positions us to think of the words, deeds, and intentions of the actors in this story. So far the opposition to Jesus has used words to entrap and snare: they look good on the outside as questions about authority of God and the state, resurrection, the importance of the commandments. Their inner intentions have, however, been deliberately foul. So part of the function of Jesus' anger is to smoke out those intentions toward him in the public space of the Temple. But what of his own actions and desires?

Jerusalem, Jerusalem! The anger of denunciation that pushed away scribes and Pharisees into hell now reaches out to the whole city. It does not change its claim: this city—and not just its leaders—murders the prophets, stones God's messengers. But the anger that cast out now becomes lament for a loss; violence becomes vulnerability. In an image reminiscent of Psalms 57 and 84 (refuge in the shadow of God's wings; the swallow rearing her brood by the altar), Jesus speaks of wanting often to stretch out and pull the children of these murderers close to his body, like chicks under the protection of maternal wings. Though he has just invited the children to finish off what their fathers started, this drawing in for care is his real desire and intention (how often *I have wished*). But they would have none of it (*you refused*). Intention is frustrated by a contrary intention, an intention so contrary that it will soon stretch out his arms and pierce his unprotected limbs, and he will not refuse.

A Private Discussion: Chapters 24–25 The next two chapters contain a long private discourse with the disciples, usually labeled eschatological or apocalyptic. It has presented major problems to scholars, who have reached no agreement over its sources in Jewish or early Christian writings or its relation to what the historical Jesus himself might have said. Having given that nod of recognition, however, we will stick with our original concern: to see what might follow, from the text as we have it, for the reader who wants to know what Matthew's Jesus believes about his own impending Passion. For all the strangeness of some of the language here, the discussion will turn out to be of help in this pursuit.

The theme is destruction, the end of the Temple (which is, of course, more than a most magnificent structure: it is the localization of religious and cosmic order), and the end of the age. The human and natural disasters of war, persecution, famine, earthquake, the falling of the heavens, all precede the revelation of the Son of Man in power and glory. Though there are signs of his coming, the signs themselves do not provide certainty, for two reasons. First, the identity of the Son of Man is not utterly transparent: there are false prophets, false messiahs, who will produce and point to signs and wonders. Since disasters are always with us, who knows whether these particular wonders are the right signs? Second, neither the Son nor any angel of heaven—let alone anybody on earth—knows the day or the hour of his coming. This privileged information belongs to the Father alone. There remains a resilient ambiguity in all signs, then, so that the time of his manifestation will be opaque even to the Son. What Jesus therefore counsels is an attentiveness that has at least three components. His followers must be ready for imposters who will attempt to mislead them; they must keep alert so that when the day does arrive they will be ready and not miss out; and given that there may be long delay, they must persevere through trials until the end. If he does not know the day or the hour any more than his disciples, this attentiveness must apply to Jesus himself, though with a special twist. He knows he must die. But will not the end of his world make impossible the manifestation of the Son of Man? He must remain attentive to the will of the Father. Should he misread the signs he may miss out, making himself a false messiah. The postponement of the kingdom may cause him to weaken in the coming trial: he must persevere, knowing but not knowing.

Much of the emphasis of this speaking is on alertness, watchfulness, preparedness for what is expected but will come unexpectedly. If that last phrase sounds paradoxical—and therefore something to be either played with or ignored—we need think only of our own death. Nothing is more certain, and nothing in the normal course of events less anticipated. That Jesus does anticipate his imminent death without knowing when to expect it is not surprising. The exhortation to stay awake through the night will be given three times in Gethsemane, making it possible for us to draw parallels between the impending betrayal and death, with the details of its unfolding unknown as yet to Jesus, and the coming of the Son of Man in glory. *That* both will happen Jesus is sure; *how* and *when* remain with the Father and are not in Jesus' possession. As the disciples are to watch for the kingdom, so Jesus is to keep on his guard for his death, making himself the wise and faithful servant who will not miss the time of his master's return. The conclusion of the parable of those wise and foolish bridesmaids, "Keep awake, for you know neither the day nor the hour," is also a speaking back to the author, who must keep oil for the solitary lamp he carries in the darkness. Not to be ready means that he may miss the only event he is waiting for. If that happens he will be shut out and unrecognized.

The story of the bags of gold (known commonly as the parable of the talents) fits into the general theme of waiting for the return of the master, though the emphasis is upon what one does with resources rather than upon the unexpectedness of the return. As in previous stories, we are drawn to the wretch who doesn't get it right: he buries the money rather than using it as intended in business, and returns at last the one bag with the words, "Here; you have what is yours." What was his motive? Fear of the master (he says), who was hard, who took what did not belong to him. If he did not really understand his master, that's of no interest because his behavior is driven by what he does think and believe. But even given his beliefs, his blurted-out fear is confusing: what more could the master have taken which wasn't his to get back? There is an answer underneath the words. The wretch must have thought it would go hard with him indeed if he risked the capital and lost money; then he would have had to make up the loss from his own resources, and his master would have taken what belonged to the wretch. The fear is the fear of failure and loss, so he opts for personal safety rather than doing what the master intends. In so doing, however, he loses his own security and is cast into darkness.

The sheep-and-goats parable privileges the reader to know that the king identifies with the insignificant, so that action directed at even the "least of the brothers" is taken to be directed at God and rewarded or punished accordingly. But it doesn't work that way *within the story.* Think about it. The ovine righteous are genuinely perplexed: they do not know how it was that they fed or clothed or visited their Lord. And the goatish are not merely pretending that they did not recognize the true object of their neglect: all they saw and ignored were the poor or hungry or ill or imprisoned, not anyone more worthy of attention. There is an assumption here worth stating: right action is not made right by its getting you the Father's blessing and a place in the kingdom. And an action is not wrong only because if you commit it you will end up in the fire with the devil and his hordes. If you live within this story, your doing right and wrong has to be in some sense blind to these outcomes. You feed and clothe just because there are needs to be met; your motivation is the meeting of human needs rather than the winning of eternal prizes. The complication comes for the *hearers* of this story, who are no longer innocent of the identity of their Lord with the poor or of the large stakes involved. They know the eternal significance of meeting needs just because they are needs, and they in consequence lose naïveté about their reasons for acting. Their motivation becomes more complex, tinged with the possibility of their own gains or losses in the kingdom.

The reigning Son of Man pronounces to the righteous from his throne: "You have my Father's blessing: come, take possession of the kingdom that has been ready for you since the world was made" (REB). Change the pronouns from the second person to the first person singular: in this sentence you have what Jesus believes to have been promised to him. Read in this way, the self-consciousness of motivation for the parable's hearers reflects back on Jesus himself as teller. His throne has not yet been won; what is instead required is that he become himself the least significant, the most humble, the last in the kingdom. He must die: but how is that, and the outcome of the kingdom, to figure in his motivation?

Silence, Intention, and Motivation

We began thinking about motivation in Matthew with thrones and the kingdom five chapters back, and it is no accident that Jesus' discourse ends on this very theme: the Son of Man enthroned in a kingdom promised though not possessed. The speaking ends so that the narrative may resume; and its plot drives directly to Jesus' humiliation and death. So one large issue as we attempt to draw together these pieces of reflection will be the relation between the talk of kingdom and the imminent Passion. That, I suggest, is the question foremost in the mind of Jesus throughout these chapters. He is in the grip of two unshakeable convictions: (1) that he will indeed inherit the kingdom, not on his own initiative but from the Father; and (2) that he must endure suffering and death. There can be no doubt that Matthew intends us to think of these two beliefs as central to Jesus, and there is no need to labor the text about the matter. What is problematic, however, is *how these convictions fit together,* for they seem completely at odds with each other. The first involves his exercise of the greatest power and authority; the second requires ultimate surrender to temporal authority and the power of death.

It is tempting for some, with a Christian reading of the whole story from back to front, to assume that Jesus sorted out these beliefs in a straightforward manner: first a death to get over with, then a quick resurrection, and then the kingdom forever. That reading receives little support from Matthew. (Indeed, as I will argue in Chapter 6, John's Gospel gives it no support either.) The elements are there, granted. But the timing is the problem; and if the timing then perhaps the order; and if the order then perhaps the necessity of his cruel death. We must take seriously Matthew's assertion that Jesus does not know the day or the hour of the revelation of the Son of Man—and just as seriously that he does sense that his appointed time is near. Further, nothing in the text allows us to assume that he welcomed the prospect of death, or that he intended to make a martyr of himself in the degenerate sense. Quite the contrary: his feelings all-too-humanly shrink from the fate he fears awaits him. Perhaps, then, just perhaps, his imminent appointment is for revealed glory rather than for death? "If possible, not the cup," he asks his Father; and he vows to Caiaphas, "From now on you will see the Son of Man coming on the clouds of heaven."

That Matthew presents these two convictions as problematically related in the mind of Jesus accounts for certain features of Jesus' language. For one thing, the anger in the Temple, the violence in the parables and the excoriation of the Pharisees scarcely suggest someone who has calmly reconciled all his beliefs about his future. The contrast with the philosophical manner in which Socrates contemplates his own death could hardly be greater. For another, a fundamental perplexity about the compatibility of his beliefs may be mirrored in the juxtapositions and paradoxes of much of Jesus' speaking in our chapters. Think of the reversals between the first and the last, those in and those out, the humbled and the exalted, the rejected stone made main cornerstone; think of that unexplained paradox about messiah as David's son and lord. What reversals and contradictions may be found in death and kingdom?

The perplexity challenges action as well as thought. Jesus was able to shut the Sadducees up by undermining their arguments about the impossibility of resurrection. The difficulty with his own juxtaposed convictions is that they require more than an intellectual sorting out, more than revised beliefs or additional premises. Although the first expectation about the kingdom does not entail action by Jesus because he cannot bring it about, the second certainty makes the strongest demand possible on him, that he give up his life. He is faced, then, with the requirement to accept an end to his life, which clashes with what he believes to be God's purpose for him. In this requirement of faith he becomes like Abraham, who must give up with his son the very condition of God's promised blessing; he is at the same time, however, like Isaac, whose life it is that must end at his father's hand. Remember Jesus' recent assertion that the God of Abraham, Isaac, and Jacob is the God of the living: no pious formula, it expresses a commitment to hope which sits uneasily with the bleak imperatives of the present.

As Abraham obeyed without comment, so Jesus resolves his internal confusion by seeking to do the will of the Father in simple obedience. Perhaps he should not attempt to sort out the Father's timetable for these things; it may not be important that he be able to say anything about that. After all, it is in the doing and not the saying that obedience consists: remember the son who went to the vineyard regardless of what he said he would or wouldn't do. And yet the matter cannot be that simple. That Jesus *intends* to do the Father's will makes all the difference to the doing; this turns what is done into true obedience instead of a mindless act. The proper intention is the wedding garment to the deed, without which action may be nothing but the rags of self-interest or self-delusion. But as soon as intention intrudes, motivation rears its self-conscious head, bringing a new temptation.

There was an older satanic temptation, mentioned when we started with thrones and who gets to occupy them: to have the kingdom without the Passion, without obedience to death. That may still lurk round the edges of a half-formed hope that God's timetable has been misread, that the clouds on the horizon are only the undersides of the clouds of a breaking glory. On top of that, though, comes the new disturbing possibility, glimpsed in what Matthew has presented about motivation. Might Jesus follow out the course of action intended for him only because he wants the kingdom more than anything else? We have seen from Matthew's language that Jesus' attitude toward death is not philosophic in the Socratic sense, nor does his own death seem to be the object of his will. Is possessing the kingdom then that object? And if so, would his eye be single, his heart pure, in handing himself over?

Jesus must not act with hypocritical blindness to inner motivation. What he really wishes to have is neither the throne, nor his death, but his sight. To walk clear-eyed into the darkness of Gethsemane is to hand himself over—to the hands of betrayers and executioners, to be sure, but most basically to the will of his Father. The first and greatest commandment is to love God with all his being, including his understanding. And to love with the understanding in this case requires that he not claim to know what he cannot know, of the when and the how of death and the kingdom. Again the answer to his enemies is not empty talk: though they did not succeed in their desire to snare him in argument, he fastens himself by his words to an obedient love of God and neighbor that will cost him his life.

Jesus thus brings together intention and motivation in obedience, not just doing what he is asked to do, but conforming his will to the will of the Father. That this speaks to his silence we shall soon see. Before that, however, we return to the narrative for an incident that objectifies in one simple gesture what we have said about the mind of Jesus.

The Passion plot picks up again in chapter 26 after the public and private discourses of Jesus. Though the focus is on Jerusalem, Matthew interrupts the train of events, placing us out in Bethany for a vignette at Simon's house. In the silent scene there is only one action, the pouring out by an unnamed woman of a very expensive perfume on the head of Jesus. Our imagination, hearing nothing, is arrested by the gesture: it is the sole moment of beauty and tenderness in the entire Passion narrative.

Then the talking erupts. What a complete loss (the word means *destruction*), the disciples complain, of a commodity with such a large cash value that it could have done much for the poor. Jesus' defense may be more memorable than the memorial of the woman: you always have the poor, but not always me; she did it in preparation for my burial. Christian commentary has struggled with this saying as setting up a Mary/Martha dichotomy, a competition between contemplation and service, devotion and social justice. Jesus must have been moved by an action that had no utility other than its expression of love; is not the woman then model for his followers? But ignore that; think instead of the self-referential quality of his answer to the murmurers. That he speaks of his burial recalls for the reader his death. That death was of great cost, and might have been exchanged for a life of service to the poor, the naked, and the hungry of the parable at the end of the last chapter. The problem is that the poor and needy would always be present, even beyond the normal span of his life. So the act that is preparation for his burial may also been seen as expressive of his own outpouring in costly obedience. His life is given without calculation of its utility for ulterior purposes, either for what he might have done otherwise or for what he will gain. Alone of his professed followers, this woman does silently in image what Jesus will do in stark reality. But the odor of his obedience will be the odor of blood.

The Silence of Jesus as the Silence in Jesus We had begun all this, remember, with the protection in silence that law affords—a protection invoked by Thomas More, who hides himself in law against those who would violate his conscience and allegiance to the supreme authority of God and Church. Agreeing from the start that the silence of Jesus in his

Passion was not a simple absence of meaning, we suspected that he was not merely keeping quiet in order to preserve his life. And we may now confirm the suspicion in the light of our reflections on Matthew's account. Jesus actively surrenders himself to betrayal, arrest, and death; so he clearly does not use silence as a legal expedient to save himself from that which he willingly embraces.

The perjury of a former friend forced open More's mouth, not so much to defend himself as to bear witness in words to the meaning of his refusal to take the oath. If he had to die, he would die because he would not speak against his conscience. With Jesus too, false words do him to death: but he does not open his mouth. This refusal to speak stands in rebuking contrast to the words of disloyalty and treachery out of which the cloth of the Passion discourse is spun: because all speech around him is degenerate Jesus will say practically nothing in his own voice. When he does utter words, they are so often associated with what is written that we may guess that what law is to More, Scripture is to Jesus: his hiding place.

With that much we will have two motives for the silence of Jesus, both negative. He will not take up the weapon of words in self-defense; he will not participate in a community of corrupted discourse. Both motives reinforce the conviction that Jesus is innocent. Although Jesus may not consciously intend to convey this in refusing to speak (obedience is his aim, not creating beliefs about himself), nevertheless Matthew's account adds innocence and victimization as ingredients to the meaning of Jesus' silence. The blameless object of gratuitous violence, "he did not open his mouth."

Silence built a wall round the well of More's self, hidden in law and then manifested in language at his trial. That Jesus should take refuge not in his own voice but in scripture and in silence prompts the question: in the well of his self, are there words of explanation to be found?

Or is the silence of Jesus in some way the silence *in* Jesus?

Silence, I suggest, is the appropriate expression in the realm of language of the obedience of Jesus to the will of the Father. Not that it always must be so; silence may be disobedient, and obedience may use words. In Jesus' case, however, the nature of his obedience does not permit speech, for it sits at the limits of understanding. Let me explain.

Sometimes silence is the refusal to utter the words that are there to be said. The weapons are not taken up, though they lie within reach; if the truth is not spoken, it is nevertheless available and understood. At other times, however, one cannot speak, in the most potent sense of *cannot:* there is nothing to be said. The words will not come—and not in the way that words have of stopping at the tip of the tongue, but in the fundamental sense of there not being any words available. Such silence is radical, and there is no remedy for it. Without the words our understanding fails, and speaking is as empty as silence without the understanding.

As empty, but more misleading. It seems almost a law that the vacuum abhorred by human nature is the vacuum of speech, so we make words do all sorts of things to keep silence away. We find ourselves using words even when we have passed beyond their proper limits, often in a brave attempt to ignore the boundaries of our ignorance. And then language does become more misleading than silence, for it creates false expectations about our abilities and leads us into all kinds of difficulties. "Whereof one cannot speak, thereof one must be silent": Wittgenstein's dictum has force even when released from a general theory about the relation between language and the world. We need not buy any one brand of metaphysics or epistemology to recognize the dangers in our tendencies to keep talking after our understanding has reached its end.

Now in the motives for Jesus' silence set out above, we were dealing with the refusal rather than the inability to speak. The silence *in* Jesus has to do with what he cannot speak because there are neither words nor understanding. And that there is such an area in his inner life our previous section has argued. We can put it in terms of two kinds of epistemological limitation, calling them (rather roughly) theological and psychological. The first is his lack of knowledge about the day or the hour, God's timetable (as we put it), with the consequent uncertainty about the relation between his death and his rule in the kingdom. The psychological problem is over motivation and intention: how can he be sure that he is acting for the right reason? These limitations mean that Jesus' knowledge does not extend all the way into the mind of his Father, nor does it encompass all the nooks and crannies of his own mind.

But there are grave dangers in speaking where one does not know. What can be said about the Father's mind that will not run the risk of sorting out the when and the how wrongly? What can be said about one's own motives that will not fall prey to self-delusion, will not be contradicted in action?

In the end, there is only one answer. Jesus is called upon to respond whether these perplexities can be sorted out or not. Either he hands himself over or he does not. But while he does not have the epistemological privilege of clarity about ultimate purpose, he does know the one thing needful: he knows which is the obedient action. And so he obeys.

This obedience is not the obliteration of his very self, and certainly not the sloughing off of responsibility onto someone else. Its moral nature as an active embrace of the will of another we must pursue in the next chapter. For these reflections here, it is enough to see that Jesus' obedience is a form of epistemological trust. It is a handing over of what he cannot know, because God has placed it beyond his reach, a handing back to God for safekeeping. And that is why Jesus is silent. To render an adequate account of himself at his trial is not something he would do, to be sure; but neither is it something he could do. That would be to retrieve what cannot be retrieved from the Father or from his own heart; that would be to speak as falsely as everyone else speaks in the whole affair.

One Last Word / One Last Silence Recall the strong, sometimes violent language of the parables. It is directed at more than one sort of offender. There are acts of revenge on those who have committed violence themselves: the tenants who killed servants and son, the prophet murderers, and shedders of innocent blood. Their judgment is severe: fire and hell. Then there are poor wretches who didn't do the right thing and who therefore get rough handling: the wedding guest who didn't come *as to* a wedding; the unfaithful servant; the cowardly servant who wouldn't risk his master's capital. They end up being bound hand and foot and flung into the dark. Even the foolish bridesmaids are unrecognized and excluded. What is of interest here is that the punishment is so often a condemnation to isolation, darkness, and speechlessness—not silence (we hear noises of wailing and grinding of teeth), but a lack of the linguistic meaning that marks community.

Now the penalties of exclusion and verbal incoherence fall upon those who are inattentive, unprepared, improperly motivated, and self-preoccupied. And with this realization comes a most poignant ending to the Passion and silence of Jesus. In his careful obedience his intentions were the right intentions, his motive only to do the Father's will. But for trusting in the one who held him dear, his reward is bitter indeed. He was prepared to accept that death must come, if necessary, before the kingdom. But the godforsakenness? The exclusion, the flinging into the dark, when he was attentive and ready, not grasping of his own safety? In shouting out the beginning of Psalm 22 from the cross, Jesus contradicts all the earlier speaking he had done about faithfulness and unfaithfulness. He dies cast out from human society and his Father's presence, with a loud cry to which Matthew assigns no meaning.

And then there is one last silence. At More's trial Thomas Cromwell called the silence of a corpse "pure and simple," signifying nothing. How can this broken end to obedience signify nothing? What could be less pure, or less simple, than this final silence of Jesus?

Socrates For and Against Words

We need a moment to adjust vision and mind as the darkness begins to lighten over a hill of execution outside Jerusalem. The scene changes, and we find ourselves in sunlit Athens. Assembled in rows is a large company of five hundred and one men, chosen by lot, who form the jury in the trial of Socrates. Opposite them stand Socrates and his three accusers, Meletus, Anytus, and Lycon. There is a public gallery, but no legal counsel, no judge—only a president to keep order. The charge against Socrates had been posted publicly beforehand:

> This indictment is entered on affidavit by Meletus son of Meletus of the deme Pittus against Socrates son of Sophroniscus of Alopeke. Socrates is guilty of refusing to recognize the gods recognized by the state and introducing other, new divinities. He is also guilty of corrupting the youth. The penalty demanded is death.

Those who brought the charge speak first. Then the accused answers the indictment. Without further summary or instruction, the jurors file up to cast their vote, placing a wheel-shaped ballot in a jar, either a hollow-axled one to denote guilt or else one with a solid axle for innocence. There are more pierced than solid counters, 280 to 221, so the accused is found guilty. Because the penalty for this offense is not fixed by law, the jury must decide between the proposals of the accuser and the defendant. Meletus has demanded death; Socrates suggests at first free state support as befits a distinguished benefactor—then, having rejected imprisonment and banishment as possibilities, proposes a fine that, though small, would cost him (according to Xenophon) one-fifth of his resources. Four of his friends, including Plato, intervene with a more serious offer of thirty times that amount, pledging it from their own pockets. The counters are cast again. This time, says Diogenes Laertius, the majority increased by eighty: 360 jurors voted for Socrates' death. After that verdict Socrates speaks one last time.

Those are the bare essentials in the scene before us. Or, at least, given our sources that's how we should think of the trial of Socrates, with one caveat. For there is a contrary tradition that at his trial Socrates said nothing in his own defense—though the sources are six centuries after his death, and not especially reliable. Appian of Alexandria refers to that tradition, although he puts it that either Socrates made no reply or he said what Plato has him say. Maximus of Tyre claims that Socrates kept silent as the safest course, since he could not speak without loss of honor. Around the turn of the third century Philostratus makes the philosopher Musonius say that Socrates was executed because he was not prepared to defend himself. Those who posit the silence of Socrates must have believed that his followers, Plato and Xenophon, made up their Defenses in order to exonerate the master. But why this late belief in Socratic silence? That is puzzling. Although I will not be able to contribute any historically plausible explanation for its appearance, I will in the course of what follows venture some suggestions about philosophy, word, and silence in Plato's Socrates.

Now because our interest lies in Plato's particular view of Socrates, it is his account of the trial that will occupy our attention—not for its historical accuracy, but for its characterization of Socrates' interests, motives, and use of language. Our chief source is, of course, the work come down to us as *The Apology of Socrates*, which purports to repeat the very words of Socrates at his trial. Apart from a few brief answers from Meletus at one point in the proceedings, the only words we hear spoken come from the mouth of Socrates. It's his account we have, not anyone else's version of his defense. We should accordingly find it a more straightforward matter to understand this man on trial than we did Jesus, whose inner experience was masked by silence.

Socrates' speaking occupies three discrete moments. The first and longest is his mounting of an explanation and defense of his philosophical activity in order to establish his innocence. Second comes his series of proposed penalties. His closing words to the jury form the third moment, with remarks addressed first to those who had voted for his death, and finally to those who believed in his innocence. During these episodes Socrates refers to other voices, positioning us to hear them through his ears, and we will turn to them in due course. But first we must attend to his own words.

Oppositions

We enter the proceedings just as Socrates begins to address the jury. In the opening words of the *Apology* Socrates harks back to the arguments of his accusers presented during the first part of the trial; but instead of opposing directly the content of their charges, he first draws attention to the dangerous effects of a certain kind of speaking. The fine and fancy words of his accusers might well have seemed persuasive to the jury, he says, even though their speaking is false. They are wrong in particular to imply that Socrates is skilled in words—unless they mean by "skilled" someone who speaks the truth, for that is the only kind of speaker Socrates would claim to be.

Effective vs. True Speaking Immediately, then, Socrates has set up three oppositions about language that reflect the opposition between himself and his accusers: between skilled and unskilled speech, between effective and ineffective speaking, and between false and true words. Significantly, these oppositions line up with each other so that the kind of speech that is skilled is effective, but it is also false. Speaking the truth doesn't go with this clever and persuasive language. Socrates warns his hearers that his own language will be simple, unadorned, and uncalculated. Partly this is a matter of long habit: he is accustomed to the vocabulary of ordinary folk in the market and has no experience with legal terminology and style. But it also seems to follow from his commitment to speak nothing other than the truth.

We have heard only the opening words of Socrates' defense, but already we are puzzled. The clustering of these dichotomies looks too rigid. Why would Plato want to make his Socrates reject the possibility of words that are both effective and true? Perhaps we recall Plato's fondness for strong oppositions and wonder whether the set we've just considered is simply an example of his overstatement. The three oppositions belong to the clan of warring contrasts found elsewhere in the dialogues, between rhetoric and philosophy, persuasion and education, belief and knowledge. Only the product of proper teaching may be called knowledge; what persuasion inculcates is classed as belief rather than knowledge; philosophy has nothing to do with rhetoric.

So, adding our set from the *Apology,* we can generate two mutually exclusive lists.

	A		B
Art:	rhetoric	*or*	philosophy
Process:	persuasion	*or*	education
Cognitive product:	belief	*or*	knowledge
Technique:	skilled	*or*	unskilled
Success:	effective	*or*	ineffective
Epistemic value:	false	*or*	true

And yet there remains something wrong. While the last three *Apology* dichotomies are close to the top three contrasts, they don't fit neatly with them on the A and B lists. Skilled and clever speaking is what rhetoric employs, and persuasion the name of the process in which it uses its tools; but though it produces beliefs, still (we want to object) there are some beliefs that aren't false. Their truth value is independent of their mode of production in the mind. Or again, it seems unlikely that Socrates would identify unskilled and ineffectual speaking with the education in which philosophy engages. Perhaps, however, we shouldn't think that Plato expects us to develop a strict and neat consistency from contrasts thrown out on a few specific occasions. And indeed there are places where Plato seems to recognize that he has overdrawn these differences. There is in the *Gorgias* a positive use for rhetoric; in the same dialogue Plato speaks of two kinds of persuasion, one of which does produce knowledge (454); and the education of Meno's slave generates true beliefs that have to be turned into knowledge later (*Meno* 85).

But if Plato will relax his juxtapositions so that some terms may move across the stark divide in these lists, that only serves to reinforce our puzzlement. Truth and knowledge may be served by proper rhetorical attention, so why should Socrates not aim at effective speaking in his own defense? Of course people can be taken in by smoothly false talk, but why can't his true speaking be skilled and persuasive, too? We understand that Socrates does not wish to speak falsely, or to employ techniques that have nothing to do with the truth—such as parading his children in front of the jury so as to cloud their judgment with pity. But isn't there something deeply wrong when true words don't work successfully to convince their hearers?

Words vs. Intentions But wait a moment. Can we be sure that Socrates seriously intends to maintain this opposition between skillful speech and true speech? Maybe he is just being modest about his own rhetorical ability. Aristotle explains in book 4.7 of the *Nicomachean Ethics* that it is better to underestimate your powers than to exaggerate them; there's something attractive about the person who plays down personal qualities generally held in high esteem. Socrates could hardly endear himself to the jury by praising his own skills; it is in better taste, then, for him to call himself, somewhat ironically, a plain rough speaker.

Well, that would be a plausible explanation for some: Aristotle, for instance, speaks of Socrates' irony as a cultivated and gentle kind of distanced self-deprecation. Unfortunately, it won't work for our Socrates, as two considerations show. First, good taste and social grace scarcely count for him. He is perfectly willing to diminish his accusers and offend the jury when he believes it appropriate. It's hard to think that he brings up his rhetorical inexperience only to ingratiate himself with his listeners—especially when he didn't have to mention the matter at all. The second, stronger, consideration concerns his reputation. The man on trial is well known for his slyness, his playing around with words and people—indeed, his accusers have just warned the jury against being deceived by his words. *That* behavior is what is meant by his "irony." Until Aristotle rewrote the meaning of Socratic irony, the term *eirôn* was entirely and distinctly negative, applied to corrupt speakers who use words in ways different from their customary meanings, and for unworthy purposes. The speech of the *eirôn* conceals his true intention; his motives thus make him morally suspect, just as unlikable as his counterpart the braggart, who says too much about himself. Whenever Plato has someone associate Socrates with *eirôneia* in his dialogues, the term retains that negative tone. Socrates' enemies accuse him of this kind of deceptive and dissembling behavior: Callicles claims he's only a mob orator, that he is wily; Thrasymachus sneers at his well-known *eirôneia*. Though Socrates' friends are more temperate in their language, they make the same sort of charge: Alcibiades talks of his "playing his little game of irony and laughing up his sleeve at all the world," and even Phaedrus tells Socrates to stop being coy about his skill with words.

Given this characterization, Socratic "irony" mustn't be thought to consist in an affectation of manner, or a habit of speech tending toward a deflating sarcasm. Nor should it be confused with the dramatic irony created by Plato, through which the reader of a dialogue understands what is opaque to the characters who converse with Socrates. Unless we appreciate that the term locates him in a morally and socially suspect territory, we will not feel its bite. The Socrates on trial is reputed (we may borrow the image from *Republic* 365c) to be a shifty fox, bent on gain. You hear his words when he opens his mouth, but you must watch out for the teeth.

It's the deep shadow of this reputation, Socrates believes, that lies across the minds of the jurors. For that reason he pulls into the light of the proceedings the submerged opinions about him created by popular rumor and by Aristophanes' comic parody. Thought to be one of those fee-collecting teachers-of-everything from atheistic natural science to the optics of argument, Socrates is called "wise," *sophos*. And when he exposes the ignorance of another person, those who observe the ineluctable direction of his questioning assume that he must himself possess the wisdom that is the object of his quest (23a). Quite simply, his protestations that he himself lacks understanding are just not believed. And once you are convinced that Socrates secretly knows the answer, you quickly attribute to him base and unfriendly motives as he goes about his business of tripping people up, diminishing their social and intellectual status. His words belie the malice of his mind; the cloak of ignorance is camouflage for the fox.

And now Socrates is repeating that he is but a rough plain speaker, interested in truth rather than the fancy talk that delivers up falsehoods. Why should the jury believe him? Isn't Socrates' very act of dressing himself in unadorned words its own kind of self-conscious and sophisticated rhetorical stance? And this constant harping on the truth: the more someone does to impress upon us his truth telling, with avowals and heart crossings and oath swearings, the more we wonder what's really going on. While we continue to be perplexed by the divorce between true words and effective words, the jury remains suspicious of Socrates' claims to veracity and to ineptitude. We need to examine whether his words do reveal the intentions of his mind.

Clever vs. Plain Speaking Socrates is aware that some of his words will be ill-taken. Twice he acknowledges that he might be thought perverse—when he explains why he refuses to bring his children on stage (34e) and when he proposes the "penalty" of free maintenance at the state's expense (37a). He also confesses that his listeners may regard him as fooling around, not serious (*paidzein*, 20d), or think him cunningly insincere (*eirôneuomenos*) in speaking of philosophy as a divine duty (38a).

This self-awareness means, I think, that we cannot quite bring ourselves to believe Socrates when he claims to speak the first words that happen to come to him. That suggests a naïveté about the effects of one's words upon their hearers, whereas Socrates is well aware of the jury's likely misconstruction of his meaning. Given the use of prepared speeches in court, it may be that Socrates intends simply to contrast his extemporaneous speech with language written chiefly for its persuasive effect. But we—and the jury—must find him self-conscious and deliberate in his diction, shaping his words for his hearers. Does it follow, however, that his entire apologia is slyly spoken through the mask of an *eirôn*, that his adoption of plain speech is unprincipled, calculated to manipulate his audience?

Of course not, since there may be a deliberate choice of language intended to serve the truth, not just one's own interests. But since Socrates is under suspicion, we may look more closely at one self-confessedly deliberate strategy he employs: his open refusal to employ a stock device known in later textbooks as the *argumentum ad misericordiam*, the appeal to pity. In summing up his defense, he explains why he has decided not to soften the hearts of the jurors by weeping and displaying his offspring, just in case someone is angry that he has not availed himself of this standard tactic.

I suppose it might be argued by those on their guard against Socratic deception that there is indeed a cunning in Socrates' disapproval of the appeal to pity as a technique to secure acquittal. In order to reject it instead of merely ignoring it, he must *produce in words* those same children and tears and pity. He confesses that he is himself not rock but flesh and blood, and that he has three sons, acknowledging thereby that human feeling has some force. Isn't that shrewd, then—to trade upon the emotional resonance of the language of pity, while at the same time proclaiming his moral superiority and innocence by presenting only words?

Some members of the jury might angrily think Socrates wants his superiority and their pity at the same time. But I don't think that's a fair reading of his intention. If we hear again his stated reasons for rejecting the strategy, perhaps we will better comprehend the relation between his technique and his principles.

If he is not about to let his children tug at heartstrings, why does Socrates bother to bring up the business of pity at all? His answer has nothing to do with gaining a more subtle pity. It's that he must explain why he does not do *everything in his power to secure acquittal.* Most of us would. We reason that our own survival takes precedence over pretty much everything else; it is the fundamental good without which other goods such as happiness, knowledge, and friendship are impossible. As long as we have some prospects for ourselves, we will fight to keep ourselves going. We will use all available weapons, especially if the threat to our continued existence is irrational or unjust. But Socrates does not regard the meaning of his life in that way at all. He is different from others, he acknowledges; he will not take improper measures to save his own skin. And he disparages appeals to pity on three counts (35c). First, they are unseemly: making a huge fuss about one's own death bespeaks a lack of courage and an unwillingness to accept mortality. Second, such appeals do not accord with justice. The proper business of the accused is to present evidence and persuasive argument; the proper business of the jury is to determine justice, not to be bribed or cajoled. And third, playing to pity isn't theologically legitimate, for it presumes to know, and therefore to determine, an outcome that must be left to the will of the god. As we will appreciate more fully in Chapter 5, Socrates must be obedient to that will.

I think, then, that we must accept the utter seriousness with which Socrates holds his principles. Given his moral and religious convictions, it would be impossible for him to get himself released by the usual means. Because he cannot wish to be freed except under the conditions of justice and the divine will, he cannot work upon the emotions of the jury for that outcome. His mention of pity, then, serves a double function. It reminds the jury of a power and tactic that he deigns not to employ—as did Jesus' words to the arresting mob, about the legions his Father would send to his aid. And it serves to make not the will of the jury but Socrates' values the location of his confidence and commitment—again, a stance not unlike Jesus' hiding in Scripture and the will of the Father.

That, I trust, dismisses the suspicion of Socrates' perversity about the conduct of this part of his defense. There is one other instance of alleged guile: his proposal that he be offered free maintenance by the state as a valued benefactor. That looks like cheek and effrontery, a bit of smart talk. It was no doubt so taken: something must account for the large swing of eighty votes against Socrates. But as I shall argue more fully in Chapter 5, that is not the case. Instead there is a principled moral rationale for the penalties Socrates proposes and rejects; and in fact the suggestion of state maintenance is itself a piece of Socratic examination.

So my conclusion is that Socrates' words—at least those considered here—are not those of an *eirôn*, cleverly concealing his true intentions in order to get what he wants from his audience. In that his values and commitments are uncommon, his strategies seem perverse; nevertheless, Socrates does speak straightforwardly and without guile in the light of these commitments.

And yet words do not necessarily deposit with their hearers the meanings assigned them by their speakers. Socrates' speaking enters suspicious minds, which turn over his words for the concealed message they want to find. In such a context plainness of speech seems an important vehicle for the honest expression of one's deep commitments. Clever talk would be out of place, reinforcing the prejudice already too eager to condemn. Still, it remains that Socrates' intention to speak plainly, and his own estimation that he fulfills that intention, cannot guarantee that his defense will be taken that way. As C. S. Lewis once remarked, in some people's minds, where there's no smoke the fire must be very carefully hidden. About the credibility of his intentions Socrates must remain impotent.

That reminds us of the puzzle with which we began, an even more significant impotence: why cannot Socrates use truthful speaking to save himself? Must true words end up being ineffectual and unpersuasive in matters of life and death?

Although we do not yet have a full answer, we must now recognize that Plato raises this problem quite directly in the *Gorgias*, where Callicles vehemently maintains that Socrates will not be able to use the words philosophy provides in order to save his own life.

The Impotence of Philosophical Speech

One of the principal themes of the *Gorgias* concerns the power and limits of language, which Plato constructs in terms of the strong opposition we encountered earlier, between rhetoric and philosophy. Socrates, naturally enough, takes the part of philosophy; the advocates of rhetoric are Gorgias, Polus, and Callicles.

Socrates vs. Rhetoric At the risk of oversimplifying the issue, what is at stake in this rivalry isn't a professional turf war. While Plato identifies a group of rhetoricians and sophists who made teaching other people their business, indeed their means of income, Socrates is presented as an individual with unique concerns that transcend the interests of a particular class or profession. And in this dialogue, Plato insists that the issue underlying the theme of power and language is the fundamental question of how we ought to conduct our very lives.

Rhetoric promises to develop skills in the use of words to accomplish whatever goals you desire. It regards language as a tool or weapon; the activity it supports goes by the name of persuasion, for it aims to change the minds of the people on which it is practiced and to produce results in their attitudes, beliefs, and behavior. The teachers of rhetoric claim, moreover, that they have brought rhetorical techniques to the level of a science, so that they can effectively train pupils in these skills.

Now there is little doubt that paying attention to the workings of human nature and behavior will yield the clever observer some useful knowledge. That knowledge may be a folk art, like the knack of selling door-to-door; or it may become sophisticated, as in the study of marketing. But whatever its form, Plato worries about it.

For the possession of rhetorical prowess does not in itself guarantee a good life. The skill may happen to be turned to good ends: Gorgias' own example is his ability to persuade his brother's patients to endure painful surgery for the sake of their health. But it may also be placed in the service of more questionable goals. Indeed, the seductions of power are such that, in petty ways or grand, you will use rhetorical skill to advance your own interests, gaining power over others who are persuaded by your words to act contrary to their own interests. That doesn't seem good for them, at least. And could it be ultimately good for you to act unjustly even if you possess that power?

The voice raising these issues belongs to philosophy. Polus and especially Callicles have no time for philosophy's concerns about justice, goodness, and self-control. They believe it best to exercise their powers in the service of desire and appetite without the conventional restraints of a timid mentality. If it is best to get whatever you want, it's also good to have sufficient power to override the social sanctions against so-called injustice. But Socrates disagrees, and engages each of them in detailed argument, attempting to expose inconsistencies and paradoxes in their positions. He also states quite categorically his opinion of the art of rhetoric: it is in fact no art at all, but a kind of knack got up for the sake of producing pleasure. (He would accordingly qualify my use of *art* as a label for both rhetoric and philosophy on my lists earlier in this chapter.)

Socrates expands this claim in a series of provocative analogies. There are certain activities that concern themselves only with the way things appear. Cosmetics and cookery, for instance, cater to pleasing effects. Contrasted to them are physical training and medicine, which deal with the body itself, the one seeking to train it into good condition, the other to heal its diseases. This juxtaposition between looking or tasting good on the one hand and being really healthy on the other may be too strong. But we get the point. And that point is transferred to rhetoric: it is no true art or technique aimed at what's best regardless of appearances, but only a trick of pandering to appetite, a base flattery that seeks out pleasure. It cares nothing about true human well-being and goodness.

So we now understand a little more fully the attitude of Plato's Socrates toward the use and abuse of language. This figure, so immersed in the world of speech, so committed to conversation, declares himself against words as well as for words. Words must be spoken on behalf of truth and goodness.

At this stage we assume that Socrates himself, representing philosophy, will speak words properly. By that we cannot mean simply that he engages in argument and cross-examination designed to bring his interlocutor into rational consistency. That's but one facet of philosophy. The philosopher—as opposed to the rhetorician anyway—must also speak the truth, and seek to live in conformity with justice and self-control. Perhaps it's easier to assess the adequacy of Socratic reasoning than to pass judgment upon his life and values: commentators at any rate have spent most of their considerable energy on the validity of his argumentative techniques. But for our purposes we need to ask about the critique of Socrates and philosophy mounted from within the dialogue; we need next to turn to the allegations of Callicles against philosophical speaking.

Callicles vs. Socrates Callicles makes his attack on two flanks, the first *ad hominem*. Knowing that Socrates has cast rhetoric in shadowy light, as feeding the dark appetites of the body politic rather than prescribing for its true health, Callicles accuses Socrates himself of using the tactics of mob oratory. Socrates, he charges, has no desire to uncover the truth; though he may not pander to his hearers, nevertheless he does intend to throw them into confusion. The accusation, then, is that Socrates' actual practice doesn't exemplify his own ideals of philosophical activity. He talks rubbish, going on about tradespeople like cooks and cobblers instead of matters of consequence.

On the other flank, Callicles attacks philosophy itself as linguistically impotent. At the outset of his interchanges with Socrates he concedes the study of philosophy to be suitable at a certain stage in one's development; but those who keep at it well into their prime are asking for trouble. They, like children, are naive about the world. And like grown children who keep lisping instead of developing proper speech habits, philosophers engage in a kind of mumbling. The words of philosophy make no difference in the real world of debate and action. In a telling image, the philosopher spends his life in a corner whispering with three or four boys, without a free strong effective voice (485e).

Callicles then drives on to claim victory over Socrates. Were Socrates to be accused where he is not guilty, be seized and dragged to prison, he would stagger and gape, not knowing what to say; and he would be sentenced to death if his accuser were so wretched as to propose that penalty (486a). In brief, though philosophy talks about justice, it is impotent in the face of injustice.

This theme persists throughout the rest of the conversation. Socrates returns to it at 508cd, recalling that Callicles thinks it most shameful that Socrates would be powerless to prevent serious injury and affront to himself in the form of fines, banishment, or even death. And near the dialogue's close the language of trial and court comes up again, in the famous image of the doctor charged by a cook in front of a jury of children. Here, however, it's not Callicles who speaks of the impotence of philosophical speech; Socrates himself acknowledges that at such a trial he would have to be silent. Since he won't make speeches to gratify the listener, he (the words are his) *won't know what to say in court* (521e). If the doctor were to try to tell the truth about the intent and outcome of his actions, done for the sake of their health instead of pleasure, the jury would shout him down. He'd be at a complete loss. Socrates goes on to apply the fable: were he to come before a court he would be able to speak neither the truth about his actions, nor anything else. The outcome would just be whatever it turned out to be, not something that he could bring about by words.

Here, I suggest, we have some material for the theme of the silence of Socrates, the tradition of his nondefense. I can't claim that the *Gorgias* is the tradition's source. (If it were, why would the tradition not appear earlier and more reliably?) All the same, the *Gorgias* might help us discern reasons why a character in Socrates' position would not open his mouth to defend himself. On Callicles' account, he would be rendered powerless by his rhetorical incompetence, his inability to use words with force to secure his place in the world. Lack of technical expertise silences him. But Socrates' explanation is different. It's not that he is *unable to speak;* rather, because of the condition of the listeners, *he cannot be heard.*

Of course, we ourselves have already been to the trial of Socrates; we know that when the time came he did speak words in his own defense. Those words are as Callicles would have it—rhetorically incompetent, and ultimately impotent to save him. The persisting puzzle—that Socrates cannot speak truly and at the same time persuasively and effectively—grows more complex. Why did he bother to speak at all?

We will come to an answer. The way is not straight, however; for in spite of Socrates' agreement that philosophy is impotent to speak in defense of the truth, *that's not at all the way Plato presents the voice of Socrates.* This is apparent in the linguistic relationship between Callicles and Socrates: it is Callicles who is brought to a loss of words, who refuses to speak or to speak in his own voice. Instead of admitting to a conflict in his beliefs about pleasure, pain, and the good, Callicles tries to say he had only been playing (499b) with his words. Socrates begs him to be straightforward, but he answers, he says, because of Gorgias and the audience (501b, 505c). When it appears that the outcome of Socrates' questioning will reverse Callicles' entire position about the silliness of imposing restraint upon desire, Callicles wants to break off the discussion, and Socrates is left to provide answers on his behalf. Philosophy triumphs over the inconsistencies of a hesitant and inarticulate rhetoric, reducing it to bluster, repetition, stammering, or a sulking silence.

I'd like to carry back to the *Apology* what we have learned about rhetoric, philosophy, voice, and silence. There Socrates speaks, but we discern and infer other voices as well, with which we can compare his speaking.

Voices in the *Apology*

The voice of Meletus, as we remember, is the only one other than Socrates' that Plato permits us to hear throughout the trial.

Meletus It is important to inspect the character of the brief replies that Meletus makes in response to Socrates' questions (*Apology* 24c–28a). At the most obvious level, his answers are terse, often in sentence fragments, and either echoes of words that Socrates himself has used or else simple affirmations and denials. We may appreciate the reason for this if we follow Socrates' strategy for a paragraph or two.

Socrates intends to deal with the two charges of corrupting the young and introducing new divinities. These are separable issues, since the young may be adversely influenced in many ways—for instance, by mimicking what Socrates does in deflating pretense, but for such ignoble ends as mocking their elders. Nevertheless, Socrates leads Meletus into a straightforward linkage of the two: it's his religious unorthodoxy which is corrupting. That's good strategy. If Socrates can defeat the second count of irreligion, he thereby defeats the first count: if it's not poison that he's feeding the young, the young are not being poisoned.

But Socrates has an independent defense against the first charge as well. He argues on the ground of credibility: it's not credible that he alone corrupts, and all other Athenians improve, the young; and it's not credible that he would do this intentionally, given that he knows he would be himself corrupted by the company he keeps. Now these are provocative claims, deserving of discussion. Yet Meletus has to have his responses pulled out of him. Socrates says at the start, "You see, Meletus, that *you are silent and cannot say*" (24d) who improves the young. Meletus won't answer a question about expert ability to improve; on the matter of whether anyone wishes to be harmed, he has to be reminded that the law requires him to reply.

When Socrates moves to the accusation of irreligion, Meletus is less reluctant to speak—but not less self-incriminating. Socrates' first move is to ask whether Meletus means by his charge that Socrates is unorthodox or instead atheistic. Seizing on the old and pervasive belief that Socrates wrongly meddles with inquiries into earth and sky, Meletus revises his published charge of introducing new divinities. Socrates doesn't believe in the divinity of the heavenly bodies, he bursts out; Socrates is an atheist. Given that revision, Socrates is able to expose the contradiction derivable from the belief that he teaches others about things divine and spiritual. He cannot do that without believing in divine beings; but that means he cannot be an atheist. The move to this contradiction involves just two very reluctant answers from Meletus: Socrates finishes off the argument for him, and we hear nothing from him again.

We have witnessed, then, a reversal of rhetorical position, very much like the reversal in the *Gorgias*. From Socrates' opening statement we had expected smooth and effective speech from Meletus, dangerously and falsely persuasive. Instead we listen to stammering and unwilling words, as Socrates pulls Meletus up from silence into self-contradiction, then returns him to silence once more. Socrates had also warned against our thinking him to have any skill in speaking; but his silencing of his opponent, in such contrast to the trial of Jesus, seems skilled indeed. We note, though, that the work is accomplished by philosophical argument—by inspecting the relation of beliefs to each other and to the evidence. If the arguments are not conclusive (irreligion is not the only corrosive, nor does just any theism count as orthodox), the inability of Meletus to grasp this serves only, in our minds at least, to diminish his status. Perhaps more to the point, Plato creates the strong impression that Meletus's reluctance to follow argument and to articulate answers is related to his having to speak the truth about Socrates. As he sees the connections and implications in Socrates' line of questioning, his words seize up. We may have suspected that Socrates, in claiming that he cannot speak cleverly and truly at the same time, was a special case. That's not so: in the speech of someone as different as Meletus, skill and truthfulness do not in fact work easily together.

Apart from these few words of Meletus, the tone, timbre, and accent of the *Apology* belong to the voice of Socrates. He alters his speaking from time to time, however, sometimes referring to voices around him at the trial, sometimes reporting the voices of others, sometimes even constructing words for other speakers. It is to these indirect voices I now turn. They belong in several different categories, and our first task will be to set them out for inspection.

Other Voices Stay with voices at the trial itself. We're able to sense restlessness and murmuring among the jury, and some outbursts of sound from its members: several times Socrates requests them not to interrupt, to let him say things that they find surprising or difficult. That call for silence is an appeal not to disturb the space in which his words may be heard; to invade that space is to destroy argument and rationality. The collective voice of the jury, then, unsettles us; it is too much the voice of the mob.

Singled out from that collectivity are four friends, named, who speak words heard only by Socrates. They offer money, thirty minas, to redeem him from death.

Those voices we may call *present by inference* from Socrates' comments. In the course of his defense Socrates draws on other voices not present on the occasion of the trial; they are *reported* voices. The one with the most to say is multiple, spoken for so long by so many people that it is difficult to distinguish speakers. It whispers publicly, privately, in the presence of the children, "Socrates is guilty of criminal meddling, in that he inquires into things below the earth and in the sky, and makes the weaker argument defeat the stronger, and teaches others to follow his example."

Other reported voices are named. Socrates recounts a conversation with Callias of Paros, slipping into direct speech in the present tense so that we sense something of his philosophical style. He quotes Homer, using again direct words of the speakers Thetis and Achilles. And again that's a matter of style, making for a vivid presentation of example and illustration.

More integral to his argument, and more serious, is his reporting of words between Chaerophon and the oracle at Delphi. This time the discourse is indirect, so that we have to reconstruct the question about anyone wiser than Socrates to which the priestess replied negatively. The vividness lies in the audacity of the conception rather than in the grammar.

Socrates relates other encounters without naming the participants, and without giving an account of their linguistic exchanges. The voices are readily *imagined,* however, in conversations that expose the limits of knowledge among politicians, poets, and craftsmen. All of these voices begin confidently; they soon slow into hesitation and come to the dead end of silence or anger.

In the penultimate category come *constructed* voices. On four occasions Socrates himself invents likely voices from among the jury. The device permits him to formulate questions that he suspects weigh upon their minds so that he can provide an adequate response. This structures their thinking for them, providing a focus that they might be incapable of achieving. The first two questions may be summarized as "Why is it that your activities have been popularly misrepresented?" (20c) and "Aren't you ashamed to lead the kind of life which puts you in danger of death?" (28b). These permit Socrates to explain and to justify his motives. The next voice proposes acquittal on condition that he cease philosophizing (29c), and it speaks up again just before the vote on the penalty: perhaps someone will ask, "Can't we get you to leave, but to live silently and keeping quiet?" (37e). To all these constructed questioners Socrates gives patient and careful reply.

I have left to the last a reported voice—some will say constructed—whose speaking we cannot imagine. Our failure could not be remedied by further conversation with Socrates about what he hears or experiences; he reports to the jury no words that this voice has uttered. It is "a sort of voice" that he has heard from his childhood, "divine and spiritual," which always forbids a course of action rather than giving advice or information (31d). We want, partly, to say that this, too, is present by inference in the trial, because Socrates refers to it at the end of his final speech. But "present" isn't quite right, when what is heard is an absence of words—though "absence" itself hardly captures the significance of an experience of such moment for Socrates. We may call this a *wordless divine voice*, recognizing how easy it is to trivialize its speaking by reducing it to a psychological state, or indeed to distort it by overinterpreting its content.

Having appreciated that, in the case of Meletus, skill and truthfulness do not sit comfortably together in his answers to Socrates, we should now inspect the success of these other voices in the *Apology*.

Clarity and Truth in the Apology's *Voices* Let me anticipate our finding: for every case but one, truth and clarity are either together absent or else inversely related in all the voices we hear, infer, or imagine throughout Socrates' defense.

This claim requires me to dispense with those reported voices Socrates invokes simply for the sake of illustration: Callias, or Thetis and Achilles. That their words are clearly vocalized by Socrates says more about him, about his powers of selection and recall, than about their own speaking.

The most compelling instance of speaking that degenerates as it is dragged closer to the truth belongs, of course, to Meletus. The tone grows reluctant, the answers curt, until stubbornness blocks all speech. The powerlessness of clever speaking is exposed, as we saw, in other interlocutors like Callicles. So the *Apology*'s silencing of the voices of those who tangle with Socrates belongs to a general pattern. Examples come readily, the most vivid being Meno's metaphor of being numbed by the stingray: his soul and mouth are paralyzed and he is unable to reply to Socrates (80b) in spite of his previous fluency on the subject of virtue. Other interlocutors conveniently remember another appointment and give up, like Euthyphro, or like Gorgias have to be rescued by somebody else. Plato strongly suggests that it is an unwillingness or incapacity to recognize the truth that brings speech to an end.

When we return to the anonymous voices reported in the *Apology*, the ones we imagine in conversation with Socrates do not achieve fluency and truth. He questions the poets about their beautiful language but discovers that they can say nothing about its meaning. Tradespeople, who use their technical vocabularies with ease, talk nonsense beyond the borders of their own craft. Public figures reputed to be wise leaders have answers for everything—until Socratic questioning brings them up short.

There is a clarity in the reported multiple voice from the past: we know the content of the old anonymous accusation against Socrates. But it speaks falsely about the object and nature of his activity, its motivation, its effects, and its legal and moral status. And as for the inferred collective voice of the jury, intruding into Socrates' linguistic space, it is indeterminate and hostile, concerned neither with clarity nor with the discovery of the truth.

One set of voices, however, does want to clarify and comprehend. Four times we hear them develop a concise formulation of words intended to advance understanding. But these are constructed voices, brought into being by Socrates himself, so they enjoy no status independent of him. In fact, their very dependence creates the impression that their attributed owners among the jurors are incapable of generating such clear words themselves. Plato does something similar in some other dialogues, when he has Socrates construct a fictional interlocutor in order to sustain the discussion. And the effect is often similar: Crito is diminished when Socrates drops him in favor of conversing with himself by giving a voice to the Laws of Athens.

I have not yet mentioned those audacious voices, of oracle and *daimonion*. Socrates has utter confidence in their peculiar speaking: the one goads him into his philosophical activity, the other prevents him from harmful behavior. Nevertheless, the pattern holds: however authoritative they are, neither voice is clear. Socrates explains his own puzzlement about the oracle at 21b. *Why does the god talk in riddles*, he asks, *what can he mean? Surely he cannot lie.* Confidence in divine truth there certainly is; but it is not born out of a clear and certain apprehension of the content of divine speaking. Socrates must discover and probe the ambiguities of that meaning for himself. Although it might be suspected that the forbidding check of the *daimonion* isn't as ambiguous as the oracle's pronouncement—Socrates, after all, knows how to conform his behavior to its negative commands—we should not drift into assuming too much clarity for the content of the divine voice. Whatever Socrates' inner experience, the discovery of its significance requires his interpretive participation. He must actively attend in order to determine the authoritative nature of the voice, and because no reasons are given in the sign, he must work out what it is to obey, only gradually coming to appreciate how obedience works to his good.

I propose, then, that the only voice in the *Apology* that speaks fluently, intelligibly, and on behalf of the truth belongs to Socrates. All other voices are insecure, or false, or too enigmatic for easy human understanding. That discovery sits strangely with our beginning, from which we expected Socrates to enjoy neither skill nor success in his speaking. And yet we are reluctant to return to the old charges that he shows perversity in slyly denying his ability with words. How do we reconcile the mastery won by his voice with his failure to persuade the jury in the matter of his death?

Philosophy, Word, and Silence

In order to answer these questions, we must come in this concluding section to some understanding of Socrates' success and failure with words at his trial, and to appreciate why he bothered to speak at all instead of remaining silent.

The Power of Socratic Speaking At the end of the *Symposium* the narrator Aristodemus wakes to the sound of cockcrow—and the voice of Socrates. After all the partying, everybody had fallen asleep except Socrates, Agathon, and Aristophanes, who carried on a discussion about comedy and tragedy while continuing to pass the drinking bowl among themselves. Aristodemus couldn't quite remember what arguments Socrates advanced, but he tells us that the other two struggled to follow until finally succumbing to sleep. The voice of Socrates prevails, its content too much for the memory but its dominance firmly established.

That instance of the power of Socratic speaking reflects, I think, the preeminent position Plato creates for Socrates as philosopher among the poets, politicians, rhetoricians, sophists, and all other crafters of words. We come with expectation, then, to the trial of Socrates: this of all occasions should be the one on which his voice triumphs.

And in a way it does. We have just recounted how masterful are his words in contrast to all others. Unfaltering, clear and straightforward, the voice of Socrates probes assumptions, exposes weaknesses, formulates positions, explains motivation, silences his accusers. It is especially good in argument, as we have seen, for Socrates is presented with no equals in philosophical inquiry. In the end, there are no other voices worth heeding. Even though Plato sets us up to listen solely to Socrates' own account of his trial, nevertheless his speaking willingly captivates us with its fluency and compelling ease.

We find the language Socrates uses to be skilled and effective in spite of his disclaimers. It was right, perhaps, that the jury be warned about his seductive abilities with words. Yet Socrates is right, too: his is not a cleverness that presses language to bring about some self-regarding end, throwing out words to deflect attention, to conceal, and to mislead their hearers. That we must grant him. So perhaps the place to direct our thinking is around the very nature of success in speaking. Whether we take language to be skillful or clever or effective depends upon what we believe the speaker intends to accomplish. If our interest is in syntax, vocabulary, image, and figure, we may judge speech rough or polished, plain or flowery; but almost any kind of speaking may be skillful if it works in its context. What it works *for* is, of course, the crux of the matter for Plato. Not all skills are morally worthy of employment, rhetoric being one of them—at least if it is deployed for gratification rather than improvement. On that count, Socrates is not a clever speaker, beguiling the audience in order to get what he wants from them.

We should ask about the truth of his words, because we began by noting Socrates' interest in true instead of persuasive speech. Does the jury hear from Socrates—as he claims—the whole truth? That's not easy to answer: how could we know what would constitute an exhaustive and reliable account of anything? One approach, though interesting in its own right, won't help us with Socrates' character. I have in mind the professional philosophic concern for right reasoning. That concern would assess the truth of Socratic language by scrutinizing the logic of his statements: what conclusions does he draw from what premises, and do these truly follow? The logician's scrutiny—surely itself a Socratic exercise—should not be discouraged. I have suggested that the interchange with Meletus cannot be logically conclusive, and in Chapter 6 I'll raise some problems with the logic of Socrates' arguments about immortality at the end of the *Apology*. Nevertheless, success in generating sound arguments cannot be the sole measure of the true speaking that we seek in Socrates. People may utter truths unwittingly or maliciously, or they may spend their time generating formally sound arguments of little human consequence. What we're after in Socrates is *a love of the truth,* an *intention* to speak all his words without dissembling or cloaking his mind in artful disguise. Truthful speech is therefore to be judged over against its opposites, deceit and *eirôneia.*

In developing an understanding of Socrates' defense as free from guile and perversity, I have argued for its truthful character. Perhaps the most significant truth-loving feature of his words lies in his refusal to take up language to save his own skin. What better test might there be of an intention to use only those words one believes to be true?

A large part of the success of Socrates' language for the reader of the *Apology* belongs to its truthful intention. So we understand now the significance of his throwaway remark about his accusers' warning against his skill with words—*unless they mean by "skilled" one who speaks the truth.* The puzzling juxtaposition that launched our exploration, between truthful and effective speech, resolves itself once we attend to the powerful voice of Socrates. Persuading us that he does speak truly, he revises for us the very notions of success and skill with words.

Lest we get carried away, however, we must draw ourselves up short in recalling that we are Plato's readers, not the jury. Their vote went against Socrates. His words failed to exonerate him; in fact, the grim irony of his voice is that he managed to persuade eighty men who had thought him innocent to cast their next votes in favor of his death.

The Failures of Hearing and Speaking Why do Socrates' words not accomplish his salvation? I'll propose two reasons, both of which will cause us to ask again about silence.

The *Gorgias* locates the problem of ineffectual speech in the hearing rather than the speaking. Plato hardly flatters his fellow Athenians by depicting the jurors as children greedy for gratification, incapable of accepting the discipline and examination necessary for their well-being. But at least he makes his belief vivid: there was something deeply wrong with the interests and values of most of Socrates' jurors. They didn't care for his message very much, or his attitude toward all accepted forms of expertise; and as for his comportment at the trial, that was positively offensive. Undoubtedly they would have preferred some recognition of the gravity of his situation—pleas and appeals, perhaps, or gestures toward a reasonable face-saving compromise. Instead, Socrates challenged their entirely human assumptions about death as evil and dislocated their ability to determine his fate, assigning it instead to the will of the god. Because Socrates does not conform to customary expectations, his words must be twisted if they are to be heard at all.

In the nature of that hearing must be sought the explanation for the strange quick reversal by so many jurors, from deciding in favor of innocence to casting their vote for death. Perhaps some, unconvinced that Socrates was guilty precisely as charged, nevertheless hoped that he would just go away and leave Athens in peace. Socrates gave them no reasonable choice, however: he rejected banishment and refused release conditional upon his future silence. Worse, he affronted them with that suggestion of honor for his civic contributions. Like the soldiers on winter campaign who resented him for walking barefoot as usual on ice (*Symposium* 220b), these jurors think Socrates is making a mockery of them. He would have been better off to have said nothing at all.

And that, of course, was how the Socrates of the *Gorgias* said he would conduct his defense—saying nothing because he could not effectively speak the truth, and allowing the outcome to be whatever it would be.

We ourselves understand that. It is true for all of us that, though our auditory equipment makes hearing possible, our basic commitments and our values determine what it is that we hear. Should Socrates wish to influence the decision of the jury, he must present himself in clothes they recognize and approve. He won't dress himself in such disguise— that really would be to dissemble. But if he won't put on a mask of false words, why does he bother to speak at all? By thinking a little about the second reason for the failure of Socrates' words to secure his salvation, perhaps we'll achieve some understanding of how the hypothetical trial of the *Gorgias* might fit with the defense of the *Apology*.

That second reason is elementary: Socrates does not want to save his own life and therefore has no interest in shaping his speech to that end. The failure to be heard is only one side of the story: there's a corresponding failure *to seek* to be heard.

Now let us not misunderstand. I do not suggest that Socrates is possessed of a contrary, self-negating, desire for death. Or that his motives revolve around hopes for an immortal reputation or more sinister thoughts of getting back at Athens by allowing it the enduring disgrace of having killed philosophy. Psychologically abnormal martyr complexes contain such tainted motives, but they won't explain Socrates—that is, Plato's Socrates, with his purity of intention and conviction. For what motivates his behavior is a small but crucial set of moral and religious beliefs that deposit outside his own control any concern about his dying.

Those beliefs, though deserving of more articulation than I can provide here, are founded on Socrates' firm conviction that wrongdoing and injustice are *bad for you*, not simply culturally conditioned concepts or socially useful notions. It's of the greatest human importance, then, to avoid wrong and to seek virtue and goodness. Unfortunately, the search is made difficult because of our overconfidence about what we know. Socrates thus counsels constant self-examination in order to avoid doing injustice; the unexamined life is not the sort of life human beings should lead.

Now if injustice is that bad, isn't it equally bad to have it perpetrated on you by someone else? Shouldn't you pay some attention to protecting yourself against being wronged by others?

We know the answer of the rhetoricians: yes indeed, and the protection you need is skill with language in order to secure your place in the world, even if weaker types think you are unjust in so doing. Socrates disagrees. Throughout the *Gorgias* he keeps repeating his dictum that it is worse to act unjustly than to be the victim of injustice. In his view the corroding power of vice works from within; it cannot be transferred onto good people by those who act wrongly toward them. So in fact you need not devote your attention to securing immunity from harm by others. In his debate with Callicles, Socrates offers three reasons for this (found at 509–13, though not in this order). The first concerns our life priorities. We should concentrate on preventing the greatest evil, making that our highest goal. Because it is worse to do wrong than be wronged, our energies must be channeled into self-scrutiny so that we act always for the welfare of our own souls. Secondly, mere immunity is insufficient. There is no point in simply preserving one's existence unless that existence is good. Our lives cannot become virtuous without our deliberately seeking goodness—so again that should be the priority for our efforts. Finally, the world seems to be such that there is no effective but harmless way for good people to keep themselves from being injured by worse people. All attempts to secure immunity require compromise with political power and are thereby corrupting.

So Socrates turns around the question of self-security: what's important becomes the skill to protect yourself against *doing* wrong. That is the concern of philosophy, not rhetoric.

Should the person bent on goodness then mutely offer no resistance to evil? What about the evil that is done to other people? Socrates does seem to be prepared to countenance the possibility that rhetoric could have a positive use were its persuasive power harnessed to proper philosophical ends. So he argues with Polus—though we're not sure how serious he is—that rhetoric could persuade one's friends to submit to the pain and discipline necessary to correct injustice in their souls. And he uses the phrase "true rhetoric" for the art of wise political rule aimed at moral welfare (517a). The philosopher may redeem persuasive language from its service to base ends in order to rectify wrongs and prevent harm in others.

Why, then, would Socrates not employ a reformed rhetoric for the prevention of an injustice done *to himself,* as long as he also devoted his attention to seeking goodness? He seems to have created too strong an opposition between mere living and virtuous living, forcing us to choose between them as competing objects of our attention. Surely, however, we could make out a case that if you have a duty not to harm yourself as part of virtuous living, then it cannot be wrong to safeguard the self against injustice from others—with the proviso that they should not be harmed by the preventive measures you take. It might even be argued that because those others do wrong in harming you, and because their wrongdoing is bad for them, for their own good they should be dissuaded from harming you. In fact Socrates makes a point like this at *Apology* 30cd: claiming that the Athenians will hurt themselves by putting him to death, he tries to make them see that he is mounting a defense on their behalf rather than his own.

We could go on about self-security as a good necessary for the cultivation of other moral excellences; but Socrates will not be much interested in following our conversation. He could agree with much of it; but he would find it beside the point. For the simple truth is this: Socrates does not regard his being condemned to death *as a harm.* Though the accusations against him may be unjust and the court's decision wrong, still what's done will not hurt him. So he has no reason to deploy the powers of rhetoric against the jury to save his life.

We must not mistake the importance of this truth for Socrates. Without it we will continue to suspect his motivation, siding with the jurors who found him perverse in not working toward his own salvation. His conviction, however unusual, is nonetheless deep, and deeply religious. Socrates expresses it this way at *Apology* 30c: his accusers are incapable of hurting him, for a worse person is not permitted to harm a better. Lying in the language of permission (harming is not *themiton*, lawful or righteous) is the belief that it's part of the divine order of things that being the object of injustice will not ultimately be bad for you. Doing injustice is the only way to bring harm upon yourself.

To give this conviction meaning, Socrates must—like Kant—posit an afterlife in which appropriate rewards and punishments are meted out. It isn't accidental that the *Gorgias* ends with yet another court and trial, in the time after death, with souls stripped of pretense and judges most just. In that trial, warns Socrates, Callicles' words will fail; he will be unable to articulate any defense.

With that other court in mind, then, Socrates need not secure imperfectly human justice from the jury. He is content to leave the outcome of the trial in the hands of the god, in keeping with the advice he gives in the *Gorgias* that we must not be anxious about the length of our lives but leave all that to the care of the god (512e). Because he sees his life as lived in obedience to the divine will, Socrates does not resist the injustice about to be done to him.

We have a grasp on Socrates' failure to speak powerfully in order to win his case. But it is not complete. To the belief that he cannot be harmed by the wrongdoing of others we must add one more thing. Given his situation, Socrates could secure his life only by doing the wrong thing. As I'll argue in Chapter 5, he cannot stop philosophizing without harming himself; and he cannot win acquittal unless he uses tactics that contradict his principles. So Socrates' commitment never to do injustice also requires him to accept the injustice of the court's decision.

Socrates' words do not effect his salvation because, for moral and religious reasons, he will not take the steps necessary to preserve his life. Why then does he bother to speak at all? The question persists, so let me suggest a reply.

Had Socrates said nothing in his own defense, his lack of speaking would not have contradicted his principles. Silence, appropriately explained, might have been a potent sign of his leaving the outcome of the trial in the care of the god. And he would bring about no harm to others by refusing to speak, or by speaking minimally if so required. Moreover, in not opening his mouth he would, like Jesus, decline to add his voice to the false voices surrounding him. Their falsity, and his innocence, would stand exposed. The *Gorgias* suggests, I think, that Plato understands something of this meaning of silence. His Socrates was tried by the wrong court, before which his words might as well have been left unspoken.

Nevertheless, standing before the Athenian court, Socrates does speak. The *Apology* situates us to hear his voice as clear, fluent, and true, so we understand why Plato wants us to listen to this defense. But his Socrates speaks out to the court for his own reason, which has nothing to do with the success or failure of his defense then or now. His speaking is *an act of obedience,* in two ways. First, the defense is another exercise in his philosophical mission: he continues to examine and warn his fellow citizens in obedience to the divine command. Secondly, as he explains to those who voted for his acquittal, throughout his speaking the divine voice, his peculiar sign, never intruded to stop him. Socrates takes this as evidence of the god's care for his final state. But we know that his attentive listening for the voice is evidence that Socrates is not silent because he is obedient.

Once set out, this conclusion seems right. But I confess I did not anticipate an understanding of Word for Socrates so close to the reason for Silence in Jesus.

Word and Silence The practice of saying or doing nothing to defend oneself has a long, if not wide, history. It is, we know, the final stance of the martyr, whose words bear witness but do not strive to protect the self against an unjust death. Those under less extreme attack may also refuse self-assertion: think of the psalmist, who prays in Psalm 38.12–15,

> Those who seek after my life lay snares for me;
> those who strive to hurt me speak of my ruin
> and plot treachery all the day long.
> But I am like the deaf who do not hear,
> like those who are mute and do not open their mouth.
> I have become like one who does not hear,
> and from whose mouth comes no defense.
> For in you, O Lord, I have fixed my hope;
> you will answer me, O Lord my God.

Though we are not entirely sure why the author makes the choice for silence, we are given a clue in the strikingly confessional nature of the psalm. Sin weighs down upon the psalmist, breaking spirit and body; friends and neighbors withdraw, and the enemy seizes upon the vulnerability of this penitent sinner. Conscious of spiritual disease and physical pain, the psalmist has no ground on which to make a stand against attack. Self-vindication is impossible; it is only God who can speak the words of defense. But there's something more in this prayer: it's as though the psalmist turns to stone, incapable of acknowledging the presence or existence of accusers. The refusal to defend becomes a refusal to accord any status to the enemy; the speaking and answering is carried on with God alone.

It might be supposed that the silence of Jesus looks back to something like this experience of divine vindication for its meaning: certainly the language of the Psalms inhabits the consciousness of Jesus in the Passion. Of course, the supposition needs the qualification that Jesus does not present himself as vulnerable and in need of defense because of his wrongdoing. Instead, his vulnerability lies in his innocence, which itself is heightened by his silence. The argument of this chapter, however, requires us to recognize additional and less obvious disanalogies between the silence of the psalmist and the silence of Jesus. In his Passion, Jesus does not turn stonily away from his accusers. He hears. He says enough to establish Scripture as his hiding place. And—though this point awaits our next chapter and Luke's Gospel—he forgives his enemies. But of most significance is the silence within Jesus. Although he places his hope in God, there is no answer that will reconcile for him his dying and his kingdom; his obedience to death is met with silence from his Father.

And in this way the obedient Silence of Jesus stands out against the Word of obedience for Socrates. Though both of them construe their use or nonuse of words in their trials as endorsed by divine authority, there is for Socrates a clarity of mission and purpose that permits him an articulate voice. His confidence in the care of the god is unshaken, and he provides eloquent witness to the power of his moral and religious convictions to sustain him in the midst of unjust and false accusations. Jesus does not work through the meaning of his arrest and Passion in the light of principles that can be articulated and defended. His intentions are set upon doing the will of his Father, even where he cannot bring into resolution the clashing elements of that will. So for him obedience resolves itself into silence.

Word and Silence thus both bear witness in their own ways in these two lives. The clarity and control of Socrates at his trial extends to his dying as well, and adds its testimony to his special character; we'll think about that, and the contrast with the death of Jesus, in our final chapter. But in Chapter 4 we turn our minds to the religious speaking—and silence—that is prayer.

FOUR

Addressing and Attending

My words fly up; my thoughts remain below
Words without thoughts never to Heaven go
—CLAUDIUS, in *Hamlet*

The true relation in prayer is not when God hears what is prayed for, but when *the person praying* continues to pray until he is *the one who hears,* who hears what God wills.
—SØREN KIERKEGAARD, *Journals*

IN ALL WE HAVE SEEN SO FAR, Jesus' relation to the Father is essential to his self-understanding and to the meaning of his death. And we have seen in the last chapter that parts of that relationship are constituted in silence, where words are not available for the speaking. Socrates, by contrast, finds language and argument necessary not only in the defense but also in the very execution of the activity fundamental to his life.

Now while silence is sometimes unavoidable or even welcome, all relationships require the mediation of language, very broadly conceived as a symbolic system of shared meanings. Without that mediation—which may involve gestures and other symbols as well as words—there is, quite simply, nothing that can be called a relationship. Of course, for the mediation to work there must be periods of attentiveness and response, not just the deployment of language. And this will have to hold for religious experience as well as for all kinds of human interactions.

In this chapter we turn to an experience, common to people of faith, that involves an unusual kind of linguistic and communicative activity, usually called prayer. If it is an authentic interpersonal experience, prayer must involve both speaking and listening. However, these poles may enjoy a difference in emphasis in particular practitioners, hence the title of this chapter. *Addressing* and *attending* continue the theme of word and silence; but our two protagonists will here change their earlier positions. Socrates will move to Silence, and Jesus to Word. For Jesus, as we will soon appreciate, addressing the Father and his being addressed by the Father are fundamental; for Socrates, prayer in the conventional sense seems less important than an attentiveness to the god that we will have to explore in the context of his religious peculiarity.

The Perplexities of Prayer

But never mind Socrates: anyone who prays looks to be caught up in a spate of peculiarities. We can come up with a small fistful without much trouble at all. First, prayer is addressed to a being not physically present in a particular location as other persons are present to us in their bodies. God does not hear with ears or look with eyes upon us, so there is no way of experiencing through physical presence his attentiveness to what we say. Second, if our prayers therefore seem like words spoken into the telephone or typed onto the screen for electronic transmission, God nevertheless does not answer in audible or legible words. He does not use language that we (or most of us anyway) think we can report as verbatim comments upon the usefulness of what we've said, verifications of our observations, or disagreements with our proposals. That weakens further the likeness of praying to normal conversation or communication, which is always shaped by response. If prayer is only one-sided speaking, it is more like a radio signal beamed into space than a telephone conversation. Third, even the usual indirect means of gaining assurance that there is a hearer are not at all easily available. The presence of a listener unavailable to normal experience could be inferred from events that serve as answers to various requests, events that might not have come about otherwise. Prayer is sometimes answered, in the collective opinion of the community of faith. But how events constitute answers rather than the mere operations of nature—that is something not obvious to those without belief in God (or even always clear, I may say, to the faithful). And though there must be many other peculiarities, let me mention just one more here: that the speaking done in prayer may seem unnecessary if God knows all there is to know. For his knowledge about others God does not depend on their efforts at communication in the same way that the rest of us do.

In spite of all these peculiarities, people still pray. And not just in lisping infant rhymes or from the usual neuroses: some pray who are in every respect admirable human beings. Among those for whom prayer holds significance we must count Socrates and Jesus. Their activity in praying can be ignored or explained away by various devices best left to those who care to use them. My interest lies in learning from these two something of the structure of the experience of praying. Because I want to uncover and display the attitudes and assumptions of the one who prays, it might be appropriate to think of this chapter as constructing a *phenomenology of prayer* (where *phenomenology* means simply a descriptive study of some facet of human experience in order to make it intelligible). Such an exercise turns out to be important in assessing the peculiarities and problems of prayer. Nevertheless, this will not be a neutral or detached description, even supposing that were possible. Given my own commitments, I'll treat the praying of Jesus as *exemplary,* the best kind of praying to do. Although Socrates does not pray in terms easily compatible with the tradition of Jesus, still he will have something important to contribute to the discussion. Both will assist us in clarifying the practices of addressing and attending in order to move toward a phenomenology of exemplary prayer. But because I will refine and endorse as well as clarify, this exercise may also be seen as a justification for prayer, especially as a response toward the evil of the world.

Philosophy and Prayer

To philosophize is not to pray: what have petition, address, and attention to Almighty God to do with critical thinking? The one activity can be carried on without the other, our collective experience assures us—in fact, probably *better* carried on, in the opinion of many practitioners of either. Philosophy trips up the praying, says the faithful heart; the philosophical mind answers that for prayer to commence the thinking must have ended.

In spite of that—or maybe because of it—prayer has always been an object of philosophical interest. The skeptic raises problems with praying as one way to discredit theistic belief and practice; but even where the existence of God is not in question, the peculiarities of prayer have been a fertile field for the growth of philosophical perplexity. The standard objections may be followed in textbooks on the philosophy of religion. They include the problems that we have just considered, over whether a divine being could hear prayer or what would constitute an answer to a petition. Critiques may also charge that it is meaningless to pray that God's will be done if God always does his will anyway, or they may condemn the selfishness of asking favors for oneself or the abdication of personal dignity in resignation to a supreme authority.

Thoughtful believers have often felt it their duty to consider such objections to prayer and to offer adequate responses. Sometimes the responses given by philosophers have turned out to be revisionary explanations of what goes on in praying, purchasing philosophical respectability at the price of denying the experience of the tradition. But sometimes, too, philosophers have attempted to practice faithful praying. They will be found on Sundays at public prayer, and may even discover themselves praying not just as Christians-in-general but also *as philosophers*. Seeking divine assistance in their work, they may end up doing that work more carefully *ad maiorem gloriam Dei.* Of course all believers aspire to do their work, whatever its sphere, to the greater glory of God. But for some kinds of questions, and for some kinds of questioners, prayer may have an appropriate role to play within philosophical activity itself.

What I have in mind is the type of philosophical problem that involves God essentially in its subject matter, and which therefore might be explored at least in part through the activity of praying. We don't have to speculate what it would be like for a philosopher to proceed in this way, for two strong and influential examples spring to mind—Augustine and Anselm. In his *Confessions,* Augustine brings before God problems about creation and time, good and evil, and lets the reader in on Augustine's side of the conversation about them. And Anselm's famous ontological argument for God's existence is uncovered in the process of praying to God. To understand the results of their philosophizing may not require the same prayerful activity, because their arguments have to stand up to public scrutiny. Nevertheless, both Augustine and Anselm seem to believe that attentive prayer discloses philosophically fruitful insights into the nature of God and our relationship to him. Their examples remind us that the addressive nature of prayer has connections with the notion of dialogue, since Plato's time a philosophical form that reflects one method for getting at the truth. But we could also look in a different direction, toward Attention rather than Address: think of the importance, stressed particularly by the French writer Simone Weil, of attending on the truth rather than trying to catch it by constant pursuit. Both dialogue and contemplation have honorable histories as philosophical practices; and both are practices known to those who pray.

No matter how suggestive, these comments on philosophy and prayer remain exceedingly general. I cannot mean by them that philosophical thinking can be an actual dialogue with God (who could hardly be an equal partner in the search for truth), or a straightforward reporting of what is disclosed in contemplating the One who is Truth. At the same time, I continue to suspect that the character of philosophizing—especially about God—may be shaped by the practice of prayer. Because this chapter is more about praying than about philosophy, instead of developing a general theory I'll discuss in the next section just one problem, though one of great importance to both activities.

Prayer and Evil

The problem of evil is a perplexity for faith as well as for philosophy. Sometimes philosophers are tempted to think of it as their problem, for they are expert in its formulation and discussion. But the question of why the righteous suffer raised itself in prayer long ago and apart from the prompting of philosophers. We need to reflect a little on how evil has been prayed about in the biblical tradition.

Think, for instance, of the Psalms, replete with petition, lament, and protest about evil. The concern of praying out of the experience of pain and suffering seems to be double, about God and about one's enemies. God, though addressed as faithful and powerful, has acted in ways that seem incompatible with his character. His people are in trouble, feel abandoned, and cry out for his mercy and justice. They don't understand how things could be this way, and they protest their lot. But their enemies also give them concern—quite rightly, because of their oppression; but more subtly, in that the enemy now thinks Israel's God to be impotent and Israel's trust to be misplaced. God, in allowing his people to be oppressed, has given their enemies evidence of his abandonment and lack of faithfulness. So there's a kind of multiplied shame in suffering: the faithful endure the shame of God's supposed indifference, and that in turn brings disgrace upon God's name in the eyes of the nations, as well as upon Israel's name by association with him.

In prayer this double concern, about one's relation to God and about one's reputation among the skeptics, is brought to God, who is asked to act openly in ways that vindicate his name and his people's confidence in him. The psalmist usually wants the unrighteous, and only them, to suffer, and to suffer in the exact measure that they deserve. The righteous, for their part, should prosper and flourish. Then all will be well.

In petitioning for this outcome, the psalmist may bring up the shame of Israel's name among the enemy partly to provoke God into protecting his friends' reputation. But the links between God's name and Israel's name are complicated. Even if Israel firmly believes that God's name has been vindicated and their shame before him removed, it wouldn't necessarily follow that their enemies would agree. Because they are the enemy, they might have their own explanations for a reversal of fortune and be unwilling therefore to release Israel from shame. If the faithful are interested in their own good name and reputation among the nations, they have to do more than pray to God; they must talk to their enemies.

And now let me apply this distinction between talking to God and talking to one's enemies to philosophy and the problem of evil. The experience of evil, especially in the form of undeserved suffering, has given rise to prayer as protest and as petition. It is also the seed from which philosophical discussion is germinated. And once that discussion has got under way, philosophers who are believers have for the most part done their talking about evil to the enemy in an attempt to avoid the shame of unwarranted trust and bad reasoning.

I don't really intend to suggest that philosophical believers have been interested only in their intellectual reputations. More often than not, their defense of the faith has been provoked by vigorous attack. The point is rather that the audience for philosophical discourse about evil has been the skeptic, by and large. Even if the philosopher has worked with the community of faith, the focus has been on sorting out the beliefs of that community by addressing its members. And so it is that philosophers who defend faith in the presence of the world's evil do much speaking *about* God, about possible divine intention, character, ability, and the like. Not professing to know the inscrutable will of God, they nevertheless postulate reasonable hypotheses about why evil is permitted—which if true would clear God's name and vindicate the believer's trust. They strive to make their reasoning internally coherent, and consistent with the accepted items of theistic belief. In this way they develop theodicies, attempts (in Milton's words) to "assert Eternal Providence / and justify the ways of God to men." Some theodicies emphasize the free will of created beings, defending the Creator's gift of freedom but showing what possibilities for wrongdoing must come along with that gift. Others speak of the necessary role played by certain types of pain and suffering in turning us into the sorts of beings God desires us to become. Still others posit necessary limitations within God's power or knowledge that account for evil, while permitting God to remain loving within the constraints of his abilities. These lines of argument are familiar to anyone with some exposure to the philosophy of religion; and the knots and tangles found in these lines by critics are also familiar. What all attempts at philosophical theology or theodicy have in common is their object of address: they speak *to* the community of the philosophical *about* God. There is nothing wrong with that; given who we are and the challenges presented to us, we (or some of us at least) will have to carry on that way. But this is very different from *addressing God,* especially when our discourse is about God. That sort of language is the language of prayer. Is it possible for it to be language that bears directly upon philosophical thinking as well?

It will take the entire chapter to achieve an answer to this question. It is nonetheless an issue that makes a difference to our expectations, as philosophically perplexed believers, about answers to the problem of evil. For answers are satisfying in relation to their questions; and, as we know, always the trick is to get the question right. What we need to take from our comments so far is that the questions themselves may differ according to their objects of address as well as their content. For think about the difference between third- and second-person discourse. It doesn't take much to recognize that discourse is always built out of the ingredients and flavors of its addressive context. Your topics of conversation, lexical choice, and tone are governed by your perception of my interests and vocabulary. Together we may speak of a third person in ways that neither of us would report verbatim to him. Or think of times when you have rehearsed what words to use to confront someone, only to find that it doesn't quite come out that way when you speak to her (as we say) *in person.* Personal address has a different quality, not just because of power and status relations (though that may play a part if you feel dependent upon the good will of the hearer), but because of what I'll loosely call "presence." Where the one spoken *about* is the one spoken *to,* then the assumptions of our speaking may be called directly into question. We must think more carefully, perhaps, about our claims and charges; we must relax our tight interpretations of motive, be sensitive to the effects of our speaking upon the other. Presence has a way of forcing an ethical dimension into our discourse, one that involves honesty, justice, and charity as well as truth. To speak to someone "in person" or "personally" about a matter of concern to him is to be confronted with his presence *as* a person.

It would be foolish to dream that what I term "presence" always makes for virtuous discourse. It doesn't—any more than being with other people makes you treat them as ends in themselves. Certainly Job's friends continued to hold their assumptions about his relation to God in spite of having sat in his presence for days. Worse, presence may release suppressed feelings of rage or hatred that will make discourse vicious rather than virtuous. I want only to claim that second-person address, in having presence as its context, may well change the nature of discourse, including the appropriateness of certain questions and thereby the nature of satisfactory answers. But that is enough.

It is enough, for when we move philosophical discourse about the problem of evil into the second person, two things happen right off. First, the enemy stays outside the temple of prayer, having no words belonging to the grammar of prayer. Second, with the enemy gone the question remaining is no longer the secondary one about the reasonableness of the believer, the good name or shame of the faithful. It is instead the primary question about the goodness, justice, and power of God— but now addressed *to* God and not about God.

And who can predict what will happen when philosophical perplexity gets translated into the language of prayer? Even if we are not competent to answer, it may help to remember that some kinds of perplexity arise because of assumptions that are challenged in direct encounter. Certainly our tradition reminds us that being in the presence of God may have a profound effect upon us, exposing more about ourselves than we sometimes want to know. At least, then, we should entertain the possibility that among the things that prayer may change is the problem of evil.

Only as a possibility, though. I have given no reason to think more than that. And even that much seems to depend upon God's being "present" to human experience in ways sufficiently like the presence required for second-person discourse—when how this itself could be so was the first of the peculiarities of prayer with which we began. To make progress, then, we must move to the main concern of this chapter, the structure of exemplary prayer. Only when we have seen what praying involves will we be able to return to the possibilities thrown out in this introduction.

Addressing

To explore the addressive nature of prayer we must consider the gospel accounts of Jesus' practice. Scarcely can there be a subject with more danger signs for the cultivated intellect: even one or two memories of any of those ghastly paintings of brown eyes in bearded face reverently raised heavenward—that will be enough to persuade us to leave this business to weak-witted sentimentalists or those so saintly that wit no longer matters. And how will the rest of us negotiate a territory of the spirit so private, or weird, that to mention this sort of intimacy in polite company would stop all conversation—though it would be perfectly acceptable, even witty, to bring up Jesus' relationship with the Magdalene in, say, *The Last Temptation of Christ*?

Yet we have to step onto this ground, if we are to understand Jesus or anything of the response of faith to the evil of the world. The itinerary includes a brief look at the evidence of the Gospels before settling down for a more detailed discussion of Luke; we will come to see that Jesus' praying, though exemplary for Christians, contains elements that are distinctive and that may well have generated difficulties for later praying. The main problem to be worked through is this: how Jesus' affirming the Father's will relates to what most of the faithful do in their feeble praying, caught up as they so often are with begging and complaining. Does prayer as address encompass petition and protest as well as acceptance? And is prayer as acceptance itself acceptable for robust minds?

Jesus at Prayer: The Evidence of the Gospels

Jesus did pray: but what is our ground for this assertion? Though we might have made it a matter of reasonable conjecture that he offered set prayers like other Jewish males of his time, there is in fact textual evidence for this. It is, however, scant. The synoptics record his participation in synagogue services, but the only ritual prayers alluded to are over food: he blesses the loaves and fish before the multiplication miracles, and he offers thanks at the Last Supper for the bread and for the cup. The rest of Jesus' praying is more private and personal.

Our sources for Jesus at prayer are uneven. From Mark we learn very little. Like Matthew and Luke, he records the prayer in the garden, and Jesus prays once from the cross; but apart from that there are only two occasions, both in remote places, where we find Jesus engaged in prayer. Matthew's Jesus gives a fair amount of teaching about prayer, including the Lord's Prayer; but his own praying is not a matter for our attention. The garden and the cross stand out, of course; but before that surprisingly little praying takes place. There is the reported prayer of thanks for his special relation to the Father at the end of chapter 11, and after the feeding of the five thousand he goes off by himself to pray. But that is all. Even when children are brought to him for the laying on of hands *and prayer* (19.13), Matthew reports only that Jesus, insisting on accepting them, laid his hands on them—and went his way.

One might wonder whether the glorified Jesus of John's Gospel will be different. But he offers only three prayers, and just one of them seems to count as address to God. At Lazarus's tomb (chapter 11), he thanks his Father for hearing him—but adds that he is saying this not to make the Father listen (he always does) but for the sake of the bystanders. And in chapter 12 when he prays, "Father, glorify your name," the answering thunderous noise is again directed at the audience. This dialogue between Jesus and his Father is thus self-conscious rather than intimate. Only in the long chapter 17 prayer, unique to John and John's Jesus, do we see that intimacy. From the cross there are no words addressed to God. Mary and John are spoken to; Jesus' words about thirst are to fulfill Scripture rather than to make a request. His last "It is finished!" is a statement for all hearers and not just his Father.

That said, perhaps we should not ignore the strong feeling over the death of Lazarus: John stresses it in saying twice that Jesus was deeply moved, that he was upset, that he wept (no calm brown eyes tilted trustingly up in this scene). So when Jesus publicly thanks the Father for hearing him, he may be referring to an internal petition in the depths of his emotion. If so, that is hidden from us.

For some reason probably related to an authorial intent I happily leave to other scholars, Luke's Gospel is strikingly different on the place and practice of prayer. That is apparent from the start.

The first couple of chapters of Luke set out the births of John the Baptist and Jesus, and no cluster of activities gets more prominence than praying, praising, and blessing. The first scene takes place in the Temple, with Zechariah offering incense in the sanctuary and the people outside at prayer. And the action starts with a most dramatic answer to prayer: Gabriel's sudden appearance is in recognition of the praying that Elizabeth and Zechariah must have done, though Luke tells us only of their uprightness and childlessness. From there on, all the characters introduced engage in language addressed to God. Mary and Zechariah sing songs in praise of God; the angels in the heavens and the shepherds in the fields, and Simeon and Anna in the Temple, all praise and bless God. When Elizabeth and Simeon bless Mary and Jesus, that activity belongs in the family of prayer even though God is not directly addressed, for God's work is explicitly invoked and praised in these contexts.

Luke ends his Gospel as he began: his final words are "in the Temple praising God." The reason for praise is the risen and ascended Christ, who after his resurrection said words of blessing over bread at Emmaus, and over his followers gathered at Bethany, and who "in the act of blessing parted from them." Luke alone among the evangelists uses the vocabulary of blessing in the resurrection, and he works it in four times.

The Practice and Content of Prayer in Luke

More to the point for this study, Luke also has Jesus himself pray more frequently—much more frequently—than in the other accounts. There are at least eleven occasions: "at least" because the evidence of the second instance in the list below suggests a regular practice.

Jesus' Practice

1. Jesus, just baptized, is praying—when the heavens open to reveal the dovelike Spirit and the voice proclaims, "You are my beloved son; in you I delight." (3.21–22)
2. After a series of noteworthy healings, Jesus would "from time to time" withdraw for prayer to remote places. (5.16) So when Luke said in the previous chapter that Jesus "made his way to a remote spot" at daybreak (4.42), we may infer that this was for prayer.
3. Just before he picks out twelve of his followers, he spends the whole night in prayer to God in the hill country. (6.12)
4. Jesus prays "by himself" in the company of his disciples, then asks them about his reputed identity. (9.18)
5. About a week later he takes Peter, James, and John up a mountain in order to pray (9.28); he is transfigured and God's voice is again heard. (9.35)

6. After the return of the seventy-two followers, Jesus thanks his Father, exulting in the Holy Spirit, in one of the several recorded prayers in this Gospel. (10.21–22)

7. Jesus gives his disciples what we know as the Lord's Prayer when they ask him to teach them to pray—after he had himself been praying. (11.1–4)

8. Jesus reports that he has prayed for Peter. (22.32)

9. In the most concentrated passage for the vocabulary of prayer (five times in these seven verses), Jesus asks his disciples to pray, and he himself prays urgently and in anguish another of his recorded prayers: "take this cup . . . yet not my will but yours." An angel brings him strength. (22.40–46)

10. Though the speaking is not called "praying," from his cross Jesus utters two prayers. The first is that his Father forgive his executioners. (23.34)

11. The second prayer from the cross is the prayer of committal, strikingly different from the cry of forsakenness in Mark and Matthew. (23.46)

These occasions provide ample evidence for the practice of prayer by Jesus. Fortunately, some of them also contain reports of what he prayed. It will help to have the texts set out for inspection, making use of titles to which we can later refer.

Jesus' Own Prayers

THE PRAYER OF THANKS. I thank you, Father, Lord of heaven and earth, for hiding these things from the learned and wise, and revealing them to the simple. Yes, Father, such was your choice. Everything is entrusted to me by my Father; no one knows who the Son is but the Father, or who the Father is but the Son, and those to whom the Son chooses to reveal him. (10.21–22 REB)

THE PRAYER IN THE GARDEN. Father, if it be your will, take this cup from me. Yet not my will but yours be done. (22.42 REB)

THE PRAYER OF FORGIVENESS. Father, forgive them; they do not know what they are doing. (23.34 REB)

THE PRAYER OF COMMITTAL. Father, into your hands I commit my spirit. (23.46 REB)

But we should also look at the words of the praying that Jesus recommends to others.

Other Prayers Of all the praying associated with Jesus, the Lord's Prayer remains the most familiar. Luke's version is shorter than Matthew's:

> Father, may your name be hallowed; your kingdom come. Give us each day our daily bread. And forgive us our sins, for we too forgive all who have done us wrong. And do not put us to the test. (11.2–4 REB)

Luke also gives us, in the parable of the Pharisee and the tax collector (18.9–14), another two prayers to compare with each other, and a clear recommendation about which is superior. So we add these texts to the list:

> The Pharisee's Prayer. I thank you, God, that I am not like the rest of mankind—greedy, dishonest, adulterous—or, for that matter, like this tax collector. I fast twice a week; I pay tithes on all that I get. (18.11 REB)
> The Tax-Collector's Prayer. God, have mercy on me, sinner that I am. (18.13 REB)

With this evidence of practice and content, then, we may now go on to reflect on the nature of the praying in which Luke's Jesus engages or which he recommends.

Exemplary Prayer as the Lord's Prayer

Christians since the earliest days have regarded the Lord's Prayer as the model for their praying. It comes directly from Jesus in both Matthew and Luke. Whereas Matthew makes the prayer part of the teaching of Jesus, Luke sets it in the context of Jesus' own praying. That is not quite the same as claiming that the words of the Lord's Prayer are something Jesus himself prayed. But his other recorded praying is consonant with elements in this prayer, in four respects.

First, Jesus' asking from the cross that his Father forgive echoes the third sentence of the Lord's Prayer, though with the object of the petition reversed *Forgive them* [not *me*], *for I forgive those who have done me wrong* seems the sense. That a plea for forgiveness is essential to prayer is reinforced in Jesus' commendation of the tax collector's petition as the appropriate words to utter in God's presence.

Second, though Jesus does not elsewhere utter the words of the final clause of the Lord's Prayer, *do not put us to the test,* nevertheless that is precisely what he asks his disciples to pray for themselves in the garden, and his words about the possibility of having the cup taken from him in the Garden Prayer are a conditional form of that request.

Third, there is an underlying theme in Jesus' Prayer of Thanks, his Prayer in the Garden, and his Prayer of Committal: the will of his Father. Jesus' thanksgiving in the first case is an affirmation of the choice and will of his Father to reverse normal expectations about the foolish and the learned; in the second prayer he explicitly subordinates the conditional request about the cup to the will of the Father; and in his last prayer, giving his spirit over into his Father's hands is, of course, nothing but the final surrender of his will to the Father's. Now only some manuscripts of Luke's version of the Lord's Prayer add "your will be done" to the first sentence, and they may well reflect Matthew's tradition. Nevertheless, this feature of Jesus' praying is entirely consonant with the Lord's Prayer as we now pray it. To acknowledge that it is *his* name that is hallowed, that it is *his* reign that must come about—that is to commit oneself to the will of the Father.

Fourth, I have kept to the end the most obvious connection between the Lord's Prayer and the recorded prayers of Jesus himself: the use of "Father" as form of address to God. Unlike the Pharisee and the tax collector, who in their prayers invoke "God," Jesus speaks to his "Father" in every prayer—and five times in the Prayer of Thanks, if indeed the reading is correct that keeps the long last sentence as part of the prayer rather than a comment directed to his disciples. New Testament commentary suggests that the Greek *pater* in the Gospel texts translates Jesus' own native Aramaic *Abba*, a term close to our "Daddy." The word thus reveals a distinct and characteristic feature of Jesus' understanding of God, expressing intimacy and familiarity. When someone uses "Father!" or better still "Daddy!" addressively to a second person, then the term doesn't just report that one is child and the other is father; the speaking also constitutes and expresses an intimate relationship.

I must add quickly that, though Jesus' relation to God cannot be understood without his seeing him as Father, not all intimate human relationships are positive and good. The experience of some believers has made the language of fatherhood problematic; and even where personal experience has been positive there remains the question of the adequacy of only masculine language about God. Given Luke's presentation of Jesus, and indeed the long history of our language, we will continue to speak here of the relationship of Father and Son. Nevertheless, I shall return to this issue later in the chapter.

To sum up, then: close relationship and forgiveness, the Father's will and confidence in that will in spite of testing—these are the essential themes in prayer for Jesus, in his own praying and in the model Lord's Prayer.

Discontinuity Between Practice and Content

But while the themes are consistently presented by Luke, there is a noteworthy difference between the praying of Jesus and his instructions to others about prayer. I have indicated that Luke's Jesus asks for forgiveness for his enemies, not for himself. Given the moral of the Pharisee–tax collector parable, that those who humble themselves in confession are the truly righteous, it is striking that Jesus does not set an example of that kind of prayer: his intimacy with the Father seems to be on a different footing. That, however, is only one indication of difference. Two more may be of interest.

The first concerns topography. A glance back at the eleven instances of Jesus at prayer will make it plain that, in almost every case, Jesus prays off by himself. The repeated pattern is in remote or deserted places, in the hills or on a mountain. When his disciples are present he nevertheless prays all alone by himself, or (in the garden) withdraws a stone's throw. By placing horizontal distance between himself and other people, he emphasizes the solitariness of prayer as relation. But what happens in that solitude? There may be a clue in the second difference: it stands out in the praying that is witnessed by others, beginning with his baptism. For where he is not removed by horizontal distance from his fellows, Jesus is marked, so to speak, by a close vertical relationship with the Father. The heavens open, the dove descends, and the voice speaks. Similarly, though more dramatically, in the Transfiguration story: in praying Jesus is radiantly transformed, and though Moses and Elijah become his peers the voice singles him out again. Finally, when he exults in the Holy Spirit in the Prayer of Thanks, Jesus himself speaks of the unique epistemological privilege between Father and Son, creating thereby a gap between himself and other human beings. As he moves away from others, then, we are positioned to suspect that Jesus enters into intimacy with the Father: horizontal distance is accompanied by vertical closeness. Even in the hour of Jesus' agony in the garden, Luke (and only he) opens heaven for the strengthening angel. Contrast the penitent tax collector, who prays aright: he keeps his distance from others, but he dares not raise his eyes to heaven to establish vertical closeness. And contrast that man again with his praying fellow the Pharisee, who sets himself righteously (but ironically) off from others: by asserting his own horizontal distance and creating vertical intimacy in words alone, he becomes the exemplar of false prayer.

Add a couple of other features that distinguish Jesus' praying from that of others. We remember that Luke's Gospel opens with prayer in the Temple and closes with praise in the same place. Jesus associates prayer with this sacred space—not just as the location of the parable we've been discussing, but also in the cleansing of the Temple (19.46). Nevertheless, while he was blessed there as an infant (2.28) and claimed at twelve that he had to be in his Father's house (2.49), not once do we see him pray in "the house of prayer." Nor, though prayer is a communal cultic activity (the Lord's Prayer is after all articulated in the plural), does Luke have his Jesus join with others in praying apart from those prayers of food blessing with which we began.

From this evidence I have to conclude that, while intimacy and the Father's will are the marks of prayer for Jesus in practice and in his teaching, his own praying is given special status in Luke. The emphasis rests on his detachment from others, his nonparticipation in his praying community, and his closeness with the Father, which alters fundamentally the recommended approach to God in humility and for forgiveness. The deficiencies of portraits of Christ at prayer in sentimental religious art are not aesthetic alone: such attempts to position us to see his face at all destroy unthinkingly the distance Luke has so carefully set between Jesus and the rest of us.

We have arrived at two conclusions about exemplary prayer. First, its marks are familiarity of address to the Father, a seeking of forgiveness, and an affirming of his will in spite of testing. Second, Jesus' own praying is intimate and affirmative, but omits the plea for forgiveness. Insofar as he is example for his followers, there is discontinuity in the kind of praying recommended and practiced in Luke. Is this discontinuity so strong that Jesus is removed from ordinary religious experience?

And in particular, is his affirmation of the Father's will so special that those who treat this aspect of his relationship as exemplary may find themselves frustrated and tripped up in their praying?

Problems in Exemplary Prayer

To advance the argument, I am going to consider in this section a couple of common problems of prayer that, though sometimes voiced by the skeptic, often give the faithful themselves cause for concern. The second problem forms a cluster around the nub of prayer as petitionary; but first I want to expose a difficulty in certain forms of submissive praying and to contrast that with prayers of protest.

Resignation and Protest Put to one side for the moment any special status that Jesus may enjoy in his relationship with his Father, and think instead of the ordinary believer who, in untoward circumstances, murmurs, "Thy will be done." The critic charges that this means nothing at all: for whatever happens or does not happen will all unfold in accordance with this ubiquitous Will. We shall worry about that sort of problem in the next subsection, and deal here instead with one thing we fear that the prayer does mean—about the murmurer, not about God. For in these words we may believe the speaker's will to be withdrawn. Verbal resignation, along with those folded hands and heavenward glances, looks so passive that we may find ourselves resisting prayer as unworthy of responsible people. The words recall a similar but less pious formulation, "have it your way"—which is surely a sign of retreat from decision making. Even if the phrase, uttered sincerely, means "You make the decision because you know best," then it still suggests a diminishment of self and a shunting off of responsibility that smacks too much for us of surrender to paternalism. Small wonder, then, if the utterance of words of resignation in prayer is thought to signal a pathological self-deprecation; small wonder if piety and psychological health are regarded as inversely related.

But that is not the whole story about prayer in the life of the faithful. Though we have not encountered it so far in Luke's exemplary praying, scripture contains a radically different style: contrast the attitude of resignation with the assertive praying done in the Psalms. It would be difficult to find anything further from passive submission to the divine will, or from the theological fatalism that has from time to time infected some believers. These prayers bristle with imperatives directed to God:

> *arise* and *save* me, *answer* me when I call, *listen* to my words, *don't rebuke* me, *rouse yourself* in wrath, *rescue* me, *strike* them, *set your hand* to the task, *don't forget* the afflicted, *break the power* of the wicked . . .

and so on; and those come in the first ten psalms alone.

Nor do we have imperatives only: another prominent grammatical feature of this praying is the interrogative, a form absent from any of the recorded prayers in Luke. *Why? When?* and especially *How Long?*—the questions express a lack of acceptance of the conditions of existence, a protest against what is assumed to be God's unwillingness to wake up and get on with his saving business:

> When will you act, Lord? (6.3) Why stand far off? (10.1) How long will you leave me forgotten, hide your face; how long must I suffer, will my enemy prevail? (13.1–2) Why have you forsaken me, why are you so far? (22.1) How long will you look on? rescue me! (35.17) Why have you forgotten me? (42.9) Why do you sleep? awake! (44.23) Why have you cast us off? Why fume with anger at the flock you used to shepherd? (74.1) How long will you fume at your people's prayer? (80.4) Will you be angry with us for ever? (85.5) How long will you hide yourself from sight? (89.46) Lord, how long? (90.13) Have you rejected us? (108.11) How long must I wait? (119.84)

Now surely there is some fiber in that sort of praying. It has at least two things going for it, over against the passivity of just being resigned to whatever is. First, as any grief-experienced person knows, it's much more psychologically healthy to release feelings than to stop them up with a religious plug: sent underground in the psyche, they seep damagingly into places where they don't belong. But more, this kind of protest is spoken from a place where there remain some scraps of human dignity. Those who cry out against the treatment they have received have somewhere to stand, a sense of having been wronged or neglected unjustly. Even if they suffer, they are nevertheless vital agents in the process, not mere shadow-extensions of an irresistible will.

Though expressed preeminently in the Psalms, that kind of tough tenacity of spirit pervades much of Hebrew scripture. It may be laudable to our generation because, given our interest in individual rights, protest wears the appearance of a claiming of rights over against authority. But for those who have been taught about the authority of the Father, talk of asserting rights is dangerously hubristic—which is why Jewish protest against God has sometimes seemed intriguingly audacious to certain forms of Christian piety. That, however, may result from a failure to appreciate the strong covenantal basis of the relationship between God and his chosen people. Having entered into a solemn agreement with them, God is bound to honor his commitments: and prayers of protest hold God to those promises (a good example is Psalm 44). Such praying has as its ground not a self-constructed dignity (who could stand when he appears, indeed?) but the solidity of covenant.

Suppose we make peace with the critic over the psychological ill health of passive resignation by recalling the tradition of dissent and lament against God. Isn't the price of peace too high, given that this tradition seems unrepresented among Jesus' own practice and teaching? And is not this absence a mark of serious discontinuity between Luke and the Psalms? For surely Jesus would have known the protesting prayer of Israel. Indeed, for Matthew and Mark it is more than "would have"; he prayed such prayer in his crying out of Psalm 22 from the cross: "My God, my God, why have you forsaken me?" Luke's Jesus, by contrast, appears to have come to unprotesting terms with the will of the Father. The Gethsemane prayer begins, "Father, *if it be your will,*" not "if it is possible"; it is offered only once while Jesus kneels on the ground. But in Mark and Matthew Jesus throws himself to the ground and has to keep praying—three times—about the possibility of not having to drink the cup, before the consequent clause of acceptance. It is easy to exaggerate the difference in these accounts: we must not overlook Luke's description of the anguished struggle (the Greek is *agônia*) in which Jesus prays, or the bloody sweat, all the more striking in the presence of an angel's strength. But that only exacerbates our problem: how can prayer that accepts the will of the Father throughout all forms of testing sit with Israel's cries of protest? Is that sweat itself mute protest, the forcing of covenantal claims against God through the pores of one's very being?

I don't think we can come to any resolution of this perplexity without moving to the second type of problem common to prayer, associated with petition.

The Problems of Petition But this is going to get us deeper into trouble. If there is something unsettling about abdicating responsibility in submission to the divine will, there is serious philosophical distress over petitionary prayer. I don't mean the question of whether petitions get answered or not; I have in mind the more perturbing possibility that this very type of praying is entirely inappropriate.

The difficulties arise for praying believers when they try to sort through their convictions. The following beliefs seem unexceptional:

1. Prayer makes requests that express the desires of the petitioner;
2. God for his part has his own will and desire;
3. Because God is omniscient, God knows everything about the situation from which the petition arises;
4. Given divine goodness, God must desire what is for the best for the petitioner in that situation;
5. Because God is omnipotent, the divine will is beyond frustration.

Though not unusual beliefs, when considered together they seem to undermine petitionary prayer. For from them—and without employing any ammunition from the arsenals of the ungodly—it seems to follow that there is *no point* in making requests at all. Praying does not contribute to God's knowledge of the situation; nor does it in any way contribute to his resolve or ability to do what he wills for the best.

There is therefore only one prayer to make: that the desires of the petitioner be brought into conformity with the divine will. If it's going to be broccoli every night no matter what you say, then at least you could ask to learn to like it. Petition, on this reasoning, leads straight back to the resignation that we have just left behind.

But—still staying within the company of the faithful—the reasoning does not always stop at resignation, and in fact may be driven to an even more radical conclusion: the dissolution of prayer itself.

If it is seriously true that there is no point in making requests because God is sovereign and accomplishes his will whatever we might say—if this is true, there is no point in making the request that our wills be brought into conformity with his, even though that looks very much like the exemplary prayer of Jesus. Either God wills this conformity or he doesn't, and our talking about it won't help him to make us resigned. Of course, given the peculiarities of our minds we might find it of some help *to us* to say the words. But the talking will easily dissolve into talking ourselves into sitting more easily with the way things are. Should we succeed, then even the ungodly may be sufficiently generous to think that "prayer" has wrought one or two things of psychological benefit.

But more than that it would be wrong even to dream of. The skeptic was right all along: those who pray address only themselves.

But such reasoning is indeed destructive of prayer, at least in the experience of Jesus as we have come to understand it here. That experience encountered a good deal more in the way things are than most of us have to deal with, of course. And what exactly he might have done in solitude to prepare his mind for his death must lie outside our confident access. But he undoubtedly spent some time in self-reflection if the material we considered in the last chapter is credible. Is that *all* that he did? Was his language entirely self-addressive? Not according to Luke, or any of the evangelists, or the witness of the Christian community. That does not rule out different explanations: just as some tidy the wilderness temptations into powerful dream images or reified internal conflicts, so one can translate "Your will be done" into "May my desires not clash with each other or the way the world is." But those who do so must not then continue to call what Luke's Jesus engaged in by the name of prayer. For essential to prayer is relation with and address to the Father. Jesus did not think that in the experience of prayer he was talking to himself in the hortatory subjunctive, first person singular.

Now when a train of thinking brings you to a sufficiently alien territory, it is prudent philosophical practice to ask before taking out new citizenship whether this particular trip was necessary—that is, whether each step when retraced was the only possible step to take. And in fact, though the kind of reasoning set out above has been used to discredit prayer on the believer's home ground, the argument does not have to slide to the conclusion that, if making any request to God is useless, prayer is only talking to oneself. For, just as it is perfectly possible to carry on pointless chatter with other people and make inappropriate requests of them, so one may continue to address God, however futilely. The conclusion must therefore be modified to this less radical but still disturbing result: that, though the believer may address supplications to God in prayer, no request or petition can be properly made of him, even the asking for conformity to his will. This is disturbing to the view of exemplary prayer we have set out thus far: asking does seem to be an essential ingredient in the praying Jesus recommends and does himself.

Perhaps then we should start again, this time not from the problems of petitionary prayer but from the notions of prayer and petition themselves. We want to see how they relate to each other, and how intrinsically they are connected in the exemplary prayer found in Luke.

Prayer and Petition Like it or not, there is something strongly petitionary in the very roots of prayer. Etymology, though never a reliable
guide on its own, still provides its evidence for this across several languages. Our English *prayer* descends by way of Old French *preier* from
the Latin *precari*—to ask, beg, request. And the Greek of the Gospels
employs several terms for praying or prayer (verbs *aiteô, deomai, erôtaô,
proseuchomai;* nouns *diêsis, proseuchê*), all having to do with asking,
requesting, even begging.

The complication arises in actual usage, where "prayer" often functions more generically. In addressing God, believers carry out linguistic
activities that do not fall into the category of petition (as our first look
at Luke demonstrated): they bless, praise, glorify, give thanks, magnify,
express love, and even make promises and commitments. So perhaps we
should conclude that proper praying, in spite of its conceptual ancestry,
should concern itself with no petitionary forms of address. There would
be one practical result that all those who have prayed without the
desired outcome will note: there is no need to expect answers if prayer
is not request. There may even be some relief in the realization that
instead of waiting in vain, one should not be waiting at all.

Only "perhaps" and "may," however; I cannot assess this suggestion
until we have done a little more work. That involves looking more
closely at the categories of petition and asking. Both of these activities
are relational. One of the parties is thought to possess the means required to bring about a desired end, and the other desires the end but
lacks the requisite means. The difference between the activities lies
partly in the kind of relationship the parties enjoy. Simple asking may
be carried on between equals, whereas petition suggests a difference in
status between the petitioner and the one addressed. Petitioning is also
employed when one believes the authority reluctant or inattentive or set
on a contrary course: you may *ask* for your paycheck, but you don't
petition for it in the way you might petition to overturn an injustice or
to win a raise.

Or that's how the concept of petition works in English, anyway.
Bring it to prayer. If praying is really addressing, a speaking *to* rather
than a speaking about, then its character will always be colored by the
nature of the relationship between the parties. It will not be surprising
if believers, reflecting on the difference in status between themselves and
God, think that any asking they do (regardless of its legitimacy) must
fall under the description of petition rather than simple request. Not a

surprising thought, I say; but we have to ask whether it is supported by the evidence for exemplary prayer in Luke. What is the place for asking and petition in the praying there recommended?

A couple of things stand out immediately. First is the theme of intimacy rather than remoteness: the address of "Father!" belongs to families, not institutional hierarchies or political structures. If this relationship is taken seriously, then the language of petition as it operates in customary English usage will be inappropriate. Second, Jesus does ask, and does commend asking. The Lord's Prayer seeks food, forgiveness, and saving from the test; the tax collector's prayer begs for mercy. Whatever the emphasis upon the will of the Father means, it does not preclude such basic requests.

But there is more. Luke has a teaching on prayer that we have not yet considered, and it is strongly importunate. There are two parables, with injunctions. Take first the one, the story of the unjust judge, which comes just before our tax collector parable, at 18.1–8. Luke makes certain that we know what it's about: Jesus wants to show that his disciples must persevere in prayer and not give up. The judge is not a laudable character; he himself confesses that he has no fear of God or respect for people. As judge but unjust, he contradicts the essential role he has been assigned. But he is forced to dispense the justice in his power to a widow simply because she beats him down by constant asking. He does the right thing not because it is right but for self-preservation: if he doesn't he will be worn out. The moral: because God is essentially just, with a patience that cannot be worn out, do not stop presenting your proper petitions; he will give justice to his chosen.

We might have concluded that persistence was unworthy of the chosen, who should themselves exercise a godly patience in silently waiting for the judge of all the earth to do the right thing by them. But Luke's Jesus seems not to want that outcome; instead he does not discourage crying out day and night, suggesting perhaps that this would be a sign of the faith the Son of Man hopes to find at his coming. While cynicism reads the moral as shoring up a groundless and unsupportable belief, the faithful look for something of importance, not about God or their own end (they brought those beliefs to the story) but about their praying. It is constant asking.

Luke's message is the same seven chapters back, just after Jesus has set out the Lord's Prayer. This time the parable is accompanied by direct teaching on the matter, and it is all of a piece. Suppose a better relationship than the widow's to the judge, this time between friends. Friends may presume upon one another in times of need, but even when friendship fails persistence will pay off. The person who has the ability to meet a need, but not the will, can be moved to answer simply by prolonged banging on the door. The friend will get all the bread he needs to feed his unexpected guests. So, says Jesus, keep asking, seeking, and knocking. And then he makes the comparison not between God and the friend with bread in the story but between human fathers as providers and his heavenly Father. The Father knows—how much more!—what is good for his children. We read that back into the story to replace the reluctant provider there with one whose will to give good things always matches his ability to supply them. Knock, then, no matter how untimely the asking.

The importunate nature of prayer for the faithful is thus unmistakable. Nor is it just the "we do not presume to come to this Thy table" in the Prayer of Humble Access: the images and vocabulary are robust. Banging on the door and crying out are not polite noises. Making your friend uncomfortable or angry enough to get out of bed, or bringing an official to the end of his tether—that takes chutzpah or hubris (or guts, to be Anglo-Saxon about it). You have to want something pretty badly to carry on like that.

In fact, these carryings on are the raw stuff of protest, not even poetically shaped into psalms.

So our investigation into the notions of prayer and petition has produced unexpected results. We have found that although it might be helpful in some ways to strain all requests out of proper prayer, the product remaining would be unrecognizable to Luke's Jesus, given the teaching we have just examined. We have also discovered an asking in prayer that does not square exactly with the English notion of petition both because it sits in an intimate relationship and because it presumes boldly upon that relationship—which is why it seemed right to use a word like "importunate" for this kind of praying. And that has brought us to exemplary prayer as protest, when we had begun with prayer as submission to the will of the Father.

I promised trouble with the notion of petition, but it does not seem possible to avoid difficulty simply by refusing to use this one term of prayer, given the strong element of asking that must remain. Nevertheless, some progress has been made. It is time to take stock of our perplexities so that we know what we have yet to deal with.

Our thinking about exemplary prayer in Luke has confirmed that it is fundamentally addressive, and that it seeks the will of the Father. By emphasizing this will and recognizing that it is almighty, we were led to minimize the contribution of the one who prays, falling into the language of resignation and passivity. Now we learn that prayer is exceedingly active: we cannot eradicate the asking, the persistence, even the protest. So there is no deep discontinuity between the teaching of Jesus about prayer and the Psalms, and that is one positive outcome so far. An unresolved problem remains, however, around the active or passive nature of Jesus' own praying as distinct from his recommendations about prayer. That problem may be generalized into this: what is it to pray that the will of the Father be done, not one's own? For the tension persists in all praying, in spite of the special character of Jesus' relation to the Father. If we cannot work this through so that there is some sense in those words, and not just the confusions that landed us in the apparent uselessness of petition, then there is something wrong at the heart of exemplary prayer.

Strangely, we have assumed all this while that petitionary prayer is asking for things to be given or to take place, without bothering to consider what sort of "things" we should have in mind. Maybe we had better turn our attention to what makes a request a proper or good request—beyond the obvious but still problematic reply that it accords with God's will.

The Object of Our Asking

Happily the gospel material set out above provides examples of what good prayer asks for beyond the generic and formal description of coincidence with the will of the Father. So we may return to Luke to look for that content.

As we have seen, the praying that Jesus commends looks for mercy and forgiveness and asks that we not be put to the test. In the light of our recent consideration of the parables of importunity, that last request looks close to a petition that we will be given strength to persevere. Now notice what sits in such asking. It concerns simply the proper conditions of the very relationship itself. Without mercy we will lack the ground on which to stand before God; unless we ourselves forgive, we will not understand what it is to be accepted by the Father. What the constant asking for perseverance is about, fundamentally, is *keeping up the rela-*

tionship rather than (as the cynic would have it) stubbornly holding some particular belief despite contrary evidence. To pray that one not be put to the test is not so much begging to escape trouble as asking to be able to carry on faithfully through whatever trouble comes. Instead of ending the conversation, the faithful keep it going, even if the only words are a crying out. Without their cries there is no address to the Father, no acknowledgment of his presence. That is why Jesus suggests that this speaking is a sign of faith: it vocalizes the address that constitutes that faith.

What about other objects of asking in Luke? There is the daily bread of the Lord's Prayer, of course—but that is followed by the parable of the friend without bread for his unexpected visitors, to which is added more talk of the fish and eggs that even mediocre fathers will give their children instead of harmful and inedible stuff. Why all this food? And to complicate the question, why does Jesus sum up this section of chapter 11 in the words, "How much more will the heavenly Father give"—not daily food, but—"the Holy Spirit to those who ask him"? The associations in the text look as though they run randomly from food to good things to the Spirit, but they share an underlying logic. For though the bread requested may be the literal thing, still it is asked for because it is a necessary condition of our existence and the satisfaction of our basic needs. Without it, we are not. And so with the Holy Spirit, without whom we have no relationship to the Father—primarily because it is God as Spirit who constitutes that relationship. It cannot be accidental that Luke brings the Spirit twice into Jesus' praying, at his baptism and in his Prayer of Thanks to the Father. We will return to this theme as Paul develops it; for now our conclusion comes to the same point as in the last paragraph. In exemplary prayer what we ask for are those things that will sustain us in the relationship itself. We address the Father in the Spirit and ask for the Spirit, the nourishment without which we perish.

Given our humanity and constant need for forgiveness, we cannot pray merely for continued relationship without also praying for wholeness. It is again no accident that Luke and indeed all the evangelists show the work of Jesus to be the work of healing. Given their view of his relationship to the Father, the sort of request he grants brings meaning to the asking appropriate to prayer. Petitions for status in the kingdom, or even for a helping hand in the kitchen, do not get anywhere. The cry for sight succeeds, as do voiced and unvoiced seekings for wholeness and life for the petitioners themselves, or for relative or friend or servant.

We need bodily health as much as we need real bread to put our teeth into. It cannot be wrong to ask for whatever is required to keep us going. But because there is no direct correlation between bodily health and the quality of our personhood (what we used to call our "souls"), it's not always clear what bodily states will make for wholeness of spirit. Without making the healing work reported in the Gospels into metaphor alone (on the contrary: a wider meaning for healing depends for its power upon the concrete and physical), we may nonetheless take from it that the proper content for petition is not necessarily physical health but whatever will make for growth into wholeness. For ourselves, but also for those in need, whoever they may be, and however unexpectedly and inopportunely they have placed themselves in our way.

And that, I submit, is about it. The object of asking in exemplary prayer is not this or that little favor to make us feel good, not events that would make life more convenient for us—though God knows we may be thankful for gestures of grace at almost any time. No. In addressing the Father we request, plead, beg, cry out (depending on our state) for the very conditions of his presence, and for all that will nourish us and others into genuine health of spirit.

Why Addressing Must Also Be Willing

Note three things about the proper object of prayer. First, there is no dissonance between what is asked, the will of the Father, and the will of the one who asks. We would not present ourselves in address to God unless we desired, however feebly, the relationship, and believed his intentions toward us to be good. This harmony of intention grounds the relationship, just as mutual desire grounds love and friendship. It does not eradicate human will, as we shall appreciate in the third point.

Second, the praying itself constitutes part of the significance of the request. What I mean is that it is fundamental to the relationship that I address God; even God cannot be present to me if I shut him out, nor can he forgive me if I will not open myself to forgiveness. So, paradoxically, the requests I make in exemplary prayer are partly answered in my very making of them, and in my continuing to make them. But that paradox is not so much a holy mystery (though it may be that for other reasons) as an everyday occurrence: my opening myself for love from another makes it possible for love to be given, is itself an expression of love, and must be continued for love to be sustained.

Third, it follows that exemplary prayer cannot be passive. All that talk of resignation cannot be read as the withdrawal of human will in the least—no more than any decent human relationship can be constituted without mutual and active personal presence. To pray is *not* to start on a list of requests that you think might be worthy of divine attention, then to remember that it's not your will that is important; then to wander through some thinking like that we set out in the section about God's knowledge of your situation; and finally to conclude that you'd better not intrude yourself into the workings of God's omnipotent will. To pray is to address the Father, and to keep addressing the Father in the very muscles and fibers of your spirit. It is (in better words than mine) to love the Lord your God with all your heart, soul, mind, and strength. And that is the work of the will.

So we swallowed too quickly the reasoning that got us from petition to resignation: that because God's will always knows the best and cannot be frustrated, there is no point in our expressing our own will. For God's will may indeed be frustrated at least with respect to ourselves, wherever we choose to ignore, or resist, or assert something other than our good. This is not the place to develop a treatise on divine sovereignty and human responsibility, so it will have to suffice to claim that God's gift of freedom is a most serious gift that cannot be withdrawn without turning us into puppets. And puppets do not pray. Their speaking is that of the ventriloquist talking only to himself. Ironically, then, the reasoning that made petition useless because of an overriding and irresistible sovereignty would likewise make prayer into self-address, except that it would be God speaking only to himself. Prayer as address needs real relationships between real beings.

Without *our* praying God cannot, in the strongest sense of *cannot*, become Father *to* us. We must ask, not because it's the polite thing to do or an effective technique, but because without our asking there is no basis for relationship. Whether the asking must be fully or only dimly conscious, and how grace moves within the asker—these questions I leave to others, though we soon consider inarticulate groanings. I must also leave unexplored the intriguing suggestion that our epistemological freedom entails that even God cannot know what our will is until we ourselves have determined what we really want. If that is true (as I suspect it might well be), then perhaps address to God involves a dialectic of willings in which one's own will is identified and related to the Father's will. But about that I can say little here, though it emerges again near the end of this chapter and will have to be considered in the next one.

We must next move to prayer as Attending, but a couple of loose ends must be relocated and dealt with first. Our pressing question was over what is it to pray that the will of the Father be done, not one's own, and we have now seen that one's own will is required in the praying. Yet we have not faced the question of conflict between what are perceived to be God's intentions and one's own desires—the issue of protest. We are encouraged to call out against felt injustice, to beg for the meeting of our needs. Why should we not instead submit without protest, as did Jesus in the garden? And that is to return to that other unresolved question of the discontinuity between his praying and our own. About the question of conflict: let me pick up a hint from the previous paragraph, and put that with what we learned in Chapter 3 about motivation and intention in Matthew. Only when we are forced to articulate to the Father our deepest yearnings will the complexities of our motivations and the limits of our knowledge become apparent. And then, perhaps—those who pray better than I do must tell us—then we will understand why at the end of prayer we are content to leave to the Father's will what cannot be sorted out within our own hearts. Not, though, until then: for in the articulation of protest we may come to see what does, and what does not, lie within the scope of our own willing and doing. For proper praying will always lead to obedience, which is why this chapter must be followed by the next one. In the meantime, Augustine might forgive a small alteration to his dictum "love God and do what you will" to make it suitable for praying: *dilige, et roga quod vis*—love, and *ask* what you will. It's all, of course, in the nature of the loving rather than the asking. Somewhere Saint John of the Cross says that those who love wisely do not wish to come right out and ask for what they desire but are rather content to hint at their necessities; in that way the beloved is permitted the freedom to do what is best for them.

And as for the submissive praying of Jesus in Luke: we must not be deceived by Luke's omission of the cry of dereliction from the cross, or by his stress on Jesus' willingness to do the Father's will, into thinking that the discontinuity between his praying and ours removes him entirely from our condition. The bloodlike sweat in Luke is unmistakable proof. Just as blushing is a sign of self-consciousness beyond the control of the agent, so sweating externalizes that internal struggle of protest against death that is part of our biology. If Luke's Jesus falls only to his knees, halfway between the customary upright stance of Jewish males in prayer and the prostrate petitioner of the other synoptics, nevertheless the sweating shows the straining of his body earthward. That, and the heightening of the strain by likening the sweat to blood, give us sufficient evidence to confirm what was only an earlier suspicion, that this is indeed a mute protest in the midst of an active and costly embracing of the will of the Father. The difference in the praying of Jesus that reflects his special relation to God does not lie in his having been provided with a will that is automatically identical to the will of the Father. Trying to imitate *that* imaginary sort of Jesus would be frustrating indeed, for there would be little we could do by way of imitation unless it were already given to us.

Attending

At the very outset we recognized that if the mediation of language is to be effective in establishing personal relationship, it requires not just speaking but also periods of attentiveness and response. We aren't able to speak and to fully listen at the same time, especially when our speaking is supposed to take into account what is being said to us. What's true in general will hold for prayer, if indeed praying constitutes genuine relationship: there must be attention as well as address.

Attention

To attend is most basically to hold on, to wait. It may seem like doing nothing at all, but that is not entirely so. The "attending" of interest here is a state of consciousness, a stance of the mind; it is an attending with an object, a "paying attention to." Insofar as attending must be placed in relation to its object, it will bear some marks of passivity. If I attend to what is happening on the television screen, I will not simultaneously be carrying on activities that demand their own awareness, such as reading poetry aloud or threading a needle, whereas I might whistle or do some straightforward ironing. The action on the center stage of consciousness is elsewhere, out there; I am "doing nothing" in the sense of not interfering with that. Nevertheless, paying attention is an activity, not an absence of doing. We enjoin others and ourselves to concentrate, to focus the mind, to be attentive—so we think there *is* something *to do* when we attend.

I don't propose to write an essay on how to improve your powers of mental concentration: I haven't thought hard enough about that to give advice. But some few comments on the nature of attending will help us with prayer. Begin with the distractibility of human consciousness. It is a feature of our embodiment that the world is given to us in the senses, largely apart from our will or pleasure. We are incapable—fortunately for our good—of altering all the content of consciousness at will: eyes and ears have their objects presented to them for attention. But given the nature of the world and experience, there is always too much going on. So the mind must learn, by trial and error, how to pay less attention to some things in order to devote more to others.

We learn to attend. But this is paradoxical, for much learning itself seems to require that we give our attention to what's presented rather than hunt out new objects. A few examples will establish that this is so. Begin with simple truths, say the elementary claim in Euclidian geometry that the sum of the internal angles of a triangle must always equal 180 degrees. This follows from definitions about straight lines and degrees, and from axioms such as the equality of angles between parallel lines. But that it follows must be grasped by paying attention to what is presented. Those who don't see the point may be given more examples and asked to confirm their understanding of definitions and axioms. In the end, though, it's the getting it for themselves that constitutes their having learned this truth. From that kind of experience philosophers like Plato have stressed that learning is a coming to see: objects of knowledge are like objects of vision, presented for inspection rather than manipulation.

We may add examples from a different category. Our aesthetic experience is refined by attentiveness that is a care in seeing, sometimes literally. The landscape painter attends to shape, shade, light, and color in ways the traveler misses. Or nonvisually, the trained ear hears intervals that untutored listening cannot pick out. (Mind you, some attention is beyond the ordinary: I once met a musician capable of distinguishing one thirty-sixth of a tone.) We could continue with the role of attentiveness in developing *appreciation* of all kinds, from the elevated to the mundane: think of the difficulty of knowing when to applaud at an unfamiliar event. Or we might move to the uncovering by attention of what's in a sense already known, as when one sees how words are related. You remember that stereoscopic glasses made pictures three-dimensional or "solid," which is the Greek root; you now see how it applies to a stereo sound system. We could also explore the role of attention in gaining self-knowledge, an awareness of the innermost springs and coils of our motivations and valuings.

But more comment is unnecessary. We may agree that some things are known only by attending; that we learn to discriminate (to see more of what's there) by attending to our experience; that the objects of attention may be out there in the world, or truths that, though independent of our will, are not literally "out there," or inner states of consciousness.

And now we can link attending to our earlier notion of "presence." I suggested in the introduction to this chapter that the presence of the person who is the subject of our discourse, particularly when we use the addressive second person, "you," heightens the ethical dimensions of our language. We can add that the way presence may hold us to account is by requiring us to pay attention *to* the one we are talking *about:* this presence becomes the object of our attention as well as our address.

That's not all. Given the multifarious forms of the objects of our attention, the "presence" we attend to does not have to be a physical human body in space or a literal voice. If that is to be useful for praying, we will have to believe that what we attend to is presented for our attention, rather than simply being reducible to our own states of consciousness. It seems to have been so for Socrates, to whom we shall next turn.

In a recent reading of some sermons by Austin Farrer, I came upon his report of a conversation between the French saint Vincent de Paul and a young peasant woman who worked with him among the poor during the plague in Paris. When asked what she did in her praying, she answered simply, "I listen to God." Vincent approved, but he added that she might better put it that she listened *for* God. Keep that in mind: presence does not have to be direct or immediate in order to be the object of attention.

The Uniqueness of Socratic Attentiveness

As we noted at the outset of this study, Socrates does pray—though if you read books on Plato rather than Plato himself, you could go through many before finding this out. He offers prayers, but his relationship with the divine is not simply constituted by his addressing the god or the gods. It is more fundamentally a matter of what I have been calling "attending."

Customary Prayer First, on his praying as a *speaking to:* there are only a few places in Plato where we are able to listen to the prayers of Socrates. One commentator has counted up a dozen occasions in the dialogues on which Socrates speaks of praying, but just four times are we given actual words. Three of these come in the *Phaedrus.* The first takes the form of an invocation to the Muses for assistance. The second is a long prayer to Eros: it asks for pardon and petitions that Lysias and Phaedrus be converted to philosophy and love. Perhaps Socrates' most famous prayer comes at the dialogue's close, where he prays to Pan and all the other gods who dwell in the countryside:

> Dear Pan and all you gods of this place, grant me that I may become beautiful within; and that what is in my possession outside me may be in friendly accord with what is inside. And may I count the wise man as rich; and may my pile of gold be of a size which only a man of moderate desires could bear or carry. (trans. C. J. Rowe)

The final recorded prayer is at his death: handed the cup of poison, Socrates asks whether he might pour a libation before drinking. He may not, for there is only poison enough for an effective dose. Nevertheless he remarks that one should pray the gods that "the removal from this world to the next will be a happy one" (*Phaedo* 117c); and he does so pray.

That Socrates participated in the customary religious rituals of his society, including sacrifices and prayers, is to be assumed from other things that Plato says—including Socrates' very last words about the cock owed to Asclepius, and his report at the beginning of the *Republic* that he went to the religious festivities at the Piraeus and offered prayers. It may also be inferred negatively from the nature of the charges laid against him, which make no mention of his breaking from conventional religious behavior.

Now it seems to me that, though the content of the recorded prayers has some additional Socratic flavor in the concerns for beauty, wisdom, and philosophy, there is nothing terribly distinctive in this sort of observance. Were this all we had to go on, then we should be left with the problem of sorting out how his activity of praying could fit with Socrates' critique of much traditional religious belief. Maybe we would conclude, as many have, that in the end Socrates discovers ethical imperatives and absolutes at the core of religious mythology—so his praying is only an accommodatory gesture to divine values rather than divine beings.

But that Socrates, congenial though he might be to some sensibilities, has lost too much of what Plato gives him. For Socrates does not easily blend in with everyone else, however often he participates in customary practice. He is religiously unusual, off-center, weird. The charge that Socrates is displaced and unique is made most memorably by Alcibiades in the *Symposium*, where the reasons include his ability to withstand temptation, hardship, and danger through his remarkable self-control. But the religious aspect of this uniqueness will serve our purpose here. I will approach it in three steps.

Silent Thought First, according to the *Symposium*, Socrates is prone to a peculiar self-absorption. This is nothing like the moods of self-preoccupation that afflict the narcissistic, who are inverted into their own personal world. Some translators refer to it as a "trance" or "fit of abstraction": that may convey something of the relative speed with which Socrates enters and leaves these experiences, but it unhelpfully suggests something of medical interest, like a catatonic state. Unfortunately, Plato gives us precious little guidance in interpreting the content of Socrates' consciousness during these times. Nevertheless, the clues should not be ignored. Aristodemus is on his way with Socrates to Agathon's house when Socrates falls behind, "absorbed in his own thoughts" (or mind), and ends up standing outside the wrong house for a time sufficiently long that dinner is half gone before he turns up. While Aristodemus knows that Socrates often does this, and for even longer periods, Agathon finds his behavior unusual. He assumes that Socrates has been working on a problem, and has got an answer he will share. But Socrates neatly turns the conversation to the contents of Agathon's mind, revealing nothing.

Near the end of the dialogue Alcibiades has a similar story. One morning when on campaign Socrates got working on a problem and stood still to think about it. When he could not make progress he did not give up, but continued there seeking. By noon people had started to notice that he had been deep in thought for some time. By nightfall he was still at it, so some Ionians took their bedrolls outside and observed him all night. At dawn he made a prayer to the sun and departed. We infer, as did Agathon, that Socrates must end his absorption in thought when he has come to some resolution: but we are not *told* this. Without any narrative comment, or any revelation from Socrates himself, the reader is placed at an epistemological disadvantage, removed from the internal consciousness of this strange thinker as surely as are the disciples removed from much of Jesus' praying by horizontal distance.

It would be foolish of me to overcome that distance by claiming that Socrates was "really" practicing meditation, or contemplating absolute goodness, or working out alternate endings to previous philosophical conversations. Certainly I am not going to argue that he was addressing the gods in some distinctively Socratic fashion.

But I do suggest that one category is not inappropriate: the idea of *attending*. Plato not only freezes Socrates' physical activity, he makes him completely impervious to external interference. While inaccessible to us, he is not, however, lost to himself in aimless thought. We are led to believe that he is *attending to* something or other, bringing his mind to bear upon an issue of some importance.

I said earlier that Socrates' strangeness had a religious dimension, but in this first way of being unusual we cannot confidently discover any religious content. Nor, however, can that dimension be excluded: we just don't know.

Divine Sign The second kind of evidence for Socratic eccentricity gives us more to go on. At his trial Socrates reminds the jury of his own private experience, pointing out that he has often spoken openly about it. He calls this experience a kind of "divine" or "spiritual" voice (*Apology* 31d), which began in his childhood and which always forbids him from an intended course of action rather than providing any positive advice. This is again not like being seized by some irrational force: Socrates is able to provide good reasons that justify the voice's forbidding his political involvement in Athens. So is the "voice" then just a personified way of casting a strong retrospective justification over what after all are only Socrates' own convictions? No: apart from the fact that this is a dangerous manner of speech at a trial, we have to take seriously Socrates' statement after his conviction. He must have counted on what he calls the "sign from the god" and his "accustomed sign" (*sêmeion*, 40b) to check him in any harmful behavior; it did not come, though it often had halted him in the middle of other speeches. So what Plato calls Socrates' *daimonion* is not a valuation of his reasoning, "divine" because

Reason is divine; it is rather something he himself experiences, interpreted as a block to his own intention and speaking. The block is not of internal origin (as what we call conscience might be), but from the realm of the spiritual or divine, which is why Socrates has confidence in obeying it and why Euthryphro links it with the charge against Socrates of introducing new deities (*Euthyphro* 3b). While the voice may come on occasions that have no special religious flavor, such as halting Socrates' departure in order to make a conversation possible (*Euthydemus* 272e), the association with the divine does continue in other contexts— as in the *Phaedrus*, where Socrates is forbidden to leave until he atones for false speaking against what belongs to the gods (242b); and in the *Theaetetus*, where he is prevented from taking back unworthy pupils in the divine work of midwifery (151a).

That this repeated spiritual experience makes Socrates unique is the opinion we are to take from Plato's dialogues; but just in case we miss the point, Plato has Socrates comment parenthetically in the *Republic*, "My own case, the divine sign, is hardly worth mentioning—for I suppose it has happened to few or none before me" (496c).

Now this spiritual experience is not at all an addressing of the gods or the divine; it is not the kind of praying we have been considering in connection with the Gospels. How the experience should be more generally described, and how it fits into Socrates' religious and philosophical beliefs, will continue to be the subject of scholarly discussion. My own point here is not about Socratic theology but about Socrates' mental state, and is very much the one made about his silent absorption in thought: that the voice or sign requires a kind of *attending*. That is especially true of the *Apology*, for he seems to have been attentive to the possibility that he would be warned off doing or speaking to his harm; but it also holds in the *Phaedrus* example because, as he confesses, he had been conscious of a vague uneasiness during his false speech. Of course, the sign may be given where he had not anticipated it, so while it demands attention it is not brought about by attending—and in that respect the first kind of experience is different from this second kind.

Divine Duty This is not all, however, that makes Socrates unusual. I want thirdly to say something about his *being addressed* in ways that are for him deeply philosophical as well as religious. He puts it this way at his defense: that he has been ordered to practice philosophy by the god "in oracles and dreams and in every other way that any other divine dispensation has ever impressed a duty upon man" (33c). The most obvious example is, clearly, the oracle's answer to Chaerephon's question: the god said there was no one wiser than Socrates (21a). Socrates regarded it a duty to the god (21e, 22a) to find the meaning of this claim—which amounts to practicing philosophy, for it constitutes an inquiry into wisdom and self-knowledge. The many references to the god in the *Apology* are well-known, but the associations with the divine are also present in Socrates' description of his method in the *Theaetetus*. And it is not just following out one particular oracular saying that Socrates has in mind as the discharge of religious duty. There are dreams as well: two are mentioned near Socrates' death, one in the *Crito* (44b) and one in the *Phaedo* (60e)—but this latter has been a recurring dream for Socrates, urging him to practice the arts. Because philosophy is the greatest of the arts, he has regarded himself as obedient to the dream, at least until his imprisonment. We cannot be sure as to the meaning of "divine dispensations," though perhaps we could place into that category the spiritual sign, at least where obedience to its negative commands has implications for Socrates' philosophical work.

It may be necessary to stress again that this language of duty to the god is not mere dressing up in religious garments of a solid philosophical commitment that Socrates thinks he could just as easily clothe in different garb. Obedience to the god consists in philosophizing, and he justifies his inability to stop practicing philosophy in terms of that allegiance (37e), even though it is most costly.

What about my category of *attending* with respect to philosophy-as-duty? It has, perhaps, its most important application here. For the duty is a duty not to the self or society or even to an activity like right thinking but *to the god*. And the god's address to Socrates is not a set of transparent commands; it is instead an oracular puzzle, a recurring dream, a prohibiting voice. Socrates must listen, focus, remember, pay attention, work things out. He does not talk back to the god; how do you question an oracle or get into a discussion with a goddess in a dream? Even though philosophy is interrogative dialogue for Socrates, its root lies deep in *attentiveness to being addressed*.

Plato's characterization of Socrates as unique, in special relationship to the divine, has other aspects, which I will consider in Chapter 6. But we may return to the first feature above, his absorption in silent thought, in light of the uniqueness of his divine sign and his exercise of philosophy in obedience to divine command. I will not reverse my caution in interpreting what was going on in Socrates' head during those still silences of the *Symposium*. But I will suggest that it is part of Plato's device to locate Socrates outside normal human society and relationships by such accounts. And if we are thereby led to associate him more closely with the divine, then we may be forgiven for the suspicion that when he is removed from the rest of us, what he is attending to may not be simply his own thinking. I am quick to add this: that it does *not* follow, from his unwillingness to communicate the content of his attention to an Agathon or a bunch of soldiers, that he was possessed of some mystically ineffable experience. We only wonder whether, given his character, his experience contained an element of address. Was that prayer to the sun an afterthought of formality to mark the end of silence, or was it a response to something presented for his attention?

The question will hang there while we return now to Jesus to consider the question of his attentiveness. And it will continue to hang: we cannot force an answer out of the evidence. Moreover, I don't think we should attempt to bring the questions of Socratic prayer to the praying of Jesus by redescribing the object of Socrates' address or attention in Christian theological terms. Regardless of the ability to do such translation from within Christian theology, that is unnecessary for my purpose. For I want to think not of the content of these respective prayings but of their *structure*. And we have at least learned this from Socrates: that prayer requires attention as well as address, and that prayerful obedience must attend to being addressed as well as the addressing.

The Attentiveness of Jesus

We've seen that for Socrates, attentiveness focuses on his being addressed by the god in oracle or dream or voice, though the content of that address is resistant to easy interpretation. What of Jesus? Until now our interest has been captured only by prayer as address *to* the Father; but given the intimacy between the Father and the Son, what of address *to Jesus,* presented for his attention in prayer?

If you return to Luke's examples of praying that we set out above, on only two occasions does God speak words of address, and both times it is to declare Jesus' identity as his beloved Son. The first, at Jesus' baptism, is directed at Jesus himself and establishes or confirms the relationship; the second, though, is for the benefit of Peter, James, and John at the Transfiguration. That means, then, that the only reported words of address to Jesus declare relationship; they do not reveal directives or advice from the Father or say anything about the content of his will. Although the vertical closeness between Jesus and the Father is uniquely intimate, we know little of what the Father says to the Son.

I write these words on Ash Wednesday, the beginning of a time of special reflection upon temptation and deliverance from evil. And I am reminded that there is, immediately following Jesus' baptism, an unusual encounter under the direction of the Spirit, an encounter that turns inside out what we have learned of prayer. Though Jesus is at marked physical distance from his society in a remote place, and though filled with the Spirit, he is confronted in his Temptation with the antitype of the Father. In the first words of address his sonship is raised, but only to be questioned; and unlike even earthly sons he is given a stone for his hunger after a long fast—but then asked to use his unusual powers to give himself his daily bread. Instead of praying that the Father's name be hallowed and his kingdom come about, Jesus is asked to do homage to the devil in order to claim all kingdoms and their glory for himself; instead of asking that he not be put to the test, he is challenged to test God's willingness to deliver him from an evil that he brings upon himself.

Although the thematic reflections of true prayer in the Temptation narrative are of interest in themselves, my concern here is to bring out the force of the fact that this is the only occasion on which we discover the solitary Jesus addressed with specific demands upon him. That his replies are all quotations from Scripture shows where his mind has been these long forty days: he has, we infer, *been attentive* in his solitude. But those replies themselves reveal little of positive detailed content—certainly no more than exemplary prayer reveals about Jesus' relationship to the Father.

So we are left with a Jesus whose closeness to the Father speaks of great attentiveness on his part, heightened by the solitary nature of his praying; but an attentiveness whose object can be spoken of in only the most general way, as the Father himself or the will of the Father. We are allowed no glimpse into direct address *to* Jesus other than the twisted words of the tempter. This privileges Jesus in ways not totally dissimilar to Plato's privileging of Socrates: what each attends to seems outside the realm of our common experience. Yet Jesus teaches us to address the Father in intimacy, to cry out for the Holy Spirit. Does the silence about how he is himself addressed mean that there is nothing for us to attend to? Remember the discontinuity that we discovered earlier between Jesus' practice in Luke and his recommendations for prayer—in which his closeness to the Father, requiring no forgiveness, may remove him from our experience. We did see that his embrace of the Father's will was not painless and unprotesting: but was his ability to be attentive to that will so different from ours that our own praying must be radically different from his?

I set myself a difficult problem in that question, for one clear answer is Yes: this is the obedient Son in whom God finds utter delight; we, by contrast, are what W. H. Auden calls "his disobedient servant / The promising child who cannot keep his word for long." And yet as the object of our prayerful address is the same as his, so the object of our attention cannot be different. If our experience of prayer is different from Jesus' praying because of our failings, nevertheless the structure of our praying must be the same as his. What then is exemplary prayer as attentive address?

Prayer as Attentive Address

In this final part I want to pull together our investigations by thinking out how prayer may be both addressive and attentive—that is, how it can be a *speaking to*, for this seems fundamental to exemplary prayer, and yet also a *listening*, in which the one addressed is present in some meaningful sense of presence as we've set that out. I'll come at this by leaving the gospel material to one side in order to look at a passage in Paul's Letter to the Romans. Because that is an unusual move for this book, let me justify it by the importance of the passage for our themes. Even though Paul's letter was almost certainly written before Luke's Gospel, Paul makes much of the role of the Spirit in our praying and of the nature of our address to God as an elemental wordless speaking.

Inarticulate Address

Of New Testament writers, perhaps none is more conscious than Paul of the power of language. To the Corinthians he writes of the deceptions of clever talk, disclaiming (as did Socrates) any rhetorical skill; he wants them to be persuaded not by human wisdom but by the Spirit who reveals the mind of the Lord. At the same time Paul (again like Socrates) does not hold back from employing effective argumentation and rhetorical device: words are his stock in trade, including words about the work of the Spirit. And his letters contain addresses to God in petitionary prayer, some with quite specific content. Romans, for instance, begins after the greeting with thanks to God, followed by Paul's report of much continual praying "that by God's will I may succeed in coming to you." He finishes near the end by asking them to pray that he might be kept safe in Judea.

So Paul knows how to pray and what to pray for.

Striking, then, these words from this apostle: *we do not even know how we ought to pray.* The paragraph in Romans 8 explains:

> In the same way the Spirit comes to the aid of our weakness. We do not even know how we ought to pray, but through our inarticulate groans the Spirit himself is pleading for us, and God who searches our inmost being knows what the Spirit means, because he pleads for God's people as God himself wills; and in everything, as we know, he cooperates for good with those who love God and are called according to his purpose. (26–28 REB)

You will recollect the context. Paul has been contrasting life in the Spirit with sin, condemnation, and death; and he has claimed that those who live in the freedom of the Spirit also have the Spirit in them, so that they are sons of God. If this is reminiscent of our earlier consideration of Jesus' sonship and the Spirit, that is no accident; nor is it accidental that the Spirit enables the crying out to God of "Abba! Father!" This addressive prayer confirms us as members of the same family with Christ and inheritors of the glory that he will know.

That glory, though, is future. What of the present life we live, in suffering, frustration, and the shackles of mortality? Paul speaks vividly of the entire creation moaning in sharp pains—and adds correctly enough that even those of us who have the Spirit also groan within ourselves. This is language about our feelings and experiences, and it deserves attention. For Paul sees, I suggest, that the suffering we witness and endure may cause uncontrollable pain and a nonverbal moaning sometimes so deep in the silent disturbance of the heart that it cannot be uttered. But that grip of pain upon us is not all that we experience. We are possessed as well of an eager longing—an expectation of birth from the dying world, of adoption into freedom and glory: exactly what life in the Spirit promises. So the sighing of our spirit also breathes out at the very same time the call of the Spirit in us: "Father!"

A redemption begun but barely; a glory whispered in the cacophony of suffering; the stirrings of hope in the turbulence of pain: how can we articulate these tensions and contradictions? How can we reconcile in language the present with the promise? The questions are familiar from Chapter 3's study of the silence of Jesus—unsurprisingly, for the structure of Christian experience descends from his life and Passion. We saw then that because Jesus could not sort out the relation between death and the kingdom, or his own desires about either, he handed over his lack of knowledge to the Father in obedient trust. And he did not attempt to recover in words what he had deposited there. If this was so for the master, whose obedience was complete, how much more then for his followers, who dare not speak where they do not know.

And yet the silence of Jesus was not utter silence toward God, for he continued to address the Father. Was his case, so special in many respects, unique in this one? Hardly: we ought to pray at all times. But with what words?

Paul's answer acknowledges our weakness. Read his paragraph above again: our weakness is not primarily the weakness of the flesh in Gethsemane, the inability to keep watch. It is instead epistemological: we *just do not know* how we should pray, in spite of the duty laid upon us to be prayerful. So we groan inarticulately away, unable to get our feelings into our language. Nevertheless—and this is crucial—*our moans are not mindless.* They are not just the exhalation of air over the vocal cords of a distressed organism, not just the linguistic expression of mental confusion. For, says Paul, *in our unutterable groanings the Spirit himself is pleading.* This gives our groans a significance we cannot ourselves assign to them, except that we know them to be part of a larger scheme of meaning. God, who searches our hearts, knows all there is to know about us. Because God and the Spirit enjoy a mutual knowledge, God understands both the meaning of what the Spirit presents and how that fits with our hearts; and the Spirit knows how what is presented fits with God's will for his people. That will seeks in everything the good for those who love him.

There may appear to be a complication of knowers here, and discomfort about such authoritative interpretation of what, after all, are *our* groanings. When our noises are so opaque to us, how can we be sure they mean what we are told they mean?

The problem with the complication of knowers is this. Why, given God's omniscience, does this other knower called the Spirit need to get involved? Doesn't God alone know what we mean in our inner lament, without additional assistance? But to ask that way is to be seduced by a picture of spatially separated divine agents—a picture that gets even more complicated by verse 34, which has not the Spirit but *Christ* doing the pleading at God's right hand. Such pictures always need the correcting vision of the unity of God. That is only a comment, however, and not a commitment to leave the subject of prayer for the tangles of trinitarian theology. Fortunately, Paul's theme here is not descriptive divine ontology but rather our experience of God in prayer. I take him to be making a link between what goes on in the depths of our experience and the activity of God. Without that link, our innermost stirrings would belong to our psyches alone, protests to nowhere and mute gropings toward an unknown god and an uncertain future. That there are such cosmic complaints and yearnings for transcendence I take as given: consult your own heart if in doubt. Paul's bold assertion here is that these stirrings are assisted by God himself, experienced as Spirit within our psyches. This need not be a causal claim, that the Spirit brings about directly our inmost emotions, seizing us suddenly without warning. The immediate reason for silent lament may well be this sorry world, or the pain of a child, or our own suffering, or a memorial service for a young tortured life suddenly ended. Faced with perplexing confusion, we groan because we don't know what else to say. To be assisted by God as Spirit in our groanings is not just to be given a little therapeutic help in unblocking expression; it is to have the assurance that there is meaning in this whole mess, as yet unavailable, but deposited within the will of God who in all things works for good.

Nor is the Spirit's help to us the help of a ghostwriter, who puts it better than we could ourselves; after praying we still do not know what to say about the details of the divine purpose. (It's not, "What your lisping servant is really trying to say here is that he would like X rather than Y": that sort of interpretation, remaining inaccessible to me, wouldn't provide me with any help or permit me ownership of my clarified wants.) Instead, we are assisted in experiencing our groanings as labor pains, as having their place in movement toward redemption and the manifestation of glory. This is faithful groaning, trusting complaint. And precisely because it is Spirit-assisted, God who knows our hearts knows this meaning of our innermost stirring: that it is a handing over to him, in love, of the pain of the world. The Spirit does not violate the meaning of my heart by presenting this to God, for I would not cry out at all if I did not want, somewhere in my depths, to seek God's will and to hold him to his promise for good.

It remains true that in one large sense we do not know how to pray in particular circumstances: because our desires cannot be easily mapped onto any plan for the world's good, we can only feel deep inarticulate stirrings. Nevertheless, in another sense we do know, if not what, then in what manner we ought to pray. We must pray "in the Spirit," knowing our constant address of the Father is not ours alone, but the cooperative work of God himself. And that recognition, I submit, requires an attentiveness in praying—of which we must now, however haltingly, speak.

Word and Silence in Prayer

Silence is required for attentiveness: but before opening up further the meaning of silence in prayer, it is important to affirm the place for words, especially because our reflections on Paul have been preoccupied with the experience of verbal inarticulateness.

Luke and indeed the other Evangelists make clear that, in the phenomenology of exemplary prayer, address to the Father is fundamental. And that address is verbal: words constitute the relationship of prayer, particularly the words of intimate address authorized by Jesus. Further, we have been unable to expunge asking from prayer, and even if the ordinary notion of "petition" does not quite fit, believers will undoubtedly continue to make and refer to petitionary prayers. Such activity is indelibly linguistic, often articulately so. The same holds for the other sort of praying for which we found strong textual evidence, protest and importunate crying out for bread and justice.

That isn't quite enough, though. For exemplary prayer in Luke contains as its refrain the acknowledgment of the will of the Father. That gave us some initial difficulties as we wondered whether there was any point to praying, but we came to understand that our own willing is essential to our asking and that we may ask in the intimacy of this relationship whatever our heart truly desires. So in the serious business of praying, requests and indeed the protests that establish our willings as our own may be offered for what they are: longings and desires, legitimate insofar as they arise from felt needs, more legitimate perhaps as they relate to the well-being of others. They can hardly be more than expressions of who we are and where we find ourselves, given the severe limitations on our understanding of divine purpose in the world. We are not heard just because we happen to remember to ask, and we are certainly not heard because we manage to get the words right.

But now consider what comes about when those limitations are appreciated. The more we reflect on what we cannot know of our own good, or the good of the world, the less we may have to say. That is the insight of Paul that we've considered in the last section—to which we must now add this, that our very speaking may distract our attentiveness in prayer. We have come back to silence. It has two aspects I want to uncover.

The first is situated on a temporal continuum between bits of speaking. We have realized all along that relationships require periods of listening and response if they are not to be one-sided—in other words, if they are to be relationships at all. Most believers find themselves thinking that God does some addressing that needs to be attended to now and then; and it would be generally agreed that the appropriate behavior at such times is to keep one's heart open and one's mouth closed. How is it that one is addressed? It is difficult to generalize about the answer believers would give to that question, but when pressed, I suspect, many would invoke such notions as listening to the Word of God in Scripture and hearkening to the voice of the Spirit in the community. And so they should: both are important sources of knowledge in the Christian way of thinking about such things. Yet that answer is not wholly satisfactory, because on its model praying is too easily assumed to consist only in speaking to God, with the listening taking place in activities that have other names. The silence this model associates with prayer is interstitial, between the speakings. And that view will not help us with the problem that moved us into silence, our inability to know what to say when we speak.

So we need to move to the second aspect. And here we must recall not only the inefficacy of words but their dangers, their power to mislead—the sorts of dangers we reflected on in considering the silence of Jesus. We may throw up words as barriers as often as we make them channels of communication. Or they may be employed as diversionary measures. Just as conversational speech is studded with semantically superfluous fillers partly because we can't get our speaking precise, so whole acts and events may be uttered because we can't stand silence. We must say something, and getting it out is better than getting it right. But not to get it right (and who among us does?) is too often to distort and mislead; and not just others but our very selves.

When presence is the normal presence of another human being, at least there is the possibility of some check on our address to that person. Response and reaction may be immediate, and our assumptions can be exposed, our formulations challenged. But when the presence is out of the ordinary, that is, when the object of our address is God, then we may too easily fall into a preoccupation with our own speaking and thinking—especially in private prayer. Though we know that genuine prayer is address to the Father, we may find ourselves wandering among our own ideas, glancing too often into the mirror of self-consciousness instead of seeking the face of God. So sometimes we need simply to stop, to shut up, to be silent. We need to know ourselves *in the presence* of God, without words of explanation or justification, without making a fuss or beginning negotiations; we need to attend, waiting on God (as Simone Weil puts it—though not exactly, for the French *attente* includes expectation as well as waiting). Above all we need to know this silence *as prayer*, and not as anything else.

How this is to be done is not for me to say. There are manuals, and no end of writings on a variety of spiritualities suited to every taste. There are even some good ones. Given the aim of this chapter, I will, however, venture something about the structure of silence and prayer.

Come at that by considering the object of attentiveness in prayer. We have just reminded ourselves of the unusual understanding of "presence" that must operate in our relationship to God; but that does not mean there is nothing to which we may attend. It is this I had in mind in recounting the story about Vincent de Paul's distinction between listening *to* and listening *for* God. It's late at night and your teenager is not home yet: you listen for the garage door, the key in the lock, the creak on the stairs. What is present for your anxious attention are sounds that are signs and symbols; rightly read they become heard as assurances of the presence of the one you love. We attend to God, likewise, in making words the object of our attention rather than our own production. In this way Scripture and the set prayers of our tradition may be incorporated into our praying. And not words alone: when we do not know quite how to pray, then often we attend to music, expressing beyond language what is to be found in our hearts. Or to the silence of art, or the stillness of architectural space: in these experiences we may wait on God as these objects of our attention become symbols of the presence of the yet-unseen one we love.

But is not this silent *attente* itself interstitial at least with respect to verbal activity in prayer? Granted that we should enlarge our understanding of prayer to include this waiting: can there nevertheless be a listening for God in our speaking to God? Yes. Given what we have seen about the structure of exemplary praying, word and silence interact in at least three ways. Most fundamentally, the speaking that is praying is addressive—that point surely does not need making. Yet what is address but the naming and constituting of a relationship of which we may be conscious without vocalizing or even verbalizing? It is not impossible to suggest that in exemplary prayer we *attend to our addressing* of the Father—which is the reason why prayer is at the same time addressive attention. Nor is it accidental that from those who pray well the counsel has sometimes been that in order to silence the static of the soul we attend only to the simplest form of address to God. For in such active attention distractibility is neglected, as is our urgent need to deploy language whether it is suitable or not. There is a stillness and silence, then, in this elemental speaking that is nothing but a situating of ourselves in the presence of God. Do not, nonetheless, be misled by the "nothing but," for however elemental this speaking, it remains addressive. The phenomenology of prayer discloses not a mindless repetition into obliteration, but a *relationship.*

Our consciousness, of course, remains human and embodied, hence distractible; there is always too much going on even in the most attentive prayer. But there is another way in which word and silence may interact in the praying. The words that form themselves around the thoughts and imaginations of the heart may be presented simply for what they are, with the invitation that they become the object of shared attention instead of being kept secret even from the self. This involves a letting go into silence, a decision not to keep speaking in order to explain or to work out appropriate petitions. To think and feel prayerfully is to feel and think not alone but "in the presence"; and that means not only an unmasking of the pretensions of the self, but—if Jesus is to be exemplary—also a handing over to the will of God that will not speak where it does not know.

And that returns us to the theme that began this section, the severe limitations on our knowledge of the divine plan, and our inability to get our speaking right about that. The problem finds its strongest expression in the kind of praying that is inarticulate groaning. But Paul provided us with a way to be attentive to such frustrated attempts at words: in the silence of the troubled spirit we listen for the pleadings of the Spirit. We attend to our turmoil to be sure (how could we not?), but our attending is an expectant waiting on God for birth, not death, from these pains.

I conclude then that prayer is structured as attentive address that involves listening for presence in experience, even the experience of suffering; speaking words of intimacy, petition, and protest; and even in the speaking, letting words go in order to wait on God.

What will the waiting disclose? The answer belongs not to the phenomenology of prayer, but to the life and experience of the faithful. In the most general terms, we may reply: knowledge of the peculiar presence of God with a discernment of the will of the Father and obedience to it. To know what that means, however, cannot be picked up by a little reading, any more than you can learn to tell chardonnays from sauvignons by memorizing a manual. And without careful attention and practice, how can we discriminate new wine from old? How else can we develop appreciation for that which we do not understand?

Other questions will continue to press for notice. A major issue in the phenomenology of exemplary prayer as I have construed it concerns the language of address to the Father as masculine language, and I am conscious of the real difficulties this raises. I could not be responsible to the gospel presentation of Jesus at prayer without employing the term Father. Nor could I begin to capture what I have claimed as essential to exemplary prayer as intimate address were I to speak of God only in impersonal neuters. One of the large disadvantages of some contemporary neither-male-nor-female addressive diction for God is that it severely diminishes the relational element in prayer. Given our embodiment and our social natures, our personal relationships are gendered. If we are to address and wait upon God who is intimate and personal Spirit, our language will have to reflect these aspects of our humanity. So there is much to be said on behalf of a fuller exploitation of maternal and feminine images warranted by Scripture and tradition. (We encountered one in the previous chapter, in Jesus' longing to gather his brood under his wings.) "Father" as address, then, is not the only term that may constitute and express prayerful relationship. If it brings difficulty or is too restrictive, one may nevertheless still pray.

Though especially important at this time in the history of the Church, working out the place of gendered language in prayer will not solve all problems. How the account offered here relates to the differences between corporate prayer and personal praying deserves thought, especially because the public practice requires a public discourse that by its nature is addressive rather than attentive. Equally deserving is the question of what follows from praying and its disclosures: we asked, but did not answer, how events are to be regarded as answers to prayer, and we have just mentioned again doing the will of the Father. None of this can be pursued here, though the next chapter will take up the last question by considering the nature of obedience.

The mention of doing the will of the Father may remind you, as it did me, of the difference between the praying Jesus does and the prayer he recommends. I have argued that discontinuity is generated by the special status of Jesus in Luke, but that Jesus was not simply handed a will identical to the will of his Father. That remains true; it is just as true that in everything he was the obedient Son in whom the Father found delight. It is this that makes his praying different, I think—so different that Luke resorts to the language of glory and radical transformation on the only occasion on which he refers to the face of the praying Jesus. We ourselves cannot imagine that face; we wake from the dream of such transfiguration and silently veil our own pale praying.

But I have forgotten a contrary incident, outside Luke. At the tomb of his friend Lazarus, Jesus did not hide his weeping. If the light was too strong for us on the mountain, here it is perhaps dark grief that keeps us from staring. Earlier we had been unable to tell from John's account how Jesus' deep upset was related to his address of the Father. Now we know; this, too, is Jesus at prayer.

Prayer, Philosophy, and Evil

At Lazarus's tomb Jesus groaned inarticulately and made no petition in words to the Father. He thanked him instead for hearing, then set about his work. Before the world's all-too-live suffering, believers groan in philosophical perplexity. How does their praying affect their philosophical work?

We began this study with the recognition that, at least for philosophical believers, philosophy and prayer need not be antithetical activities; we saw, too, that discourse in the second person might shape the nature of questions because of the effect of presence upon the questioner. Evil breeds questions about God's love, justice, and power, questions that theodicy attempts to answer in order to preserve the believer's good name and indeed to protect God's reputation. It would be utterly wrong to deny the force of these questions, to insinuate in any way that they can be easily answered, or especially to minimize the human suffering that cries out in their asking. Nevertheless, it is time to face up to one hard fact to which both philosophy and prayer give the same witness: *we cannot generate a fully satisfactory answer to the problem of evil.*

Now it may be inappropriate to expect philosophy to arrive at fully satisfactory answers to any problem, let alone this one: given the nature of philosophical activity, what satisfies one philosopher will always be problematic to another. Maybe theodicy is only like philosophy itself, in that we are doomed to attempt it but never really to succeed at it, while still being able to get on with our lives. But given our reflections so far, we must ask whether there isn't something more to be considered.

Does addressing God attentively over the perplexities of suffering make any difference? And if so, is the difference philosophical? I must ask the second question, because someone might claim that a believer could find a consolation in prayer that was pastoral, spiritual, therapeutic, and so on, all without properly philosophical consequence. And indeed, the first part of the rejoinder should not be underestimated. Whoever, after praying, does not succumb to despair or multiply evil by retaliation, whoever thereby bears suffering with stronger resolution— that person has been helped in ways even the skeptic may admire. Nevertheless, prayer may yield more than this: it may indeed be philosophically consequential.

Although my analysis of praying has been concerned more with structure than with content, I have said enough to permit three observations about what happens to philosophical perplexity in exemplary prayer. First, our attentive address to God expresses a trust in God's love, goodness, and justice: otherwise we would not pray, but instead end the relationship. Our perplexity thus begins to move from the *whether* to the *how* of divine concern; this distinguishes the believer from the skeptic. I suggest that talking with the enemy puts the believer on the defense about the very possibilities of God's power and concern; but once the discourse shifts to second-person address, that question takes on a different cast. The grammar of the simple interrogative mood may persist in our speaking, but as soon as one asks directly "Are you just, O Lord?" one knows the answer called for by the relationship of trust. Exemplary prayer affirms divine justice but groans for its manifestation and confronts God with the incongruities of suffering. Philosophical prayer searches for the meaning of that justice it has yet to find.

To be sure, merely shifting perplexity from one category to the other, from the *whether* to the *how,* might be considered small progress. But notice the second feature of praying, taken from Paul though compatible with Luke, and related to silence. Prayer in the Spirit is prayer that acknowledges our epistemological weakness, our lack of knowing what to ask for in accordance with the good will of God. This is of first importance: it places the *how* firmly beyond our comprehension. We may spin our possibilities in other places, but when we turn to God we fall silent, confessing the limits of our knowing. Maybe we will continue to ask *how* this piece of suffering or that irremediable injustice accords with the well-being of the world. But in prayer we may also find ourselves not negating but rather suspending the question, handing over our perplexity into the keeping of the Father. Because the *how* admits of no present answer, it turns itself into the *how long* and the *when* of those psalms of lament and protest. The grammar in which we speak of exemplary prayer as waiting on God, waiting expectantly for God, always slips into the future tense, moving toward that hope for redemption which Paul overhears in our groaning. That we no more know *when* than did Jesus know the day or hour of the revelation of the Son of Man—that makes no difference to the significance of the change in question. For asking *when* instead of *how* betrays the trust that there is an answer to be manifested on that day.

These shifts in questions, and therefore in the answers we expect, mean that in a sense the consequence of prayer for philosophy is that this philosophical perplexity about evil is ended—not by providing answers, but by revealing the impossibility of answers. This outcome looks "philosophical" in the popular stoic sense of recognizing limitations and becoming resigned to them; but that is wrong on two counts. For one thing, the perplexity is ended only in the sense of being suspended and given over to God. Answers are impossible—at present, not in principle. God's justice and love will be vindicated. So it's not that perplexity ceases because the questions are themselves wrong, or because we give up the search for what is resolutely undiscoverable at any time. We give *over*, not *up.* Although this sort of relinquishment provides psychological benefits (think of letting go a grudge), this way of dealing with perplexity is founded on epistemological convictions about all human knowers and is therefore a philosophical stance, not just a bit of pastoral advice.

The other reason that praying does not end in stoical resignation may be discovered in the third observation I promised. Exemplary prayer asks for forgiveness and leads, as we have seen repeatedly, to doing the will of the Father. In other words, although our epistemological limitations are apprehended in prayer, human sin is also exposed and our wills provoked into the discernment and fulfillment of God's will. We come face to face with the complicity of our nature in evil, and our responsibility to do something about it. If no one can practice exemplary prayer without this consequence, then addressing God with one's philosophical perplexities over evil will have an unsettling way of turning the questions back in our direction. I do not mean (one shouldn't have to say it, but let's be clear) that the burden of the world's evil descends entire on the backs of those who pray, or that prayer is the recognition that one deserves everything one gets. Prayer is often protest against innocent suffering where nobody's to blame. Even where praying reveals some kind of implication in evil, the lines between sin, responsibility, and guilt are not always easily drawn. All the same, it is difficult to speak to God about God's role in the suffering of all creation without becoming aware of the not-so-innocent secrets of the human heart, and of the need for one's own contribution toward the good. Wherever those who pray understand better the human condition, experience forgiveness, and amend their lives, practical benefit obtains. But philosophy is also affected: we cannot be content simply to unload our responsibility along with our perplexity. That means we are not excused from hard thinking about the world's evil, including thinking about how prayerful philosophy may provide both challenge and consolation in the face of suffering.

Whether I'm right or not in these observations, thoughtful believers will continue to work on the problem of evil. If for no other purpose than to defend against skeptical attack, faithful philosophers will write in the third person about the world's ills and the ways of God; some will, I am sure, draw new designs for theodicy. I've argued that exemplary prayer holds something of importance in reshaping the questions that theodicy attempts to answer. Shifting the discourse into attentively addressive language does not end philosophy's work; unsurprisingly, it only poses its own kinds of questions. The shift, nevertheless, brings to the best end available to faith the perplexities all of us experience over evil: it surrenders them to God in tenacious and cooperative trust.

FIVE

Obedience and Authority

. . . I shall obey the god rather than you	—APOLOGY 29d
. . . the wind and the sea obey him	—MARK 4.41
. . . obedient even as far as death, death on a cross	—PHILIPPIANS 2.8

THIS CHAPTER IS ABOUT what it says it's about, obedience and authority; but whether it's about what those words usually evoke remains to be discovered. Although it would be better, for reasons I will presently discuss, not to hear anything at all about obeying authorities, that does not, however, seem to be an option for this study. Early in the book those martyrs got us involved with witness to an absolute that must be obeyed beyond the interests of the self. Insofar as they saw their deaths as acts of obedience, we cannot ignore the idea if we are to do them justice. In particular, Jesus obeyed the will of the Father as the only way to resolve the conflict between the hour of death and the day of his manifestation in glory; as for Socrates, he could not mount his defense without speaking of obedience to the god. And when in the previous chapter we inquired into the nature of prayer for both of them, we had to employ the language of obedience frequently. Socrates attended in order to discern and obey the divine sign; Jesus sought to follow the Father's will rather than his own. Obedience, like prayer, seems to be a positive notion for each of them; but because like prayer it is for us problematic, we had better devote a chapter to it and its corresponding term, authority.

The Troubles with Obedience

Obedience is a virtue—in dogs. That puts succinctly what I take to be the late-twentieth-century attitude toward obedience, at least in the societies most of us are familiar with. Whether our behavior matches our talk is a rather different question. Stay first, though, with the reasons why we are suspicious of the cultivation of an obedient attitude in members of our species.

Maybe the underlying reason is as simple as this: every obedient dog has, necessarily, its master. And if a little phrase could capture the recent history of large parts of our kind, it would be *Getting rid of the master.* That would be true especially from the eighteenth century on, in political revolutions, the antislavery and anticolonial movements, the emancipation of women, and campaigns for gender equality and human rights in our own time.

So obedience, in that it always looks toward some master or authority, diminishes the freedom and autonomy we think the inalienable possession of mature moral agents. This fundamental understanding of moral agency as autonomous is thus responsible for our pervasive suspicion that obedience can be a desirable moral trait only in small children (and these days we don't seem to be very sure that it's even appropriate for them). In fact, the prizing of autonomy extends beyond moral agency; we think that it's important for our general well-being and social advancement, as a host of therapies and psychological theories will attest. Obedience has many of the same problems as the attitude of resignation we considered in the chapter on prayer. It doesn't belong to people with initiative and creativity, to those who can make independent judgments. To use the word "obedient" in a letter of reference would be tantamount to labeling the candidate immature, indecisive, and other-directed.

There is a more specific reason why we do not think obedience a virtue, arising from the sordid history of war in this century. For we know too well what has followed from obeying orders without question, just because an authority has issued them. After Nuremberg the excuse that one was simply following orders does not absolve from responsibility but only adds to the horror. And not just in that world war for one group of people: we have had to face the fact that masters on both sides of conflicts have commanded those under them to commit atrocities beyond moral imagination. The result is not just a distrust of obedience but an outright condemnation of it. Compliance in these circumstances is a terrible weakness and a pernicious vice.

Obedience wears another troubling aspect that cannot be ignored in a study like this one: praised and promoted as a virtue in religious life, it has often worked directly against human flourishing. Only a few reminders are required. First, think of how the emancipation movements mentioned a moment ago had to work against the stern authority of Scripture and Church. Slaves are to obey their masters, states Colossians 3—and, Ephesians 6 adds, with fear and trembling as though obeying Christ. Wives must be submissive to their husbands, who are their heads as Christ is head of the Church. Where oppressive institutions have been shored up by making compliance a duty to God, we have every reason to be deeply troubled by religious obedience. Second, within ecclesiastical hierarchical orders, obedience has been regarded as a special obligation, with the result that conduct and beliefs have been regulated by an overriding authority. This sits ill not only with convictions about freedom of conscience but also with the obvious fact that the Church has reformed itself on many occasions. Surely there's something unsettling about an obedience that would ignore inconsistencies and incompatibilities in its own history. And third, there's a kind of religious mentality that feeds on dependency, being content to let personal and moral responsibility rest with a parental—perhaps especially paternal—external authority. We may find ourselves thinking of extreme pathological examples of other-directed religious psychologies, but elements of this mentality are common: otherwise there would not be so much history around my first two points. But isn't it worrisome that (to put it crudely) some religious people don't ever really *grow up?*

So given the social and personal dysfunctionalities of compliance with authority, and the positive duty to disobey wrong commands, we have a large handful of problems over obedience as a praiseworthy quality. If it is to appear on a list of duties and virtues, it would be under the Canine and not the Human, part of "What Makes a Dog a Good Dog" but not listed in "Good Traits Among Humankind."

Or so we seem to think. But having left the duty of obedience to dogs, maybe we should be willing to inspect a little more closely the way in which it actually works with them. If we just assume that dumb dogs obey commands mindlessly, as canine bodily responses to the stimulus of the master's voice, then naturally we wouldn't commend such behavior in human beings; as full moral agents we must not jump, fetch, and sit upon command. Yet that assumption does disserve to well-trained animals. For if you have developed a relationship with domestic animals or read the work of a reflective trainer (such as Vicki Hearne's articles in *Harper's Magazine*), you will know that successful obedience learning must exist in the context of a mutual respect between animal and human being. They must heed each other: the animal attends to voice and gesture, but the trainer also pays attention to the movements and responses of the animal and makes appropriate adjustments. Only in a relationship of trust will there be mutual communication and understanding. In such a relationship the dog will return the respect of obedience and develop the fulfillment of its canine living in the virtues of loyalty and courage. As with any heeding and learning, things can go wrong, which is why it makes sense to talk of disobedience and to take seriously whose fault that might be. It's not always the dog's.

In healthy canine obedience, there is therefore something to be learned about shared responsibility. If so, then perhaps we might be willing to reconsider our discomfort with even the mention of obedience among our own kind. Not that we should sweep away the troubles we've been recounting: I mean only that we should suspend our distrust of obedience in order to inquire further into its nature.

What It Is to Obey

When you look up our term in a few dictionaries, you will discover that lexicographers employ two clusters of terms around *obedience*. One set includes words like *rule, authority, law, command*, and *bidding;* the other has notions of *submission, compliance, performance*, and *doing.* So (you can work out the combinations) in obedience one *does* the *bidding* of an *authority, conforms* to a *rule, submits* to a *command*, and so on. Now what's of interest here is that obedience involves first a certain kind of performance in the realm of action, and second a particular state of mind, an attitude which informs that doing. The first ingredient seems always to be present in obedience and can be expressed as follows: an obedient action *conforms* to a law or command. That doesn't look as though it's enough, however, for we want to know what agents think they are doing when they act in conformity with a command. Their intentions matter. To take an extreme example, somebody whose authority you don't accept orders you to do something that, independently, you have already determined to do (an obnoxious pupil shouts out, "Shut the classroom door!"). Your action has the same shape as the one commanded, but because you don't see yourself as doing it for that reason, you don't construe the act as *obedient.* Nevertheless, this second ingredient of intentionality is complex and not precisely measurable. To act in obedience, you don't have to set out to follow in full awareness some rule or order. You can *disobey* by not acting in conformity with a rule through absentmindedness. And obedience may still be obedience even if it is half-hearted, reluctant, habitual, or even a reflex (like ducking at a command as the boat nears the bridge). Children know about this. When told for the third time to clean up the room or to apologize, they understand quite capably what would constitute minimal compliance with the order and are able to claim that they are obeying without seeing themselves as entirely caving in to parental authority.

Contrast that with what you might, in memory's retouching, have been yourself: a child who usually acted *obediently* when told to do something. The adverb is important, for it signifies a disposition and tendency of character, an intentionality that goes beyond bare conformity with commands. Dispositional obedience is compliant and does not assert its will against the will of the other; it can be relied upon to participate willingly in following instructions, to be cooperative. Obedience in this sense does not simply act in conformity to command; it acts that way, *knowing its place in the world.*

One more comment. It is essential to the obedient mind that it accept the rule, decree, order, command, law, bidding, or what-have-you *as authoritative.* In saying that, I'm drawing on a difference between *power* and *authority.* You may be forced to comply with the wishes of someone who holds power over you; you obey, but without granting any legitimate authority to the compelling force. So yours is not an obedient mind. Where we acknowledge another's authority, we signal an agreement to participate in the process of compliance. Maybe it's just this willingness that contains the trouble with obedience. However distasteful an *enforced* obedience may be, at least we can relocate responsibility for our behavior in the enforcer. But *acting obediently toward an authority* involves an attitude of mind in which, paradoxically, we hand over to another the authorship of our actions, letting someone else write our lines for us and direct our movements. Because in our view submissiveness is inappropriate to a free agent who enjoys dignity and self-possession, the obedient character seems deficient in human virtue.

It's not, of course, that simple—as a little reflection upon our actual practices will reveal. Before moving to that, however, we need to slip into a corner of our minds a philological comment about the term under investigation. Our English word descends from the Latin *obedire,* itself from *ob* + *audire, to give ear to* (or to slip dangerously into the colloquial, *to listen up*). That is worth noting, not only because we might not have guessed it, but also because something of a similar nature goes on in Greek, the language in which our sources for Jesus and Socrates were written. It has two principal root ideas for obedience. One uses the basic notion of *persuasion,* so that to obey is to be persuaded by someone *(peithesthai),* sometimes by someone over you *(peitharcheô).* The other root has to do with listening or hearkening to someone *(hupakouô,* to obey, heed; *hupkoos,* obedient). Of course, these ideas aren't far apart: the first has an eye on the persuader who is successful in getting the complying agent to believe something; the second has an eye on the attentiveness of the hearer who is so persuaded. The philological history of obedience, then, places it on the side of the intentionality of the one who obeys, assuming that action in conformity with command follows as evidence that the agent has indeed been persuaded or has listened well.

The Practice of Obedience

We must shortly move from this discussion of the meaning and history of terms to the significance of obedience for Socrates and Jesus. Before doing that, however, it's important to juxtapose our troubles over the language of obedience with our own behavior. Our practice doesn't match up with the impression conveyed by the words I have been using.

It doesn't take much to establish this, so I will not belabor the central point: we could not survive or flourish without the widespread practice of compliance with authority—that is, without obedience, whether we use that label or not.

The sphere of most obvious compliance is the legal, where we happily praise the disposition to obey the law. But even if we don't think of ourselves as "obedient" citizens ("law-abiding" sounds better), our movements stay well within the law. When we stray, most of us fortunately have a highly developed sense of the limits of tolerable nonobservance. We might speed or park illegally, but we will refrain from driving on the wrong side of the freeway. We also want others to act in accordance with law. When they do not, we ask for the protection of the law: we hire experts to argue the meaning of strict observance, and we demand that those in the wrong be forced into compliance.

While in our speech the typical objects of obedience are law, court orders, injunctions, and the like, our practice of compliance with authority extends far beyond the legal. Our behavior in all forms of social organization, from business corporations and educational institutions to sports teams, has to be governed by rules. (Were it not, there could be no organization.) In very large measure, success requires not just respect for rules in general, but also conformity to authoritative decrees that interpret and apply those rules. We therefore practice obedience in all the territories of our social existence. How, then, can we continue to dismiss the conforming behavior or the intentionality of obedience as inherently vicious or immature? Obedience is too essential to be thus banished.

It's worth adding that in the face of our practice it's difficult to preserve the fiction that the self can get rid of all masters, becoming sole author of its actions. We cannot reconcile our autonomy with our obedience by claiming that, having figured out independently what we should do, we conform only because the authority has arrived at the same conclusion. That would be impossible in practice almost always, simply because we do not enjoy access to the necessary information (as when we follow expert instructions). It's also often impossible in principle: what we should do depends on the authority, not on us (as in arbitration or team sports). Not only do we conform, we often intend to do so without apology.

Although the structure of our practice in shaping actions to authority covers a wide territory, it is puzzling that our use of the term *obedience* maps so unevenly upon this structure. I don't have an easy explanation for the fact that the word for a practice this fundamental remains submerged in so many areas of our speech. Often we ignore it or pull it up with distaste; in few areas can it surface with our approval— and then it gets used as a duty to be imposed on others. Moreover, obedience is unlike other terms for which we have developed distinctions between acceptable and unacceptable forms: belief slides into credulity, love degenerates into lust, courage into foolhardiness. But we have no distinction in English usage between exemplary and degenerate forms of obedience.

Yet we should be able to commend its good practice. Given the importance of the issues posed by authority and obedience, and the nervousness of our language, we need to examine with care some telling examples of lives in which obedience plays a central and positive role. We will find that Jesus and Socrates must be called obedient—there is no other word for it. But their practice is not like the practice I've been pointing to here, in which we obey the voices around us to secure our place in the common good. They don't fit comfortably within their societies; their listening is from some other place. Neither of them will help us, then, to sort out the duties and vices of obedience as a civic or social practice. They will take us instead to that most troubling and demanding obedience of all, obedience to God.

The Obedience of Socrates

At the beginning of his Defense, Socrates makes a comment that takes us directly to our topic. Speaking of the tension between what he wants and what will happen, he says that he wishes to defend himself against false accusations, but he knows this will be difficult. Things will turn out as it pleases the god; what he must do is obey the law and make his defense (*Apology* 19a). In his acceptance of the requirements of the law and the will of the god we will discover how authority and obedience work in the life and death of Socrates.

The Tough Independence of Socrates

Let's be clear about one thing: although we need the category of obedience to understand this man, Plato does not present his Socrates as a compliant personality. To draw a portrait of the dispositionally obedient person we would have to sketch a type who fits in easily with authority figures, doesn't make waves, has little independence of mind—someone with soft and pliable boundaries of the self.

But Socrates is tough.

And not just in his physical constitution, though I will discuss that later in this chapter. For now it's the toughness of his social and intellectual independence that I have in mind. Earlier I mentioned that Socrates is strange and eccentric, and the *Apology* delivers his own explanation for this. He doesn't fit in because he has no pretensions to knowledge, whereas everyone else's claims to know are misguided or fraudulent. Socrates has spent his public life creating distance between himself and every other class: neither politicians, nor poets, nor craftsmen were able to justify their alleged wisdom to his satisfaction. And he didn't merely notice that this distance was somehow there. Socrates actually *created* it, arriving at the conclusion about his ignorance not by quiet observation but by an active interrogation and cross-examination of his victims. As he recognizes, it was impossible for others to accept his self-deprecating profession of ignorance, and they assumed that he really thought he held the knowledge he denied to everyone else. So this intellectual distance, perceived as superiority, brings about in its turn social isolation—exacerbated by the irritation that his imitating followers caused when they attempted to discredit their betters. Not appreciating Socrates' own motivation and mission, the Athenians resorted (he says) to stereotypical charges against him.

The rest of his speech is an attempt to defend himself against those charges in their current guise, formulated by Meletus, Anytus, and Lycon: corrupting the young and acknowledging new deities instead of accepting the city's gods. Of course, the very accusations mean that Socrates cannot be regarded as a Good Citizen, observant of custom and the social space of others, respectful of religious convention. But instead of trying to close the gap between himself and his fellows, Socrates deliberately reinforces distance by the defense strategy he adopts. We considered much of this when we reflected upon the ways in which words work for Socrates. Here it is sufficient to remind ourselves that he seems to go out of his way to prevent the jurors from developing any sense of identification with him. How, he asks, can he alone harm the young, when the many (with a glance at the jury) know less about what's good than the expert? How can he be irreligious if he believes in divine activity—though that activity is the voice of his own private *daimonion,* inaccessible to others? People in general hang on to their lives at any price through fear, but how can he be afraid when he cannot share their inflated and unsupported belief that death is a great evil? Socrates claims that his strategy has not been adopted out of personal arrogance or disrespect for his fellows, but his words serve only to underline the distance that his reputation and philosophical activity had created.

Even though his life is on the line, Socrates cannot bring himself to fall in with the expectations of conventional behavior or belief. He suspects that he could get off with banishment as penalty; instead he provokes the jury with the suggestion of state support in recognition of his service. It's his friends who, too late, bring him round to proposing a credible fine. Why does his life mean so little to him? What is it that holds power over him, drives the deep concerns of his life? It cannot be social status, purchased through wealth or political influence. But it doesn't seem to be personal attachments, either: his unwillingness to parade his sons in front of the jury locates his fundamental allegiance outside his family.

Faced with such resolute refusal to be like the rest of us, we find ourselves believing that Socrates displays none of the traits of obedience. The obedient personality, we earlier decided, is one that conforms to authoritative decrees, knowing its place in the world. Socrates' place cannot be located in common social space. And wherever his edges are, they remain too tough to be molded by the norms that define decent and respectable human living, by the values that hold power over the rest of us. But if his scores rise off the scale on tests for independence of judgment and inner-directedness, and if he can't get any marks for social adaptability—still he characterizes himself as obedient. And more: as law-abiding. What is this peculiar Socratic obedience? Is it as perverse as the man himself?

Philosophy as Religious Duty

We can't understand Socrates without reflecting on what motivates him to philosophize and how his motivation springs from experiences we'd have to label broadly "religious." The way into this is through watching how he speaks of what's of fundamental importance once the jury has rendered its initial verdict (*Apology* 36a–38c).

The Problem of Integrity Socrates has a problem. He now knows that the jury has found him guilty, and further that Meletus has demanded the death penalty. He is permitted to make one counterproposal, after which the jury will vote again to choose between the two penalties. He needs only to convince about ten percent of those who thought him guilty that he doesn't deserve death. But that's not the problem on his mind. For even to think that way would betray everything his life had stood for.

Socrates believes that the point of his life has been the search for moral goodness, which must take precedence over temporal benefits, including social position and bodily health. It is essential to moral goodness that one not do or agree to anything known to cause one harm. (We can see why: to agree to harm yourself is to participate in the diminishment of your moral worth, as well as to act on an unworthy principle.) Now, given his convictions, he cannot hang on to his life at the price of goodness; but given his situation, what alternative penalty could he propose that would not harm him? That's the problem he faces.

It's natural for us to think of death as the greatest harm, so that it would be worth paying some price to escape that fate. Not Socrates, though: he claims that he *cannot know death to be a great evil.* Against that doubt he places a large certainty. A life spent in careful moral examination of one's own self and others is the greatest good; an unscrutinized life is not worth living. Not to live that way, then, is to do oneself great harm. So Socrates must think how he may propose with integrity a penalty that keeps his doubt and his certainty in their right places. It also has to be a penalty that will be accepted—and there's the difficulty, for the Athenians quite clearly want him to stop doing what he cannot stop doing. Imprisonment would harm him, not because it restricts freedom of movement but because it stops free philosophical conversation. Banishment would harm him, not by exiling him from those he loves, but because, given his reputation, philosophical inquiry will not be possible anywhere. Only a fine he can afford will not cause harm, and that turns out to be but a small amount.

That is the kind of reasoning I find in this section of the *Apology.* Socrates begins, of course, by pushing back the sympathies of his listeners, suggesting the penalty of free state support in recognition of his civic contributions. Athens rewards its athletes in this way; why not one who has their true benefit at heart? This proposal clashes not just with their sympathies but also with his own manner of life: when before has he cared about such amenities? But though it cannot be seriously intended it is nevertheless deliberately constructed to call into question the kinds of activities the Athenians think worthy of honor. So it is itself a piece of Socratic examination, an activity in the only life worth living, even though it contributes to his death.

What therefore looks like perversity on Socrates' part actually arises out of the integrity of his moral life. If we put it that he cannot refuse to practice philosophy, we must be clear about that duty.

The Duty to Philosophize What Socrates must carry on isn't the sort of philosophizing done by teachers and scholars these days, part of a large academic enterprise in which students are graded and articles published. People stop doing that, and quite rightly. They may even have a duty not to philosophize in this manner when their interests wane or their powers fade, or when the arguments themselves become sterile.

But Socratic philosophizing is not about imparting knowledge or advancing the interests of a discipline. It's the search for an excellence of life and mind that cannot be taken for granted, that is lost as soon as one stops being mindful of the manner of one's living. It is not one duty among many, like generosity to be exercised only on certain occasions, so much as a duty that defines what it is to be human.

Now this duty may be thought to be *foundational,* with nothing more basic to support it; if so, one simply sees that it is to be embraced, not something to be argued into or out of. Socrates could have given, or assumed, that kind of justification. But he doesn't. Instead he adds a claim until now ignored in my presentation: that not to live this way would be *disobedience* to the god.

Moreover, he remarks that his audience will believe that in saying this he is dissembling, not revealing his true mind. The verb is *eirôneuomai,* to act in the manner of an *eirôn,* speaking insincere words. We've already considered this Socratic "irony," and here it returns over the sincerity of Socrates' religious commitment. He was right to raise the issue. Even among the commentators there are those who read Socratic duty as nothing other than the commitment to be moral and rational, so that this talk of the god should be seen only as metaphor, dressing up the serious language of Philosophy in the garb of religious Mythology to make it better understood by the popular mind.

Those thinkers who have already arrived at the conclusion that "obeying God" means just *being sincere about your basic human duties* will not be required to posit an authoritative will to which human wills conform in religious obedience. They have their reasons for so viewing the world. But they should not use those reasons to impute their view to Plato's Socrates.

For Socrates brings up the suspicion of a dissembling irony only because the jury has been told that he is *ir*religious: they will not incline toward a sincere reading of his claim to obedience. Now, if he doesn't truly believe in the god himself, he must be *a self-conscious dissembler.* But why would he mislead? If it's to escape penalty by creating a mistaken belief in his religious commitment, then that would go against his fundamental decision not to place temporal advantage above goodness. And how would deliberately false speaking be welcome in the morally good life of self-examination—especially if that is (as it is for the thinkers just mentioned) the life of sincerity? Translating absolute duty into popular mythic language might be something a Socrates fashioned in some other image could do, but not *this* Socrates of Plato's *Apology*.

Furthermore, we actually need the category of obedience to make sense of Socrates as he presents himself to the jury. Ask why Socrates practices philosophy. Obviously it's not for the money (he doesn't take any) or for professional prestige (he doesn't get any). Nor does it seem to be done for Aristotelian intellectual rewards: if Socrates' mind starts out wondering, it doesn't quite achieve the satisfaction of arriving at knowledge. Socrates remains wisely ignorant. I suppose we could say that for Socrates, philosophizing is (like eating good food) both an ingredient in the good life and a means to the betterment of that life. You do it for your own good. But what *he* says is that it's a religious duty, owed not to himself but to the god.

The Experience of Religious Duty: Sign and Oracle It's important to see that Socrates' characterization of philosophy as religious duty arises out of reflection upon his experience. There are two aspects to this experience, the oracle and the sign, and both, I think, reveal something about the philosophical enterprise. Start with the oracle.

Socrates must have been for some time an impressive thinker, else Chaerephon would not have been moved to inquire about his wisdom at Delphi. What were his intellectual pursuits the reader of the *Apology* doesn't know, for Socrates starts the story with the oracle's answer. Philosophy for him begins in puzzlement, not about the world or his own mind, but about the discord between his epistemological condition and the claim of a god who wouldn't lie. He can believe neither that he knows nor that the god doesn't know. How then could the god claim that there is no one wiser than Socrates? Ignoring or denying this bold assertion requires him to be sure that the oracle is wrong; but he knows that he doesn't know that. The only way to figure out the meaning, then, is to investigate the limits of all human knowing to learn where he fits in this picture. That turns out to cause hostile resentment among those subjected to his probing and prying. So he's faced with some rather basic choices: will he keep on alienating people, or will he conform to the norms and expectations of his society? Will he follow the god or save his own skin?

In a way it's too late for this to be a real choice. Socrates believes that he has discovered in the epistemological quarters of the human psyche not ignorance but the inflated pretensions of conceit. To save his skin, then, he'd have to go along with claims to knowledge that he thinks mistaken. But note: the god has something to do with this recognition. Socrates doesn't himself go to Delphi about it. Instead he tells us that he asked himself *on behalf of the oracle,* and replied to himself *and the oracle,* that it was best for him to accept his own ignorance (22de). In this self-questioning in the presence of the god, Socrates came to see that real wisdom resides with the god, and that human wisdom is of little or no value (23a).

Could he have left it there, quietly pulling the weeds of pretense from his own garden? No: having interpreted the oracle as addressing the human condition itself, Socrates believes that he has a responsibility to bring other people to recognize the cluttered growth in their own minds. Because no oracle has spoken to them, it is Socrates who must assist the god in proving that they—whoever they are, citizen or stranger—do not know what they think they know (23b). Socrates speaks of his service *(latreia, hupêresia)* to the god and many times refers to himself as being appointed by the god, as the god's gift to the city for its good. (We see a similar sense of *being sent* in Jesus.) As we noted in Chapter 4, Socrates insists at 33c that he has been ordered by the god in oracles, dreams, and every possible kind of divine dispensation to human beings. And that brings us to the second type of experience on which Socrates must have reflected in coming to appreciate his religious duty: the divine sign.

I gave some reasons in the last chapter why this "spiritual voice" should be regarded as something external to Socrates' consciousness to which he attends. It is, you recall, always negative: it blocks an intention or direction that Socrates would otherwise have followed. We can now add that this lack of content is consistent with Socrates' conclusion about the oracle's meaning. He himself doesn't know, cannot put into words what belongs only to the god; but the god does have wisdom. So divine care, while not relieving human ignorance, shows itself in preventing that ignorance from doing harm to itself. It is also significant that Socrates experienced something like a negative vocation to philosophy: it was because the sign blocked him from public life that he turned to philosophizing as private conversation (31d). Kept from the harm that political confrontation would have brought him, he has been free to call individuals to account in the matter of goodness. Sign and oracle thus work together in Socrates' experience, causing him to view philosophy as religious duty.

Beyond this I need, however, to make it quite clear how philosophizing requires *obedience* for Socrates.

It has to do at heart with Socrates' conviction that the god does know and care. That's why he can have the assurance that in the end goodness will come to no harm, that (as he puts it) it's not in the order of things that a worse man should harm a better (30d) or that a good man's affairs will be neglected by the gods (41d). No mere postulate of thought, this assurance must carry Socrates in his living, as we've seen. He can't *know* that he will escape harm by refusing to live in the realm of pretense, forsaking temporal advantages; nor is he in any position to judge the outcome of following, or not following, the divine sign. He has to treat oracle and sign as commanding and forbidding from the place of wisdom inaccessible to him. And therefore his response is correctly called obedience.

But this is no easy conformity to command, no surrender of responsibility to an imposed will. For one thing, Socrates has to figure out what it means to obey the oracle. As the Greek word suggests, obedience is for him a *being persuaded* in his own mind through a long process of interrogation in which the oracle is tested. For another, the outworking of obedience lies in hard-nosed examination and scrutiny: it is the call to that sort of activity that he heeds. And finally, there's an integrity to his life of obedience, so that following the god provides assurance that the principles he has embraced will not fail him.

Obeying the Laws

We began with the tough independence of Socrates, the distance interposed between himself and others that makes it difficult to count him among the obedient. Now that we understand the nature of his obedience to the divine call, we're tempted to view that supremely private loyalty as making even more apparent his social isolation from the authorities which govern normal life. It would be wrong, however, to think that we'd captured Socratic obedience completely by looking only in the direction of the god. For there is another most noteworthy feature of this man: his law-abidingness. Surprisingly, in light of his toughness, Socrates thinks he should obey the laws of Athens.

Obeying Authorities Maybe we should straight off dispose of one suspicion: that Socrates follows the laws of Athens because he believes it right always to obey the person set in legitimate authority over you. There is no doubt about his recognition of authority relationships in general, or about his use of imagery—usually military—that trades upon such roles. He himself followed orders while on military campaigns, sticking to his post in spite of danger (*Apology* 28e; cf *Symposium* 221ab); so, he says, how much more should he stay with the order to practice philosophy. Among his friends on the day of his death, he speaks of suicide as a desertion of one's proper place in a garrison or an attempt to escape from prison (*Phaedo* 62b); it seems to be wrong because it usurps authority. What's behind this language? An abdication of moral or personal responsibility for action by submerging one's agency in the greater will of a superior?

Although Socrates does think it wrong to disobey one's better, whether god or human (*Apology* 29b), we cannot read him as advocating an unquestioning obedience. But we don't have to be content simply to infer that from his general character, for three specific considerations tell against it.

First, some of Socrates' examples turn out to be really concerned with the *motivation* for obeying and disobeying, not the rightness or wrongness of authority. Take staying at one's post: he *assumes* that there's good reason for the order, but that fear or cowardice might drive you to flee for your life. Given his basic convictions about wrongdoing and harm, Socrates must hold that where the order is a good one, you shouldn't try to escape harm by doing wrong. Wrongdoing might save your skin, but will in the end get you into more trouble. Obedience in such contexts, then, would be a form of the virtue of courage, a sticking to one's convictions instead of being pushed around by instincts and passions. Further, paying obedient attention to a right command in difficult circumstances requires a self-control that, far from surrendering agency, enhances it. As for the *Phaedo*'s treatment of suicide: there's a similar concern with the grounds for accepting or rejecting a proper command, predicated on the conviction that only the gods know when it is appropriate for you to leave your posting in the world of embodiment. At issue is why suicide should not be actively sought if philosophy has been a continuous preparation for death and the soul's disembodied state most to be desired. Socrates claims it is wrong to bring death upon yourself without some sign of its necessity (62c), couching his explanation for this wrongness in the language of the gods' property rights over their creatures. But he needn't have put it that way.

For it's the *care of the god for us* that's important. To leave when *you* think you are prepared is to presume too much upon your meager knowledge. You know that you've been ordered into embodiment, but without another necessity (that is, a countermanding order) you must pay attention to the way in which you conduct your life—versifying Aesop if need be. In these cases of obeying orders, then, the focus is upon sticking to a commitment already accepted as right and proper; disobedience would do the agent harm, for it would be predicated on fear or false belief.

A second reason why we can't see Socratic law-abidingness as a simple obedience to the orders of superiors is that on occasion he himself went against duly established authority. As he reminds the jurors, under the democracy he voted against an illegal proposal to try the ten commanders *en bloc;* and under the Thirty Tyrants, he simply went home rather than go with four others to arrest Leon. Now it may be pointed out that if Socrates wanted to uphold the law and constitution of Athens in these cases, he had to take sides against those in charge at the time. What's interesting, however, is his own way of talking about these decisions. For he uses the same language as in the obeying-orders cases: the requirement to avoid wrong even at the cost of one's life. On both occasions he experienced conflict over the consequences of doing right: but he determined that it was his duty to side with law and justice rather than give in to fear of prison or death (32c), that government should not terrify him with fear of death, but rather he should do nothing wrong (32d). Socrates clearly recognizes that political power may lack moral authority and that sometimes it is imperative to disobey because compliance would be not only illegal or internally inconsistent with the constitution but plainly wrong and unjust. That's why, instead of arguing respect for law, he makes so much of the need to escape wrongdoing.

Third, we know Socrates is not promoting an unconditional loyalty to duly established civil authority because he promises that he will disobey at least one order. There's no doubt about that. In his defense he raises the possibility of acquittal on condition that he stop philosophizing—and then shuts that out firmly by claiming he owes greater obedience to the god than to the jury (29d). When canvassing alternate penalties later in the proceedings, he returns to the proposal that he should simply mind his own business, and once more calls that disobedience to the god.

The Laws and the God Now if, as I believe, these considerations establish that Socrates does not accord ultimate authority to law as embodied by the decrees and decisions of the state, then what is going on in the *Crito?* For there, you will remember, his friend Crito (who arrives with the distressing news that Socrates' execution day is imminent) attempts to persuade him that he should take advantage of arrangements already made to spirit him out of prison into exile. Socrates rejoins that this is impossible: he must comply with the law for a series of reasons that appear to make it impossible to disobey in the name of any other authority. The arguments are placed in the mouth of the personified Laws of Athens, who argue that the state cannot continue to exist if private citizens disregard laws and legal judgments. They also claim that Socrates has an obligation to respect the law, on several grounds. The state gave him protection and education from birth and deserves the recognition appropriate to a superior. Socrates has willingly accepted the state's benefits, making explicit in deed if not in word his agreement to live under its jurisdiction. Were he to leave prison without permission, he would therefore harm the state and break knowingly a long-standing commitment. Civil disobedience, on this view, contradicts fundamental Socratic principles about never doing or returning harm and always keeping agreements. So it does indeed seem to be the case that the *Crito* elevates law-abidingness to unexpected heights—as high as the *Apology*'s obedience to the god. How can its Socrates live in harmony with the Socrates we've just been discussing?

The question has a long history that cannot be traversed here; our interest is in Socratic obedience rather than Plato's political philosophy. But I will comment that some answers just won't work. Two, for instance, trade on some unusual features of the *Crito*, the last section of which does come across as atypical of Socrates. He makes up questions for a fictional entity, the Laws of Athens; the questioning quickly slides into sermonizing; and Socrates pronounces himself so in the grip of these words that he cannot hear the other side. Perhaps, then, he has just given up on his characteristic searching to become reconciled to his dying, and the *Crito* signals that change. Or (as a different suggestion) perhaps he is employing persuasive techniques not to reveal his own mind but in order to reconcile his friend Crito to his death. These suggestions are not utterly implausible. Nevertheless, I cannot think either that Socrates is mesmerized by the counsel of an unconditional obedience to law for reasons arising solely from the psychology of dying, or that he is simply saying what Crito wants to hear. If we take six steps we will be able to arrive at a more satisfactory account, dealing along the way with the issues just raised.

First, it has to be said that within the *Crito* itself there is no argument for an unconditional obedience to law in general. The Laws of Athens four times stress an alternative: persuasion that laws or judicial decisions are unjust. Remember that to obey is to be persuaded, so the alternatives have a parallelism that doesn't come across in English: the citizen is to persuade the state or be persuaded by it. There's also the right of voluntary exit from the state should the citizen find its laws and institutions unsatisfactory. Decrees and decisions of legal authority are not therefore automatically worthy of obedience.

Second, think about Socrates' psychological state over his approaching execution. He retains a remarkable self-possession in contrast to Crito's distress; in a reversal of normal expectations, his is the calm center around which Crito's anxiety flutters. So it's clear that Socrates has accepted his death; the question is how that acceptance relates to his decision to obey the law. If Socrates really believes in civil obedience at any cost, then *the jury's decision* dictates his acceptance. Every other consideration aside, it is enough that due process has issued in this decree, so he'll abide by it. For our part, however, we find it not credible that someone should break himself solely on an unbending respect for law-abidingness, so we suspect other motives in Socrates' psychology— a martyr complex, or (as Xenophon has it in his version of the Defense) a desire to get out before senile decrepitude sets in. Are those the motives that make him so unusually respectful of law?

We'll find a different answer in the third step. It involves, though, a move back to the *Apology* in order to collect up our understanding of *who Socrates is* so that we can regard the *Crito* in that light. (Though it's a good idea to take each Platonic dialogue first on its own terms, the *Crito*'s terms have evidently clashed with the *Apology*'s, so we shouldn't have to forget what we know of Socrates' motivations from the defense in figuring out why he stays in prison.) Now the *Apology* makes clear (at least on our reading) that Socrates has no choice but to accept the death penalty, given his overriding commitments not to harm himself and to practice philosophy, and given the jury's resolve to stop that practice. The necessity of his death arises not out of their decision to impose capital punishment, but from *who he is* and *where he is situated.* Much like Jesus, Socrates embraces his own dying as that which is given him to do. And also as in the case of Jesus, death has a double determination—the work of divine as well as human will.

Socrates cannot believe his fate to be determined only by legal process, for he sees his death as the will of the god. He has concluded his initial defense to the jury by leaving judgment about what is best (for him and Athens) to them and *to the god* (*Apology* 35d). When that judgment becomes the death sentence, he interprets the silence of his sign throughout the proceedings as divine permission to go to death as a blessing instead of a harm. Socrates remains in this frame of mind as the *Crito* opens. His death will turn out for good, if that pleases the gods (43e); his dream, announcing the time of his departure, confirms the goodness of his destination (44b). And he ends his discussion with Crito by affirming that "the god leads the way" to his death (54e).

There's another piece of reasoning that, I propose, reinforces this understanding of Socrates' attitude. Beginning at 46b, Socrates sorts through Crito's arguments in favor of his escape in order to refute them, and he asks whether popular opinion ought to determine the rightness of a course of action. It doesn't in the case of physical well-being, where we listen instead to the expert doctor or trainer. So our soul's health, being that much more important, should be entrusted only to the one who knows. It is the person who knows justice and injustice, the truth itself (48a), who should be feared and followed and not (the language is repeated) disobeyed. Think about this. Who, pray tell, is this expert? Maybe elsewhere Plato positions the figure of Socrates in that place, but this identification won't work here. It's Socrates, after all, who himself needs expert help to reject popular advice. But he has found it—in the wisdom that belongs alone to the god. The ground of his obedience to death lies in the care and knowledge shown by the god to Socrates, who will follow because he cannot stop philosophizing any more than he can harm himself by escaping death. In all these ways, then, the Socrates of the *Crito* lets us know that he still attributes his imminent death to the ultimate will not of the Athenian people but of the god.

It follows that Socrates' respect for law is more complex than we might have supposed. Because he knows on those other grounds we found in the *Apology* that his death is necessary, he cannot bring himself to escape from prison. But the kind of obedience that he owes the Laws of Athens, though not unconditional, serves to provide an *additional reason* for not taking up Crito's offer.

This brings us to the fourth step. What is new in the *Crito* is the extension of the principle of doing no harm to include more than oneself. Where before Socrates had found it morally impossible to do anything intentionally to his own harm, he here adds that he must not harm others, even when they have harmed him. That's why, I think, the Laws stress the damage to the state that disobedience causes, and why they introduce some extra considerations about the harm an illegal escape would likely inflict on his friends and family. Socrates develops this approach largely because Crito had argued the case for escape on the basis of the harms Socrates' death would inflict on others.

We can now recognize—as our fifth step—that Socrates makes use of arguments that Crito needs to hear, not rhetorical devices with persuasive force but no personal significance for their author. Socrates actually believes that it is right for him to die because he should harm no one—not himself, not his associates, not the state. But it doesn't follow that he needs always to obey whatever the state decrees.

And that's the sixth step. We should be aware of the particularity of Socrates' decision to remain in prison in obedience to the law. He has already attempted to persuade the jury of his innocence, already rejected voluntary exit from Athens as a possible penalty. Perhaps for those other reasons we've explored, he has closed off these routes that may lead out of obedience to unacceptable laws and decrees. More: it isn't clear that Socrates misreads the harms that would follow upon his disobedience to this particular legal judgment about his fate. He could be quite right in thinking that *his* disrespect for due process would create damage. It's best therefore to read the sermon of the Laws of Athens not as a discourse on civil disobedience in general but as a pointed bit of preaching to Socrates, applying all his principles to this one decision that Crito asks him to make. With other decisions in other circumstances, those principles might well play out differently.

There's much more to be said about the *Crito,* and commentators will continue to argue about the shapes of civil obedience into which Plato's materials may be pressed. Nevertheless, we have enough on Socratic obedience for our purposes. We know that Socrates accepts the duty to be law-abiding where disobedience would be harmful to himself or others. We have no reason to commit him to promoting civil obedience above considerations of harm; indeed, he gives us evidence that he would disobey certain orders even if they resulted from due process. And finally we have seen that his refusal to break out of prison stems not from law-abidingness alone but from his acceptance of death as the will of the god.

Socratic Obedience

A brief summary is in order before we move on to the themes of authority and obedience in Jesus.

The paradox who is Socrates occupies a social space that is markedly his own, independent of the usual concerns and norms of his fellow citizens; yet he exhibits a commitment to obey the laws of his state that is more important than his life. His tough independence is expressed in his philosophizing, carried out in obedience to the god who commands him, in oracle and sign, from a place of wisdom inaccessible to human knowledge. Socratic obedience is thus *a being persuaded by* the god, a carrying out of his fundamental principles in the confidence that the god cares for his true welfare and will not fail him. Put that way, the obedience of Socrates flows from the nature of Socratic prayer as a kind of attentiveness.

Such obedience diminishes in no way the moral or personal status of its agent. On the contrary, it requires intellectual initiative in seeking and questioning the will of the god, the virtues of courage and trust, the full participation of the agent in exercising self-control.

But a Socrates obedient to an authority beyond the limits of human society and knowledge must inevitably clash with those who are persuaded by other voices. And so he does: that's the short reason for his trial and death. Yet in setting out the meaning of his death, he does not locate his sole authority in the god, as he might well have done. Instead he turns back to his city, preaching his duty to abide by its laws.

Although law-abidingness cannot be written out of Socratic obedience, my account requires it to be subservient to the religious duty of philosophizing. Can we provide any reason for its prominence, then, in Plato's presentation of Socrates? There is, of course, good practical justification for keeping laws: Socrates could, I'm sure, appreciate that his invocation of the law in the conduct of his trial commits him to playing by the same rules. But that line of pursuit won't account for the moral seriousness with which the *Crito* treats civil obedience. So I'll make a different, if tentative, suggestion.

The law-abiding side of Socratic obedience functions in a quasi-sacramental fashion. There's a point to this claim beyond its abrupt introduction of Christian vocabulary. For a sacrament is, among other things, a concrete and visible sign that accompanies an inner divine grace. For our purposes, it has an epistemological role to play, bearing witness to an experience otherwise inaccessible to onlookers. Now the crucial thing about obedience is that it must involve conformity to an authority beyond the self. What could serve as the outward mark of an authority that is so private and inward for Socrates? What *sacramentum* might manifest the fact that he is persuaded from beyond his own desires and wishes? Conformity to publicly proclaimed law and acceptance of the outcome of recognized judicial procedure. This is especially true of Socrates' death, for (to appropriate the language a little further) the jury's will becomes the vehicle for the will of the god. That, I propose, imparts a sacramentlike seriousness to Socratic obedience as law-abid-ingness.

I will return to obedience and the divine will before we finish. Our next task, though, is a large one: to bring our questions about obedience and authority to Jesus, or more specifically the Jesus presented in Mark's Gospel. We'll discover that the material calls upon us to think more about authority in the case of Jesus, around his person and his teaching. That will, however, turn out to have important implications for obedience. We'll also find it helpful at a couple of places to bring back Socrates into the discussion.

Authority and Obedience in Mark's Jesus

In earlier chapters we have encountered a silent Jesus whose inability to sort out the relation between death and the kingdom nevertheless did not stand in the way of obedience to the Father's will, and a Jesus for whom the meaning of prayer has the same outcome, the discerning and doing of that will. We cannot escape, then, the category of obedience if we are to understand the motivation and action of Jesus. But in this statement we are only acknowledging what must have been recognized very early on, even before the writing of the Gospels. In a section of his letter to the Philippians, Paul makes use of lines that scholars consider one of the first Christian hymns:

> He was in the form of God
> yet laid no claim to equality with God
> but made himself nothing, assuming the form of a slave

Bearing the human likeness, sharing the human lot
he humbled himself
and was obedient
even to the point of death, death
on a cross (Philippians 2.6–8, REB)

This Jesus became an explicit model for his followers: Paul goes on to say, "So you too, my beloved, must be obedient as always."

Now as we've seen, obedience requires a relation to some authority or other, so in order to pursue our topic, we have to inquire into the nature of authority for Jesus. Only when we have achieved that understanding will we be able to assess the obedience that the early Christian writers think characteristic of his life and death. For although the general theme is simple enough—he was obedient to the Father's will—nevertheless, the actual evidence for his attitude and relation to authority is not at all simple. In the conviction, then, that we must be guided by the material in our texts and not just the assumptions we think are embedded in a general claim, we turn next to Mark's gospel.

And here we see why the material is not straightforward. For although Mark does have ten occurrences of the word for authority, *exousia,* and although there are many instances of commands and of compliance, along with a couple of explicit references to obedience, Jesus is not presented as living a life of obedience to authority. Quite the contrary: Jesus is the one who holds authority and is obeyed.

Authority Exercised

The very first chapter of Mark sets out in quick strokes the peculiar relation of Jesus to everything else. Although we start with a prophet, John, who is announced by an earlier prophet, Isaiah, we move at once to someone who is mightier than that and of greater worth: Jesus appears on the scene. Immediately his special connection with the Spirit and with the Father is established. He is straightway removed from human community and civilization, placed among wild beasts, and made the special object of Satan's attention and of angels' ministrations. Without his having said a word, or having done anything but submit himself to baptism and to the agency of the Spirit, we are nevertheless positioned to expect his actions to be of the greatest significance.

[184]

And we do not wait long. With the simplest of words, Jesus begins to preach and to exercise an authority of enormous scope. He commands two pairs of men to follow him; they obey at once without question. When he teaches he does so with an unparalleled authority, twice remarked on. More: screamed at by an unclean spirit, Jesus orders that spirit to shut up and leave its victim—and the spirit obeys. Not just that one: that evening, and later throughout Galilee, other demons are driven out. Illness cannot withstand his touch; fever, leprosy, "various diseases" all retreat before him. So in this opening chapter, commands and compliance, authority and obedience (*exousia* occurs twice, *hupakouô* once), are essential to the activity of Jesus. Mark makes certain that his reader knows the authority of Jesus extends over nature and the demonic, over human lives and traditional teaching. The only failure of Jesus' power is with the leper who, despite a strong order to keep quiet, spreads the word of his cure far and wide.

For the rest of the gospel, or at least until the Last Supper narrative, the authority of Jesus continues to be exercised in all spheres. Although another disciple follows his compelling call, perhaps the Marcan "crowd" best exemplifies the power of Jesus on others, with 9.15 epitomizing the relationship: *and suddenly the whole crowd, catching sight of him, was amazed and ran forward to welcome him.* The miracle stories establish his authority over bodily illness and disease of all kinds, as he repairs capacities to move limbs and to see or speak or hear, stanches the flow of lifeblood, or restores life itself. Natural forces fall under the scope of his ability: loaves and fish are multiplied, a fig tree blasted, wind and waves stilled—in obedience, it is said at 4.41, to his command. But perhaps the most revealing spheres for Jesus' authority in Mark's account are the demonic and the religious.

It is practically impossible for us to read straightforwardly the Marcan stories about demon possession and exorcism; it's therefore easy even for the faithful to pass quickly over them with thoughts of epilepsy at the edges of one's mind. Given different assumptions about metaphysics and the aetiology of mental disease from those that the ancients held, we reinterpret the stories as examples of healings not properly understood by them. But if we suppress our superiority to let Mark tell the story his way, it's striking that there are *so many* references to unclean spirits and demons in this gospel. I count more than thirty occurrences, with Satan getting half a dozen additional mentions. (Not that Mark is unusual: Matthew has only slightly fewer references, and

Luke three or four more.) The account of the Gerasene demoniac possessed by Legion in chapter 5 takes up more space than any other healing narrative, and indeed more than the crucifixion itself; and other memorable vignettes include the demon-inhabited daughter of an astute Gentile woman (7.25–30) and the possessed boy whom the disciples were powerless to help (9.14–29).

More to our point, the accounts of the demonic employ the language of *authority*, referring to a special power to expel evil spirits: twice (at 3.15 and 6.7) Mark tells us that Jesus gave that particular form of *exousia*, remarked upon at the very beginning of his own work in 1.27, to the Twelve. As we've just noted, one spirit was too much for them; we also learn from 9.39 that they weren't the only ones to perform exorcisms in Jesus' name. Such observations from Mark heighten the power surrounding Jesus: his very name has sufficient authority for some cases, while the tough ones requiring prayer yield only to his own voice. But (I submit) that is what all this talk of demons and spirits is about: it's about the limits of our human ability, individually and together, to keep ourselves, our fellow citizens, and our loved ones from harm and evil. We fall prey to disorder and chaos brought about by causes we can't understand. The ancients succumbed, but so do we, and so will our children. This morning's news reports the arrest of a suspect in the murder eight months ago of a three-year-old girl: forensic science was able to match DNA in material found in the suspect's apartment and on the water-submerged little body. There is so much we know and yet so little we can understand or do about the iron grasp of evil on the human mind—which is why we mustn't demystify the stories into something we think we are now able to figure out. If our minds associate the gospel accounts with those medieval etchings and carvings of devils, we may fall into the comfort of making what are representations of the imagination into something simply imaginary; but when we so comfort ourselves we miss the point. Nothing is solved by rubbing out those hideous faces and leering grins. We should stop at the place where we do not know and confess that just as evil is greater than any of us, so we cannot fully name its causes or make it malleable to our will. In restoring demoniacs to society and family, Mark's Jesus did what no human ingenuity or skill or attention could accomplish. Those Gerasenes couldn't fashion chains of sufficient strength to restrain the demoniac, or do anything to prevent his self-mutilation; that little boy kept heading for the destruction of water or fire. Mark has no surer way to extend the authority of his Jesus beyond the dark edges of the human.

Now the ability of Jesus to command obedience in the human, natural, and demonic orders is matched by his authority in word and teaching. That teaching, as we saw from Mark's first chapter, is notably different in its effects from the words of the professional scribes; and in the second chapter the stakes are considerably elevated as Jesus claims the *exousia* (he uses the term at v. 10) to forgive sins, then pronounces forgiveness and heals the paralytic. Much of his authority sets itself against other religious expertise. He disagrees over such authorized religious observances as those about the sabbath, food preparation, fellowship, and fasting; he reinterprets the keeping of law, the traditions about divorce. Much of this speaking appears to carry the not completely unfamiliar stamp of prophetic utterance, and Jesus himself makes that association (in the saying that "a prophet is not without honor") in chapter 6 when the synagogue in his hometown couldn't locate the source of his wisdom and power ("Where does he get it from? What is this wisdom he has been given?"). But Mark continues his opening theme of elevating Jesus above the recognizable class of prophets, both in what his Jesus claims and in what he does not say. Another example, beyond the authority to forgive sins, of a striking claim: after Peter comes out with the messianic identification of Jesus in chapter 8, Jesus lays down for his followers the requirement of self-denial and life-losing for his sake. In this he demands a level of personal allegiance not appropriate for prophets in his tradition. As for what Mark's Jesus does not say: he never claims that he is speaking the word of the Lord, as every legitimate prophet does announce. There is, surprisingly in this context, no message from God of which Jesus is the herald and proclaimer. Whereas prophets seek to authenticate their speaking with divine authority, Jesus speaks in his own voice. Not that this voice is different from God's: twice the heavens open, not to reveal something for Jesus to pass on, but to confirm his Sonship and to announce to others that they should listen to this beloved Son. Mark presents him as the one who can say what the kingdom of God is like, not only in public parables but also in authoritative private interpretation of the meaning of that teaching. In short, Jesus is much more than the announcer of an authorized message. He carries a kind of personal authority constituted by his identity, and that identity is of greater importance to Mark than the content of his teaching.

We shall have to inspect in more detail just how the identity of Jesus is disclosed and how he himself regards his own authoritative role. Before that, however, we must come to the climax of the story in the final week of his life. For—though we may have forgotten it momentarily in this talk of Jesus' authority—that climax is a taking back of everything we have said about his power, a shrinking into nothing of the wide authority he has exercised throughout Mark's Gospel. If, as we saw two chapters back, the Passion is a handing over into silence, it is also the emptying out of authority.

Authority Emptied

This is Holy Week in which I write. It is now Christian custom to call the first day of this week the Sunday of the Passion, rather than Palm Sunday, to emphasize that the entry into Jerusalem marks the start of the end for Jesus: the Liturgy of the Palms is introduced with such lines as, "The people welcomed him with palms and shouts of praise, / but the path before him led to self-giving, suffering and death."

True enough: the Entry was a purposeful making possible of those actions on the part of others that procured Jesus' death; so it marks the giving of himself over to the designs of his enemies. All the same, it would be wrong to take from this that Jesus slips swiftly into passivity: Mark refuses to permit his authority to drain away that quickly. Instead, the Entry narrative of chapter 11 reasserts the wide scope of the power of Jesus, functioning therefore like a repetition of and response to the opening chapter of Mark's Gospel. If there are no longer diseases or demons to be dealt with here, nevertheless Jesus is the one in control. He has privileged information about the whereabouts of the colt; the mere report of his need secures the compliance of its owner; the colt submits to this, its first rider. And the people voice their recognition: finally the sentence of the Father at Jesus' baptism is acknowledged with shouts of blessing on earth, as the crowd throws at his feet palm branches and cloaks, the products of nature and of art. The public acclamation of his status and authority peaks in this event, and Jesus does not accept it benignly. Instead the peaking seems to unleash power—quite physical power—as Jesus' curse withers the fig tree and his anger cleanses the Temple the next day. He even states that sufficient faith could hurl mountains into the sea. If we let ourselves suspect hyperbole in order to tone this Jesus down, we might be reminded of

Mark's report that the leaders were frightened of him: he affords no easy target. Nor will he comply by turning himself in after these scenes. In the battle of wits—we saw this in Matthew, and Mark's version is similar—Jesus gives as good as he gets, fencing with Pharisees, with the Herodians, the Sadducees, the scribes, and holding his enemies at bay.

Nevertheless, we are conscious of the looming shadow of Maundy Thursday over these expressions of status and power. Even in the first part of that night, Jesus is able to exert some control over events. He has arranged the Passover location, knowing that his reported words ("The Teacher says, where is the room?") will once more be efficacious in securing compliance; he understands the impending betrayal, predicts the disciples' dereliction and Peter's triple denial. But this authority is largely a matter of privileged knowledge. The sphere of his superior power is reduced to his own consciousness—where, poignantly, the knowledge is a knowledge about his imminent loss of power.

So the one who was obeyed by wind and sea, by forces beyond human naming, submits himself to the authorities of Temple and state, who think that they hold power of arrest, conviction, and execution. I suggested in our discussion of Word and Silence that Jesus' speaking at his arrest discloses a deliberate surrender of control as he hands himself over in the Passion, that the strange incident with the fig tree demonstrates a power in his very language which is yielded up as he goes to death. What our present reflection on Mark helps us see now is the larger picture, a much bigger canvas of authority and power exercised from his submission in baptism to the Father until his willing surrender to death at human hands.

I know of no better way to appreciate what this abdication of authority means than by watching what happens to the body of Jesus in his Passion, later throwing that into relief with Plato's presentation of the body of Socrates. Although I cannot bring myself to reduce persons to their bodies alone, still our identities are closely entangled with our embodiment, given the sorts of persons that human beings are. To be a person is to have agency, to be able to do things; and to be a human agent is to have control over one's bodily motions. That's why (for instance) incontinence in older children and the elderly is so painful: not just because it is unpleasant but because it tellingly announces an erosion in the boundaries of the self beyond the socially acceptable. More generally, although self-control is a virtue, it is more than that: it is a necessary metaphysical condition of selfhood, without which we are only embodiments at a distance of blind forces or somebody else's will. Further, reflection on how people relate to their bodies reveals a good deal about personal identity and status. It will turn out that there are striking differences in what we may call (with convenient shorthand, using the Greek word *sôma*, body) the *somatic characteristics* of Socrates and Jesus, differences that are crucial for their identities.

Mark's Somatic Presentation of Jesus Recall that Mark has no birth narrative, but begins at the Jordan with John the Baptist: the first act of Jesus is thus the presentation of his body for baptism. Immediately after this the Spirit drives him into the wilderness. But if we thereby expect the story of someone whose bodily presence expresses the will of another—in a continuation of what we might call gestures of somatic submissiveness—our expectations are reversed right away. As we have just recognized in looking at authority in Mark, Jesus' bodily presence is one of great power. His words and deeds restore bodily integrity to those who had lost it through disease or possession; he brings somatic agency to the paralyzed, somatic control to the demon-driven. All agency resides with him, so much so that to touch even his clothing (5.27; 6.56) is sufficient to participate in that power. (The Baptist had warned us: John was unworthy to put a finger on the sandals of the Coming One.) This body has such presence that Mark is constantly moving Jesus around, trying to preserve him against the crush of the crowd both indoors and out: we see his body standing in boats a little way from shore, crossing the lake several times, seeking remote places, moving inside to be alone with his disciples. There is such attraction to his somatic presence that, unless this distance were laid down, Jesus might quite literally have been handled to death. He retains his bodily integrity only by not submitting to the wishes of others, by dispensing power as much as he can on his own initiative. (Only with the hemorrhaging woman is he caught off guard.) Against this remarkable somatic integrity, sustained across his ministry and expressed again (as we just noted) in the Entry to Jerusalem, it is striking to witness Jesus' willingness to permit the woman at Simon's house to anoint him. This is a gesture of submission reminiscent of his baptism: as he stood still for the water, so he does not draw back as the oil is poured on his head. Indeed, if we want an event to foreshadow what I'm about to call the somatic relinquishment of his Passion, we should think not of the Sunday of those Palms but of the midweek day of the Anointing. For this is the first time since the opening of Mark's Gospel that Jesus lets anybody do anything to his body (others had touched only his clothing); and he defends the woman's action by referring to his own burial. That is where we will end up: with his lifeless linen-wrapped body, unanointed and for all Mark says perhaps unwashed, laid alone by Joseph of Arimathaea in a rockhewn tomb.

We are not yet there: as I have pointed out, Jesus does retain at least epistemological authority up until the time he enters the Garden of the Agony. Then, however, the handing over of himself to the will of others begins in earnest. And even before Judas arrives. He places himself at a distance from his disciples and in one dramatic movement of his body signals the disintegration of his somatic control: Mark says he falls to the ground. (Matthew's words are that he throws himself on his face.) Three times he prays, displacing his own will with the will of the Father. Though it is to Peter and the others that he addresses his comment on the willingness of the spirit and the weakness of the flesh, the primary referent must be to himself: he may not fall asleep, but the weak body is just as much his as theirs.

Perhaps the term I mentioned, *somatic relinquishment,* will capture this grief-laden weakness of body that is not so much an unsought affliction as a deliberate outcome of his determinate purpose to embrace the Father's will. Remember our exploration of Word and Silence: Matthew's account presented an agent who actively hands himself over instead of being overpowered at the sole initiative of the arresting mob and its leaders. Mark gives much the same flavor to the scene, especially in Jesus' locating the arrest in the fulfillment of Scripture. Watch more particularly now how all the action impinges on his body.

Lips first brush his cheek; hands then seize his arms, holding him fast. Jesus no longer moves at his own pleasure. His body is led away, transferred from one authority to another, bound, handed over, led out, brought to the place of crucifixion, fastened and hung up, then finally taken down, laid out, and sealed in.

There is special emphasis on Jesus' face. Twice, Mark reports, violence is directed there: before the religious authorities, and again in the Roman Praetorium, Jesus is spat upon and beaten about the head. In the first scene he is spat at and struck while blindfolded so that he can be ridiculed about the religious power of prophetic speaking. (Mark, remember, had Jesus use his spittle to loose a tongue and open eyes.) In the second the soldiers do their spitting and striking, having crowned his head with a plait of thorns, in order to mock him over the political authority of kingship. Previously we remarked upon the silence of Jesus through these indignities; to that we now add Mark's lack of comment upon any physical response at all on Jesus' part. We know nothing of the look in his eyes, even less of the face of the victimized Jesus than of the face of Jesus at prayer.

We cannot understand human bodily identity without thinking of the role of clothing. Apart from its necessary protective function, our apparel expresses identity in sometimes subtle combinations of difference and sameness. Our clothing is our own in quite complex ways, providing us with recognition and social location. Though we undress to take care of our bodies or for intimacy, to be undressed against our will is to be diminished and dislocated. Jesus' body, we remember, was stripped. It must have happened twice in the Praetorium if he was first flogged, then dressed in purple, then undressed, then put back in his own clothes. One last stripping, in public, gave away to his executioners the last layer of personal protection he had, the only things we know him to have held as his own.

This is the somatic relinquishment of Jesus: his withdrawal of agency and control over where his body was moved, what it wore or suffered, what indignities it was made to bear. He couldn't even carry his own cross. In becoming victim, Jesus gives up what is so essential to our embodiment—our ability to initiate action, to mark out our selfhood in the world. And insofar as he remains a silent victim, Jesus makes it difficult for us to interpret whatever presence he retains in this passive body. We saw earlier from Matthew that in his words at the arrest and in speaking to Caiaphas, Jesus makes it clear that this is an active relinquishing of power; and Mark's account permits the same point. But neither gospel helps us much once the handing over is complete. We cannot forget the haunting words of dereliction and the loud wordless cry, so we know that Jesus has not withdrawn completely, that he continues to experience whatever it is that is done to him. Indeed, his refusal to drink before being crucified may (but only may: there is some uncertainty about the nature of the drink) be a mark of his deliberate desire to remain conscious of his relinquishment. What his experience is, other than of passivity and absence, stays out of our secure reach.

Scholars in working out a theology of incarnation speak sometimes of *kenôsis*, an emptying, picking up the language used by Paul in Philippians 2.7, quoted above: Jesus "emptied himself," or "made himself nothing" although he was in the form of God. Mark's account considered here does not use this term and makes no comment on the metaphysics of incarnation. But there is a kind of elementally human *kenôsis* in the draining away of Jesus' control over his own person through somatic relinquishment, in his refusal to be a bodily agent, to defend the boundaries of personhood, or to express in anything but the most minimal way an embodied self through language or gesture.

Mark's presentation of the body of Jesus requires at this point the contrast of Plato's embodied Socrates. The journey back to Athens places us in very different space from the Garden of the Agony and the Garden of the Tomb: but leave the lifeless body of Jesus at rest, remembering the care with which it was treated—a care Bach captures with tenderness in the closing of his *Saint Matthew's Passion*. Remember, for the somatic Socrates will turn our minds in another direction altogether.

The Somatic Socrates While thinking of prayer as attending, we had occasion to remark on the weirdness of Socrates, the difference Plato creates between him and other human beings—a difference we described as "tough independence." The strangeness of Socrates is marked by somatic characteristics as striking in their own way as the relinquishment that we have been describing in Jesus.

If we know more of the physical appearance of Socrates than of Jesus, still the details are sketchy: they amount to his being physically unattractive, with prominent eyes and snub nose (*Theaetetus* 143e; cf. *Phaedo* 86d). In his drunken speech in praise of Socrates in the *Symposium*, Alcibiades reinforces this image by emphasizing Socrates' outward likeness to satyr images sold in the marketplace; he also quotes lines from Aristophanes' *Clouds* about the peculiar gait of Socrates (walking with his head high) and his habit of glancing sideways (221b). Socrates' physical appearance, then, does not fit any cultural ideal—which only makes his personal attractiveness to his followers more intriguing and compelling. The few other details the *Symposium* reveals about Socrates' bodily life we can set out quickly. We have already dealt with his strange trancelike stillness, to which we now may add his imperviousness to sexual temptation (Alcibiades' attempts never succeed, 217a–219c), to intoxication (no one has ever seen him drunk, 220a), to cold (he walks barefoot on the ice, 220b), to physical danger (he doesn't panic and run off, 220e), to the normal need for sleep (he outlasts all the guests and does not go to bed till the next evening, 223d).

Now if we had to employ but one category for Socrates' relation to his body, it would be self-control. This notion (as Plato well understood) requires a distinction within the self—whereby one part or aspect, though belonging to oneself, is mastered, ruled, or governed by another part. In the examples just set out, bodily appetites and needs that are successfully insistent in the rest of us have been tamed and managed by Socrates so that he is not at their mercy; indeed, the basic instincts that drive human behavior seem under his deliberate direction. The ruling element in Socrates' psyche, we are led to believe, is reason. Helping to lead us to this belief are those paradoxical Socratic sayings that form themes throughout many of Plato's dialogues—that virtue is knowledge, that vice is ignorance, that no one does wrong voluntarily. Knowing the right thing to do is what's required for human excellence, because no one could possess this knowledge and fail to act upon it. Many of us are, of course, resistant to this view, finding weakness of will not only theoretically possible but frequently present in human experience; and scholars argue about Plato's own reaction to a doctrine that looks as though it came originally from the historical Socrates (especially because the moral psychology of the *Republic* is more complex than this, recognizing that agents sometimes are aware of doing the wrong thing because of lack of spirit to reinforce reason). Whatever pursuit of such questions will uncover, I think it defensible to hold that Plato's presentation of Socrates is such that we find ourselves thinking that in his case at least appetites never won out against right reason. As one commentator earlier this century put it (though a little too enthusiastically for our current taste), "If Reason ever has been incarnate on earth, it was in the person of Socrates, and those who wish to see her face can see it in him."

We can appreciate, I think, how such toughness of character might be developed through discipline by a resolute personality—by a moral athlete, if you like. And we can applaud both the goal and the performance without assenting to an entire theory built on one striking example. Nevertheless, somatic self-control will not capture everything that Plato gives us about Socrates' attitude to his own body. There is more, and it starts to push him out of our league altogether.

Come at this by going back to the argument in the *Apology* that answers the question of why Socrates would not simply stop philosophizing, if that will save his life. He replies, we recall, that some things (such as not avenging a murder) are worse than self-preservation, and that disobedience to the god's command to practice philosophy is too high a price to pay in order to escape death. This conviction is sufficiently strong to provide him with the remarkable composure exhibited in his trial, but it also reveals an attitude to embodied life: not simply that bodily needs and desires must be kept in their place but that their place is not ultimately important. Socrates doesn't seem to make his continued bodily existence a matter of concern; rather, the object of his interest is the single-minded pursuit of goodness. It is true that he preaches self-examination. That process, however, reveals the need to demote bodily concerns and possessions in favor of the welfare of the soul (30b). Only where goodness is realized will other and lesser benefits follow in its train; whether it turns out well with the good man who seeks not his own advantage but to do the right thing—that may be left to the god. If Socrates himself is convinced that goodness is sufficient protection against harm, that is because he seems not to include bodily death within the notion of harm to the essential person.

The *Apology* bears marks other than expressed beliefs that reinforce this kind of indifference in Socrates. I have in mind the ironic superiority over rhetoric that he claims for his own speaking, the challenge that he would not comply with an order to cease philosophizing, his deliberately provocative proposal of maintenance at state expense for a penalty, his distancing of family relationships, the concluding speech about death's not being that bad after all.

So I now suggest that we use a phrase like *somatic indifference*, not just somatic self-control, to characterize Socrates' attitudes to body.

And with that idea in hand, we may comment briefly on the *Phaedo*'s account of the last day of his life. It is unnecessary to set out at length the strong dualism that Plato speaks through his Socrates here, a dualism that focuses almost exclusively on the soul and its immortality. Socrates spends some time at the beginning of the dialogue explicating the negative features of embodiment and arguing that philosophy is best seen as the practice of dying—that is, separating the soul from the body—in order to escape bodily distractions. Somatic indifference would seem to be the appropriate attitude for the true philosopher, then. And Socrates exhibits this as well as preaching it in the *Phaedo*. For obvious reasons this dialogue rivals the *Symposium* for its attention to Socrates' body; we begin with his massaging his leg, just released from irons. The release motif is metaphor, of course, for his death: but notice the detachment from his own pain that Socrates manifests by using the occasion to philosophize about pleasure and pain in general. The same employment of body as illustration for philosophical purpose occurs when he later refers to his body in the autobiographical passage: though having a body is a necessary condition of his doing what is best in his circumstances, reference to his bodily states can never explain the reasons for his staying in prison. It is in the final scene, however, that Socrates' relation to his body is most succinctly expressed. Most obviously, somatic self-control reappears to great effect. It is Socrates who washes his own body in preparation for his death; he discusses calmly the administration of the poison; he himself takes the cup and drains it in one breath; everyone else, including the jailer, breaks down. Socrates is fully present in all his actions, the only agent of his own release. And yet this presence is not quite *somatic* presence, for Socrates is not present *as* body. His words to Crito make the point: it is not Socrates they will bury, but only a body which bears accidental relation to the one who is really Socrates. And they can do with that what they will. The self-control is indeed a control of the passions and emotions that carry other human beings away, but it is control through a cultivated somatic indifference.

One way to put all this is by asking about the locality of Socrates' concern. On what is his heart set, his attention fixed? If we answer with language that employs the vocabulary of the body, we'll find that it doesn't work, but the same is the case, I think, with the vocabulary of the self. I have just referred to self-examination, but of course the famous phrase is about the unexamined *life;* and what Socrates is after is not self-improvement in any of the obvious senses (he doesn't expect to become better organized or to widen his appreciation of the arts, for instance). What he cares about is goodness, and the nature of wisdom. He is more concerned about living out the right commitments than he is about the consequences of his choices for his supposed well-being. And this basic commitment that sends him to his death in the *Apology* is consonant with the object of his love in both the *Symposium* and the *Phaedrus,* where Socrates' heart is set not on this or that person or object but on the Beautiful itself. In a word, then, the locality of Socratic interest is (to use Plato's term) the Forms. That is the reason for his eccentricity, his displacedness.

At his death, the poison does not work as it works on other mortals. Death by ingesting the poison known as hemlock was, by ancient account and in modern toxicology, a difficult exit. The poison affects the arms and the legs; it also attacks the throat, so that the victim chokes and retches; the body is subject to spasms; speech grows thick and incoherent. With Socrates it is different. Having walked around until his legs are numb, Socrates lies on his back. He cannot feel the pinch of the man who administered the drink; covering his face, he stays perfectly calm as the coldness moves up toward his heart. Then Socrates, still in control of hands and speech, uncovers his face and asks Crito to offer the cock to Asclepius. There is silence, one bit of stirring, and he is gone. Plato's memorable writing thus emphasizes to the end the remarkable control over his body that Socrates exercises. At the same time he is able to suggest Socrates' ultimate somatic indifference as the real Socrates gradually departs from his body, leaving it cold and lifeless by degrees. We could almost believe that the poison does only what Socrates wills it to do, that death, as it were, has no dominion over this man.

We will have occasion to visit again the manner of Socrates' dying in our next chapter, and to hold that up against the death of Jesus. For now, though, we should return from Socrates' bodily self-control and indifference to the relinquishment we have discovered in Jesus.

Indifference vs. Relinquishment Look back on the territory of the body we have traversed. Jesus has moved from the exercise of more-than-human power over forces that threaten the bodily existence of others to the abdication of power over his own body. It is worth pausing over this movement. For Jesus did not simply step out of authority roles by ceasing to exercise control over disease and demons and nature, withdrawing from conflict and contact. Stepping down is one thing; it is common to all those whose terms in power have come to an end. But handing over one's own self into the will of others—that is entirely another matter. Jesus' somatic relinquishment involves what we'll later call an *inversion* of authority roles, in which power that worked beyond the edges of the human shrinks into mortal weakness. I think this turns out to be fundamentally different from the kind of indifference to bodily concerns that Socrates exhibits, in spite of the fact that both he and Jesus are rightly called obedient. Before facing that directly, however, I want to return to the question we raised earlier about identity and authority in Jesus. We had said that he carries a kind of personal authority constituted by his identity; we wanted to explore further how that identity is disclosed and what clues may be found in Jesus' words for his understanding of the nature of authority. His words, we'll see, have a kind of indirection about them that will remind us again of Socrates.

Hiddenness and Indirection in Authority

The two terms I have just used, *identity* and *authority*, have, of course, close ties. In fact, where one's identity is connected to a particular role or status, the recognition of identity is also a recognition of the authority belonging to that status. To identify yourself in certain contexts as a doctor, or a priest, or a prince in peasant garb is to license behavior and legitimate claims that would otherwise be unauthorized. Again, when the power exercised over others is questioned, one way to answer is to locate the relationship of the agent to established authority.

I've said that Mark presents Jesus as more than a prophet, with wider scope of power and stronger demands on followers than is customary for people holding prophetic status. I've also noted that he does not invoke the usual prophetic authorization, an appeal to the word of the Lord, for his teaching. By what authority, then, does he say what he says? Where is his identity located in relation to that authority?

That issue is explicitly raised in the Gospels by the Jerusalem religious leadership. Mark's report at 11.27–33 includes four uses of *exousia*, so the passage is of central concern for our understanding of authority. You will remember the incident from Matthew's account when Jesus maintained his silence about the source of his authority. Mark's version is practically identical: the leaders put a double question about Jesus' authority to him. He counters that he will answer if they first address *his* question about the baptism of John; the leaders refuse to reply, so Jesus will not answer them about himself. The significance of the passage for our study lies in the inference that the reader is invited to make about Jesus. It is Jesus who sets out the alternatives in his counterquestion: authority is either human or from God. If human, one's word is as good or bad as anyone else's, but if the authority comes from God, then the messenger must be accepted. About John, Mark tells us, the leaders did not want to say anything publicly because of political considerations (if his baptism was from God, they would have to believe him; but they could not answer that John's was merely human authority because they feared the popular reaction). So one obvious ploy for Jesus to follow about his own authority would be to ask the leaders what he'd asked the disciples back in chapter 8: if you can't say about John, can you at least say about me? Who do *you* say that I am? He would have won their silence about himself on the same grounds as their silence about John. If his authority was from God they should believe him; if only human they would fear the people who have acclaimed Jesus as much as John. Instead of asking this question, however, Jesus uses their professed ignorance about John to maintain his silence about himself—and thereby, I think, Mark creates the impression that Jesus is hiding something about authority (this holds for Matthew and Luke, too): "You *do not know,* but I *will not say."* And here, then, is the inference that we are invited to draw about Jesus. Were he to come out with a direct answer about his relation to divine authority, it wouldn't be quite like the answer in the case of John; John was not, after all, the beloved Son.

If I am right about this—that a hidden answer engenders the belief that it would be different from the standard answer of prophetic authority—then we are faced with another issue: why does Mark's Jesus bother to hide his authority or identity at all? This is not just a question about one passage in Mark, for Jesus does this hiding consistently. We must add to our earlier understanding of the silence of Jesus—which was confined to his speaking and not speaking in arrest, trial, and death— that Jesus remains frustratingly silent about his identity and authority throughout his public life. In Mark (and again in the other synoptics) it is the descending Spirit, the voice of the Father, the shouts of demons, and the confession of Peter that disclose Jesus' messianic sonship. He does not reject the attribution and relationship (what is rejected is the imputed relation to the prince of demons in 3.22), but he does not license it explicitly and certainly does not want it proclaimed.

Think a little more about that. On seven occasions in Mark, Jesus orders that his works or words are not to be divulged to others, and he performs his healings in private when he can. The only person permitted to talk about his healing is the Gerasene ex-demoniac, who (perhaps as a Gentile) is not to follow Jesus but to stay home to witness to what the Lord (not Jesus) in his mercy has done for him. This warning into silence does not seem to arise from modesty, and it seems unnecessary to view it as a device of reverse psychology designed to generate underground attention. Is it politically motivated, to avoid conflict with religious authorities? Hardly: the conflict is sufficiently provoked in other ways. To avoid prosecution on charges of blasphemy? That's not a satisfying explanation simply because Jesus does not shrink from death. It is more promising to look for something about the nature of Jesus' authority in this silence, especially because we have just seen that he might well have answered the direct question about his authority differently. The reason Jesus does not want others to proclaim his identity is the same as his reason for being so indirect about it himself: there must be something wrong with the very attempt to put that identity directly into words. Just what the problem is will emerge over the next pages, as we work through the indirection characteristic of Mark's Jesus.

Indirection in the Discourse of Jesus By "indirection" I mean a feature of discourse that is opposite from directness in speech, where words are used plainly to state the mind of the speaker. It's difficult, of course, to sort speech neatly into these two categories (what's poetry, for instance?); the distinction makes sense only where something that might be stated straight out is instead hinted at or implied. Attempts to interpret, say, the Delphic oracle may be seen as attempts to make direct what was said indirectly.

The hiddenness of Jesus' identity is an example of his unwillingness to speak directly. But there are several other characteristics of the discourse of Mark's Jesus that seem to belong to this category of indirection. One of the effects of indirection is that it demands a translation effort on the part of the interpreter to arrive at the intended meaning. And this seems to be the case with the words of Jesus: they do not do all the work necessary in order to disclose his authority and identity. Something more is required, to be contributed by the hearer.

Perhaps that is why Jesus is so interested in what goes on, or doesn't go on, in the listener. Mark 4 sets out those memorable sayings from Isaiah, that *they may look and look, but see nothing; they may listen and listen, but understand nothing.* The sayings are associated with Jesus' parables as a public form of discourse, and Mark seems to imply that this form is deliberately used to *prevent* understanding. But read in their earlier context, the phrases place the responsibility for cognitive malfunction on the receiver rather than the presenter: *these people,* Isaiah had said, *have stopped their ears, shut up their eyes.* That surely must be Jesus' point—that the teaching may be presented, the works performed, all to no avail unless the receiver is receptive. What else is the sower parable about? (Note its irony—that if you don't get its point you are not yourself the right kind of soil.) Why else in explaining that parable does he revert to the sayings with his own "if you have ears to hear, then hear"? Or does Mark use language about the shut-up hearts of the disciples in chapters 6 and 8? Such language might appear to belong to direct rather than indirect communication, for we tend to think of visual and aural experience as occurring apart from our will. The bright light, the loud noise are difficult to ignore. Nevertheless, as we remember from our last chapter, *what it is* that we see or hear depends very much upon the attentiveness we bring to bear upon our experience. The appreciation of art or music requires much active looking and listening by the receiver.

That Jesus wishes activity on the part of the listener may explain his fondness for the parable form. Parables have this advantage over plain speaking, that they invite an interpretive contribution from the hearer, a contribution that the hearer then owns. Their indirection lies in the fact that their intended focus of attention is not presented but only pointed to; parables are always "about" something that is unstated within their structure. What is pointed to will be susceptible of more direct formulation: Jesus spends time alone with his disciples explaining his public parables. Curiously, though, even to them he is not forthcoming about his identity and authority. He remains resolutely indirect about this: there does seem to be something wrong with direct words on this subject. Why this is so I shall endeavor soon to explain, but first we need to introduce another vehicle of indirection that depends for its success on the viewer's own condition, and like parable demands the activity of interpretation. This vehicle is the *sign;* it plays a prominent role in a puzzling incident that will reinforce our understanding of the kind of indirection Jesus employs.

The puzzle comes in chapter 8, after the feeding of the four thousand. (Remember, this is a second incident, after the five thousand in chapter 6). Jesus and his disciples have left the area by boat; when they land, the Pharisees are there to argue, asking for a sign. Jesus lets out one of his groans, states that no sign will be given to this generation, and gets back into the boat. On the return trip he warns the disciples to be on strict guard against the "leaven of the Pharisees" and of Herod. What this "leaven" is to mean, apart from its obvious symbolism as a pervasive influence, is itself puzzling: Matthew calls it the teaching of the Pharisees (16.6), Luke their hypocrisy (12.1). The disciples certainly got it wrong: their thinking slid associatively to bread, and their forgetfulness to bring enough on the trip. Jesus fastens instead on their forgetfulness about what he had done—twice—with a few loaves, and asks them—twice—whether they still don't understand. In words repeated from chapter 4, they have eyes but don't see, ears but do not hear. On arriving at Bethsaida, he then takes a blind man outside the village and touches his eyes—twice—until he sees clearly.

To put the puzzle succinctly, if the disciples were wrong to associate leaven with bread, what are the proper associations between signs and leaven and bread and seeing? Who knows? The very nature of the material is open-ended, but here is a reading that at least coheres with what I have said so far about the nature of Jesus' authority. When Jesus sighs at the demand for a sign, it is a groan of exasperation in the face of a cognitive condition he is powerless to correct—a kind of mental obstinacy about what constitutes a sign. Signs are not events that sport their meaning on their sleeves; they are events regarded in certain ways, "invested with" a significance. They are, if you like, *parabolic* events in which something more is pointed to for discernment and recognition. Now given his recent activity, what *more* could Jesus do? Any action he performed could be subjected to competing interpretations, attributed again to the prince of demons. This utter inability to give a sign to those who will not receive the giving *as* a sign weighs on Jesus' mind. He remembers the earlier dullness of the disciples, their inability to grasp the significance of his first feeding of the five thousand (Mark's account here recalls his comment in 6.52 about their closed minds—in a boat after a feeding miracle). So Jesus warns them against the pervasive mind-set of the Pharisees—and immediately discovers that his own followers continue to participate in this lack of discernment: they think about bread as food instead of bread as sign. Getting out of the boat, he is able to exercise his power over physical blindness in answer to a request for healing. But his ability to give sight cannot penetrate to hearts and minds that will not open themselves to the seeing. Perhaps that is why Mark's Jesus is so relieved in the next chapter to find an openness in the possessed boy's father, whose cry, "I believe; help my unbelief!" (9.24), parallels the blind man's honest confession that he could see people only *as* walking trees, and his *looking hard* (Mark's verb stresses attentiveness) in order to see clearly after Jesus' second touch.

We're now in a position to appreciate one large reason for Jesus' indirect approach to his identity. It has to do with his *powerlessness* to control what it is that his hearers hear. They may shut up their ears; his viewers may will a blindness that he cannot cure. Just as the leper could not be ordered effectively into silence, so disciples and critics alike cannot be made to see what is before their eyes. We could call this a recognition of *epistemic freedom* on the part of Mark's Jesus, an acknowledgment that his authority cannot override the interpretive decisions of his listeners. But we shouldn't think that somehow Jesus makes a gift of this freedom to some, as though it's something he could deny to others. That does not seem to be within his competence at all. Storms, demons, diseases—over these he holds power, but not over unbelief. Because belief and unbelief both depend upon an unforced contribution on the part of the listener, indirect presentation is the only appropriate form of discourse.

There are two other features of discourse in Mark that to my mind betray an unwillingness or inability to dictate precise formulations of belief. Where understanding is won by attentive looking rather than telling, then devices to draw that attention are required. Maybe this is why *repetition* is important for Mark, and not just in the double actions I just noted. There are two sabbath questionings, two commissionings of the Twelve, two storm stillings, two blind men healed, two child blessings, two discussions of greatness. It's as though Mark's Jesus wants to be sure that the attention of his followers is focused by repetition on events and conversations that yield up material for reflection. (Mark himself perhaps worries that his readers may be as dull as the disciples.) And there is another device to downplay pedagogical authority by inviting contribution from the hearer, this time in the very syntax of discourse. Although I have emphasized above Jesus' use of commands that are immediately obeyed, it is important to see that these commands are usually for healing in the spheres of the natural and demonic. When his own identity and authority are at stake, or when he is attempting to communicate his teaching, the dominant syntactic form is not command or statement but question. If his is not quite the serial questioning of Socrates, designed to expose ignorance, it is questioning nonetheless. Mark's Jesus looks for deliberate response that will participate in coming at answers, not a simple negative or positive response.

Parable, sign, questioning, repetition: all of these devices require or invite the hearer to play a determinative role in arriving at understanding. I have suggested that Mark's Jesus proceeds in these ways because of a powerlessness to control the cognitive choices of his listeners, but there may be one other necessary reason for his indirection.

Suppose that someone's identity is difficult to put into the right words, partly because of its uniqueness, partly because the most appropriate language would be readily misunderstood and rejected. This supposition doesn't have to be far from experience. Think, for example, of a young child who has lost a father and whose mother is recently remarried. The new husband gains an ambiguous identity for the child, which may be difficult to express in appropriate language if he is to be *in the place of father* to the child. For in order truly to be in that place, he cannot simply constitute the relationship by announcing it. The child must recognize and accept; and such acceptance is often won only through words and behavior that open up possibilities instead of demanding a particular response.

Now, the example cannot be squeezed too hard. Nevertheless, there is something of importance in it. To recognize who Mark's Jesus is means according him a unique place and relationship, one that he cannot simply constitute by naming it himself. Were he to name it, our cognitive guard would go up so quickly that we wouldn't be able to see or hear properly. Of course, the more theoretically minded followers of Jesus quickly got interested in the naming, from which has grown a thick-stemmed, many-branched discipline called Christology. I'm impressed, though, that the indirection of Jesus in Mark leaves the full determination and disclosure of his identity outside his control. He surrenders that work to his hearers.

It is not irrelevant that although the truths he is interested in are not truths about himself, Plato's Socrates also employs indirection in his philosophical work. After giving Socrates a little time on his pedagogic approach, we will summarize what we have learned about pedagogic authority as hidden before returning to the obedience of Jesus.

Socratic Indirection For the present, our guiding concern must be the way Socrates exercises the authority of his philosophical vocation in Athens. He has some sort of status: a circle of followers grew up around him, young men felt his influence, and his words carried enough weight to bring him to trial. How does he regard his own authority?

Of little account, it seems. Socrates refuses to identify himself with those professional teachers, called sophists, who command a fee for their expertise. Their very label suggests that they have some kind of wisdom to impart. And with knowledge, it's assumed, comes pedagogic authority: those in the know should speak the content of their minds, and those who need that content should listen and accept it. Teaching is the transfer of contents from one place to another by a licensed mover—or, to use the hydraulics metaphor proposed ironically in the *Symposium*, it's the syphoning of wisdom from one vessel to the next.

Socrates, though, prefers to talk in the city's public places to anybody willing to take part in discussions on topics about which it is difficult to find experts. Although some assume that he thinks himself expert because he can poke holes in the answers he gets, Socrates (as we have seen) denies such authority. His own ignorance won't allow it. If he has nothing to impart, he won't charge a fee.

Plato's readers, like the jury in the *Apology*, sometimes doubt that Socrates can be serious about this. He does have convictions: we saw that he is willing to die rather than to abandon the fundamental principles that govern his life. Moreover, he wants others to share those convictions and to change their way of living. True: but it doesn't follow that Socrates believes that the best pedagogic activity is a straight telling on the part of someone considered an authority. I have three points to make about that.

First, we can't get very far in setting out Socratic beliefs before we encounter what scholars (not the character Socrates or Plato himself) call *Socratic paradoxes*. Among these are the claims that nobody does wrong willingly (or intentionally or knowingly—the term is hard to translate); that no one wishes evil; that virtue is knowledge; that vice is ignorance. The list may be expanded to include questions about the teachability of virtue that depend on virtue's relation to knowledge and on how knowledge gets taught. Naturally enough, commentators debate formulations and interpretations and are unclear about what the historical Socrates might have spoken on these matters. Here, though, we worry only about Plato's presentation: and his Socrates must be said to promote a series of terse claims like the ones just mentioned. Even if they are not all paradoxes strictly speaking, still they generate puzzles for the mind to turn over. My point, then, is simple: the aphorisms propounded by Socrates can hardly be said to be fully articulated theories or beliefs in his mind. They don't enjoy a developed meaning to be taught—and at least in this way they function much like the parables of Jesus. Both need that interpretive contribution from the listener.

My second point is about the devotion of Socrates to the question as his primary form of speech. His mission begins in interrogation, of course, as he seeks to know who is wise and who is not. But Plato keeps him asking throughout the course of his philosophic life. To ask is to get the other person to do the telling, so that Socrates doesn't need to uncover the contents of his own mind. More, it permits him to expose the muddles and inconsistencies in the answers he gets, so that the results of his investigations are invariably negative. But he does have a genuine reason for this approach, beyond intellectual modesty or argumentative perversity. He is convinced that you are in no fit state to appreciate your lack of hold on the truth until you have undergone the kind of refutation that he's so skilled at. Telling you will do no good if you are deafened by inflated judgment. You have to repent, change your mind, and open yourself to seeking the truth.

Third, Socrates would keep to the question even if he knew the answer. I don't mean by that claim to abandon Socrates' peculiar ignorance of matters on which there are no human experts. Rather, what's on my mind is the well-known episode with the slave in the *Meno*, in which Socrates extracts from an untutored boy the geometric truth about doubling the area of a square. This is often regarded as a neatly characteristic example of the *Socratic method*, whereas in fact it is highly unusual just because Socrates does in this case know the answer to the problem he poses. Still, he keeps saying throughout the episode that he isn't *telling* the slave boy anything; instead of teaching him, he is asking him questions to help him get out what's already within his mind. Now again, scholars write much about the justice of Plato's description of what Socrates is up to—but I do think we can appreciate the difference between rote repetition of theorems and solutions and a coming to see for oneself the way a solution works. Socrates has at least that difference in mind when he points out that the answer has come from within the boy's mind and can be turned into knowledge through repeated questioning. So part of what Socrates' method involves is getting the hearers to work it out for themselves, following the argument instead of the teacher. Questions demand that sort of participation.

For these reasons, then, we cannot place Socrates in the role of pedagogic authority who serves up things to be believed. In spite of his striking personal presence, he hides himself by the indirection of his teaching so that his hearers come to bear responsibility for what they themselves learn. Undoubtedly the most memorable image for this Socratic pedagogy comes in the *Theaetetus*, where Socrates calls himself a midwife who assists at the birth of wisdom in others. Why this is only *assistance* we'll consider later, but here we need only to note that the image of knowledge born in the soul decisively rejects the content-transfer model of learning. Behind this image lies a larger Platonic vision of soul and the nature of knowledge, in which human learning is characterized as *recollecting* what the mind saw most clearly in a discarnate state. And in Plato's theory of education, it is impossible to put knowledge into someone else's soul, as impossible as giving blind eyes their sight. All one can do is to turn the soul around, convert it from attention to the wrong realm, so that it can employ the power of vision it already has (*Republic* VII, 518).

We could pursue more ways in which Plato's Socrates attempts to tease understanding out of his interlocutors; we could also raise important questions about the success of his method, when hardly anybody seems to be able to deliver healthy intellectual offspring in a discussion with him. Nevertheless that's another day's work.

Hidden Authority For we can now agree that indirection marks the discourse of Jesus and the philosophic interrogation of Socrates. Both are to be found asking questions as a way of diverting attention from their own minds; when they make assertions, both tend toward the terse, cryptic aphorism or the parable that points beyond itself. Plato makes his Socrates speak of a turning around in order to see; Mark's Jesus engages in repetition in order to hold up his words and deeds for inspection. Hearers must attend to parable, viewers to sign, with their own ears and eyes.

In the case of Socrates as well as Jesus, indirection is used to hide authority for compelling reasons. Neither wants to be made use of as an Authority in the realm of faith or knowledge. Were it otherwise, they would have provided clear answers to perplexities, answers to be taken on trust because of their expert identities. Socrates is no expert, so in a deeply serious fashion he would claim to have no authority to be hidden. Instead, he hides his own mind in order to bring to birth knowledge in those whom he questions. For Jesus the matter is different. Mark paints vividly his power over things in heaven and earth, but in spite of that authority, Jesus hides his identity. Partly, we saw, that's because his identity is difficult to get into the right words without misunderstanding. It is also because of the powerlessness of Jesus over the kind of seeing and hearing that constitutes belief or unbelief. Though Mark would not agree with Plato on the impossibility of putting sight into blind eyes, his Jesus would understand well the need for viewers to do the looking for themselves. The authority of Jesus must be hidden because it is properly constituted only in the work of discovering for oneself what it means.

There are, you may guess, implications in hiddenness and indirection for what it means to listen to Jesus or to be persuaded by Socrates—that is, implications for our understanding of obedience. We'll come to that after we return to the obedience of Jesus.

Obedience as Authority Inverted

I have claimed that a good reason for indirection would be that there's something wrong with attempts to put one's point plainly: the hearer, for example, may have erected defenses against the message. But I have also suggested that indirection works where it is difficult to get the point into the right words, and that this might be true of the identity of Jesus. It is time to move this suggestion to the matter of the *authority* of Jesus. For, in fact, what Jesus says about power is paradoxical; and by the end of Mark's Gospel the ways in which he exercises his own personal authority demonstrate an inversion of our common assumptions. This inversion turns out to be another reason for the hiddenness and indirection of his authority with respect to his hearers and viewers.

Consider the teaching of Mark's Jesus about power. He says some simple but hard things about that—twice. When he and his disciples arrive at Capernaum in chapter 9, Jesus ingenuously asks the group what they'd been arguing about on the way—generating embarrassment, because he had caught them discussing who among them was greatest. With his arm around a child, Jesus identifies receiving a little one with receiving him (and the one who sent him), having stated that it is the last of all, the servant of all, who is first. The disciples don't get the point: a while later (10.13–16) they try to keep children away from Jesus. And James and John still don't get it, for on the way to Jerusalem (in that incident we considered earlier in Matthew's version) they ask to sit on the right and left hands of Jesus in his glory (Mark 10.35–45). Jesus uses the misunderstanding to speak specifically about authority. The common pattern ("among the Gentiles" is the way he puts it) is this: *rulers lord it over their subjects, the great wield their authority over them.* That is not for the followers of Jesus: *their great must be servants, their first the slave of everyone else.*

The paradoxical saying is so simple and at least to Christian believers so familiar that its implications for authority and obedience slide too easily by. Three things are worth stressing. First, though a paradox, the saying does not hide anything about Jesus' view of authority. If he won't come out with his own identity, nevertheless he does not conceal his mind about the exercise of power among his followers. Second, what is revealed in this mind is nothing less than the abdication of authority, the surrendering of status, the placing of oneself under obedience. And third, the view would remain a paradox of language alone, were the saying not followed by the actuality of the next verse: for indeed *the son of man did not come to be served but to serve, and to give his life a ransom for many.* Jesus did not come to be obeyed but to be obedient, even to death.

These observations may be filled out a little. Mark uses repetition to provoke reflection upon power, as we have seen, with two child blessings and two discussions of greatness. But other sayings of Jesus convey the same paradoxical inversions. Think of that wealthy man of impeccable conduct whose heart was in his worldly treasure (10.17–22): his status will not buy him a place in the kingdom. The disciples are completely amazed at this (10.23–28), for it is the privilege of the rich to enjoy whatever goods (including therefore, they suppose, eternal goods) they desire. Not so, for Jesus: wealth must be given to the poor, and the privilege of position emptied out. A like point is made in the losing-life-to-save-it saying (8.34–37), where the paradox extends to the release of control over one's own self. And were we to leave Mark to put the question of status to Matthew or Luke, the evidence of the Beatitudes would reinforce the conviction that this is a message of reversal in power and rank.

But we should not misunderstand this reversal. That the mighty should be thrown down and the humble exalted—this may appeal to egalitarian instincts, even (more often than we are happy to admit) to the desire for our turn at the trough. Reversals in position, our history tells us, usually mean only different players in the same game. What Jesus seems to be after is giving up the game altogether, an inversion in the very meaning of power. We use whatever authority we can garner in order to preserve our lives and advance our individual and collective interests, even when we do not act crassly and in disregard of the welfare of others. We often obey just for the same reasons, because our own welfare depends on those who have authority over us. Maybe, just, we could comprehend a redemptive deployment of power that would serve human need without thinking of personal reward or gain: we do have examples of such selfless behavior in a few saints even in our own day, despite widespread cynicism about political power. But Jesus goes further. He abdicates all power and control, even the good kind that can make a difference to the world (like the ability to create bread from stones), and hands himself over in obedience. That's why this is an inversion, not a redemption, of authority.

And Jesus does exemplify this inversion. Without that, we would be tempted to read into his sayings the cyclical view of power reversals. Instead, Mark's story put in a sentence comes to this: power great beyond imagination empties itself into unthinkable weakness. In our need to translate the gospel accounts of healings and exorcisms into words that taste better in our mouths, we run the danger of distorting the fundamental line of this story. ("Crowd turns against popular rabbi," or "Well-known teacher miscalculates extent of his support"— you can no doubt write other headlines.) That Mark's Jesus exercises authority beyond that of any teacher or prophet is essential to our understanding of the emptying out of his power. Authority, however divine, seeks to serve by turning into obedience.

There are two icons of this paradox in chapter 15, complex in their irony. The first icon uses the trappings of regal power, a purple robe and a crown. Jesus is stripped of his own garment, once so charged with power that touching its border could heal; he is invested with clothing supposed to signify supreme authority, but the robe is borrowed and the crown thorny. The second icon is a literal sign, lettered to read HO BASILEUS TÔN IOUDAIÔN, the King of the Jews; the words are not an acclamation but a charge against him. The perpetrators think they're being mockingly ironic because Jesus must be the victim of a grand delusion. The irony for the reader of Mark sits in the misunderstanding of these mockers, who truly do not know what they are doing to one whose authority extends far beyond their imaginings. But under that lies another and more troubling irony: these icons really do signify what the inversion of authority means for Jesus. It is a stripping off of his own power, a submission to the distorted misreadings of his identity, an uncompromising obedience even to the death of the cross.

Such is the obedience of Jesus. It is, and it is not, like Socratic obedience. We can appreciate some similarity in their locating the grounds for obedience in the divine will. Jesus does all that he has to do because it is the will of his Father that he drink this cup. Socrates knows, through the meanings of oracle and sign, that the death in his cup is the will of the god. While we cannot pretend that both of them would share identical beliefs about the object of their ultimate allegiance, still we see that this commitment functions to relativize all other authorities.

Yet two differences beg for notice, the straightforward one leading to a more radical dissimilarity.

For it's clear that Mark's Jesus does not exhibit the kind of concern to be *law-abiding* that Socrates shows. In large measure we can account for this by remembering that their trials are presented very differently. Socrates has recourse to due legal procedures, even if he does not manipulate the situation to his own immediate advantage. Although the jury reaches the wrong verdict about his guilt, he at least has taken the opportunity to convince them about what's right. Having participated in the process, and knowing independently that the outcome is the god's will, Socrates is able to hold up respect for law as an outward sign of his obedience. Not so with Jesus. Mark has told us several times before the Entry into Jerusalem that Jesus will be put to death by the religious and civil authorities, so there is no uncertainty, no suspense, around the trials. It's not even a question whether fair judicial procedures could be employed to save him, and as we well saw in Chapter 2, he makes no defense. Scripture and the will of his Father form his hiding place, not law. Not that Jesus had been especially observant of law and custom before his arrest—quite the contrary. When Socrates went against duly established authority, he did it quietly and without challenging the rules themselves. He manifested that tough independence from others in what he claimed to value and to know. Jesus, however, takes on the rules and regulations directly, breaking with custom about sabbath observance and ritual washing in particular. His challenges to established authority are pointed, hard, and (in the Temple cleansing) even violent.

And that leads to the recognition that Mark's Jesus acts this way because he appropriates for himself a kind of authority that a Socrates would find puzzling, inappropriate to a human being. Socratic obedience maintains a consistency across his life, trial, and death; it is born in an intellectual humility that conforms to the will of the god because he does not know what may be to his harm and what to his final good. Socratic law-abidingness, then, makes sense as a sacramental expression of this state of mind, in order that his unique social location may be seen to spring not simply from his own desires and perceptions. But the hiddenness and indirection that we've seen in Mark's Jesus creates the strong suspicion that for him it is entirely different. His unique location is close to the Father, replete with that sort of authority; from that place he challenges the forms of lawfulness cherished by religious leadership. Only in his Passion does Jesus relinquish his privileged position, so that there is for him (as not for Socrates) a turning toward obedience as his authority is inverted. Instead of retaining sufficient presence of mind to mount an argument about what obedience means in his circumstances, Jesus explains nothing. He empties himself.

And the outward and visible marks of this elemental conformity to the will of his Father? The visibility takes the form of all those signs of powerlessness we've recalled in his somatic relinquishment, the marks of his Passion. The sacramental expression of obedience for Jesus is nothing other than the cross.

One last comment about the nature of obedience as the inversion of authority. Surely it is significant that this is no ordinary authority that Mark presents for our attention. We see here the nature of divine authority and might, so commonly understood as temporal power extended into ultimacy. Because we often feel that temporal power subsumes our little lives in its own ends, we experience powerlessness and insignificance in the presence of the Almighty. But that's a misapprehension built out of attending only to our own limitations, if I am at all on the right course with Mark. For his Jesus discloses the self-imposed *powerlessness of God* as the Son becomes obedient to death. There is Divine Authority to be sure, but its form is Divine Obedience. And it has our good as its end.

We had seen that Jesus is incapable of putting the eyes of faith into those who are determined not to see. He hides his identity and authority because their very constitution depends upon the activity of looking and looking in order to discover. And now, having looked again at the exercise of his authority and its emptying out in relinquishment, what we've discovered is nothing other than obedience. His turning of power upside down to drain into weakness so controverts our all-too-human notions of authority that, unless we had seen, never would we have believed.

Exemplary Obedience

There are things to be learned about obedience from both Socrates and Jesus, some of them not easy lessons. Neither of them makes it possible to regard obedience as unworthy of exemplary human beings, commendable only in most dogs and some children. But neither justifies obedience to authority by asking us to conform in the name of a greater social good. Both maintain a pronounced independence of thought and behavior: they are not woven neatly into their social fabric, as obedient personality types should be. Yet because they obey something other than their own voices, they call us to reflect on how we might come to understand not just that sometimes obedience is a duty but more importantly that there are virtues to be cultivated in a form of obedience for human lives. In the remainder of the chapter I'll try to sketch the broad lines along which obedience should be rehabilitated as a virtue. That will be difficult in two ways: it's not easy to overcome our suspicion of the very term, and it also takes work to develop the practice that a better understanding would commend.

In setting out, then, we have to dismiss the easy hope that obedience belongs only to a chosen few, martyrs like Jesus or Socrates. Those who die as witnesses do exhibit a heroic obedience, hard because of its great cost, but the rest of us may find that carrying on with a truly responsible living requires an obedience alike in kind if not degree.

Obedience as Listening

The most important thing to be said at the start, deserving of its own paragraph, is deceptively simple:
Obedience is a kind of listening.

We knew that, of course, from etymology: the main root of the idea in Greek, Latin, and English is aural, and even the business of "being persuaded" requires a hearing. But the ancestry of the word aside, the very experience of what I'm now going to call *exemplary obedience* has to involve something like listening.

This means that, of the two aspects in obeying that we uncovered early in the chapter, I have to stress the intentionality of the agent over the conformity of action to command. In other words, the obedience that we should be interested in isn't merely the following of an order. That can be done out of habit, grudgingly or minimally (as when made to apologize to your sister), or even in mocking and ironic fashion, with raised brow or exaggerated attention to detail. We know many devices to preserve our independence while appearing to fall in line. And maybe it's because we so often experience this dissonance between what we ourselves really want and what we have to end up doing that we regard obedience as a bad compromise. The actions and attitudes we praise as virtuous can't have such a flavor; they must proceed from a whole-hearted willingness in the agent. So if obedience is to be exemplary, it has to be characterized by the right attitude—if we can find it.

That attitude is expressed, I claim, in *listening*. Although it is a kind of aural experience, I haven't called it *hearing*, so I need to explain a distinction not always preserved tidily in English usage. The point is straightforward: hearing may go on without our full awareness, but listening requires that we pay attention to what we hear. If you need an example, think of the difference between hearing snatches of conversation at the restaurant table next to you, and actually listening to that conversation. To listen, you must stop doing other things in order to concentrate on what you hear. We have already considered something of what's involved in attentiveness in the chapter on prayer, so we know that, though we become quiet to listen, listening requires *our activity*.

That's important. Being truly obedient doesn't mean becoming the passive extension of somebody else's will. Its somatic gesture is not the bowed head or exposed neck; it's the cocked ear.

Another simple feature of obedience as listening is equally important. What's listened to is a voice not your own. Otherwise you are just paying attention to your schemes and desires, trying to listen to whatever your own self speaks. Sometimes we have to do that, but those who follow only their own interests or instincts are egocentric and self-indulgent. We don't find them morally praiseworthy. We do, however, regard with moral admiration those who pay attention to needs and desires beyond their own, who advance plans for the good of others. Such selflessness requires a listening to a place outside the self. And that's a necessary ingredient in obedience. Of course, degenerate forms of obedience also listen to outside voices, so we must add that it's crucial to turn one's ear in the right direction. Included in the activity of listening, then, is a discrimination among authorities demanding our allegiance.

One more feature of this listening: it is also *heeding*. The voice heard and attended to is found, upon reflection, to be persuasive. And therefore we act. When we lack resolve, we can be great explorers of the gap between what goes on in our heads and what goes on in the world, between what's right to do and what we actually get done. In the notion of heeding, however, are brought together the listening and the doing, for heeding makes true in the world the words addressed to us. We can hear deliberately and consciously, then fail for some reason to act—but then we don't heed what's said. In order to heed we must both listen and do. That's exactly what is involved in exemplary obedience: the hand accomplishes with resolve what the attentive ear hears.

The Work of Exemplary Obedience

Unworthy voices counsel things to our detriment or the diminishment of goodness; we can heed those voices in foolish or vicious acts. But there's no point in throwing out all forms of obedience along with the bad, for sometimes we are morally required to listen and heed. There are several spheres within human experience where a virtuous obedience becomes a necessity and should be cultivated. I'll explore next what an exemplary obedience might accomplish when we already know in some sense what's right, when we are puzzled about that, and when we are faced with conditions that seem to contradict our good.

The Word in the Heart Here's a hard confession: more often than I'd like to acknowledge, I know what it is I should do. I don't do it not because I am ignorant of the good or perverse about seeking evil but because I give my time and attention to lesser tasks.

Now if observation serves me, this is a pretty common feature of human moral psychology. In more obvious form, the phenomenon becomes known as weakness of will or moral weakness, where I am somehow powerless to accomplish the good I approve. Whether it's a Phaedra confessing the domination of passion over clear knowledge about the good or a Saint Paul complaining that the good he wants to do he doesn't do but that he does the evil he doesn't want to do, they speak for all of us who have found ourselves paralyzed in that gap between knowing and doing.

Plato's Socrates tackles the problem of moral weakness by proposing that there's something wrong with our claim to know the good when we get into these fixes. Had we a firm grasp on the good, we'd find our knowledge strong enough to get us through the distractions of pleasure or fear or cowardice. Because Socrates himself exhibits unusual self-control, it's credible that he considered ignorance the cause of wrongdoing. The rest of us aren't so sure of this diagnosis. But I don't think it helpful here simply to claim that, say, lack of listening is a better explanation. It would be true, of course—by definition—that we do wrong because we *don't heed* the right. But instead of trying to come up with a fully adequate explanation for our behavior around moral weakness, we need to come up with a cure. And that's why I am interested in obedience as listening and heeding.

For it does seem true, if I move away from extreme cases where I'm morally paralyzed by an alien grip on my will, that much of the time I suffer from a kind of moral laziness or distractibility. Lots of other good things need doing, by which I can always justify my putting off this one needful thing. What I need may not be as strong as deliverance from a foreign power but simply the disciplined exercise of my own half-hearted will.

The cure, then, is a matter of exercise rather than strong surgical intervention. And that exercise is the discipline of exemplary obedience.

Not that talk of discipline goes down more smoothly than the language of obedience—on the contrary, it may stick in the throat as dry fiber foisted on us by those nutritionists of the soul who know much better than do we what's supposedly for our good. Still, it's adolescent to continue to indulge our appetites just because we may have broken away from an imposed joyless regimen. Socrates calls us to a life of self-examination, asking us to face up to our own responsibility for our soul's health. Jesus calls us to repent and to seek the will of God in radical trust. If we hold up either of these figures against our own practices, it's impossible to escape questions about how we bring some order and discipline into our lives.

I'm not competent to answer in this kind of writing questions that require different harmonies for different lives; but it is possible to hint at a context in which they may be played out. What's important, I suggest, is the way we see our moral practice, how we are willing to characterize it to ourselves. It's one thing to regard your life as accountable in the end to nobody else; it's quite another to live it as a member of a community, interlocked with the welfare of others. For in the latter case, my failure to do the good isn't my concern alone; it has an effect upon those I care for and who care for me. It's also important, I think, that we see the goods we espouse as something more than personal preferences to be modified at will. Otherwise, it's too easy to rationalize my failures to heed the right voice by telling myself I've just decided to do things differently. We need to become morally serious about our good, and the intertwined good of our community, if we are to overcome the temptation to fiddle around with lesser things.

When we view our moral practice as exemplary obedience, we move some distance toward this goal. For—as Socrates believed—what's right for us may also be what God wills for us. Forget the distraction of whether the divine will actually determines the right; focus instead on the simple fact that our ultimate good cannot be other than what God intends. It follows that, whenever and however I conclude something to be what I *really ought to do,* I may also regard this as a listening to God from beyond my self. That means my heeding is done as to God, not merely to a set of shifting interests whose configuration has no importance for others. This invests what I already know to be right with moral and religious seriousness and makes my practice accountable to God as well as myself. For some, such language may well dredge up the memories of a stultifying fear of God promoted by stern parental or ecclesiastical authorities. It need not be that way. Listening to what's right, and heeding it, may be acts of courage in which divine grace and power are discovered because they are carried out as though in the presence of the God who cares.

For us to accomplish what we know we should, then, may require a virtuous obedience. I've titled this section "The Word in the Heart" after a phrase in the conclusion of Moses' extended speech about obedience in Deuteronomy. He there sums up the instruction he's been giving by pointing out that the commandment is not too difficult or too remote. You don't have to climb into heaven to discover it, or cross the seas to find it: "No, the word is very near to you; it is in your mouth and in your heart for you to observe" (30.14 NRSV).

It's that *word in the heart* to which I must attend in virtuous obedience, listening for more than my own voice in its speaking. This is especially so when I fear the truth I half-know and refuse to speak to myself the meaning of the word lodged in my heart. In the cacophonies of anxiety and dread, I need the courage to listen faithfully. If that puts us back a chapter into the attentiveness that is found in exemplary prayer, should we be surprised?

The Discerning of Signs Suppose what's most unlikely: that I could act in accordance with what I know to be right much more often than I now do. Such obedience might help me to see more clearly by overcoming the petty self-deceptions whose companionship I welcome when the way ahead looks too difficult. Nevertheless, the moral life would still present problems requiring another step in obedience. For I do not always know what I should do, even when I have tried to listen faithfully. Or to put the point in religious terms, the will of God remains on many occasions frustratingly opaque if not entirely inaccessible. What could it mean to be obedient when you're puzzled about what to do?

The first thing to note is that this is indeed our human condition, and especially our condition as believers. We pretend, it is true, that it's otherwise. As nature abhors a vacuum so our minds abhor unknowing: we make up our certainties out of whatever's at hand. If some believers claim to know details of the Divine Plan unavailable to the rest of us, they are only presenting their local symptoms of a widespread affliction. And one can see why they hold to the will of God as Divine Plan. For one thing, it's part of the faith that God is sovereign over nature and history; it's also part of the teaching of Jesus that God's care extends to details of our existence we don't think of ourselves. If human intelligence can do the work of planning lives, surely an omnipotent and omniscient deity must have a model or blueprint that may be followed in obedience.

I've let it out that I think this a misunderstanding. Experience doesn't support the claim that human beings may enjoy such privilege; in fact, such contrary things have been attributed to the divine will that we'd be in a hopeless mess if we tried to heed all voices using God's name. Instead of such clarity we have only what T. S. Eliot calls "hints and guesses, / Hints followed by guesses." More, even assuming a divinable Divine Plan, there's no good reason to suppose that it would set out all the right choices for our lives. We do not think it proper to map out the minutiae of life for our children: they couldn't be said to live *their* lives if they only and always followed in detail what we told them to do. So we need an appreciation of the will of God that creates authentic space for our own willings—as indeed we recognized in thinking how prayer may be not limp resignation but protest, and how seeking the will of the Father clarifies our desires.

The implications in this for obedience are not insignificant. But then that's no surprise, given what we've learned of the relation between authority and obedience in both Socrates and Jesus. Go back to that for a moment, for each will help in a different way. Socrates impresses upon us our responsibility to give birth to knowledge from within. He holds up puzzles for our inspection and prods us with questions but refuses to do the work of giving out understanding—only because that's not work a teacher can do. It's up to the learner to seek and to find. Perhaps disturbingly for anyone who takes religious faith to mean believing things on divine say-so, we learned much the same from the indirection and hiddenness of authority in Jesus. Jesus is as incapable of eradicating unbelief as is Socrates unable to hand out knowledge. Mark requires us to look and to look, to uncover for ourselves the identity of Jesus. When we do that we discover a difference from Socrates, for Jesus exercises such large authority. Yet if we grant him authority for our lives, so that we try to live in obedience to God through him, he turns the questions back to us. We've got to make the interpretative moves about the will of God; it's up to us to do the reading. And what we are given is not map or blueprint; it is *sign*.

It's worth pausing over that word for a moment, in order to let it correct a very different view of the will of God. This is a view reminiscent of the interpretation of Socratic obedience to the god as nothing more than moral sincerity. In Christian context, it confesses such agnosticism about the mind of God that it reduces God's will to those general moral principles and precepts that can be established on other grounds. We know that truthtelling is obligatory, that torture is wrong, that generosity is a virtue; so as religious people we can also attach to these items the label of the divine will. Such thinking overcomes the embarrassment of too much confidence about God's specific intentions and may seem appropriately humble. Unfortunately, it does not show how it is possible for God to have intentions about real people in concrete situations, or how the divine will is related to the divine love that seeks not good-in-general but our own good. That love, I have suggested, is manifested not in the giving of orders but in the presentation of signs, a great grand mixture of parable, clue, irony, paradox—words and events that have to be looked at and listened to.

It is wrong, then, to let models of obedience as following somebody else's orders infect our understanding of listening to and heeding the will of God. Exemplary obedience participates in the determination of what it is that God wills.

Why, however, should we regard this as obedience and not something else? In a way, the term isn't appropriate to a situation much more complex than simple conforming response to command. The outcomes of a process of investigating the meaning of signs are too precarious to be placed alongside the "compliance with orders" notion of obedience. Nevertheless, I propose that there remains a role for the virtue of obedience in the responsible determination of the will of God.

The obedience lies *in the seeking.* While the discernment of what it is we ought to do in the will of God must be partly up to us, the decision to undertake that very exercise may be made in response to the call of God. We heed that voice from beyond ourselves, having listened (if we may return to the previous section) to the word in the heart that confirms what we already know, that this seeking is for our true good. Obedience is that stance from which we see the events of our lives as signs and puzzles that may disclose the divine will. Were we not poised to listen, there would come no word to hear; conversely, when we are so poised, then we are ready to heed the word which does come.

I conclude that exemplary obedience is necessary when I am puzzled about what to do, for only by obeying the call to interpret the signs will I discover whether there is the word in the heart for my situation. That demands persistence and faithfulness in the face of ambiguity, a trust that God's good will may be discerned. So again such obedience is no easy virtue; again its exercise requires discipline.

The Discoveries of Suffering What, though, of those most difficult experiences that remain impenetrable? I'm thinking of the hard conditions of life that are laid unevenly upon us, and that do not feel like the works of a loving care. Chronic pain, the wound in the soul, an untimely death—you will be able to write your own list. They eat dangerously at our centers, threatening if not utterly to destroy then to damage and disfigure us. Should we grant them the character of signs, they would look only readable as counting against the goodwill of God.

Now in fact, we think of such intractable suffering in many ways: our sorry lot; our fate; the cross we have to bear; just bad luck; what we deserve; the blind intersection of processes running their natural course. But this "thinking of" discloses a range of attitudes we take up toward the events and meanings of our lives, and among those attitudes is the stance of listening. It's possible, I suggest, to learn obedience in such situations.

That's obedience, not resignation. The last chapter disposed, I trust, of the misunderstanding that seeking the will of God in prayer requires the surrender of one's own willing. We do not obey by giving up. In spite of the admirable discipline of someone who can settle and silence all emotion, withdrawing from the presence of pain or suffering, that way does not look to me the path of obedience. Instead the faithful are called to the activities of paying attention, of puzzling out significance, of discerning the signs—and of heeding. That may well involve the protest and persistence of prayer. Almost certainly the learning of obedience will situate us not among the impervious gods but within the fragilities of human existence, where we can join hands with others and listen to their voices. We may even find, if we sit down and get to know the hard things, a double grace: the power to change a little some things we had thought intractable, and the ability to persevere past the limits we feared would destroy us.

In proposing that we might learn obedience in our suffering, I haven't fully identified what or whom we are obeying. The object of "listening to" and "heeding" remains incomplete—something in our wounds and our pain, but let us be blunt: is their voice the voice of God? If I say No in order to protect divine goodness, then how can I continue to view my response as a prayerful obedience in which grace may be discovered? If I say Yes, how can I bear to see so much suffering within the will of a loving God?

From this Yes and this No springs a large part of philosophical theology, where God has been challenged or vindicated in a welter of attacks and theodicies. Although we seek an accounting for suffering-in-general, and for a theoretical consistency in our beliefs about God and human experience, I cannot here contribute to that search. For what we hear in our suffering is *partly up to us* and need not be determined entirely by some theory or other. (That's not unusual: theory is often inadequate to experience.) And when I take seriously what faithful people claim, I learn that they *listen for God* within their suffering. They might not (or might, for that matter) believe that God permits or sends suffering, but in a way that isn't for them the question. Maybe they *just don't know* how their hard afflictions figure in some larger scheme. They seem, though, to be willing to leave that knot unpicked and deposited with God. They would instead claim that their experience has a givenness that makes it appropriate to take up the attitude of obedience toward it; further, when they attend to their suffering, they discover within it divine grace and love. Theirs is an unshakable trust, whose very source springs from outside themselves; it carries them past blame, past even the discerning of signs, into the place where they share their suffering with God. Because many who speak this way lead lives of admirable moral depth, I cannot easily dismiss their witness. Indeed, we could do worse than to listen to them, if we are moved ourselves to learn obedience. They tell us that, although this learning requires much discipline (and why not, when any developed appreciation demands effort?), once taken upon us this yoke is easier, this burden lighter, than we might ever have thought possible.

Obedience and Love

The trust shown by those who listen for God suggests that the attitude of exemplary obedience may also be the attitude of love. As long as we remain gripped by the picture of a morally suspect submission to authority, we won't remember that it's possible to heed the voice of another not from fear or ignorance but out of a desire to delight the beloved. Such desires can themselves be unworthy, of course; nevertheless, that love's service may be rendered unwisely should not throw suspicion on all its forms. Because lovers do not order each other around, we don't usually think of loving relationships in the vocabulary of obedience. The structure of experience captured by the concept is not, however, foreign to love. There is a mature listening and mutual heeding that can rightly be called love's obedience. Think of a simple thing like planning and preparing a meal together. In that activity, likings and preferences are expressed, modified, and harmonized; each listens to what the other wants and finds satisfaction in fulfilling desires that are invested with the character of love's small imperatives. Or move from the pleasures of the table to the physical intimacies of love, where again mutuality listens to the other and fulfills those desires it knows only by attending to them. Without assertions of authority or submission to power, we may be tempted to miss the deeper marks of obedience in loving relationships. But where what's listened to with attention is the voice of the beloved, there obedience has been redeemed and become virtuous.

Could we carry the idea of a loving obedience back to the business of obeying the will of God? Almost certainly so: the two examples of obedience we have considered in this chapter encourage us to think of divine commands as the expression of love. Socrates regarded the necessity laid upon him as an expression of the care of the god; Jesus sought to follow not some impersonal duty but the will of his Father. Especially in Jesus' case obedience sits in the context of a loving relationship: as we will see in some detail in the next chapter, his obedient dying expresses the depth of his love for the Father and for his own followers—who show their love for him by keeping his commandments. If one conforms freely out of love to another's will, regarding that will as authoritative without being forced to do so, then it's hard to call that kind of obedience degenerate or morally unworthy.

All the same, my "almost certainly so" hides a small reservation about the appropriateness of placing obedience to God within the context of loving relationships. For the loving obedience I've pointed to requires a mutuality of concerned listening and heeding. Where power and authority are distributed unequally, mutuality is difficult to achieve. Sometimes in human relationships gone sadly wrong, the weaker creates a self-deceiving fiction about acting in love under the influence of the stronger. So even if there's a loving conformity to the will of another, we would want some assurance that obedience was intelligent and that the will so freely obeyed did wisely intend the good of the other. Now given the unimaginable disparity between human weakness and divine strength, it's difficult to rid ourselves of the suspicion that obedience to God is servile rather than freely offered in love. Yet without the confidence that God heeds our good in what we are given to do, a cosmic cognitive dissonance will infect religious obedience, forcing it to shore itself up with false promises and hopes. We must therefore ask: do those who trust God's good intentions in their suffering trust wisely?

I wish I could write words of easy assurance about that. Scripture and the collective experience we call tradition do provide examples of a willing obedience carried out in the confidence of divine love. Yet there remains a dark side in obedience to God, an unconditionality in divine command that must not be sentimentalized away.

Maybe the simplest and starkest way to face this comes in the demand for a supreme allegiance that God lays upon his people. This allegiance overrides all others, including the natural affections we think should be valued in families. And this theme, be warned, leads to an even more problematic demand.

God and Family How we order our affections and loyalties in families, and how natural attachments may come into conflict with wider social and religious duties—these have been enduring issues in human life. From our earliest literature and across many cultures, the entanglements between the bonds of kinship, morality, fate, and the divine have held peculiar fascination. Think of Abraham, required to sacrifice his only son, Isaac, or of unwitting Oedipus, who slays father and marries mother; think of our own preoccupation with parental sins against innocent children and our quest for therapeutic redemption. What our kind desperately needs is a weaving into harmony of our duties, our loves, and our ties, whereby we may enjoy the intimacy and acceptance of family affection as an intrinsic part of the fulfillments of the ethical life. Indeed, such relationships are enjoined as religious duties, both in the fifth commandment and in apostolic teaching.

And yet our tradition contains disturbing stories of an obedience to God that cuts against the natural grain of family affection. The Genesis 22 demand addressed to Abraham is best known: he is to offer to God the child of the promise, born beyond his and Sarah's expectation, his only son, *the son* (in an unnecessary emphasis) *he loves*. But there are other stories, too. In Exodus 32, Moses, having forced the disobedient Israelites to drink their calf-god ground into powder and mixed with water, calls upon those loyal to God to slay all who will not come over to the Lord's side. The Levites obey, killing three thousand of their own relatives and friends. Moses says to the Levites, "You have been installed as priests to the Lord today, because you have turned each against his own son and his own brother and so have brought a blessing this day upon yourselves" (32.29 REB). That is a hard saying. How can you be blessed because you slaughter your own children or the children of your parents? How become priest of this God not by ritual initiation but in carrying out orders that cut across all natural affections?

It would help late twentieth-century Christians to keep their God of Love purified of such bloody-mindedness if we could tuck these stories back into a more primitive, misunderstanding time or excise them from our working canon *(if the text offends you, rip it out)*. Unfortunately, when we try to trim the cloth of our Scriptures into something more comfortable to wear, the unconditionality of divine command continues to stick like pins into our vulnerable places. For the demands of Jesus are not themselves free from problematic claims upon our natural attachments. Think first of some tensions over family relationships.

Mark's Jesus stresses by deed and word the importance of these relationships in several places. He heightens the value of children in chapters 9 and 10. Although he has not permitted anyone to touch him, he himself overcomes this somatic detachment by throwing his arms round these little ones (9.37, 10.16). Mark tells us he healed two daughters and a son, restoring them to their parents. Jesus excoriates the Pharisees for practices that deny the intent of the commandment to honor father and mother (7.9–13); and in chapter 10 he moves to the relationship between husband and wife, seeing this as constituted by God and inseverable by divorce. (We can read Mark's chapter 6 story about Herod, Herodias, and her daughter's dancing for the head of John the Baptist as a gruesome example of family relationships gone wrong.)

That's all on the one hand. But on the other, Jesus comes up with difficult sayings about families, and for someone who apparently values them he behaves strangely himself. He doesn't fit well into his own family—whatever that is. With no birth narrative, Mark characterizes Jesus' first and final family identity in terms of his status as beloved Son of the Father. That's where Jesus centers his life and allegiance. So when Mark mentions Jesus' natural family, it's to report tension and nonrecognition. They come to take charge of him because he's thought out of his mind (3.21); he, however, keeps them outside the house and outside his acknowledgment: who is his mother, who his brothers (3.33)? His neighbors could not situate him among the members of his family, provoking Jesus' saying that a prophet is not honored by his kin and in his own home (6.4). If we are tempted to think him like Socrates, who does not himself show much interest in his family, that will soften his much more radical message. Socrates had his circle of followers: but they were not like James and John, who got up out of the boat and left their father behind. Nor are those two unique: in chapter 10, Peter says they all have left everything to follow Jesus. And Jesus acknowledges in reply that he and the gospel have required the leaving of home, siblings, parents, children, and property. Moreover, relationships will not improve: in the eschatological section of his Gospel, Mark's Jesus prophesies that those loyal to him will be hated and betrayed, brother by brother, child by father, parent by child (13.12–13). So the turning away of Jesus from his own family gets replicated in the leaving and the hating that he requires and predicts for those who would follow him.

Of course, what Jesus has in mind isn't fragmentation and isolation but a different kind of family. I have reported the severing of natural ties; Jesus, however, goes on to create an unusual new kinship. Who are his relatives? Whoever does the will of God—that is what makes a mother or sister or brother of Jesus (3.35). (He does not include father in his list, for there is only one Father, obedience to whom undercuts all natural relationships and establishes these new ones.) There's a like promise in chapter 10 to those who have left everything and everybody: they will receive siblings and children and mother (again no mention of father) as well as property, all a hundredfold.

It's difficult, I confess, to know what to make of this. Mark doesn't present the relationships among the disciples and Jesus as particularly good instances of a new intimacy: Jesus doesn't seem to treat them as family, nor do they employ family names for each other (though he does call the hemorrhaging woman healed through her bold faith "Daughter"). We'll have to wait until John's Gospel, and the next chapter, for the disciples to become beloved friends. The emphasis here seems rather on the authority of Jesus to lay upon his followers high demands for allegiance beyond the ties of nature, and to do this in the name of God.

Obedience to Death I had warned that this call for allegiance leads to an even more problematic demand, and it's now time to face that. For I cannot simply say that the old bloody obedience to God has been softened by a Jesus who calls us to abandon what's unproductive in natural affection so that we can extend family love to a wider fellowship. That would be a nice reading for the urban cultures that most of us know, preoccupied with relaxing family ties and joining up with the right (and therefore unrelated) people for meaningful relationships. No: the message about following Jesus cuts more deeply, past what we call ties of blood into our very flesh.

Mark gives us two painful images of this, all the worse when put together. The words are familiar: from chapter 8, *who wishes to follow me must take up the cross;* from chapter 9, *if your hand or foot or eye causes you to stumble, cut it off; rip it out.* I can't write out the violence from these sayings. The cross borne is the instrument of my death, not some little drudging duty interfering with my pleasure. The mutilation to my body is no accident in the workplace but self-inflicted dismemberment. Socrates exhibits a self-control over passion and appetite so effective that we saw it leading to a somatic indifference; Jesus calls us in the unsettling language of somatic disfigurement.

That is profoundly disturbing—more so as we remember the sick self-loathing of people who have imposed the image literally upon their own bodies. That literalness is not at all the way to conform our lives to the image. There can be no misunderstanding. Let me nonetheless repeat: the images, though bodily, have as their object our way of living, our "souls" and not our physical flesh.

For what Jesus calls for is the denial and rejection of the self, the losing of the soul. There are those who strain their wills to hold onto their souls, those who set out to gain all that's to be had. They lose what they grasp for: if what they win costs their souls, they have no profit. These are paradoxes of possession, pulling up for scrutiny our assumptions about value and intention. There seems no escape: we may value supremely either our soul or the world, but grasping for one or the other will lose us our soul. We win only by giving up the grasping itself—that is, we live by dying. The command in the much ado about nothing that is human existence comes in three words: "die to live."

Mark will not help us if we throw all our questions at his text: what is the meaning of "soul" here? and does the reflexive in self-denial require the notion of a "self" that could in any meaningful sense be nailed to a cross? and does the world gained include family affection or just material possessions? and so on. But if we stop throwing and start listening, we might hear these words in the voice of the obedient Son. His is a distinctive voice, not the impersonal echo of a timeless wisdom; it belongs to the one who exercised a power over the world beyond our reach, but who emptied out all authority in his obedience to death. The cross is his cross; the mutilated body belongs to him.

To be at this place is to have moved some distance from the start of this section. We had worried about the bloody orders of a God demanding allegiance at the cost of natural family affection. Although I have not alleviated all concern about those stories, Mark's Jesus has shifted our attention, twice. He has transferred the locus of violence and death from those near us to our very self; and he has asked that we follow not an alien supreme will but the path that he himself has taken. We discover the meaning of complete and final allegiance to God, then, in the Passion and death of Jesus.

I've already said that the images of dismemberment and crucifixion cannot be transferred literally onto the bodies of the followers of Jesus. How, then, do these images get worked into their biographies? To answer, we must look for the model of exemplary obedience in the complete conformity of will between Father and beloved Son. But we move into trouble whenever we forget that this conformity is not the submission of one human will to another finite will. The troubles with obedience, especially religious obedience, arise from superimposing divine authority on temporal and limited masters. In another day we should have called that *idolatry;* but the term's offense to our cultural sensitivities today shouldn't blind us to our practice. The critical distance between Jesus and religious leadership, even the tough independence of Socrates, remind us that exemplary obedience has its locus outside temporal authority.

What's heeded, however, is *not the self.* That's what I find so compelling about this deep, intense listening. We understand well the search for autonomy and independence, the capturing of authority for the individual alone; we know intimately the desire to fulfill personal ambition, petty or grand. However necessary this appropriation of power for the self, we should not be deceived. Those who think they can live out of the resources of the self alone *do not know their place in the world.* The evidence for this we have all met in the faces of the arrogant. The truly obedient listen, and in their listening they give up grasping after the self's own schemes, let go their grip on the self's meager resources. We might say that they make their place in the world God's place. We might even say that they die to live.

An obedient death in love to God this radical must be given as the work of grace. But must grace move inscrutably, or is there anything that permits us to believe such obedient trust to be a wise trust? Only this: that the exemplary obedience of Jesus is also the obedience of God toward us. If divine authority conforms itself to our need and empties itself into divine powerlessness, then isn't there something foolishly ironic in our struggles to fortify our own little places in the world? What if those who are given to appreciate the obedience of Jesus as the work of divine love toward them—what if they find themselves so loved that they follow love's lead past the interests of the self and into God's place? Would their obedience be death? or life?

A Borrowed Epilogue

> Men's curiosity searches past and future
> And clings to that dimension. But to apprehend
> The point of intersection of the timeless
> With time, is an occupation for the saint—
> No occupation either, but something given
> And taken, in a lifetime's death in love,
> Ardour and selflessness and self-surrender.
> For most of us, there is only the unattended
> Moment, the moment in and out of time,
> The distraction fit, lost in a shaft of sunlight,
> The wild thyme unseen, or the winter lightning

Or the waterfall, or music heard so deeply
That it is not heard at all, but you are the music
While the music lasts. These are only hints and guesses,
Hints followed by guesses; and the rest
Is prayer, observance, discipline, thought and action.

—T. S. ELIOT
"The Dry Salvages," from *The Four Quartets*

SIX

Love and Death

Love is strong as death, passion fierce as the grave. —SONG OF SOLOMON 8.6 (NRSV)

Come, lady, die to live.   —FRIAR FRANCIS to HERO, in *Much Ado About Nothing*

LOVE AND DEATH: the conjunction does not state the way we want the world to be. We'd much prefer to do without the death.

But because our preferences make very little difference in matters of mortality, at least we may be grateful for whatever love we know in our lives. In loving and being loved we make a world worth living in. The trouble is that the more we love the more we open ourselves to the wounding loss of those we love, so that we cannot simply get on with our loving by closing our eyes to death. Our loved ones die, and pass beyond our ability to cherish them except in memory and imagination. And we, too, we ourselves die, regardless of the intensity of our love for life. Deathlessness belongs to the divine; we all-too-humanly live not in that realm but among the creatures of time and dust.

There comes about in loving, then, an impetus toward immortality. Love strives to reproduce itself and to live forever, declares Plato; passion is fierce, the Song of Solomon announces, as fierce as the grave; love, says Paul, never fails. We want to believe that love can overcome death. We hope, sometimes with a depth of self-forgetful sorrow, that the transcending experience of love portends a glory that will not fade.

In the midst of contradictory fears, longings, hopes, and losses, we must fashion a way to live. One part of our minds plays with metaphysical thoughts of our selves as persisting and indestructible souls, created by God never to go out of existence. Another part sifts through all the objects of our interest, looking for just those things to love that won't ever disappoint us. Yet another part objects to salvation through metaphysics and reminds us that love can't be directed only at the perfect as long as we ourselves need to be loved. Somehow in all of this we've got to get our thinking and our loving right.

It may help to consider the loving and the dying of Jesus and Socrates. We have seen how their obedience leads to their deaths, but neither of them can be understood without attending to the objects and the character of his love. For each of them there's an important sense in which love does overcome death. That is connected with an understanding of immortality in Socrates' case and of resurrection in the case of Jesus. We'll find, moreover, that we must do some extensive work on how love relates to the divine, especially in John's Gospel, as we consider the themes of death and glory, but also for Socrates—who, we shall discover, turns out to know less fragility in his loving than does Jesus.

Jesus: Death and Glory

In our reflections we have so far spent time with the three writers of the synoptic Gospels, interrogating each of them around a particular concern. How does the silence of Jesus reveal his own motives and intentions as he goes to his death? What is it that he does when he removes himself from others to address his Father? Who obeys his authority, and what is the nature of obedience demonstrated in his own life and death? For each answer we have remained within one of the synoptics, using its materials not for historical speculation but in order to construct a reading of the character of the Jesus we find in that text.

But there is one more Evangelist and a fourth Gospel, to which we now turn. John's writing, though classified as a gospel because it gives another presentation of the life and Passion of Jesus, doesn't fit neatly alongside Matthew, Mark, and Luke. They enjoy much more in common with each other than does John with any of them. The differences are well-known. John's prologue is perhaps the most strikingly different feature; but distinctive, too, is the great amount of speaking that Jesus does, in public about himself but especially in private on his last night. What John's Jesus *doesn't* talk about, or *doesn't* do, also piques the interest of the reflective reader. Where are the parables and sayings about the Kingdom of Heaven, or those unclean spirits and demons that keep appearing in Mark and the other synoptics? We will have occasion to note additional contrasts between the synoptics and the Fourth Gospel—and because it makes such comparisons, this chapter treats its gospel text somewhat differently from the previous three chapters.

In comparing John with the synoptics, I do not wish to make strong claims about the author's own knowledge of the synoptic traditions. Although it would be strange to think that his audience had no prior acquaintance with events in Jesus' life (think how John presupposes a memory of the anointing story in 11.2), nevertheless my interest does not lie in reconstructing what the author or the audience believed about Jesus before the creation of this text. So I shan't be trying to explain how or why the writer of the Fourth Gospel wanted to shape traditions about Jesus. Instead, I want to explore what may happen in the minds of present day readers who do have this text alongside the synoptic writings, and who therefore cannot read the Fourth Gospel without being reminded of the other three.

There is another difference in this chapter's approach: it draws upon our believing something about the author of the Fourth Gospel. Questions about who wrote this work can grow extremely complicated and subtle. I'll be simple: the author is, for my purposes, *John the beloved disciple*. Again, I must be clear about this. Debate has been extensive over the authorship of all the gospels. Ancient ascriptions must assign Matthew and Mark to their gospels, for nothing internal to the text discloses authorship. The Third Gospel opens with a statement of authorial intent without giving the author's name, but its association with the Acts of the Apostles, with its first-person narration by the companion of Paul, provides some evidence for assigning authorship to Luke. In the case of the Fourth Gospel, again the author doesn't name himself, so we must come up with his identity by other means. Is he the disciple John, prominent with Peter and James in the synoptics but curiously unmentioned in this Gospel? Or does some compelling evidence make that long-cherished identification impossible? Rather than sitting down to that discussion, however, I want to point to what's different about authorship in the Fourth Gospel, and to why my claim can continue to be a simple one. The difference from the synoptics is this: the author identifies himself as a player—indeed a significant one—in the story. He is *the disciple Jesus loves,* an intimate and an eyewitness during those central events of betrayal and arrest, crucifixion and resurrection. This identification is made quite explicitly at the end of chapter 21: *it is this same disciple* [the one Jesus loved, who asked him about the betrayal, v. 20] *who vouches for what has been written here. He it is who wrote it* (v. 24, REB). Naturally, I cannot use this claim as sufficient evidence for its own historical truth, or to dismiss postulations about other hands involved in the authorial process. (Who, it will be asked, are the "we" who know his testimony is true?) I only mean to say something unstartling: that the author, however related to the actual followers of Jesus, intends us to identify him with one special follower whom we know as *the beloved disciple* and whose name has for long centuries been John. Whether he is the same John of the synoptic trio need not matter for my purposes. I will argue that this Gospel's presentation of Jesus is illumined by the identification of the narrator with the beloved disciple; but this understanding may be compatible with differing beliefs about the author's own historical identity.

How the author's own experience works in his understanding of Jesus will have to await the unfolding of the themes of this chapter. In the end we'll see that the clue lies in his epithet as the beloved disciple: he is able to write what he does because of his being loved. That love enables him to recognize the identity of Jesus; it informs his seeing and his witnessing. In fact, it will have much to do with another large difference between John and the synoptics, over the relation of the death and resurrection of Jesus and his glory. Whereas they see his resurrection as the locus of his glory, John discovers glory in his death. Of all the Evangelists, his is the boldest reading: he claims to have witnessed, visually, the glory he attaches to Jesus.

Our themes, then, are large indeed: love, death, glory. But John starts us off on the grandest possible scale himself. The prologue of the Gospel situates his reader from the outset in an audacious context: John starts the world all over again from the beginning.

And who is there, in the very genesis of all that has come to be? It is not God who receives first mention; instead it is the Logos, the Word. The Word was with God, and was indeed God. Nor is it the Spirit who moves over chaotic waters to call out light and life: it is within the Word himself that light and life are to be found, and who is the agent of all else.

And who is the Word? That, for John, is the question for the world to answer. I use "world" advisedly, for John sets up an important opposition between Word and World. The World, though made by the Word, lies at an alien distance from the Word: it did not, indeed does not, know him. If for other thinkers the cosmos is the ordered product of mind, responsive to mind's rational plan, it is not so for John: he invests the world with its own resistant will, able to close its eyes to knowledge. The world's lack of recognition turns out to be a dominant theme of the Gospel, and the bringing about of faith as that response which constitutes recognition John's chief reason for writing.

The Word, he continues, became flesh and took residence among us; and we saw his glory, glory as of the Father's only offspring, full of grace and truth.

"We saw," John says, as though the "glory" were some halo or aura shimmering around the man John the Baptist pointed out as the Lamb of God. What kind of seeing is this, and what is this thing seen?

"Glory" in John

One answer suggests itself today as I write, for it is the Feast of the Transfiguration. Luke twice uses the word *glory* in chapter 9 for the appearance of Jesus, Moses, and Elijah on the mountain, and the same word is picked up later in Second Peter in reference to that event, witnessed by the impulsive apostle of that name. This radical change in physical presence was just the sort of thing to be seen with the eyes even if difficult to believe. But John the Evangelist does not record the Transfiguration story in his Gospel. What John claims he saw does not seem to be the splendor of a visible transformation.

Truth to tell, explanation becomes more difficult the more one compares John's talk of glory with the way the synoptic writers employ the term. The difference is obvious at the level of word count, for John seems seized of the notion in a way the others are not. Mark has only three references to the noun or verb; Matthew has twelve. Luke almost doubles that with twenty-two. John, though, uses the term twice as many times again, with forty-five occurrences. But there is a more revealing difference. The proper home of the term isn't terrestrial: as we shall see in the next section, glory belongs to God. Most commonly, then, the evangelists speak of glorifying God. The only other context for the synoptics' use of glory proper and divine is apocalyptic. They apply the word to the future revelation of the Son of Man, who will come (as we remember from our reflections on the inability of Jesus to know the day or the hour) with his angels in great power and glory on the clouds of heaven. Such glory has to do with resurrection, adumbrated in the Transfiguration. Luke puts it simply in the postresurrection Emmaus story: first the suffering, and then the glory—and the same locution recurs in First Peter 1.11: the sufferings of Christ are followed by the glories. John, however, sees it not at all like that. He has no apocalyptic discourse before the Passion, no prophecy about the imminent destruction of the Temple or the coming of the Son of Man with power. Instead the glory of God is associated with death—the fatal illness of Lazarus (11.4) and the prophesied death of Peter (21.19), but preeminently in Jesus' own death (especially 12.23–33). How this death can evoke glory is what must occupy our attention in this chapter.

Glory and Glorification It was once raised in my hearing as a criticism of a poet of high standing that she used too freely the word *glory.* The justice of the comment aside, it does trade on the possible gulf between language and experience: this small word may indeed fail to evoke the power to which it is supposed to point. Whether our English term has become banal beyond hope, or whether contemporary human experience has been so shuttered by self-absorption that there is little for the word to point to—these are questions to be deliberately ignored in order to try to recover something of what John might have meant about Jesus. Forget, then, the last time you thought of a dinner or movie as "glorious," or of the "glory" of a lavish production—even a sunset, I'm afraid. Think instead of God.

When we have spent more than an accidental moment thinking ourselves in the presence of God—that is, to use the language of Chapter 4, when we have been attentive to God, or have addressed God however feebly—then we find ourselves in need of some conceptual markers to plant squarely between God, on the one side, and on the other ourselves and the created order, sunsets included. Holiness is one such marker. So are many adjectives declined in the superlative, and moral qualities stretched past their most perfect examples. Our spiritual ancestors fashioned yet another indicator, primarily visual. It emphasizes the limits of vision at both ends, so to speak: that which is too obscure to be seen and that which is too bright to be observed. Cloud and fire, darkness and light—these form the images of glory. They are there in the flash of the cherubim guarding against reentry to Eden, in the guiding pillars of fire and cloud at the Exodus, in the smoke and fire, the storm and brightness, of the visions of Isaiah or Ezekiel; they may be read compressed into the small, expanding space of Psalm 97. Whatever its language of presentation, *glory* is about what we can't visualize when we try to look at God. And the reason is that there is *too much there* to be seen with the kinds of eyes we have, eyes that cloud over in the presence of so much light.

If this is so, then *glory* is a *perceptual* term, pointing at something present in the object of its ascription, but requiring also perceivers of that something without whom it wouldn't be quite right to say that there was glory—or wasn't, for that matter. (This requirement of perceivers might help explain why the Greek word used by biblical writers is *doxa*, which means outside Scripture "reputation": it is part of the divine glory that God's people believe him to have these qualities and ascribe them to him.) And the perceptual nature of glory in turn will permit us to make sense of *glorification*.

We do need to think for a moment about the activity of glorifying, because in one sense it seems pointless. How can the perfectly complete be improved upon, or mere mortals add anything to the glory of God? As Socrates gets Euthyphro to acknowledge, holiness cannot be ministry to the gods for their betterment (*Euthyphro* 13c). But that is to think of glorification as an activity aimed at change in its object. It would belong to the same class as something like *fortification*, which strengthens what's thought to be vulnerable. There are other *-ification* words more apt to our case, such as *amplification* or *magnification*, that belong with the perceptual. Those activities leave the structures of their objects unaltered but enhance their perceptibility for hearers and viewers. It's something similar, I suggest, with glorification. The activity of glorifying doesn't alter the nature of God. Yet without that activity, acknowledging as it does the divine otherness and splendor, it wouldn't be quite right to say that God has glory. And something does change in the act of ascribing glory: the relationship between the glorifier and the one glorified.

Some Johannine Peculiarities That said, we must get back to John's use of "glory," *doxa*, in relation to Jesus, and to its peculiarities. In much of John's text, of course, the word functions just as we would expect: it is God who is the proper object of glory, and it is God who is glorified. That is how Jesus uses the term on several occasions throughout the Gospel. It is true of the deaths of Lazarus and Peter, and John also reflects this use in the charge of the Pharisees to the blind man of chapter 9 to give glory to God for his sight, not to this sinner he talks about.

But if there is nothing surprising in these instances, John's *doxa* language at some other places strikes me as unusual. It may appear that he is merely continuing his interest in the matter of glory's proper location (with God and not mortals) in chapters 5, 7, 8, and 12; but I think that the meaning of *doxa* shifts in such passages. John comments at 12.43 that several leaders were unwilling to acknowledge their belief in Jesus, valuing the doxa of human beings rather than the doxa of God.

This same conflict sits between the Pharisees and Jesus: he does not seek doxa from humans for himself (5.41) as do they, for they do not look for the doxa that is from God alone (5.44). Nevertheless—here is the point—at issue is not so much the glory that belongs to God as the good opinion that God would hold of them. The meaning of the word must therefore be closer to its extrabiblical sense of "reputation," or "honor," as some translations have it, than to "glory" in any full-blooded sense. (This more commonplace use isn't completely foreign to the synoptics. The term means the less-than-divine "splendor" of the kingdoms of the world in the Matthew and Luke Temptation scenes, and Luke applies it to Solomon in the lilies of the field passage. Luke also comes close to John's meaning of "honor" in speaking at 14.10 of the doxa shown in banquet seating placement; compare Matthew 6.2.) When John uses the word again in chapters 7 and 8, his reasoning about the proper location of doxa shifts slightly once more as he refers to doxa and the self. Anyone who speaks on his own behalf must be seeking his own doxa, so the right thing is to seek the doxa of the one who sends him (7.18); Jesus does not seek his own doxa, which is nothing (8.50, 54). Here "reputation" might work as meaning, but perhaps something like "authentication" will better capture the sense. We seem at some distance from doxa as glory.

Now, if Jesus wants to be authenticated and honored by God, having doxa in that sense, it is also true that he wants "to be glorified" by the Father. It might be thought, from the material we've just considered, that the process of being given doxa means simply being accorded the kind of honor that comes from God rather than one's fellows. But no. The instances I've set out in the paragraph above all involve the noun *doxa*, but the verb in John bears the stronger sense, which returns us to divine glory. There can be no doubt about that, for Jesus sees the relationship between himself and God in intimate and reciprocal terms. He refers repeatedly in the prayer of chapter 17 to the glory that he had with the Father before the world began; and he wants to be glorified in order to glorify God:

> Now the Son of Man is glorified, and in him God is glorified. If God is glorified in him, God will also glorify him in himself, and will glorify him now. (13.31–32 REB)

> Father, the hour has come. Glorify your Son, that the Son may glorify you. . . . I have glorified you on earth by finishing the work which you

gave me to do; and now, Father, glorify me in your own presence with the glory which I had with you before the world began. (17.1,4–5 REB)

The uniqueness of Jesus' glory is thus established; it is clearly more than an "honor" that is available to other mortals. And the importance of his glorification may be remarked in the fact that John records more references to Jesus' being glorified than to the glory, or glorification, of God.

Having seen how seriously John takes the glorification of Jesus, we may return to a consideration of its peculiarities. We started on this in the first place because of John's association of glory with death rather than resurrection, but I want to draw attention to a different matter now. It is the question of John's assignment of temporality to the glorification of Jesus. We know he believes Jesus to have had a kind of atemporal glory from eternity (John claims that Isaiah saw Jesus' glory and spoke of him, 12.41), but he also speaks as though there is a time at which Jesus is glorified—a Before and After for this one event. At a couple of places John comments that Jesus had not yet been glorified (in chapters 7 and 12), so we know there is a Before. At two places glorification is associated with the future coming of the Spirit (7.39, 16.14): if that is a temporal indicator, we would have to place the event after the resurrection, in the upper room where Jesus breathes on his disciples as he says, "Receive the Holy Spirit" (20.22). In the Lazarus story, however, Jesus says that the Son of God is to be glorified through that illness; and this seems to link naturally with John's remark in chapter 2 that it was through signs that the glory of Jesus was manifest so that his disciples believed in him. Glorification looks like an ongoing process rather than a unique event, then—and indeed Jesus speaks of it in the present tense in 8.54, *"It is the Father who glorifies me."* Yet there are unequivocal statements in chapters 12, 13, and 17, and they are unmistakably about Jesus' death. His hour has come; this is to be the occasion of his glorification. After chapter 17 there are no references to the glorification of Jesus, so John must believe that whatever constitutes glorification is to be linked to the events of the Passion.

So we're left with questions about how to map the glorification of Jesus onto his biography. If his glory is eternal, how does glorification work as process and as event? Moreover, thinking about that raises another peculiarity, which resides in the uniqueness of glorification for Jesus. Although his doxa is reciprocal with God's and therefore unlike human honor, his glorification nevertheless seems to be asymmetrical with the activity of glorifying God. There doesn't seem to be any temporality in connection with glorifying God, in that God does not change from Before to After in being glorified. The temporality relates to the glorifiers and the changes in them. But with Jesus, there is anticipation of an event in which his glorification will consist: something happens to him in this event in a way in which nothing changes in God as a result of our glorifying him.

This talk of time and the Hour needs more explicit attention if we are to advance toward an understanding of glorification: through it we will be able to appreciate something of how John sees the death of Jesus.

Time, Hour, Death

We noted when beginning upon the Fourth Gospel that John presupposes in his reader familiarity with a set of particulars about Jesus, upon which he wants to throw additional light. He does more than situate these details in the large context of his prologue, of course; he recounts several incidents and encounters not found in the accounts of the three synoptic Evangelists. But where events are common to all four Gospels, the reader sometimes finds a significantly altered chronology. Simon is renamed Peter as soon as he is called (1.42); the Temple merchants are cleared out at the very beginning of Jesus' public ministry (2.13 ff.); the anointing at Bethany takes place before, not after, the Entry into Jerusalem (12.1 ff., 12.12 ff.). Different readers will find widely different explanations for chronological disparities in John: he didn't know the synoptic accounts, or he didn't care, or he did care and wanted to alter time to make a nonchronological point. I have no special interest here in determining what approach should give most satisfaction. Rather, I want to place alongside this striking feature of changed temporal order a less dramatic one: in other respects John has a strong interest in time. Among the four Evangelists, John and Luke seem most interested in recording details about time. Both of them tell us specific temporal particulars outside the sequence of events in the Passion and Resurrection that all the Gospelers report. Luke, for instance, gives us the ages of Anna and Jesus at the Temple incident, the year of Tiberius's reign, and the age of Jesus when he began public teaching. John reports the claim that the Temple took forty-six years to build, that the lame man had been crippled for thirty-eight years, that Jesus' audience exclaimed that he was not yet fifty years old. This precision may be an expression of a more general interest in numbers on John's part: he counts six stone water jars, each holding two or three measures (2.6), four soldiers at the crucifixion (19.23), two hundred cubits (21.8), and one hundred fifty-three fish (21.11). Perhaps so, but there is more.

For John seems to me to have a special concern with days and hours. Among the frequent temporal expressions used by all the Evangelists, "the sabbath" has particular significance because of Jesus' healings on that day; "the third day" occurs in connection with the resurrection, as does "the first day of the week." But geography matters more than chronology in the synoptics. While we are often told in what region events took place, there are few clues (beyond the occasional reference to morning or evening) as to dates or elapsed time for much of the public work of Jesus. His teachings and healings take place at unspecified times, "one day" or "once when." It's not that John makes possible a better chronological construction—we've seen the complications with that already—but he does provide details that others do not. For instance, we get four references to day sequences by 2.1 and three mentions of elapsed days in chapter 11. Of most interest, though, are the four specified hours in his Gospel, timing events and encounters (the tenth hour, 1.39; the sixth, 4.6 and 19.14; the seventh, 4.52). The other Evangelists never bother with locating incidents on the clock (so to speak), *with the notable exception of the crucifixion.* Mark puts that from the third to the ninth hour; Matthew and Luke both mention the darkness from the sixth to the ninth hour.

Now what's of interest about this is simply that John does not follow the others in specifying the hours of the crucifixion. Although other events—including Pilate's noontime judgment—are locatable by hours, Jesus' death is not.

Why, especially when there is so much about the "hour" of Jesus? I think the answer lies in the nature of this Hour, in its being seen not as elapsed time, which measures any and every event, but as something else.

The Hour as Death To understand this we must look at John's idea of Hour, and how it relates both to glory and to death.

It's perhaps unnecessary to remind ourselves that the Greek term *(hôra)* translated "hour" in our texts has a broader meaning than the space between numbers on a timepiece—unnecessary because English usage is similar. "That was our finest hour" on the lips of a Churchill refers to something more than sixty minutes; on the lips of a basketball coach to something less. One's Hour in this sense is a time of large significance in which decisions, actions, and events determine the very shape of one's life and history. The chronological duration of the Hour is irrelevant, for what matters is not how long but how much change there is between the Before and the After.

Fortunately, Hours for most of us are few in comparison with hours, and we don't usually know when or even that they are coming up. Jesus, however, knew *that* there was an Hour for him: this seems to have been as much a part of his consciousness as was Socrates' divine voice part of his. About the *when*, though? That seems more difficult to determine if we recall our reading of motivation and intention in Matthew. For I argued back in Chapter 3 that Jesus' words about not knowing the day or the hour are to be taken with great seriousness. He cannot retrieve from the Father the chronological time at which the Son of Man will be seen coming in glory on the clouds of heaven. And yet he does know that his hour of death is approaching: "The hour has come! the Son of Man is betrayed into the hands of sinners" are his words in Matthew 26.45. Will that hour be transformed into The Hour? Will the kingdom be possible without crucifixion now that he has gotten this far without surrendering to the temptation of shortcuts? These were the questions that we saw settled by obedience to the Father, a handing over of what Jesus could not sort out by himself. And we saw him die dismissed from the Father's presence in spite of that obedience. The hour of his death was not the hour of his glory.

John's Jesus, however, does not experience the perplexity of separation between two hours, and he knows not only the *that* but also the *when* of his Hour.

Or at least he starts out knowing *when it is not.* We learn of his Hour first at Cana in chapter 2, in that not atypical interchange between mother and son, where mother expects son to do something that son is not entirely comfortable with, and where mother knows son will end up doing it anyway. (Ignoring his answer, she says to the servants: "Do whatever he tells you" [2.5].) The reason Jesus doesn't want to solve his host's problem about wine is that his "Hour has not yet come." Now we should note John's editorial comment on the incident: that this was the first of the signs that made apparent his *glory.* Most of the guests, including the master of the feast and the bridegroom, had no idea of

Jesus' contribution to the occasion; only the servants, his mother, and his disciples knew the provenance and youth of this surprisingly good vintage. The Glory is therefore veiled, a secret from those who enjoy its benefits. Did Jesus give this sign *in spite of* his Hour not having come— and if so, is that why the Glory isn't public? Or is the Glory veiled but present because the sign anticipates in some way his Hour? If we find ourselves asking such questions, John has created tension over Hour and Glory for us in this account.

The difficulties continue next time Hour crops up in the text, in chapter 7. Having said in the Temple things outrageous to many listeners, Jesus is about to be seized; but no one could lay hands on him *because his Hour had not come* (7.30). Jesus seems to have known that: he has told his brothers that he would not attend the festival in Jerusalem because the right time hasn't come (7.8: here the word is *kairos* rather than hour, *hôra*, but the sense is the same). They go to Jerusalem by themselves; he arrives later in secret, and halfway through the festival starts teaching in the Temple. Our problem is the same as in chapter 2: if attending the festival is a mark of the right time's arrival, is this his Hour or is it not? Why the denial, the secrecy, the ambiguity? And John seems to have altered the meaning of the Hour. Whereas it was unclearly associated with Glory in chapter 2, the Hour is now said not to have arrived because nobody could seize Jesus—a clear reference to his impending arrest and death, reinforced at 8.20 with the same explanation about his Hour's not having come.

By the second half of chapter 12, and through the prayer of chapter 17, the relation between glory and Jesus' death starts to get sorted out. In this stretch of text we have six references to Hour and twenty-one to glory or glorification. At 12.23 Jesus announces that the *Hour* has arrived for the Son of Man *to be glorified;* he repeats that the Son of Man is glorified in 13.31, that God will glorify him *now* in 13.32; then (as we have seen) begins his prayer in 17.1 by announcing that the Hour has come and by asking the Father to glorify him. And the events in the Hour have to do with his Passion and death. Jesus speaks of the dying of the grain of wheat (12.24), his turmoil of soul that raises the possibility of his asking to be saved from the Hour, a possibility to be rejected because it was for this that he came to this Hour (12.27); John comments that the Hour means that Jesus was to leave the world (13.1); Jesus alludes to the Hour as labor-pain, grief made bearable by future joy (16.21); he warns that the Hour has arrived when he would be left alone by his scattered disciples (16.32).

So what we have is this: the Hour's content in time is death by crucifixion, events that are given by John no chronological fixing because their temporal significance is immaterial. What is material is the meaning John assigns to these events: they are Accomplishment. Four times in the account of the crucifixion in chapter 19, John uses the notion of fulfillment—as he had already at 18.32. On three occasions the Scriptures are fulfilled in what takes place: as we have seen, Psalm 22 lies behind Matthew's account, and John, too, quotes its verses in connection with the casting of lots and Jesus' thirst. He puts together Psalm 34 (compare Exodus 12) and Zechariah 12 as fulfilled in the final scene with the spear. But the central fulfillment is not of Scripture so much as of Jesus' own life in his final cry, "It is accomplished." What is completed is the work which his Father had given him: *I have glorified you by finishing the work you gave me to do* (17.4). The Hour has arrived, is Now, because Jesus has embraced his death, has placed himself in that space. But the Hour's significance is also Glory.

What is it for the Hour to be the hour of glorification, when it is the hour of death?

Dying as Glorification The two hours are the same Hour: that is the message of John. It is worth remarking on the ways in which John's language in chapter 12 reflects this identification, partly through a kaleidoscoping of synoptic chronology. As we've seen, John omits the apocalyptic discourses found in Matthew 24–25, Mark 13, and Luke 21, where in the last week before the crucifixion Jesus predicts the destruction of the Temple and the coming glory of the Son of Man. (He also omits Jesus' reference to the future glory of the Son of Man in the trial scenes.) Between the Entry into Jerusalem and the Last Supper, John records only one event, and he alone records it. Significantly, it does contain a reference to the glory of the Son of Man. Some Gentiles in Jerusalem ask to be taken to Jesus, who tells Andrew and Philip in response to this request: *the Hour has come for the Son of Man to be glorified,* and he goes on to speak of his death. Onto this little encounter John superimposes the manifestation of the Son to all nations, the drawing of other sheep not from Israel's fold to the One lifted up from the earth in crucifixion. It's also here—not in the garden—that John locates the *agônia* of Jesus over his death: his soul is in turmoil and he wonders whether he should ask to be saved from this Hour. The answer is No; rather, the Father is to be glorified in this Hour, which is also the Hour of judgment for the world (again an apocalyptic theme).

Death and glory fall together for Jesus. How can this be?

The idea of a glorious death is not unfamiliar, having been around as long as leaders have called men to war. The sweet fittingness of *pro patria* dying lies in the worthy end to be realized—the preservation of country and culture—and in the memorial of an altruistic courage. If this end of the twentieth century finds that kind of glory worn thin, that is because we have discovered the contaminant of political self-interest in the smooth rhetoric of self-sacrifice, not because no deaths have ever been noble. All the distasteful waste and horror of war cannot eradicate the honor in much of the dying of friend and foe alike; indeed, it is that honor which makes war tragic where it is not senseless. Nevertheless, this is not the honor and glory of the death of Jesus, in any straightfor-ward way, at least. So we should inquire not about war and politics but about any good dying. What is it to "make," as our forebears had it, "a good death"? And will that lead us if not to fame then to glory?

Good Dying: Socrates—and Jesus?

Our contemporary interest in good dying has been caught up with issues generated out of medical technology, like the prolongation of life and the control of pain through palliative care. Concerns peculiar to our current technical capacities may be situated, however, in the larger context of the kind of dying we have for long centuries seemed to admire. It's true—often urgently true—that we would include on our list of ways *not* to die, dying in great physical pain, or dying a long and slow death; and most of us would prefer not to die after prolonged unconscious connection to life support systems. So when someone dies without warning we find a little consolation in their abrupt escape from the suffering that we have witnessed elsewhere. "At least," we say, "it was quick." But that is not the kind of death for which many believers pray. In their petitions for deliverance, Christians have asked to be saved from "lightning and tempest; from earthquake, fire and flood; from plague, pestilence and famine; from battle and murder; *and from sudden death*"—or in recent revision, *"from dying suddenly and unprepared."* The addition of *preparation* seems right, for that is what unexpected death does not permit. And if we reflect on it, we do want to have our affairs in order for the sake of family and friends; we also want to have our *souls* prepared, whatever that means.

Part of what it means, I think, is that we have come to accept our dying; and such acceptance means that our dying becomes something that *we do.* There is a huge paradox here, is there not?—my death as my *activity,* when it is the cessation of my bodily functions and therefore of my human agency, the end of all my doings in this life. Our very biology drives against death, so we might expect dying to be the most basic experience of struggle against what is being done to us. Nevertheless, in the activity of accepting our death, we paradoxically win rather than lose control, not over our death itself but over our dying. By embracing we make it our own, not something foreign to us. If the shape of this paradox has a faint familiarity about it, perhaps that is because it is much like the most active embracing of the Father's will that we considered in the chapter on prayer. What we saw there may be applied here: there is a large difference between just *giving up* and *giving oneself over* to death. In giving up there are no positive virtues; in giving over we may show self-control and courage in the process of dying.

Now if *dying prepared* means accepting our deaths and having some involvement in what goes on as we die, it also means for Christians that we die *in the faith.* Making a good death will involve making our peace with God and neighbor and will include the sacramental expressions of grace in our tradition. Among our funeral prayers we ask "that when we shall have served you in our generation, we may be gathered to our ancestors, having the testimony of a good conscience, in the communion of the catholic Church, in the confidence of a certain faith, in the comfort of a religious and holy hope, in favor with you, our God, and in perfect charity with all."

That characterizes good Christian dying. Those of other faiths have similar aspirations for deaths suited to their ways of living and believing. Perhaps, then, the general point to be made is that we all wish that our deaths will be fitting expressions of the kind of life we have led.

So making a good death will mean time for preparation of our affairs and our souls; peace with our loved ones and with our God; inner acceptance of our dying; final rites and ceremonies expressive of our deepest convictions; where required and possible, sufficient prolongation and palliative care to enable us to do these things, but nothing beyond that.

I have not stated one other necessary condition for good dying—that one dies full of years rather than cut down at tender age or in one's prime. There is better and worse dying at any age, to be sure; but a good death comes at the right time, after a life fulfilled. When all of these features characterize one's dying, it becomes exemplary for others. For as there are exemplary lives that witness to values we admire and emulate, so are there exemplary deaths.

Socrates We're now in a position to return to Socrates' last day and the dying he does in the *Phaedo,* something we thought a little about in the last chapter when considering what I called the "somatic Socrates." Few readers remain unmoved by Plato's account of this admirable death; the reflections just set out may help us to appreciate why that is so.

Plato structures the account to evoke admiration from the start. Phaedo takes the role of eyewitness, and reports his own unusual experience: he felt no sorrow because Socrates met his death so fearlessly and nobly (58e). The dialogue closes with the famous lines about the end of our friend, the best and wisest and most just man of his time. And it is not only the more than a dozen of Socrates' companions present who are moved by these final moments: remember the jailer, who can contain neither his praise nor his tears as he calls Socrates the noblest and best and gentlest of men he'd ever had to deal with (116c). What are the features of nobility in this dying?

Perhaps the most important is the *self-control* that Socrates displays throughout the day—indeed somatic control characterized his entire life. Every other character breaks into tears by the dialogue's end. Socrates had sent the women away so as to banish weeping, but none of the men can keep from crying except Socrates himself. He had spent most of his final hours in good-humored philosophical discussion about the immortality of the soul without betraying any personal fear of dying, and when the time comes to drink the poison he does not prolong his life to the last possible moment as though it were something to be grasped at. Instead he receives the cup "quite cheerfully," "without a tremor, without any change of color or expression"; then "quite calmly and with no sign of distaste, he drained the cup in one breath."

Such control is also *courage,* for it persists in the face of the most fundamental fear we mortals know. Both these virtues (Socrates mentions them together in connection with death at 68d) demonstrate Socrates' great *presence of mind,* as we might ourselves put it; and this presence is an essential ingredient in *being prepared* to die. But there are other marks of Socrates' preparedness. He discharges his responsibilities to others: he tells his friends to continue to care for themselves as he has always taught (115b), and gives final wishes to his sons and the women of the household (116ab). As an expression of concern for the women he washes his own body (115a)—a gesture that enhances his participation in his own dying. His careful observance of religious ritual further marks out the deliberateness of his actions: he wants to be sure that he has followed all possible meanings of his recurring dream, so he writes poetry; when he is not permitted to pour a libation from his cup of death, he nevertheless offers a prayer; "We owe a cock to Asclepius— pay the debt and don't neglect it" are his last words.

It is true that some acts of preparation may be performed distractedly, that last arrangements may be made under compulsion without accepting wholeheartedly our death. This cannot, however, be true of Socrates. For Plato makes certain that we know at the beginning of the dialogue that for Socrates philosophy itself is a kind of dying. His entire way of life has been preparation for this final day. However we appraise the stark Platonic dualism of the *Phaedo* (and Plato himself did not always speak this starkly), we may still appreciate Socrates' point. If philosophy seeks the wisdom and truth that is to be found in soul, not body, then the final separation of soul from body may be welcomed as the fitting culmination of the philosophical quest.

In Chapter 5, I concluded that Socrates' self-control in the *Phaedo* doesn't quite require a *somatic* presence because of his indifference to his body. All the same, I want here to reaffirm that Socrates *the person* is very much *present* in all his actions related to his dying. The notion of personal presence is better, I suggest, than a more abstract term like *autonomy:* while Socrates makes his own choices, what's significant about them is not their bare source but their color and texture as his. Because of that personal presence we know that he has accepted death as *his* death.

It appears, then, that Plato has given us Exemplary Dying. Though we had illustrated the marks of making a good death from Christian sources, those marks also appear in Plato's account of the death of Socrates. He also has the benefit of right timing. Plato does not remark on Socrates' age in the *Phaedo*, but because Socrates himself refers to his being advanced in years and near natural death in his Defense (*Apology* 38c), the knowledge that Socrates has enjoyed a long and fulfilled life plays a silent part in our estimation of his death. Moreover, the *Phaedo* presents this as a painless end: the agonies of hemlock poisoning do not cloud Socrates' presence of mind or distance him from his dying.

Exemplary praying and exemplary obedience are to be found for the Christian in Jesus, though they are not utterly foreign to the Athenian Socrates. With dying, however, it seems otherwise. For—as long as the last offering were an offering to Christ and not Asclepius—would not the Christian believer aspire to die in the manner of a Socrates?

And, by implication, not in the manner of Jesus. For we must now take what we've learned back into John's Gospel to see what comparison between these deaths will yield.

And Jesus? We should pause to remind ourselves that we are in pursuit of the meaning, for John, of the glory of Jesus' death; that is why we have been searching for marks of goodness or nobility in dying. But because John's Jesus differs from the synoptic Jesus in being glorified in his very death, inevitably our comparisons must include the three other Evangelists and not Socrates alone.

Socrates died in the privacy of a prison surrounded by his friends— which suggests an additional feature of the dying we might wish for, namely the character of the space and the company in which we die. The synoptic writers are concerned to let the reader know how *public* an event is Jesus' dying, the sort of event open to anybody's intrusive observation. Jesus arrives at the place of execution having had his cross carried by Simon. There he is crucified. No writer uses more than that simple verb in describing the process; this is not a sensational account about nails or hammers or dropped wood thudding into place. Each adds several other particulars: the inscription over his head, the disposition of his clothes, his criminal companions in death, his refusal to drink the drugged wine. But because each records those details in few words, the weight of their accounts seems to tend toward more dramatic effects and aspects of this dying. All three comment on the jeering and mocking that went on—the crowds, ecclesiastical leaders, the soldiers, even the two criminals took part. All three report a loud cry from Jesus. And there are answering effects from nature: all three mention darkness at noon; Matthew reports an earthquake; Mark and Luke join him in claiming that the curtain in the Temple was ripped apart. By the end, this dying has made its deep impression on witnesses: the centurion must have been forced into unusual reflection, for when it was all over he confessed that this man must have been a son of God (Matthew, Mark), an innocent or just man (Luke). Luke tells us that the crowd who had come to watch left the scene beating their breasts.

John's account feels, to me at least, very different.

Two of the small details reported so tersely by the others are expanded into their own paragraphs—so we hear about how the chief priests tried to get Pilate to turn "King of the Jews" (in three languages, we learn) into indirect discourse rather than proclamation, and about how the four soldiers came to toss for the tunic (in fulfillment, remember, of Psalm 22). John moves the women closer to the scene (again we learn more, this time names and number), and instead of Luke's anonymous and indefinite "those who knew him" to watch with the women from a distance, John places the disciple whom Jesus loved there as eyewitness. The death scene has an effect for them that we shall return to: it is highly personal, not at all public. This absence of public reaction, in a most public space, is in striking contrast to the synoptic stories.

There is, to start with, no jeering. John tells us that the inscription was "read by many Jews," but we have no indication that any of them belonged to the clamorous mob of the first part of the chapter. For all we know, they read in silence and went on their ways. The chief priests do their talking to Pilate and do not address Jesus. The thieves say nothing. The soldiers talk only to themselves. Nature is quiet or unmoved. We would expect John to bring in the midday darkness, so concerned is he with the imagery of light, but he does not. The ground does not shudder, the Temple's curtain goes unnoticed. We are not told that Jesus does any crying out in his speaking. There is no mob to beat its breast. The account ends with what one of the executioners does—but this man is resistant to awe and makes no confession. For him the only thing remarkable in this dying is that it is over so quickly, so he doesn't need to break this man's legs—but irrationally, in an act of gratuitous violence, the soldier expresses a final contempt not with words but with a spear.

So John's account of Jesus' death is strangely muted. There is less noise—no one speaks at all to Jesus—and less effect upon those present, again with the exception of the small group near the cross. John has not rewritten the crucifixion into the dying we would wish for: water and blood from a desecrated corpse do not make for a story about good dying. Socrates does not bleed; *his* executioner weeps with the others for his death. Still, John has mitigated some of the harshness and hatred of public exposure in the other accounts, concentrating contempt into one man's action after Jesus is dead.

What of the more central features of good dying? Does Jesus die having made adequate preparation? Socrates spends his last day in long conversation with his followers, attempting to assuage their fears. John's Jesus on the night of his betrayal likewise prepares his friends for his death with an extended discourse taking up four chapters. So set is John on the content of this speech that he pays no attention to the dinner location or preparations that interest Mark or Luke. Nor does John include the institution of the Eucharist, though he has in common with the others Jesus' distress over his impending betrayal and the prediction of Peter's denial, perhaps because of an interest in relationships that we will later consider. By the end of chapter 16 the disciples understand that Jesus is leaving to go to the Father, and in the next chapter Jesus addresses his Father directly, claiming that his work has been accomplished. These twenty-six verses constitute the most sustained and intimate presentation of Jesus' praying. In that the prayer expresses acceptance and completion rather than struggle over what is to come, it could not be more different in tone from the synoptic *agônia* prayer in the Garden of Gethsemane. And given that it would make no dramatic sense to move away from such acceptance of the Father's work and will, John places the *agônia* back in chapter 12 rather than among the events of chapter 18. Instead, the reference in the arrest scene to the cup continues the tone of the chapter 17 prayer as Jesus asks Peter, "The cup the Father has given me, shall I not drink it?" (18.11). The cumulative effect, then, of chapters 13 through 17 is one of closure upon Jesus' life and relationships. He has left his disciples his own peace and said his final words to his Father.

It is difficult for the other Evangelists to achieve that sense of closure because in their accounts the disciples don't understand the attempts of Jesus to reconcile them to his dying, and they desert him. John does not portray a death of abandonment and inner loneliness: there comes no cry of godforsakenness (Luke omits that as well); neither is the absence of the disciples other than the beloved one presented as a forsaking. The scattering of the sheep is not desertion, as it is in Matthew 26.56 and Mark 14.50. Luke includes neither the saying nor the running away, but John gives the scattering prediction in 16.32—then has Jesus add that *he is not alone because the Father is with him*. Further, what's seen in Matthew and Mark as the disciples' abandonment after the arrest is made into their *release* in John 18.8–9: let these others go, says Jesus, in order to make good his promise to his Father that he had lost none of them. What may have been experienced for Matthew and Mark as the shame of desertion (and perhaps on that count ignored by Luke) becomes for John evidence of Jesus' care at the last for his friends. He goes to his death having made preparation for them and with his Father.

In his dying he makes one last arrangement. There are four people near the cross, three Marys and the beloved disciple. In the *Phaedo* Socrates speaks with his family and the women offstage in another room (116b), out of our earshot; John tells us directly as eyewitness and participant how Jesus dealt with his family. The words are simple: "Mother, look, your son" and "Look, your mother." And the effect is stated simply as well: from that hour John took Mary into his own home. This focus on an intimate address resulting in a new relationship fits well with the muted tone of the account.

All of this attentive preparation is itself testimony to Jesus' own acceptance of his death. Indeed, if we turn to ask more directly about his inner acceptance, the very question seems strange. Because most of us are bent on living as long as we can live—or, rather, live well—our dying must be something that requires the work of acceptance, a result hard to win. In the case of Jesus, the very point of his bodily existence seems to be his death. And that point is not something gained in retrospect at the end of his days—as might be the case for a seriously ill benefactor with a generous bequest, who comes to appreciate that the good consequences of his dying will outweigh that of his prolonged living. The purpose of Jesus' life as bound to his death is constantly present in his own consciousness. John presents him as *the one who is to die.* So in the very first chapter of this Gospel, the Baptist calls him with sacrificial significance the Lamb of God; and from there on we cannot read much at a stretch without encountering anticipations of his death. More, there is a *double determination* of this death. At one level, it is at the agency of human will (unlike those born as children of God in the prologue), beginning with "destroy this Temple" (said of his body, 2.19) and continuing after chapter 5 with repeated talk of plots to arrest and kill Jesus. On another level, his death is something he must perform, for it is the Father's work. He refers often to his dying as his going, or returning, to the Father—a journey he will undertake, not an event pressed upon him. Most explicitly in chapter 10, Jesus claims that no one takes his life from him; instead *he lays it down by himself, under his own authority* or power (10.18). The language of "authority" must carry political overtones, contrasting his power with that of his opposition; in this it anticipates his response to Pilate about the source of Pilate's authority (19.11), itself determined from above. Given this purposefulness toward death that pervades what John tells us of his life, we cannot but read Jesus' dying as unmistakably *his activity.*

Are there any other signs of what in Socrates' case we called presence of mind? Plato commented explicitly upon Socrates' bodily preparations, his steadiness of hand and gaze witnessing to his inner control. It's difficult to exhibit that sort of control over your body when you are bound, dressed up as an object of mockery, and thrust skyward pinned to a cross. Mark has helped us appreciate how the somatic relinquishment of Jesus expresses the draining of his personal presence in the Passion; we observed earlier that Mark's Jesus refused to be a bodily agent, to defend the boundaries of personhood, or to express in anything but the most minimal way an embodied self through language or gesture. Nevertheless, John's account mitigates this relinquishment. One small mark of this: in John, Jesus and not Simon carries the cross. Or more accurately, the point about his agency would be that double determination enters again, for he is "led out" *and* he "goes out," carrying the cross on his own. But a more noticeable mark of the greater presence of mind in the Johannine Passion comes in the speaking that Jesus does. For the arresting band, the force of his words is quite physical: at his identity-disclosing words "I am he," John says, "They drew back and fell to the ground" (18.6). John's Jesus does not invoke the possibility of his calling for legions of angels from his Father (as in Matthew); there is no need for such words. In the trials, Jesus remains present in his speaking. Only once, with Pilate, does John's Jesus not answer a question (*"Where have you come from?"* [19.9]). Had John rather than Matthew been our source, we would not have addressed the Silence of Jesus in Chapter 3. Unlike Matthew, who gives but two replies in the trials (one to the high priest, one to Pilate), John has Jesus speak to half a dozen questions (one from the high priest, one from the police, and four from Pilate). His answers prickle and prod, surrendering nothing at all.

We might by this stage find ourselves concluding that there are some discernible features of a good death in Jesus' case, more than we had initially suspected. Shouldn't we pull ourselves back to the stark facts? For Socrates, and for us, good dying means dying full of years and without debilitating pain. In Jesus' case neither of these conditions is met. But in a highly curious way, this doesn't matter for the Gospels as much as it should. None of the Evangelists makes anything of—or even mentions—the age of Jesus at his death, so it is sometimes hard to think just how young this man was, not half the age of Socrates. Of some other person cut off near the start of a promising career we would expect the biographer to comment on how much more might have been accomplished in a doubled lifespan. John, though, ends his Gospel speculating that the world could not contain the books required for a complete account of what Jesus had done. As for the pain we fear would constitute a bad death: the manner of this dying must surely have been—the word, after all, comes from it—excruciating. But none of the Evangelists dwells on this. The Gospels do not sanitize crucifixion in the way the *Phaedo* rewrites poisoning: John mentions the thirst, as well as the blood and water. And placing Psalm 22 as backdrop to Jesus' dying situates his death for familiar readers in a context of distress. Nevertheless, neither Jesus' age nor his pain are as prominent as we would expect—or, one could add, as later piety has made them.

It is now time to bring to the surface a suspicion engendered by all the differences in John's account of the Passion and of Jesus' dying: that for John the Hour of Death is the Hour of Glory because it was a noble and good dying, at least for this kind of death by crucifixion. Jesus wasn't alone: his Father was with him, but so were his mother and the other Marys and the beloved disciple. Jesus wasn't helpless in the face of murderous intent or crushing authority: he accomplished his own death by participating in it and embracing it. Jesus died having fulfilled his life work and having successfully prepared his disciples for his departure. In the circumstances it was, we may say, a satisfactory, even exemplary, end.

Were we to permit this suspicion to survive as an explanation of the glory of death, then the glorification of Jesus would be the product of John's narrative activity, arising in the mind of the reader through comparison with the synoptic accounts of the Passion. I do think that his narrative details have something to do with glory, but it is not that the glory *consists in* their mode of presentation. It's rather (if I can put it this way) that the glory *conditions* the mode of presentation. John's account of how Jesus dies does not *create* the glory of his dying; instead it *reflects* that glory.

We can explore the connection between narrative and glorification by pointing out where, for John, the glory is *not* to be found. Two negatives immediately suggest themselves. First, though the Hour of

Death is the Hour of Glory, that glory cannot be associated with *suffering per se*. The narrative does not permit it: the mental anguish is put behind Jesus in chapter 12, and the physical agony of crucifixion is not exploited. If this conclusion flows fairly easily from what we've seen in John's account, its ease should not diminish its significance. There have been readers who, recalling a Pauline phrase about "glorying in suffering" (from Romans 5), link that to another of Paul's sayings (from Galatians 6) about "glorying in the cross of Christ"; they then conclude that there must be something mysteriously good and glorious about suffering in itself for Jesus and therefore for them. That is not John's view of the death of Jesus. (It's not even what Paul meant.)

The second negative also arises from John's narrative presentation. The glory cannot be found where we might expect to discover it—in large-scale publicly impressive features of the event. Such expectation is entirely reasonable, given that divine glory has to do with cloud and fire, with that which overwhelms our ability to see and know. The glorious goes with the grand. But for the characters in John's crucifixion story there is nothing to attract public attention to this dying; nor does his account provide information about their reactions to it. Instead, the story reads (to repeat) more intimately and personally, as told by one who was actually present. If there was glory to be experienced in Jesus' death, it was the beloved disciple, not the other players in the drama, who saw it.

But it will not escape you that here we find ourselves again in the place where this chapter began: what is it for John to *see the glory?*

Recognition, Love, and Glorification

I'm going to propose the following. "Seeing the glory" of Jesus is bound up with coming to recognize his identity. As I mentioned earlier, the theme of nonrecognition pervades this Gospel, and we will think a little more about that next. More: John keeps before his reader the theme of relationships, especially love. So (to give away the ending now) for John the very epithet *"beloved disciple"* contains the clue: love discloses identity, and glory is revealed in love. As for Jesus' glorification, it has something to do with his loving and his being loved, which is why it can be an event and a process, something that happens to Jesus with a Before and an After, but also something that reveals his essential character. Interestingly, love also figures prominently in the relation of Socrates to the divine, but that aspect of his story must wait a bit. For now we are in search of the meaning of this compressed statement about seeing the glory of Jesus.

Nonrecognition At the outset of this part, I claimed that John invests the "world" with its own resistant will: it shuts up its eyes to knowledge so that it does not recognize the identity of Jesus. John writes in order to bring about in his readers that faith which is recognition of Jesus' relationship with his Father. It's time now to see just how pervasive is this theme.

If you reread this Gospel, marking phrases for ignorance like "does not know" or "did not know," you will discover dozens of occurrences. The prologue's charge that "the world did not know him" announces what becomes a constant refrain, repeating itself especially in the farewell discourse chapters 14 through 17 (see 14.17, 15.21, 16.3, 17.25). Given John's preoccupation with those he calls (too simply) "the Jews" and their leaders the Pharisees, we might expect the Evangelist to reserve nonrecognition for this group alone. That is so when the Baptist charges the Pharisees with ignorance at 1.26, "In your midst stands one you do not know," and when Jesus continues in chapters 7 and 8 to accuse "the Jews" and "the people of Jerusalem" several times of not knowing the one who has sent him, or his own identity (see especially 7.28 and 8.14–19). But John does not make the matter that simple: strikingly, it is the disciples themselves who are constantly prone to misunderstanding. The Baptist himself starts off by confessing twice that at first he did not recognize Jesus (1.31, 33); and this unknowing extends to all the disciples. None of them understands the meaning of Jesus' actions (say, in the Entry to Jerusalem, 12.16) or words (to Judas, for instance, 13.28). John gets more specific, naming names: Peter does not understand the footwashing (13.7), Thomas where Jesus is going (14.5), Philip his relation to the Father (14.9). If it is true that by the end of his chapter 17 prayer Jesus has made his name known so that his disciples are no longer in ignorance like the world (vv. 25–26), the problem of identification and knowledge does not go cleanly away. For the theme of nonrecognition repeats itself in the resurrection narratives at the Gospel's end. Twice Mary of Magdala "does not know" where they have laid her Lord (20.2, 13). The disciples "had not understood" the Scriptures (20.9), and they "did not know" that it was Jesus on the beach (21.4). More words and actions are required to bring them to recognition.

The ubiquitous difficulties of understanding Jesus as Word made flesh have worked themselves deeply into John's writing. He finds a range of devices, literal and metaphorical, to make the point. It may be that Jesus hides himself, as when he goes to the Feast of Tabernacles not openly but in secret (chapter 7). Or the unknowing may be visual: John implies at 6.2 that the disciples did not recognize Jesus walking through the storm to their boat. A story can play upon the theme, as when the steward and wedding guests do not know (2.9) the source of the miraculous wine. Or John can spiritualize: the disciples do not know (4.32) the food that sustains Jesus in doing the will of the one who has sent him. Even the claim of Caiaphas (that the Council "knows nothing" of the national interest in Jesus' death, 11.50) gets pressed ironically into John's theme, for he sees this as a prophetic utterance not understood by the high priest.

There are, of course, narratives of successful recognition, but in them John's point persists. Jesus is not known or understood at first; the movement out of that initial lack of recognition is always a coming-to-know through some kind of disclosure. Think of the crippled man of chapter 5, who could not name his healer until Jesus found him later, revealing his identity in his terse advice to sin no longer. Or of another anonymous man (blind this time) four chapters later, whose coming-to-know John details at some length—from lack of knowledge through growing apprehension into full faith and worship. Also among the anonymous belongs the woman at Sychar's well who moves from suspicion and puzzlement to recognition and faith as she asks questions about Jesus. The pattern is similar for a Nicodemus, whose private perplexity is somehow resolved (how we are not told, but we can see the results in chapters 7 and 19), and for a Thomas, whose doubt dissolves into faith in the actual presence of the resurrected Jesus.

The Word came to his own, but they would not accept him; he was in the world he made, but it did not know him. So John says, and goes on to demonstrate in case after case. But there is one exception to his common theme of nonrecognition, out of which some come to know: the narrator himself. Not only does he enjoy the narrator's epistemological privilege whereby he knows what his characters cannot appreciate; he does at least two more things to privilege his position. First, he speaks in his own voice words of recognition. "We saw his glory," he says at the start; we witnessed with our own eyes the spear and the water and the blood, he claims in chapter 19. Placing himself in the position of one who has seen truly (19.35, 21.24), he twice makes plain his authorial intent (19.35, 20.31), that his readers should come to believe—that is, to recognize what he recognizes. Second, John by the end has disclosed his own identity as the "beloved disciple." This one "loved by Jesus" is set apart from all the others, not just by the epithet but more significantly by the knowledge he enjoys. Only he understands Judas as the betrayer: because of his physical closeness to Jesus he gains privileged information. Perhaps because he is special, rumor has it that Jesus said John wouldn't die; but John is the one who understands the meaning of the saying to Peter (a call to mind his own business) and sets the record straight.

Is John's understanding related to his being loved? We could choose to regard John as something like the teacher's favorite, possessing a particular relationship with Jesus not open to other disciples. There's good evidence of strong attachment in his willingness to follow Jesus into the high priest's courtyard, his decision to go with the women to Golgotha, his eagerness to reach the tomb before Peter. Still, John doesn't quite permit us to think that he gains his knowledge only because of an especially good friendship. For his Jesus speaks often about love in ways that open up wider possibilities for everyone.

Recognition and Love Straight off we should note that love must be another of those distinctive centers of John's attention in the writing of his Gospel. Although his most frequent Greek term is the characteristically biblical *agapaô* and related forms, John occasionally employs *phileô* in ways suggesting near equivalence. It is not my purpose to wring a subtle definition of *agapê* out of his account but instead to chart something of its use and importance for the enterprise we have undertaken here.

I think it helpful first to situate Johannine love in the person of Jesus and his relationships. That is, as we've seen, how John himself experiences it, five times over identifying himself as the object of that love. (My shorthand reference to the "beloved disciple," though common enough, doesn't do full justice to John's own locution, since he always uses the active verb, "the one Jesus loved," stressing the identity of the lover.) Not John alone, however—and here the idea of special preference for John gets qualified—for he tells us that Jesus loved Mary, Martha, and Lazarus (11.5). So important was this love to Jesus that he weeps at Lazarus's grave, his tears readily interpreted as love's grief by those who

were there (11.36). We shouldn't overlook the significance of this personal and intimate love, a deep friendship between Jesus and others. For
it is unique to John's Gospel. The other Evangelists include sayings
about loving God and neighbor, but only once—in Mark—does Jesus
love anybody in particular: a young wealthy man who moves Jesus with
his candid innocence about law keeping. But as he is a stranger (Mark
10.17) who goes away instead of following Jesus, the love is not experienced as friendship.

Now, were we to plot the appearances of our term across John's text,
almost all of them (a good thirty) would bunch up in the privacy of the
farewell discourse, with a little group at the Gospel's end. This is in
keeping, I suggest, with the intimate nature of love for John. In the
ending, you will remember, Peter is interrogated three times about his
love for Jesus. The synoptics leave Peter with the bitter taste of tears or the
haunting memory of Jesus' look after his denial. Although his name gets
mention in some resurrection accounts, only John explicitly puts Jesus
and Peter back together, affording Peter the somewhat painful opportunity to profess his love through repetition and to reestablish a relationship thrice-denied. Love particularizes and singles out its object, John
emphasizes, and not only in the comparison Peter is forced to make (Do
you love me more than these others?), but also in the rebuked impropriety of Peter's curiosity about the beloved disciple's manner of death. So if
we use a term like *intimate* for John's view of love, we cannot mean that
its "deep friendship" is simply familiar and cozy. Or even, as we shall see,
that it is like Aristotelian friendship between two who are "other selves"
alike and equal in their virtues. It has its own exacting demands.

Nevertheless, there is no other word for it: Johannine love remains
profoundly intimate. Those whom Jesus loves are called "his own." In
chapter 13, John prefaces the farewell discourse with the prologue's
opposition between the "world" and Jesus: Jesus is about to leave the
world, but always having loved "his own" within this world, he continues to love them to the end. Before these five chapters of private conversation Jesus is not said to have loved anyone other than his Bethany
friends; now during this conversation there are half a dozen references
to his loving his disciples. And them alone. Neither the Sermon on the
Mount saying about love of enemies (Matthew 5.44, Luke 6.28) nor the
Lucan parable about the way neighbor-love includes strangers and victims (10.25–37) finds any distinct echo or instance in John's vocabulary
of love.

Perhaps that is because John's mind is fixed on love as the best characterization of the relationship between Jesus and his Father. Of course, Jesus' form of address to God, as Father, establishes this relationship as intimate throughout the synoptic Gospels—we saw that at length in the chapter on prayer. Nonetheless, the general injunction to love God aside, the synoptic Jesus never reports or expresses *love for the Father;* nor does he acknowledge that the *Father loves him.* The closest we come is in the three Evangelists' use of the phrase "beloved Son" in the voice from heaven at Jesus' baptism or in the Transfiguration. Matthew draws on a version of Isaiah 42 to call Jesus the "servant" whom God "has chosen, my beloved on whom my favor rests" (12.18); so maybe for him, at least, the epithet has messianic associations. With John it's different. He does not draw on the phrase "beloved Son" (his Baptist doesn't even baptize Jesus) but instead makes the love between Father and Son entirely reciprocal. Already from his prologue we know of the closeness between the Word and God, of the unique relation between the Son and the Father; but by 3.35, John says it for the first time: "the Father loves the Son." He places the same words on Jesus' lips in 5.20, then has him say at 10.17, "The Father loves me." The private discourse continues this language, especially with three references at the end of Jesus' prayer; and at 14.31 Jesus speaks of demonstrating through obedience his love for his Father. Moreover, although hunting for places where "love" crops up in the text helps us understand the closeness between the Father and the Son, it isn't the only way to get at that. The very notion of "closeness" in love employs spatial language, either literal or metaphorical; so we can also advance our understanding of John's Jesus by noting the very many, entirely simple, locative terms associated with Jesus and the Father. Most prominent is the preposition *in:* one is "in" the other, making for near-identity of description (if you see me, you see him). But there is also what gets translated as "dwelling" or "abiding" in one another, signifying the permanence of the relationship. Lest we collapse the two into an identical one, we must remember that John speaks of the one "with" the other, and of Jesus "having come from" and "going to" the Father. Although this language leads in short order to theological speculation on trinitarian matters, I am content to let it go into other hands for that kind of treatment. It's enough, here, to think of this spatial language as describing a kind of *family space.* Family members inhabit a shared terrain of identical interest, common memory, reciprocal concern—or at least, in aspiration they do. I propose, then, that John's paradigm of intimacy is Father/Son, who are so close as to collapse spatial differences. And his word for this intimacy is love.

If that is so, then it's difficult to make the vocabulary of love work properly in the context of strangers or anonymous victims or enemies. It does not follow that, for John, treatment of nonintimates or the hostile must be radically different from that prescribed by the synoptics' Jesus. One may still show mercy and compassion. It's just that, in spite of weighty theological treatises on the subject, this way of acting would not, *for John,* be called agapistic. Love is among friends, shared in the family.

I want to come back to ask who gets to participate in this intimacy between Father and Son, and how familial relationships are extended. Before that, though, we should pick up the claim that Johannine love must be characterized by exacting demands rather than a cozy feeling of belonging.

We might have guessed as much from the prolific association of the language of *commands and obedience* with love. Jesus speaks of love for one another as his new commandment; he makes the test of love for him obedience to his commands. It works the other way round, too: keeping his commandments creates friendship with him and means that his followers will dwell in his love. Now it may be objected that it makes as much sense to *command love* as it would to order somebody to sneeze. I can feign sneezing behavior, and pretend to act in loving ways, but my genuine feelings of love remain as much outside my control as the tickle that triggers the real sneeze. But the objection is too simple: it misses the complexities of how feelings follow from having deliberately taken up certain attitudes, how love as appreciation is cultivated through experience, how delight may be disciplined and increase thereby. Besides, it detracts from a more urgent matter: what it is that is commanded. It is not enough to answer "love" *tout court,* and to end up in some kind of empty circularity in which it's loving to love, and love means loving. What is commanded has strong content for John's Jesus. The Father loves me, he says, because I lay down my life, of my own accord, in obedience to the command I have received from him (10.17–18). It is that exacting, and that simple: love manifests itself in dying. The grain of wheat that must die is like one's life; love must not seek to preserve its own life in this world (12.24–25). That Jesus must die we have already considered in seeing his dying as his activity; now we know that this is the activity of love.

Not that Jesus himself is the only one who is to love in this way; the same is required of his followers. This is John's reading of the Last Supper—instead of bread and wine as love's body and blood, he gives us the basin and the towel, love's exemplary work in the service of others. Where the synoptics' Jesus wants us to recall the new covenant in his death, John's Jesus requires us to follow him in the sacrificial action of the new commandment. There is no greater love, he says, than that one should lay down his life for his friends (15.13).

So in place of a pointless order to experience certain feelings, we have a most pointed command; in place of an empty circularity of meaning, we are given a paradox. To love is to act in the interest of the other, and so to act though that means dying.

One more observation about love's work for John. It is in love that Jesus is recognized and known. Midway through chapter 14 comes the key: who obeys Jesus' commands loves him; who loves him is loved by the Father; moreover, *"I will love him and disclose myself to him"* (v. 21). The world, he continues, neither loves nor heeds him. So it does not know him (17.25); indeed, only when the love between Father and Son is seen to be shared by Jesus' followers will the world learn the truth about Jesus (17.23). What gets in the way of successful recognition is lack of love, the wrong kind of relationship, as Jesus had publicly charged earlier: you do not accept me because you have no love of God in you (5.42–44); were God truly your Father, you would love me (8.42). Or as John explains, because of their evil deeds, people love the darkness rather than the light (3.19).

The role of love in opening up knowledge of Jesus enlarges our understanding of some of the matters that we have been thinking about. I'll mention three, the first of which is the closure John achieves with the disciples before the arrest and crucifixion. Why is it, we may wonder, that what Jesus does in chapters 13 through 16 works to a successful end, whereas his public statements about himself in the Temple and else-where (chapters 5 through 10) bring no illumination? The question is a real one. John's Jesus uses most of his public time to make personal affirmations rather than to preach the news of the kingdom in precept and parable. So we already know by chapter 13 such claims as his being sent by the Father as bread from heaven and his going away where he cannot be followed; his closeness with the Father and their mutual indwelling, so that if he is known the Father is known; his gifts of living water, his flesh for the world, eternal life, and resurrection. Though we could elaborate, the point doesn't require more: whatever insight happens on the night of the arrest is not due to an exposure of new teaching about Jesus. At most the disciples are privately reminded about what Jesus had publicly proclaimed. So what makes the difference in bringing them now to believe that he had come from God (16.30)? I think John would answer that there *is* something new: that *new commandment* about love. What he seems to be stressing in the privacy of Jesus' deeds and words on the Last Night is the meaning of Jesus' "going away" in death as an expression of love for the Father and for his own. Somehow the disciples' seeing his work as *for them*—and as continuing for them in his sending of the Spirit—enables them to grasp his true identity. That grasp may be imperfect (their love will quickly falter, as Jesus wryly notes in commenting that they will soon leave him alone [16.32]), but at least they have begun to enter into an appreciation of his love.

Second, what's disclosed about Jesus is his loving relationship with the Father *and* with his followers now called friends. This extension of the intimacy of Father/Son "family space" to Jesus' followers colors strongly John's telling of the Gospel, not just in the private discourse but also in other details. I said earlier that John has an interest in relationships, and these, quickly, are what I have in mind. One: John's Judas does not kiss Jesus, as he does in all three synoptics, nor does Jesus call him friend (as in Matthew). Instead, he is distanced in the arresting band, thrown back by Jesus' powerful speaking. The betrayer, placing himself outside the family, may not express the signs of intimacy. Two: perhaps a similar reason sits in John's identifying the anointing woman as Mary of Bethany: only someone who loved may be that intimate. Three: John's account of Peter's denial is subtly different from the synoptics'. Whereas they report Peter as denying his *knowledge of Jesus* ("I don't know the man"), John won't permit Peter those words. How could he, when Jesus has successfully disclosed himself to all his disciples? Rather, denial—like betrayal—is a negation of family relationship: asked whether he is one of the disciples, Peter answers "I am not" (his repeated *ouk eimi* in 18.17, 26 is for John perhaps an echo of Jesus' repeated *egô eimi*, "I am," in the garden at 18.5, 8). Four: go back to John and Mary at the cross. "From that hour," reports John, the disciple Jesus loved took her "into his own." (Our translations add "home," but the words *ta idia* are the same as in 1.11, where the Word comes to what's "his own.") The dying Jesus establishes a new family closeness for these two, John now seeing himself as son in place of Jesus. The new commandment is repeated and fulfilled in this hour, the Hour of death. John's use of *hôra* cannot be accidental: that was the most immediate meaning of the Hour *for him,* the meaning of being loved and loving.

My third comment on love as disclosing Jesus? It can be mercifully short: we can see now why John's knowledge of Jesus doesn't arise simply from an "especially good friendship," as had been hinted. True, his relationship with Jesus is privileged; but the new commandment so essential to Johannine love makes hard demands. Gaining knowledge of Jesus in loving and being loved is much more than having one of the best seats in the inner circle.

It is time to draw to a close these reflections on a Johannine understanding of how love works in revealing and constituting relationships. Two questions will finish the section. First, we've said that for John love is intimate, but that it is also self-sacrificial: how do these two features fit together? Surely it's the intimacy that is important in disclosing knowledge. We can imagine—indeed we will see this with Socrates—that loving someone opens up new possibilities of knowledge closed off by indifference or dislike. Partly that's because love is *attentive* and notices more; partly because it *singles out,* discarding stale generalizations; partly because love is *creative,* generating new experiences to be known together. For the kind of intimate personal knowledge he seems interested in, John surely needs only to keep love within the family, so to speak. The demands of love for obedience even to the point of death—don't these sit ill with knowledge and intimacy? It would seem so, in more than one way. For even small acts of self-sacrifice will, if done on behalf of the ungrateful or ignorant, make the context of intimacy unnecessary; and large sacrifice, if it lays down life, will bring intimacy to an end.

The second question has, I fear, a too-familiar ring. Even if we could weave coherence from these double strands of Johannine love, how would that help with glory? How is it that Jesus is glorified in his Hour of Death?

Love and Glorification At long last we are in a position to appreciate how John's answer to our question might be unfolded—and how in the unfolding we may find help with the problem over the duality in Johannine love.

If sometimes the weary are easily satisfied, then the length of our reflections on John's Gospel might make a short resolution too attractive. It's important to face up to the bristle of questions that we had about glory and Jesus. Here are the issues, in a handful of sentences. At first, we expected John to mean by glory the divine splendor, that which presses at the edges of our perceptual capacities because God cannot be contained in our viewing. But to ascribe this glory to Jesus is problematic, mainly because he is unrecognized and unknown—and how can that much light be so darkly hidden? We found nevertheless that John does not thin down the glorification of Jesus into mere honor or acknowledgment; he keeps a robust relation between the glories of the Father and the Son. Yet this cannot be a symmetrical relation: while glorifying God effects no change in him, the glorification of Jesus takes place in time, as an event with a Before and After, and changes him. Yet the event is also part of a larger process, difficult to map onto his biography—especially because his glory is also atemporal, with the Father. We know this much, that the glory is associated with his Hour of Death; but also that this glory lies not in his dying the exemplary death of a Socrates, not in the suffering itself, not in the large effects on others of his dying. It remains hidden. And yet John saw it.

I've been arguing that what John saw was an intimate, self-giving love; and that love is the means whereby Jesus is recognized and known. And so the resolution, simple though it is, lies in the relation between love and glory. Once we catch on to that, things start to fall into place.

For instance, it strikes us that, for all John's talk of creation and light in the prologue, his images of glory are relational and personal, not perceptual after all. The glory he saw was the glory befitting *the Father's only-begotten,* the son *in the bosom of the Father.* The generative and even maternal associations in these phrases carry the meaning and should not be downplayed. Recent translations like "nearest the Father's heart" introduce an inappropriate comparative element and dilute the sheer physical intimacy in John's language. Though obviously not literal, the metaphor must be permitted its elemental closeness, because for John glory has that kind of divine love as its content.

But it also has something else. This glory is *full of grace and truth,* a fullness from which we all have received grace, indeed grace upon grace. What John saw he also participated in. Curiously, he does not continue with the vocabulary of grace past the prologue (or maybe the curiosity lies in his having used it there at all); nevertheless, it's not difficult to see into what language grace is translated. For what may be the mode in which love as glory becomes grace, if not in love as gift? The disciple

Jesus loved and for whom Jesus laid down his life—this is the author of these lines. If he cannot quite place himself within the same sphere of love as the only-begotten, still he knows what it is to experience this love as grace. It was he, if you remember, who lay *in the bosom* of Jesus on that Last Night (the same word as in 1.18, this time with literal signification, also not captured in recent translations using simply "close" or "near"). The image of unique Son in the Father's bosom gets replicated as disciple in the bosom of the Father's Son, but though the loves are both intimate, the second has the character of grace.

So the double strands of Johannine love, as family closeness and as self-giving, may be picked up even in the prologue's viewing of glory.

Moreover, though I will not here argue each case, I propose that all of John's references to glory and glorification—at least as it pertains to Jesus—may be rewoven with one or both of those strands. There is no better place to see this than in Jesus' prayer in chapter 17, where he speaks of glory and love together. The *doxa* he participates in belonged to him before the world began (we are back to the time of the prologue), given in love by the Father. Now, we cannot imagine this doxa as an objective thing, a sign or even symbol of love to be bestowed (or not) at the pleasure of the giver. The glory must be intrinsic to the divine life itself, and for Jesus as Son to "have glory" is simply (strange adverb) for him to share in the intimacy of the Father. It's impossible to be *that close* and not have glory. And yet Jesus also speaks of *glorification as process,* in two ways that I think are distinct. In the first, God has been glorified in the completion of the work that Jesus has performed; in the second, Jesus asks the Father to glorify him. The distinction relates to the changed status of the Son when he is sent into the world, distanced from the Father. For Jesus to be glorified, then, is for him to return to the full realization of the Father's presence. That return, however, can only be along the way of obedience to death, as Jesus' own expression of love. This in its own way glorifies God by making apparent the extent of the Son's love for the Father. The same event, the death of Jesus, thus glorifies God as Father and Jesus as Son differently—the former is shown to be worthy of such love, while the latter, displaying the magnitude of his love, is restored to full intimacy.

This reading of love and glory extends to the disciples. They share in the glory given to Jesus by being completely "one" through their love; they participate in family intimacy. And Jesus prays that they might be with him where he is, so that they may witness his glory. A like process of glorification is possible for them through their inhabiting together the same interpersonal space, for which John's name is love.

Concerning the explication by love of other references to Jesus' glory in John, some hints must suffice. Think of a couple of miracle stories that John claims manifest his glory—water vinified, or Lazarus raised. Is it bright sparks and spangles that make these events visible signs of perceptible glory? Not at all. In the one, nobody knows the right person to thank for the gift of good wine. Among the meanings of the account must be glory as self-hiding giving, a love (not intimate here because anonymous) that is sheer gift for no self-related reason. There's much more drama in the Lazarus story, but John employs it to display the strand of love's closeness. The narrative line might have built to Lazarus resurrected, finding its climax in the report of whatever glories he experienced. That kind of interest John leaves to Robert Browning's imaginative construction in "An Epistle from Karshis." His own focus is on family love and friendship, on private conversations and the sisters' trust, on the peculiarly emotional Jesus, deeply moved, weeping, giving a great cry. Among the story's meanings (plural: it must unroll the plot toward the arrest and foreshadow Jesus' resurrection as Mary's anointing portends his burial) is the closeness between Father and Son, such that whatever is asked—even this—is performed.

If John's witness of the glory works as I've suggested, so that his viewing and experiencing involves familial closeness with a Jesus himself obediently intimate with God, then some of our puzzles over glory may be sorted out, especially those having to do with time and change. The *atemporal* glory of Jesus seen by Isaiah refers to the Son in the bosom of the Father, whereas the *process* of glorification comes in the acts of obedience by which Jesus demonstrates love and returns to the Father. Because the supreme act is the laying down of his life, there is a Before and After to this process. But because obedience is manifested in a series of steps toward that end, the process stretches a little untidily over time, being discernible wherever love's strands appear. It extends even to the giving of the Holy Spirit, for the Spirit is sent as continued family presence, so to speak, once the process of glorification returns the Son to the Father.

Just as love is condition, disposition, and process, a state enjoyed and activity performed, so then is glory and glorification for John's Jesus. What, however, of the hiddenness of glory, and of its strange, poignant association with the Hour of Death? These things, too, follow from love as glory.

The first follows from the opposition between private and public experience, intimate and open space. Although Jesus made no secret of his origin, mission or destiny, John claims that he was neither believed nor received. Belief requires more than a public hearing. I've argued that it involves for John a more personal seeing of Jesus' life and death as the work of love, a responsive seeing that places oneself within the family. The hiddenness, then, is only this: that it is not possible to see the glory without that response, and conversely, that it is impossible to respond without seeing the glory.

And the dark Hour of Death? If the glory of Jesus lies not in his suffering, not in the public effects of his crucifixion nor quite in the manner of his death, then we may best look for that glory in his dying *as an expression of love.* John experiences—or so I postulate—in the death of Jesus the marks of a self-sacrificial love so compelling that he associates it with divine glory.

Now how, we may ask, does this kind of emptying love achieve its association with the fullness of intimacy with God? That, of course, is our earlier question about the relation between John's two strands of love. It may be put another, though still Johannine, way: why did Jesus have *to die* to return to "the bosom of the Father" and to invite his followers into that divine affection?

I cannot find in John an adequate account of the necessity of the death of Jesus—or at least one adequate to the questions most often pressed out of theorizing on that death. If the idea of expiation or atonement arises, we need corresponding concepts of sin, guilt, punishment, substitution, satisfaction, and the like. John doesn't work any of that out. Although he speaks of belief in Jesus as the means of moving from condemnation into eternal life, he does not see Jesus as taking upon himself that condemnation, or even as dying for sin. He lays down his life for his friends, to bring together the scattered sheep from many folds into one flock. But John will not easily permit a less-cluttered reading of Jesus' death as exemplary instead of sacrificial. His dying does indeed function as prime example of the new commandment for his disciples, but it is more: it is the drinking of the cup given by his Father and the reason why his Father loves him.

Maybe, though, there's a good explanation for why we cannot discover in John a necessary reason for Jesus' death. Something freely offered in love needs no further justification; love is itself sufficient motivation and meaning. Damaged, fallen, and broken as we are, we may find it difficult to accept love in its freely given form, so we will sniff for causes in obligation or ulterior motive. But if what is offered is *just a gift,* love's own cause explains all. For John, the glory is that this lifting up in death is sheer gift, inviting those who are so loved into the divine family without more argument or explanation.

Why, though, does love require self-sacrifice in any form? Is it not possible to issue a less costly invitation into intimacy? Surely one can have decent personal relationships, even take turns washing a few feet now and then, without this disturbing escalation into the laying down of one's life. Well, in that way lie common sense and safety. But love? Consider how love plays its paradoxes with the self. If my sense of self is such that I believe I deserve your love as a matter of right, then I do not understand love. I cannot think that what you give is only done out of a necessity I have imposed, or in the measure of my worth. To receive love as love the self must give up its claims, relax the guarded territoriality that marks it off from other selves. Or to entertain another metaphor: we cannot enter into intimacy without taking off our clothes. But love also requires another kind of self-emptying, for it must give freely in return. Paradoxically, a self without center cannot love; but to live in love selves must be decentered. Undressed and unarmed, I must direct my protective attention not primarily toward my own privacy but around the vulnerability of the other entrusted into my power.

Our practice of love, of course, is always more muddied than this. Sometimes we are bold to make claims upon another's love and friendship; but maybe that works only where, having secured love's concern, we relax that initial self-assertion. Or again, romantic or erotic love may be engrossed with the self's own feelings, and want (in familiar metaphors) to absorb, eat, devour the beloved. That looks far from self-giving, so far that many thinkers have labeled the erotic generically different from the agapistic. Whatever the distance, though, erotic love cannot escape the paradoxes of the self. For where it is requited, this love will seek to dissolve the hard edges of the self, to be eaten as well as to devour. The goal of union must mean, after all, a kind of dying into a new creation. It is not for nothing that the release and forgetting in sexual experience gets called a "little death."

So intimacy needs giving and receiving, which in their turn require some surrendering of the self. Nevertheless it cannot be that intimacy demands death, real and final death; such a paradox would degenerate into nothingness, like the relationship itself. That is so: with permanent loss the closeness lives in memory alone. And yet—and yet people do die for one another, out of love. Not knowing in my own experience what that is like in any immediate way, I may only call upon fictive imagination for help; but would it not be possible to see through the loss and the guilt an affirmation of incalculable worth? If in love's little gifts I experience myself as the subject of another's delight, how much more would I be shaken into awe by the final sacrifice?

Who knows? I can only postulate this as an ingredient in John's seeing the death of Jesus as *for him,* and therefore as love's gracious glory. However, his experience gains its shape from two other factors that make it unlike the *being died for* that I have just attempted to describe.

Both factors have to do with the unique relation, for John, between Jesus and the Father. The first harks back to the notion of Jesus' being sent by the Father and pulls into our focus one important aspect of Johannine love that we have till now ignored. I have maintained that this love is in the family, among intimates, and not for stranger or victim or enemy. This view inevitably excludes, drawing a circle around Jesus and his friends that leaves "the world" outside the sphere of his concern. Though this is so, one most familiar saying stands out against it: for it is this very world that is *so much the object of God's love that he gave his only begotten Son* (3.16). Here is a love that gives the gift of one who is so closely beloved that it is costly to the giver. In the very character of God's love itself, then, flows not just intimacy but also the grace of giving. Whether John here conceives "the world" that is so loved as hostile or indifferent to God, or rather as belonging to God through creation, I cannot determine. If the former, then John does have this one uncharacteristic instance of the synoptic Gospels' love-of-enemy; if the latter, then God intends to embrace the world as his own in the giving of his beloved. Perhaps it's a difference that doesn't much matter, for John may continue to hold that God regards the world as his own, but that the world in refusing God's gift turns away from the divine embrace. In any case, the death of Jesus as not only his gift to the Father but more significantly *God's gift to the world* imparts divine glory to John's experience of being died for in love.

We must conclude with the second reason why, though life-sacrificing friendship must be extraordinary, this particular death for John reveals a love so unique as to be glory. Jesus' dying is a return to the Father as well as the Father's gift: intimacy, only temporarily severed by death, is fully recovered in resurrection. Though we've said very little about it, Jesus' resurrection has a central part to play in John's appreciation of glory, for the person whose glory he saw was not done in by death.

Now this association of resurrection with glory recalls us to this chapter's introductory comments about the synoptics' use of divine *doxa* for the Transfiguration and the Son's coming on the clouds of heaven. But in being reminded of that connection, we appear to move away from John's particular understanding of the Hours of Death and Glory. We need therefore to think a little about John's experience on Easter Day.

That requires us to look for John himself in the Easter account. I had pointed earlier to John's privileged position as narrator throughout his Gospel, heightened by his claims as witness and by his special closeness to Jesus as beloved disciple. There I had argued that he does not seem to belong to the general human condition he depicts, to a world that does not recognize Jesus but out of which some come into a place of knowledge and acceptance. John's own knowledge seemed to me then to be a matter of privilege rather than something won over time, with its own before and after. But there is an important clue that corrects this impression. On that first day of the week something happened to the beloved disciple: *he*—and not just the inclusive "they" of the disciples—*he saw and believed* (20.8). Strictly speaking, it was what he *didn't* see that made the difference: there was no body in the tomb. That absence rearranged what he had known and experienced of Jesus, lining up that knowledge with what he knew of the Scriptures. He came to faith, a faith subsequently confirmed in three encounters with his resurrected Lord.

But note: what John saw that morning was not what Mary or Thomas saw when they came to faith. They met and saw Jesus for themselves. John's seeing was a perceiving and a believing that reinterpreted all that he had previously witnessed of Jesus. From that difference follow two things. First, we can preserve the Johannine understanding of glory as having to do with death: it's not the visual seeing of the resurrected Jesus that produces the experience of glory for John. But second, we now understand that knowledge of the resurrection colors indelibly all that John knew in retrospect about that death. What he bears witness to in writing his Gospel is illumined by the backward cast of Easter's light. That's how he knows that Jesus' dying is a return to the bosom of the Father. John does not wait for that return on a separate

Ascension Day. Jesus ascends to the Father immediately upon revealing his risen presence to Mary, so that it becomes impossible to separate his resurrection from that return. And the crucifixion becomes itself, in a telling repeated Johannine phrase, a "lifting up" or "exaltation" (the word is the same).

So the dying of Jesus for John cannot be contained within an explanation making it a noble example of a friend's supreme sacrifice. In this death God gives in love to the world; by this death the Son overcomes death and is lifted back into the Father's love.

On this reading, then, resurrection becomes the clue to John's realization that what he saw was glory, and that the glory lay in the intimacy and grace of love. Before we end, however, we might try to dispel a small worry creeping out of a Johannine appreciation of resurrection. For we could be asked whether the early prediction of John's Jesus that he would rise again after three days (2.21) doesn't detract from his death as the sacrifice of love. Isn't it much easier, and therefore less costly, to give something if you think you're going to get it back again? Well, maybe, and sometimes, with some kinds of giving. If I wash your feet you'll wash mine—that could make it easier, and, of course, less loving. But dying cannot be that kind of gift. Because it is loss of all the conditions of existence, it costs everything. Nor can it be that the promise of resurrection would make any difference to John's Jesus. He is the eternal Word returning to the Father. That return, however, is through a giving up of his life, a letting go in loving obedience and trust that places himself entirely within Another's will. And if we think not of hurt or uncertainty but of cost to the self, what could be more costly in love than that?

There is as well another kind of risk in sacrifice. The love in Jesus' dying extends horizontally as well as vertically, toward his own as well as to his Father. His resurrection must be *for them,* so that (as he tells Mary to announce) he may ascend to *their* Father and *their* God. And because it is up to them to do the receiving and the believing, John's Jesus can have no guarantees that his dying will be seen as love's gift. Divine love takes that costly risk with the world. Some will indeed come near the cross and be welcomed into the family. But there will be others who just want their version of events in the record or their fair share of the gains—and some who can only treat love's final sacrifice with a pointed contempt.

With that understanding of the intimacy and costliness of divine love, we must now leave John's Jesus. Socrates awaits us once more.

Socrates: Love and the Divine

In the experience of love, John the beloved disciple came to recognize divine glory in Jesus. We find in Plato's Socrates these same themes of love and the divine, but around them the largest differences between Socrates and Jesus have been drawn. It is commonly believed, for instance, that the Greek understanding of love and friendship cannot capture the New Testament view of love as agapistic. If *erôs* strives only for the beautiful while *agapê* embraces the sinful, then what Jesus displays differs radically from what relationships are about for Socrates. More centrally for Christian belief: whatever Socrates' associations with the divine, Jesus remains in a wholly other category as the beloved Son of the Father. Believers who get to know their Plato might come to admire Socrates; but they do not sing hymns or pray to him. They believe in one Lord, Jesus Christ, who alone with the Father and Spirit is worshiped and glorified. Although Socrates died in obedience to the god's command to practice philosophy, philosophers have not died for Socrates. (Aristotle set their example in escaping from Athens in order to remove the opportunity for its sinning twice against philosophy.) Jesus died in obedience to the Father; for twenty centuries countless numbers of martyrs have followed the example of Stephen and have died for Jesus. And so on: with little difficulty we can go over all the strong dissimilarities in belief and practice around Jesus and Socrates.

I have to confess, however, that the exercise of rereading the Gospels and Plato's dialogues for this writing has thrown up an unexpected contrast between these two, one obscured by centuries of theorizing about the nature of Jesus as Son of God. In two words: Plato's Socrates is *less human* than the Jesus of the Gospels.

Now, rather than wondering about the Christian orthodoxy of such a claim, I want to use it to provoke reflection on how Plato situates his Socrates in the cosmos, so to speak. Hints have fallen out of our earlier examinations of Socrates that he is set apart from the normal run of our kind, with an unusual relationship to the divine. We'll undertake to work that theme through and to discover what love has to do with it; but first I should explain why I have found Jesus to be more human than Socrates. Starting there may have an advantage in that it should be easier to determine what it means to be human than to set out how a human might be divine.

Jesus: Incarnation

It is possible to attribute some of the dissimilarities in the portrayals of Socrates and Jesus to a difference in the literary forms of dialogue and gospel. Plato represents self-contained conversations among philosophical types; the Evangelists, though not writing what we widely consider standard historical biography, still give us more narrative detail than philosophic dialogue contains. The differences should not be discounted; nevertheless, in each form we have a sufficiently strong characterization of the protagonist to draw out significant comparisons between them.

The character of Jesus across the four Gospels consistently reveals the marks of our common humanity. I'll point to perceptible differences between him and Socrates in three areas. The first has to do with the expression of empathy: that will uncover part of the emotional life we think essential to human beings. Those who express nothing of their feelings we relegate to the edges of our species in the metaphors of rocks or stones, or in spatial notions like aloofness and remoteness. To show empathy it's necessary to be one of us, participating in the experience and the expression of our common feelings. Whatever the gospel writers believe about the authority of Jesus, his closeness to the Father or his sharing in the divine glory, they all portray his identification with human frailty. If sometimes textual reticence means we have to read compassion into his face, at other times we know he is deeply affected in the presence of evils. He groans over the blind or the deaf and weeps by a grave for his friend. It's not only suffering that calls out his response, however; he is moved by love for the young rich man observant of the law, reaches out to make physical contact with children, and demonstrates the care for his friends that we've just been considering in John's Gospel.

With Socrates it's different, I think. Remember how Plato sets him as foil against the confused anxiety of Crito, or the fears about death voiced by his friends in the *Phaedo:* Socrates seems more concerned to prove those emotions groundless than to enter into their experience. He's too self-possessed to weep along with those who love him. In fact, throughout the bits of his life Plato sketches, Socrates never reaches out in sympathy or tenderness to another person. Ask Alcibiades about that, and he will answer in the charge of the *Symposium* that especially to his friends Socrates is guilty of aloofness, disconnectedness. Socrates talks much about love, as we'll shortly see; but the only gesture that I can remember of anything approaching tenderness comes just before his death, when he plays with Phaedo's hair. Plato sets even his farewells to his family offstage, beyond our observation. So when Socrates tells the jury that he did not spring (in Homer's words) "from an oak or a rock," we want to believe that he has human feelings as well as human relatives: but he just doesn't produce the evidence. When he does make claims to participate in human cognitive failings—with his forgetfulness and his ignorance—these turn out to be taken as ironically cultivated expressions of his superiority rather than as an empathetic identification with the rest of us.

Return to Jesus for another contrast, still in the area of emotional expression but this time on the negative side, in feelings of anger and hostility. I don't have in mind anything as mild as his frustration with the disciples over their dullwittedness. It's the overturning of Temple tables, the lashing out at moneychangers, the cursing of fig trees: these are the articulations of anger, and they find no parallels in the life of Socrates. Nor does the language of Socrates contain anything approaching the violence in the parables of Jesus, the murdering and the gagging and the throwing into darkness that act as verbal anticipations of his own death. Socrates' illustrations are commonplace, too boring for some hearers; and when characters like Callicles or Thrasymachus push against the bounds of decency or civility in argument, the restrained conduct of Socrates stands out in relief. He does not treat his opponents as does Jesus. Plato has no love for the Sophists, yet his Socrates maintains a coolness in verbal combat with them. He is able to diminish his opposition by the sheer force of seemingly inexorable reasoning, while they lose control into incoherence or humiliation or even once or twice into gracious defeat. Maybe we shouldn't forget that Jesus was up against something more dangerous than a contest between intellectual sparring partners; still, his response to opposition goes well beyond a skillful use of Scripture, parable, and questioning into a denunciation, even excoriation, that has high emotional charge. Socrates feels compelled to prophesy against those who voted as his executioners, warning them of disaster unless they change their ways; but his words are measured. One suspects that Socrates would have found intemperate Jesus' anger and his calling down of repeated woes upon hypocrisy. He would have preferred the gentler if no less certain deflation of religious pretense through irony, as with Euthyphro.

Empathy and passionate engagement characterize Jesus, then, in ways that don't seem to be suited to Socrates. For the third area of difference, reflect on their respective mortalities. Not for nothing do we call ourselves mortals, or seek immortality in the heavens. Jesus takes full part in the apprehension of human mortality. As we have seen over and over again, his Passion is told as the too-human story of betrayal and denial, of recoil from agony, of mockery and malice, of a final godforsakenness. If our humanity carries the burdens of weakness and wounding, Jesus the victim expresses our meaning without reservation. His cross is our sign.

And Socrates? Where do we seek him? Not in the emptying tomb that is his body—"try to catch me" he laughs to Crito, rising as he dies.

That Socrates is not his body shouldn't be read only as an instance of a general metaphysical statement about the identity of persons with souls as distinct from their physical habitations. Socrates, as we have come to understand, exhibits such detachment from and indifference to his body that he is different from the rest of us. He already began long ago the disengagement which is dying. He won't answer what should be done with his body, and though Crito is permitted to close the eyes and mouth, Plato, too, leaves Socrates' body. It is of no further use or interest. Jesus, by contrast—but you know his story, and the care with which a few women and a couple of men prepare his body for burial and, unwittingly, for so much more.

The Word became flesh, writes John, and took up his dwelling in our midst. That's incarnation, and it means that this flesh is our flesh, not Socratic flesh. However puzzling for theory, incarnation for Jesus is matched by a different puzzle for Socrates: divinization. It's time now to assume the task of explaining how a human might become divine.

Socrates: Divinization

Some in every generation have sided with the old accusers of Socrates, thinking him as sly and slippery in argument as any sophist. Against their opinion stands the dominant belief that there is something special about this figure that marks him off from the common run, something worthy of admiration.

For philosophers Socrates has always incarnated the philosophic quest, the driving spirit of inquiry. Although Thales gets first mention in the history of Western philosophy because his was the earliest recorded attempt to develop a single explanation for the complexity of the world, that explanation was soon replaced by a series of new ones, each proclaimed somewhat better than the previous. That has been the story of philosophers: the latest sees the holes in the fabric of previous attempts, themselves improvements upon earlier efforts. Some philosophers mend old garments; some know they can patch no longer and weave brand new material; some sketch daring designs. Curiously, all this activity can never produce The Philosophy to suit the human condition: even if by some impossibility it did, philosophers would have to pick it apart and try again. So perhaps the perennial interest in Socrates lives in his never having come up with a product, but only with questions about how it should be made, what should go into it, and so on.

We could add that insofar as philosophical questions belong to our humanity and not simply to a small class of people receiving pay for working on them, Socrates can capture the imagination of almost any reader. This, however, won't explain how his reputation gets to be so high. I want to say something about its height, and then to offer an explanation about its source in Plato's dialogues.

Socrates Sanctified Here's a small curiosity about Socrates and Plato: that their philosophical followers celebrated their birthdays in the ancient world. The chosen dates of the sixth and seventh of Thargelion were also the birthdays of Artemis and Apollo, respectively, so each is associated with a divinity. How extensive was the practice we don't know: our evidence goes from the second to the fifth centuries A.D. in Plutarch, in Porphyry's Life of Plotinus, and in Marinus's Life of Proclus. We do know that the fifteenth-century Platonist Marsilio Ficino revived the custom in Florence. In Ficino we see marks of veneration: he kept a flame burning before a bust of Plato, but more to our point he speaks of Socrates in biblical images. Socrates has a compassionate concern for the salvation of his followers, freeing the young from wicked men as a shepherd keeps his lambs from the ravage of wolves. This Good Shepherd keeps moving into the Christian tradition: half a century later one of Erasmus's characters in *The Godly Feast* reports that he is so overcome by Socrates' attitude toward death that he wants to exclaim, *Sancte Socrates, ora pro nobis.*

It's that attitude, I think, which heightens Socrates' reputation beyond exemplary practitioner of philosophy and brings him in some minds close to sainthood. For reasons familiar from our study of martyrdom, his death also brings him close to Jesus, and this association elevates his reputation further among readers in the Christian tradition. There is plenty of evidence for this: the most accessible comes in the one-volume English edition of Plato's *Collected Dialogues*, with intro- ductions by Edith Hamilton. For the *Phaedo* and the *Gorgias* she picks up gospel phrases for Socrates' death (he entered into "life more abun- dantly") and teaching (it amounts to "Turn to him the other cheek"). She goes further in her note to the *Phaedrus*, attributing to Socrates the description of the suffering servant applied to Jesus: "Again and again his snub nose is mentioned, his protruding eyes, and so on. 'He had no form nor comeliness that we should desire him.' His wonderful beauty was within." But Hamilton is not alone. Referring to beliefs about similarities between the fate of the just man and the death of Jesus, Paul Shorey defends his use of "crucified" for the translation of a verb in the *Republic* meaning "impaled." And his is only one further instance of this kind of retroactive hallowing of Plato's Socrates in the light of Jesus.

The appropriation of Socrates deserves study in its own right, but it's enough here to conclude that his special status in the ancient world has been successfully translated into something approaching sanctificat- ion among a significant number of readers in the Christian West, and not just in the Renaissance. This process of sanctifying Socrates, how- ever, assimilates him to the Christian tradition of saints and martyrs; it does not explain my observation that he is less human than Jesus, and it pulls Socrates out of his original home in Plato's dialogues. So we must return him there, asking how Plato has constructed a special place for his Socrates, and why it is that I associate him with the divine.

Plato's Divinization of Socrates Begin with the familiar idea of Soc- rates as midwife. Found only in the *Theaetetus*, it's a striking image, apt in form (Socrates liked homely metaphors) and content (he himself doesn't produce but only assists at birth). To our ears it also nicely reverses gender roles. What's not commonly noticed, however, is a *difference* between Socrates and midwives. Their patron goddess Artemis is virginal and would prefer that state for her devotees; that won't work, though, because weak human nature requires actual expe- rience for knowledge. So to assist others, midwives must be women who have themselves borne children; but to be more like Artemis they must now have passed childbearing age. Socrates claims himself to be barren of knowledge and its mere midwife: but how can he get his skill if he has not ever experienced personally the birth of knowledge?

The answer may be found in the repeated linking of Socrates' work with the divine in this passage of the *Theaetetus*. Sometimes his *daimonion* forbids his work, but otherwise the god compels him to practice his skill, grants progress to his pupils, and works together with Socrates. ("The god and I are the cause of delivery" [150d].) More: when countering accusations of malevolence toward some pupils, Socrates points out that *no god* is ever malevolent toward human beings. This is strong language, and places Socrates on the side of Artemis herself, a goddess who may oversee childbirth without personal experience because she is not subject to human weakness. Socrates' birthday may have been celebrated on Artemis' day because she was his patroness; but in associating him with her in this account Plato elevates his Socrates beyond the human.

However, on the basis of this passage alone it would be difficult actually to use the word "divine" of Socrates. Plato stops short of that attribution, here and to my knowledge elsewhere. What he presents is rather a movement toward the divine, expressed in my term *divinization*. To understand this requires comment on how the adjective "divine," *theios*, functions in Plato.

Some of its uses won't help us with Socrates, at least if we try to keep them working separately. Sometimes Plato means simply to reflect a popular way of commending by hyperbole. (We have done likewise in calling opera singers or parties divine. Plato pokes playfully with the term at the Spartans in the *Meno* or Prodicus in the *Protagoras*, and wouldn't attach it in this way to Socrates. A second venue for "divine" is poetic or prophetic inspiration, in which the gods take mortals for their mouthpieces. But because Plato thinks poets the passive receivers of true beliefs from outside their psyches, his Socrates would have to have more content to his mind were he rightly classified among them. Moreover, Socrates found poets wanting in his search for knowledge; and his own experience of the divine was only negative, in the checking of his *daimonion*. So he could not be linked to the divine through this kind of inspiration. The third context of *theios* may be more promising. Plato calls divine those objects that are (to use terms from the *Phaedo*) unchanging, immortal, invisible, pure, and completely intelligible. He has in mind preeminently the Forms, but the god or the gods are also in this class (though not the Olympian deities of popular piety). Soul, too, is a candidate for divine status; and if soul is divine and Socrates is his soul, then Socrates—you can do the rest. But alas, so is everybody else, even tyrants; and this gives no way to account for the special status of Socrates, his closeness to the god.

There is, though, one group of mortals who do eventually attain that closeness. Plato's eschatological myths in the *Phaedo*, the *Gorgias*, and the *Republic* all place in the company of the gods those souls that have been purified by philosophy. They dwell in the Islands of the Blessed, having escaped the cycle of transmigration. That means philosophers have undergone a process of elevation from mortality toward immortality and the divine. It can work that way because for Plato what makes the gods divine is their unclouded apprehension of the Forms. Without bodies to compromise their understanding, the minds of the gods (in the words of the *Phaedrus*) are nourished by reason and knowledge. In Plato's view reason itself is divine, sharing in the nature of its objects, so the soul fully possessing and exercising reason participates in true being and becomes godlike. Among mortals, philosophers are those who have so directed their love toward wisdom that they come to glimpse the Forms. In life they remain seekers rather than possessors of wisdom; after death they enjoy the same vision as the gods. In that they once were embodied, philosophers are not gods; but their share in divine reason makes them godlike, and in reason's breaking free to return to the Forms they are divinized.

It will be clear that Plato's scheme permits a process of deification not available in the Judeo-Christian tradition, with its fundamental ontological bifurcation between uncreated God and the created order. Forms are the ultimate Platonic units, and because the quality of relation of souls to Forms determines degree of divinity, human-souls achieving the same vision as god-souls are entitled to the epithet "divine."

But it will also be clear that Socrates, though exemplary philosopher, still inhabits the realm of mortals throughout Plato's dialogues. He has not yet returned to the Forms, not yet enjoyed the beatifying vision. Or has he? There remains something unusual about Socrates, something that provokes our suspicion that he is not tied down to this world. What accounts for our reaction, and how does that situate Socrates in relation to the divine?

I want to suggest that Plato employs two strategies of divinization in his presentation of Socrates, one having to do with what Socrates knows, and one about the objects of his fundamental concern, his love.

It's strange to think of knowledge as distinguishing Socrates from the rest of us when his profession of ignorance is so important to his identity. But what I'm after is perhaps best called his *epistemological privilege;* it has to do with his multifaceted advantages for viewing things not available to others. Right from the start of his mission, Socrates enjoys those privileges of oracle and sign that we spent time considering in the previous chapter; even if what they teach is negative, nevertheless Socrates sees what his fellow citizens do not. His confidence in the care of the god and his critique of popular piety continue to set him apart from them. Then there is the sure force of his intellectual skills, manifested in the success of his arguments but also in the control he exercises over his own life. Whatever it is Socrates knows may remain inaccessible, but it has power. And the sense of privilege grows stronger through such literary devices as foreshadowing and narrative perspective. In the *Euthyphro, Meno,* and *Gorgias,* for example, Socrates creates the impression that he foreknows his trial and death; and in the many eschatological myths he relates, he speaks in spite of his modesty from a place outside the experience of mere mortals. He tells us in the *Phaedrus* that god alone knows the nature of soul, yet Socrates is able to give us those resemblances that are as close as any human being may come to its nature. Whatever his professed ignorance, then, Socrates charts the limits of human knowledge with the certainty of an omniscient narrator. His elevation beyond human weakness in these ways is the product of Plato's literary art. It should not surprise us that the midwife Socrates shares in the nature and work of the divine Artemis.

There is a second strategy that yields the same conclusion, this time centering on the ultimate object of love and Socrates' relationship to it. Plato's best presentation of this strategy comes in the *Symposium,* for there he portrays Socrates' character and behavior as well as his words about love.

The *Symposium* makes much of Socrates' difference. His friends witness to those extraordinary powers we considered in the last chapter when describing his somatic control, so we know he is unusual. But the prophetess Diotima goes further: she characterizes the daimon Eros, halfway between mortals and gods, in terms that fit Socrates himself. As the embodiment of this spirit, Socrates is neither darkly ignorant nor fully wise, but instead a lover of a wisdom that the gods alone possess. We might leave it there, with a Socrates begun on the road to divinization in the "lesser mysteries of love." He would come to the end of the road only when in another world he might come to gaze on beauty itself—for then he would become the friend of god and immortal. That is our expectation of the philosopher in this life, seeking but not yet possessing divine wisdom. Plato, however, does not end at that expected place with Socrates: he brings in Alcibiades. And from him we learn that Socrates has indeed passed beyond the human already. No ancient hero, no contemporary, is like Socrates, claims Alcibiades; he may be compared only with satyrs and sileni—and not just for his appearance, but for the images of the gods within. Socrates is full of the divine in speech and in virtue's images; and only the language of divine devotion and religious frenzy will capture his effect upon his followers.

And now comes the point of most significance: Socrates does not return to others the affection that they bestow on him. Alcibiades calls on all who know him to bear witness at this new trial among his friends. Socrates is remote, withdrawn, unattached; his attention is devoted to some place apart from his friends.

But all this comes out only in Alcibiades' drunken speech. Isn't it just the product of befuddlement and a wounded pride, rubbed with the salt of unrequited love? Or does Plato really mean us to suspect that, although Socrates himself won't say it, already his heart and mind have been captured by the austere and impersonal Forms? Is Socrates far advanced in dying in the midst of his life, and grown that close to the divine?

The answer is crucial to our understanding of love, death, and the divine. For if Alcibiades is right, here too Socrates may be less human than Jesus.

Socratic Love and the Divine

I mean to turn to *Socratic* love, not the much more familiar (if not always well understood) *Platonic* love. We will say something about Plato's own theory of *erôs,* but for now I want to look at the way Plato constructs his Socrates around love. Because the dialogues develop characters and their interactions, it is possible to watch how Socrates relates to others—what attitudes flavor his speech, which concerns elicit what response. Socrates' actions can then be held up to his more explicit words about the nature of love and friendship. So by Socratic love I mean to refer not just to a theory but to love as spoken about and displayed by Plato's Socrates. We all know (perhaps with self-knowledge) people whose talk about human relationships is more impressive than their actual practice. With Socrates we'll discover that his life misses something from his theory, and that in this curious gap evidence of his divinization may be discovered.

Some Socratic Relationships Were we devoting a whole book to Socrates alone, we'd be able to engage in a systematic analysis of his relationships, his style, attitudes, interests, motivations, and beliefs. Instead, I'll have to sketch the broad lines of a portrait assembled from observations about his treatment of acquaintances and friends in familiar dialogues such as the *Euthyphro,* the *Apology,* the *Crito,* and the *Gorgias.*

Begin with a linguistic clue: the large number of times Socrates uses terms like *friend* or *companion,* along with friendly epithets like *good* or *noble fellow,* for his interlocutors. It's not mere conventional courtesy that explains his habit, for these terms are made to carry a variety of emotions and attitudes. Take Euthyphro: Socrates praises him on many occasions, but not long into the dialogue we suspect Socrates of playing around with this deluded victim of inflated epistemological confidence. The purpose of their discussion is highly serious, for if Socrates can learn from Euthyphro the nature of the holy he will be able to defend himself against the charges of impiety at his trial. The dialogue's failure to discover the holy should then be tragic. Instead it is ironic, ending in the intentional diminishment of Euthyphro. He's no friend at all.

Nor is Polus. The vocabulary of friendship is peppered throughout Socrates' encounter with this brash interlocutor of the *Gorgias;* but here the terms are downright sarcastic as Socrates wrings the truth out of Polus, giving him as good as he gets in the tricks of argument.

We might expect better from the *Crito,* as a dear friend and longtime companion visits Socrates to persuade him to save his own life by leaving prison. Yet Socrates quickly brushes aside the evident distress of an old friend, paying no attention to his feelings but focusing only on impersonal moral principles. When Crito's emotional state prevents his continuing the discussion, Socrates turns to the Laws of Athens to carry on—only Socrates' own imaginative creations seem worthy partners in this argument.

And as a last bit of evidence, recall our earlier discussions of Socrates' defense before the jury. What is most striking about the *Apology* is Socrates' refusal to save his own life. His commitments are to truth and goodness, but unlike our commitments—which include self-preservation—his are absolute and override all interests. Nothing is more important than goodness, nor can any human bond or feeling stand in the way of this single-minded pursuit.

The portrait that emerges is of a man whose consuming passion is the goodness of his soul. He is in love with goodness and truth, obsessed with getting things right, his conduct as well as his ideas. His goodness matters more than reputation, than wealth or position, than life itself. And it certainly matters more than family or friends (especially family, for they don't seem to be of much help in the search). But for all his self-possession and self-containment, Socrates is not turned utterly inward. Just the opposite: he can't stop talking to people. That might suggest that he needs their contribution to his quest: indeed, he sometimes claims as much. Yet we are not really convinced by his behavior that this is so. Everybody who talks with Socrates turns out to be at a disadvantage; nobody is invited into the conversation on equal terms. As we found it hard to think of him as conforming to his society, so it's also hard to give Socrates many marks on any scale for decent friendship. No one is allowed to share equally in his life.

Nevertheless, these characterizations are not sufficient for constructing a notion of Socratic love. For we have not yet considered what Socrates actually says himself on the matter: surely his words must figure largely in any assessment of the nature of his kind of love. For that we return to the *Symposium.*

The Theory and Practice of Love Although this dialogue contains a full account of *erôs,* we find that Socrates says little in his own person: his understanding of love is not his own, but comes from his teacher, the prophetess Diotima. Diotima tells the young Socrates that she is confident that he will be initiated into the "lesser" mysteries of love: so we should recall what these involve, and ask ourselves whether there is enough evidence about Socrates' character and pursuits to assess her prediction.

Socrates' own report to the dinner party makes it clear that he got to understand the basics from spending time with Diotima. He got straight, for instance, that one must not characterize the loving in the same way as the beloved. The object of love is variously called goodness or beauty or wisdom. The experience or process of loving, because it is a felt lack of these objects, is intermediate between their utter absence and their complete possession. He also learned that the desire which is love is a desire to possess its objects—that is, love is not appreciation at a distance but a desire to turn into something better, to give birth to something, to become a certain kind of being; and to become this forever, in a stable and unchanging way. That state of perfection is the immortality that humankind seeks but in which no human being can fully participate. So we substitute lesser creations—children, poetry, laws, institutions—in attempts to find enduring happiness. All this Socrates reports himself as having learned; of its truth he is convinced.

It is nonetheless one thing to agree with the theory and another to begin to practice it. The theory requires that the seeker locate the good and the beautiful and bring them to birth in beauty. And it offers, in these lesser mysteries, some steps to take. The path seems to be this: one must discover within a great desire for the birth of wisdom and goodness. Not everyone has this. But if it is there, one must search for the beautiful that will bring goodness to birth. The ugly cannot generate goodness, so beautiful bodies will be attractive. But something else is better: a beautiful soul in a beautiful body, in whose company one may give birth to an enduring goodness.

Has Socrates indeed begun on this path? Has he become skillful in love, as Diotima predicted and as he himself wanted to be? We can believe that Socrates' soul is striving to bring to birth wisdom and beauty: we could not imagine a better candidate for love's work. But (and here is the point crucial to my reading) we know of no close association between himself and another person, no intimacy in which beauty has begotten beauty. The character Plato presents seems better placed in the next steps, among the "greater" mysteries. Here the attachment that produced the birth of beauty is released. The lover better appreciates the beauty of soul so that physical beauty is less important; then particular beauties are left behind as he enters upon contemplation of that "great sea of beauty."

That Socrates belongs near the threshold of the final mysteries is confirmed in the similarities between his persona and Diotima's description of the daimon Eros. That daimon is impoverished, spends his time outdoors, goes barefoot, is tough, not tender, is neither human nor divine, but intermediate between gods and men. In characterizing Socrates as Eros, Plato removes him from normal relationships between lover and beloved, isolating him as Love itself. Think how different is Socrates from the lovers the others have praised: for Phaedrus, for

Pausanias, for Aristophanes, the virtuous and healing benefits of love come only through relationships, relationships that are special and even unique. But Socrates has no such relationships. How, then, has Socrates' goodness come about? Not from any attachment Pausanias would recognize: we hear of no satisfactory teachers for Socrates in, say, the *Phaedo*'s autobiographical account; and here in the *Symposium* his teacher is a woman—who, though she gives him instruction, is not at all presented as the possible object of his erotic interest. Socrates has managed to make it up the ladder of love: but he has gone beyond the human in ways inaccessible to our understanding. By some heroic feat he has managed to do it on his own.

All this is confirmed in Alcibiades' drunken speech, which charges Socrates with *hubris* and displacedness: he doesn't fit. Worse, he refuses not just Alcibiades' erotic advances but also the exercise Diotima recommends—he doesn't allow Alcibiades to acquire virtue through intimacy between lover and beloved. Though Alcibiades' complaint does express the pique of his particular relationship to Socrates, nevertheless Socrates' character is accurately reflected here. The object of his affection, indeed his passion, is not this or that beauty, but the beautiful itself—because goodness and wisdom are there as well. Socratic love, if the term means the love that the character Socrates exhibits, has nothing of the personal in it. His supposed interest in others is an ironic verbal masking of his inner preoccupation with goodness; he neither appreciates nor delights in other people, nor does he actively help in their seeking salvation or improvement. He loves but is not loving.

I earlier remarked that Socrates doesn't get high grades for friendship with other people. Now we can appreciate that this is not because he is uncaring, passionless, or self-absorbed. It is rather because, in removing himself from our world to care about the eternal, Plato's Socrates has passed over to the realm of the divine. I stress again that we have no idea how he has managed this, because he hasn't followed his own prescriptions gotten from Diotima. In this way Plato heightens his idealization of Socrates as perfect lover and grants him godlike status.

Platonic Love, Socratic Love, and Johannine Love

And how does this view of Socratic love fit into what's more commonly known as Platonic love? I propose that Plato's own understanding of love comprises the entire series of ascending steps in the

Symposium, including the non-Socratic experience of intimate and productive friendship between two lovers of beauty. In the theory constructed for Diotima to hand on to Socrates, Plato gave an important role to this element of attraction between individuals, for it is to be channeled into an ascent to the beautiful and the good. The lover delights in another beautiful person and brings goodness to birth with him. "Such men share an intimacy with one another," says Diotima, "which is far deeper than one coming from children and enjoy a surer affection, because they have taken part in the creation of more beautiful and immortal progeny" (209bc, trans. Groden). Plato wrote extensively and compellingly about this in the potent imagery and sexuality of the *Phaedrus:* there he contemplates the possibility of an inner transformation into goodness through a disciplined and redirected sexual energy, in company with another like-minded friend. It is true that the final goal of *erôs* in Platonic love remains the eternal Forms, so that its object is the divine and unchanging rather than changeable human beings. But personal relationships between suitable lovers have a crucial role in Platonic love, a role absent from Socratic life and love.

Curiously, however, I cannot find any example in Plato's dialogues of characters who actually practice Platonic love in ways that prize unique individuality. The problem, I suspect, lies in finding the right people as plausible Platonic lovers. Socrates should be one of them; and certainly he gets regarded as special by Alcibiades and a host of other followers. They are devoted to Socrates, sometimes fanatically; they cherish him as irreplaceable; they extol him as divine. That their deep affection is of uncertain reciprocation makes it no less love on their part. But just because Socrates directs his own devotion to the Forms rather than to their beauty, their love cannot be manifestations of the intimate stage of Platonic love.

What, then, is it that they love about Socrates? Not the little idiosyncrasies that make people lovable in their particularities; rather, it is Socrates' unwavering commitment to goodness, his exemplification of the virtues in a life that has already begun to pass beyond the human. What Socrates loves is inaccessible to those attracted to him; but in him they find the images of that reality which he seeks, and they love in this one unique and peerless place that which he himself loves. So Socrates is loved *as* an individual without being loved *for* his individualities or particularities; he is loved rather for his embodiment of those transcendent values to which, Plato believed, we aspire for the sake of enduring happiness.

That, I suggest, is the meaning of Socratic incarnation. Inner goodness and beauty find themselves hidden in this eccentric, unhandsome snub-nosed flesh. And they are disclosed only through the operations of love. In his own divine beauty Socrates mediates between the Beautiful and those who long for it. So in a way he is like Jesus, who mediates the love of God; he who is in the bosom of the Father makes the Father known, welcoming the beloved disciple into his own bosom. But beyond this mediating relation between the eternal and the individual, Socratic love looks very different from Johannine love.

Come to this by thinking how love discloses identity for both Socrates and Jesus. In being attracted to Socrates his followers discover that, in spite of outward appearance, he instantiates true beauty and goodness. And in following Jesus, John comes through love to see a glory unrecognized by the world. Nevertheless, I have argued that for John it's the *experience of being loved by Jesus* that discloses divine glory. Plato's characters simply don't enjoy anything like that experience in the presence of Socrates. Alcibiades puts his arms around him, but Socrates will not receive him.

It's in the intimacy of loving, then, that Johannine love is set apart from Socratic love. John names those who know what it is to be loved by Jesus and to love him: Mary, Martha, Lazarus, Peter, the beloved disciple, indeed, all his own. Further, this family space (as we called it) has both divine and human dimensions. The relation between Father and Son is paradigmatic intimacy, a sharing of reciprocal love and divine glory. But it is extended most humanly toward the friends of Jesus. We remember that incarnation for Jesus requires not Socratic flesh as a temporary vehicle for self-containment but vulnerable human flesh— and tears and blood as well. At Lazarus's grave and in Mary's anointing, John gives us bodily gestures of shared intimate love. Socrates, by contrast, washes his own body to save the women the bother of caring for him.

Plato, as distinct from his character Socrates, does understand, as we have seen, something of intimacy between lovers who enjoy beauty and the images of the divine in each other. So we cannot say of *Platonic* love that it is utterly unlike Johannine family intimacy: it's unhelpful to place *erôs* and *agapê* in complete opposition. The likeness, though, cannot be carried very far. For in the end Plato's lovers are driven toward immortal Beauty, while John's Jesus lays down his life for his friends. This second strand in Johannine love, the grace and giving and self-sacrificing, cannot be forgotten; it's the very way into the intimacy of love. Plato's beloved could never experience Platonic love as grace. Even more, for Plato divine love could not be extended to an imperfect world; only the perfected are worthy candidates for god-belovedness, because they have become like the gods immortal. If Socrates experiences the care of the god, that must have something to do with his unique relationship to the divine. God, however, so loves the entire world that he gives his only Son; the Son so loves the Father that he surrenders his life to glorify him, and in this same act loves all his own to the death.

"Love is strong as death," affirms the Song of Solomon; passion flares fiercer than flame, unquenchable by flood. So strong is our hold on the objects of our love that we will not surrender them to the inevitable. But can we succeed? Socratic love overcomes death by directing its attention only to the immortal; Johannine love gives up its own life—but resurrection and glory follow upon its dying. In our final section we must confront our own deaths and loves along with Socrates and Jesus.

Love and Death

On any list of items about which we are absolutely certain, our own deaths will have high place. For creatures so thirsty for knowledge that we will run toward its mirages, something this certain might be expected to play a significant role in shaping our experience. But in spite of our professed love for the truth, this one is not easily embraced; we much prefer to think it the mirage upon which we may safely close our eyes.

Or at least that is so for our own deaths. About human mortality in general we can afford to feel differently. After all, there seems no universal judgment grounded in better empirical evidence than that all human beings are mortal. We can hardly deny the continuous passing out of existence of the members of our race, whose lives are outspanned by fir trees and tortoises. The incontrovertible dead give silent witness to the mortality of those yet living. Upon their witness we have shaped significant social and economic practices; we have even developed sophisticated ways of predicting rates and patterns of dying among our various populations. Yet the simple incontestable move from "all" to "I" remains difficult to confront. For the certainty of my death *is experienced* in very different ways by me and by, say, my insurance company.

One difference that might seem a trifle academic is that I don't have the same epistemological relation to my death as to anybody else's. Less tersely: I come to know that others have died by observing their deaths or by believing the witness of those who have access to the appropriate evidence; but I cannot verify through a similar observation or witness that I have myself died. There's a deeply felt tension, then, between my certainty of this future event and the way it lies beyond the usual conditions for my knowing that an event has come about.

It seems, moreover, that my apprehension of my mortality has different roots than my insurance company's certitude. The company achieves its knowledge through observation and calculation, I through raw and unbidden experience. About most of what I know I have to be educated—about the function of my liver or the location of my spleen—but untutored experience itself discloses a basic fear of my ceasing to be. Philosophers and psychologists will refine accounts of this feeling, arguing whether it should be called dread or angst or ontological anxiety or something else but we all know what it is. Some of us can date it: it gave me a bad summer around my twelfth birthday after I watched a man collapse past resuscitation during a silly picnic game. Ruptured spleen, they said; but they could have said anything about internal organs, or tumors, or humors or spirits or strokes—I still would have felt the precariousness of my own existence, its dependence upon causes outside my control. My guts knew this, apart from whatever cognitive desires or aversions I had. Our apprehension of mortality grows from roots in our biology, pushed up by adrenaline and hormones.

Because I experience the eventuality of my death in ways not available to a corporation, that corporation and I behave differently in the attention we are willing to accord its certainty. My insurance company works my death into its actuarial tables, assigning me numerical values in a complex set of statistics. It behaves in a highly rational manner in assessing risks, setting costs, calculating dividends, and so on. But my behavior over my certain dying is very different indeed. I think about it when I review my insurance policies (though my agent is careful to be guardedly hypothetical about its timing), on Ash Wednesday when my priest smudges darkly with her thumb across my forehead, and in other confrontations—unwilled as at that summer picnic or at funerals; or willing, as in this act of writing. But otherwise? Not often; I love life.

To render a detailed account of what it is to love life would be tedious and happily unnecessary, for two points will suffice. First, it's *my* life that's dear to me, not life-in-general. What death threatens is that locus of experience which is mine: call it my "soul" or my "self" or my "world," as long as you qualify it by the "my." Yet this possessive has strange features, even beyond the logical oddity of an "I" as bare, blank owner separable from "my" thoughts, feelings, and experiences. I stand in a unique relation to my life that nobody else can enjoy, and that characterizes no other object. My life is precious to me not as any other possessions—I might or might not own them—but as that which is ineradicably my own. You and I might share parts of our lives, but shared experiences aren't divided like pies cut down the middle: there's a *completeness* to my place in the world, which might be the object of your empathy but never your habitation. So in loving my life, I cherish a structure in which nobody else could ever dwell.

A second point. That structure is more than a bare self, for included in my life is a large tangle of interests and loves. In loving my life I don't necessarily love only myself over against other people and things who aren't so favored. Sometimes I catch myself growing selfish or inattentive; but by and large what's dear to me reaches past my self to family and friends, the solving of problems, cooking, music, the poignancy of the world—but I said such details were unnecessary. In caring sometimes distractedly, sometimes passionately, my love turns toward the good of others and can seek that good without always having regard for my own welfare.

Anxiety over my death, then, shakes the foundations of my own being as that structure without which I have no experiences; but it also shakes everything within this structure. Though I care about not being around, the strong flavor of that care is *loss* of every last thing, regardless of how much or how little it is loved.

Our biology blindly urges us to survival and the propagation in perpetuity of those just like us; Amen, answers our caring humanity, Amen, Amen. And yet all the laws of our striving and loving can never prevail against the gravity of death: down, down we go.

And then?

But what voice speaks this *And then?* Surely it's only the echo of love's futile hope, unwilling to acknowledge the finality, the nullity, the unquestionableness of death. Perhaps so. We cannot in this study become too dismissive of love's hope, however. In the liturgy of commendation at a Christian funeral the voices of faith join together:

You only are immortal, the creator and maker of all;
and we are mortal, formed of the earth,
and to earth we shall return.
For so you did ordain when you created me, saying
"You are dust, and to dust you shall return."
All of us go down to the dust;
yet even at the grave we make our song:
Alleluia, alleluia, alleluia.

These words paradoxically give death its due, but not the last word. They suggest that in singing to God with loving confidence we may also sing to our anxiety over our own dying.

Both Socrates and Jesus reveal love's work on anxiety over death. We'll find some contrasts, though, in how they would have us approach our dying, contrasts that will turn on the difference between immortality and resurrection. So it's time to shake off the weight of dead certainties in order to learn what we may, first from the example of Socrates.

Immortality: The Remedy of Socratic Love

Throughout our studies Plato's Socrates has epitomized rational self-control over both body and emotions. When thinking about the good dying that he does, we commented on the way his somatic containment manifests itself as courage in the face of death. Here I want to probe further into the nature and ground of Socrates' attitude.

We may return to the *Apology* first, where, as the reader knows, death's sentence waits to be spoken at the end. Neither here nor in the other dialogues about his last days does Socrates let slip any sign of uneasiness. It's not until he is well into his defense that the subject of death comes up. He introduces it as a possible objection to his persistent philosophizing: why continue an activity that will bring about his death?

Socrates answers that it's inappropriate to engage in calculating likely outcomes of one's actions; attention should rather focus on the rightness of action and on goodness. But he then goes on to explain why death should not be avoided at any cost—that is, why self-preservation is not an overriding good. First, we know that some kinds of disgrace are worse than being killed (not avenging a friend's death is his example from the *Iliad*). Second, disobedience to one's superior out of cowardice is wrong, especially when that superior is the god. Both considerations place bare self-survival within a hierarchy of values, ranking it lower than honor and obedient courage. But there's a third point, about our beliefs rather than values. People think death to be the greatest evil; but it may in fact be the greatest of goods. We *just don't know*. So to fear death is act without epistemological warrant; it is the greatest and most culpable ignorance, a thinking oneself wise when one is not.

That's how, it seems, Socrates handles his anxiety about dying. He does not value the kind of disgraceful life that he would lead by avoiding death; and he deflates unwarranted beliefs about the evils of death. Because Plato permits Socrates no anxious thought, we are inclined to accept that this strategy succeeds in drawing death's sting. Nevertheless, it's difficult to prescribe it widely as a remedy for others. This calm Socrates, master of his words, does not seem to appreciate the diseased nature of our fear of dying.

That fear is not helped by subsuming it under Fear as Expectation of Evils, then undercutting our claims to know that death will be a really bad thing. For suppose we yield to Socratic questioning: we won't be able to conclude that it's a really good thing, either. Only the not-knowing will remain. And, we want to point out, the disease of our fear lies precisely there, in the not-knowing. We cannot simply order ourselves to be indifferent about our ultimate fate: as we've been considering, it's all that we have and are that's at stake. Nor does the cure come by knowing the disgraces of fleeing death, simply because we cannot compare this disvalue with the unknown values or disvalues of death. Besides, even when I clearly value something like health above other states, that doesn't by itself necessarily dampen down my quickening fear of the surgery I'm sure is necessary to that end.

These words of Socrates cannot argue us out of our fear, then: but perhaps Plato knew that. For the *Apology* closes with different words about death. Socrates mounts another argument, of this form: Death is either A or B, but A is not bad and B is even better; therefore there is reason to hope for good in death. That seems to contain more certainty than his earlier ignorance permitted, for a reason I'll come to next; but first let's flesh out the argument itself. Socrates proposes that death is either cessation of awareness or else removal to another world. The first would be like a dreamless sleep, which by all standards is better than most of the nights, and the days, that we have spent. The second would locate us in a world of the immortals, where real justice would be done and Socrates could carry on with philosophy. Now it doesn't take prodigious skill to generate perplexity about these alternatives. The analogy between dreamless sleep and death isn't secure: there's *no waking up* in this alternative, and that makes all the difference to whether it's good. Nor is the dreamlessness in the alternative secure, as Hamlet feared. As for the other world: on what grounds may hope believe the old stories about the immortals? Why posit real justice and philosophy instead of their mere shadows among the thin shades of Hades? Is this the best Socrates can do—to chase fear with such words?

It's important, I think, to remember where his argument comes in the *Apology*. Socrates is no longer answering objections about his conduct; he instead opens his mind to the members of the jury who had believed in his innocence. Since they don't think him guilty of irreligion, they are in a position to understand the care of the god, under which no harm will befall a good person in life or death. That's the confidence that displaces fear in Socrates. More: Socrates advances his argument after his revelation about the amazing silence of his sign during the whole proceedings. His confidence receives its confirmation from his own experience of what he regards as divine care—or, in terms from our last chapter, from his obedience to the god, his readiness to take the outcome of the trial as an expression of the divine will. It is this confidence that closes off those negative possibilities that I raised about his postmortem condition. His words are employed not to chase the fear of death by themselves but to work out the likely meanings of his hope.

This reading of the *Apology* finds, then, that for Plato's Socrates the fear of death is not cured by words alone. Not that this is surprising: the *Phaedo* has quite explicit evidence that Plato understood our fear to be sometimes resistant to the operation of reason by itself.

Of course, the *Phaedo* contains a great deal of reasoning about death and the soul. But after Socrates has set out a couple of arguments for immortality, he senses that Simmias and Cebes remain fearful like children that the soul will not survive its separation from the body. Cebes laughs, but confesses of a child within who fears death as if it were a bogeyman. In response Socrates prescribes the singing of spells every day to charm this child—adding that when they have searched Greece for a charmer, they may find that they themselves are best capable of that task. In bringing back to the self the responsibility for handling the fear of death, Plato discourages the search for an external remedy that would excise or mask that fear without our having to confront it fully on our own.

The language of song, spells, and charms reminds us that the confrontation must engage something other than reason. And the notion of spell recurs at the end of the eschatological myth Socrates relates: although we can never be sure that we've got right the story about our postmortem fate, still we should repeat it *to ourselves like a spell.* That, he says, will give the virtuous person confidence about his own soul.

We may not be sure about getting such stories right: yet we continue to need them because we cannot be confident, either, about the powers of reason to get right the hard things about the afterlife. Simmias worries that certain knowledge about death and the soul is beyond human capacity, and even when the final argument seems to prove immortality to everyone's satisfaction, his embrace remains conditional because of human weakness. Socrates' own attitude is similar: because full knowledge is impossible in our embodied condition, we must constantly scrutinize our thinking. Nonetheless, our inability to achieve rational closure harbors a temptation against which Socrates warns us. It's *misology,* coming to hate argument itself. Finding this or that piece of reasoning inadequate, we might slip into suspicion about the whole rational enterprise—and then blame argument for what is rather our own misuse and misapprehension. There is truth about the soul's fate to be won, and we must not lose courage in the search.

But is even good Socratic reasoning sufficient to allay mortal anxiety? Imagine a community of readers who found themselves persuaded by the cumulative efforts of the *Phaedo*'s arguments to establish the immortality of the soul: they would have put to rest for themselves Cebes' worry that the soul would not persist with agency and intelligence. Would they, however, be satisfied with the grounding of Socrates' own conviction, expressed so categorically at the dialogue's beginning, that he will enter the presence of gods who are wise and good? That conviction is the only one that permits him to welcome death without resentment or fear. How does he come into his certainty about the quality of his experience after death? And how does this certainty operate upon anxiety and fear?

The answer is to be discovered not so much in the *Phaedo*'s arguments as in its claims about the way Socrates has been living his life all along. In pursuing philosophy he has already *practiced dying* for some time. That, we understand, builds upon the meaning of death as separation of soul from body; Socrates has not been rehearsing what it would be like to fall into nonexistence. Soul does the knowing; body gets in the way of coming to know because of the distractions of pleasure and pain. Seeking wisdom thus requires the philosopher to place distance between himself and his body. What is it to die, then, but to finish off this leaving of the body? And because soul is thereby placed closer to the objects of its knowledge, why should the philosopher fear to gain that which he has so long sought? Besides, as an emotion that clouds and distracts the soul, fear in Socrates' account has a physical basis. And if one is withdrawing from the body, the power of fear recedes; fear becomes a counterfeit coin, given away for the true value of wisdom.

So from the *Phaedo* we understand that what matters in facing death is what one has loved in life. Where that is not one's physical place in the world, but rather the immutable objects of knowledge, there anxiety about the shaking of conditions of mortal existence loses its grip. Love casts out fear; or at least fear is banished in loving (as Augustine will later put it) what one cannot lose. It matters, then, where love is directed.

How would Socrates rightly direct his love in order to overcome mortal anxiety? The *Symposium* yields an answer, as we remember from having considered Socratic love there. The separation of soul from body in the practice of love's lesser mysteries is driven by the longing for beauty. Directed first at a particular beautiful body, love moves up the ladder to bodily beauty in general; then to artistic and institutional expressions, and to the beauty of science. The movement of Eros is a drive to overcome death, to seek not mutable objects but the changelessness of immortality, of knowledge, of beauty, of good. As the hold on all particulars is relaxed in the greater mysteries, the lover comes at last upon the vision of Beauty itself. The result is that one enjoys true virtue and contact with truth instead of their images, becoming if possible immortal and beloved of gods. The Socratic quest for goodness in all its forms, even holiness as that which the gods love, here finds its fulfillment. In causing us to suspect that his divinized Socrates has already entered into this fulfillment, Plato has secured him against mortality.

Anxiety about our death has a Socratic remedy, we may conclude. Its biological roots cannot continue their growth if we release attachment to our bodies, recognizing that the physical manifestations of fear are separable from our true identities. As for psychological dread over the certainty of our dying, it needs a wide-spectrum treatment. Argument discloses a rational belief in the immortality of the soul, so that we need not agonize over its continued existence after death. But our fears for what awaits us are addressed by directing our love in this life. We center right now our longings upon the immortal, withdrawing from the contingencies of the human enterprise, the entanglements so bound to disappoint us. We realize our immortality even within the time of this mortal life, and so for us death itself dies, or at least fades into a mirage. More particularly, Socrates himself experiences signs of the care of the god for him as he approaches his own dying; and although he cannot say with accuracy what form that care will take, he advocates singing to ourselves likely tales of charm and enchantment.

The Loving in the Dying of Jesus

In returning to Jesus and Johannine love we change the objects of loving: not the eternal Forms, but Jesus' own friends and the eternal Father. We also reclothe ourselves in the vulnerabilities of human flesh. Amid this mortality and intimacy, death reasserts its power: death matters more for Jesus than for Socrates. The better to understand this, we will recover here some of our observations from the synoptic writers as well as from John.

Jesus does not bring to his dying the kind of speaking Socrates employs. To put the difference succinctly: Socrates spins arguments and tales about the afterlife, while Jesus says practically nothing about it. True, John's Jesus repeatedly promises that the eternal life he brings means resurrection from the dead; and he raises Lazarus in that anticipation. But what any life beyond this world would be like isn't hinted at in Platonic-type myths or stories in the Gospels, nor are there other Socratic remedies for anxiety. In John, Jesus goes "to prepare a place," about which it is sufficient to know only two things, that it is the Father's house and that there's room enough for all the family. As for the Jesus of the synoptics, none of the power of his language in parable is ever put into the service of images about life after death. All of his talk about the kingdom of heaven places that territory not in some postmortem space in the skies but unsettlingly across the geography of our human living. We can't quite say that gospel language falters in giving us clues to the afterlife, because the attempt is hardly made at all.

Nor does Jesus have available for himself the kinds of charms and enchantments Socrates recommended as antidote to anxiety. The Jesus of Matthew and Mark sang with his disciples on the night of his betrayal before leaving for the garden. But what he sang had in all likelihood dark tones. It is fair to assume that the singing was of the hymns prescribed for Passover: Psalms 113 and 114 in the first part of the evening, then after supper and more wine, Psalms 115 to 118. Read sometime these words for yourself in this context: in place of the sweet consolations of an afterlife, you will discover layered ironies about a divine deliverance from death, which Jesus must have longed for as he entered Gethsemane.

As for arguments about the immortality of the soul, there are none in the Gospels—naturally enough, for that is not a metaphysical belief we could attribute to Jesus. Yet we don't find arguments for the resurrection of the body, either, despite the fact that all of the Evangelists give Jesus this firm conviction. Because the Sadducees deny resurrection, the synoptic Jesus takes on their challenge about its incoherence; this brief bit of reasoning, however, serves not to establish the belief but only to clear away one misconception about it.

No: the logical ground of Jesus' conviction about resurrection remains hidden from the gospel reader. It seems that Jesus just knows it, as he just knows that he is to go up to Jerusalem and be put to death. Yet we can add one observation of great importance: his belief has the character of confidence in God. That comes out in his counter to the Sadducees, that God is God of the living and not the dead. And it is clearly the Johannine view about Jesus' own glorification as return to the intimate love of the Father.

It's worth stressing, I think, that Jesus' confidence in God is not at all like Socratic thinking about the nature of soul, designed to get at whatever truth about immortality is available to human intelligence. There's a conventional picture of resurrection as an event on the Day of Judgment, in which bodies get raised up or reconstituted to reunite with souls that have persisted since death—a picture that incorporates biblical resurrection with Greek metaphysics in order to come up with an account of the current status of the dead. But we have no textual reason to put this thinking into the mind of the Gospels' Jesus. Metaphysics doesn't provide him even minimal comfort.

What must be said in addition, however, is that Jesus' confidence in God does not bring with it anything like Socratic calmness about death.

For Jesus, to die is not to slip out of a temporary covering for the journey home; and therefore to fear death is not anxiously to anticipate that the separation might be painful, the destination inhospitable. Jesus' attitude seems to have no purchase on any notion of a perduring self. Instead, his language and behavior suggest that he faces the prospect of death not as separation but as disintegration and dissolution, the loss of the self.

Given all the talk of glory in John, the claim that death is self-loss may be clearer in the case of the Jesus of the synoptics. Recall our study of the silence of Matthew's Jesus—his preoccupation with violence, muzzling, throwing out, contrasted with watchfulness and perseverance for the right moment. What makes sense of Jesus' struggle over intention and motivation is the utter incompatibility between his death and the glory of the kingdom. It's not, I've argued, that he sees the first as the cost of the second; rather, he can't sort out how both can fit together in the will of the Father. So the spilling of that costly perfume becomes the symbol of his death: the loss of something precious, without utility for another purpose. Only fear of a loss this great explains his Gethsemane *agônia,* his plea to let the cup pass if possible. And only an experience of tumbling into that loss in spite of his faithful obedience could unleash that last godforsaken cry.

As we've seen, John's account of the Passion and crucifixion gives us a Jesus who has prepared himself for death and who dies in a more intimate setting, without public clamor and the sympathetic reactions of nature. That sense of control over his dying might be thought to betray a view of death softer than self-disintegration. We should not be misled. Although the time of his *agônia* comes before the garden, John's Jesus is still troubled, and must pray to set his own anxious heart at rest about his impending hour. Moreover, his very imagery about his body discloses the same sense of loss we have found in the synoptic Gospels: think of the grain of wheat that must fall into the ground and die, of the bread which is his flesh. These are images of the disintegration of identity: seeds rot so that something new may grow; bread and drink sustain by being consumed. The real flesh-and-blood Jesus must face the dissolution of the constituents of his being if he is to give life to the world.

That, I submit, brings his facing of death close to the kind of fear I experience before that dead certainty. Because the same degree of certainty is never achieved by arguments about my own immortality, reason can't quite manage to pull death's sting. So I want to know how it is that Jesus overcomes this too-familiar anxiety.

As we know well from Matthew and Mark, the anxious struggle of Gethsemane resolves itself into silence and the emptying out of agency; from Luke we understand that this is also a most active embracing of the will of the Father. Jesus handles anxiety, then, through prayer and obedience. That's important: the not-knowing that feeds mortal fear does not have an easy remedy. Rather Jesus must move toward death able to say only *that,* and not *how,* his dying fits with God's will. Attentively waiting upon the Father he addresses, he hands over uncertainty into silence.

John adds: all this Jesus does in love. We suspected as much, for he must have seen his obedience in light of the Great Commandment to love God and neighbor. But only John shows us what a difference love makes to the dying of Jesus. Love glorifies his death. And where love of that sort is, there can be no room for anxiety. Socrates was right about the potency of a properly directed affection; Jesus, though, does not withdraw from human contingencies to center his love upon the immortal objects of knowledge alone. He is able to confront the radical loss of self through a complexity of loving that has three distinguishable aspects.

The deep ground of the loving in the dying of Jesus is, I propose, his own experience of *being loved by the Father.* That this characterization of the relation of Jesus and the Father is unique to John we established earlier; we also noted at that time John's creation of an intimate family space through his use of locative prepositions and his notion of dwelling or abiding in one another. Though this closeness is best manifested in the eternal time of the prologue, the Word with God and the Son in the Father's bosom, nevertheless the Son who is in the world and away from the Father still knows that love. More to our point: he is able to locate his dying within that love. Precisely because he freely lays down his life, the Father loves him—and in addition, his own initiative of self-giving brings with it the ability to receive his life back again: *this command I have received from my Father* (10.18). That suggests a loving obedience, in which Jesus discovers the confidence that his unconstrained self-surrender will be answered by the gift of his life returned. He doesn't predict his resurrection on the basis of a metaphysics about the nature of the self, then; instead, he sees resurrection as the gift of a love that cherishes him so much that it will not permit his loss, real though it is, to continue.

Such a "seeing" itself requires a loving, for Jesus could not freely surrender his life unless this gift were also an expression of his own love back to the Father. His loving has the character of trust, whereas his Father's love is experienced as a sustaining and creative cherishing. Trusting love casts out fear, not exactly because it loves what it cannot lose but more because it knows and returns a love that will not permit it to be lost.

To these two movements of love, from Father to Son and back again, we must add a third: for the loving in the dying of Jesus is directed also horizontally, to his own, his friends. And this third aspect has itself a double characterization, in that it is also God's love manifesting itself to the world. The name of this love is self-sacrifice for the sake of another's good, a giving so that others may come into the family of love. It may have its own contribution to the alleviation of mortal anxiety, in that love for another tends to displace inwardly focused attention. About that only those faced with the call to final sacrifice should testify, perhaps; but our own clumsy ministrations in the service of a less demanding love do teach us that extending a hand to another person has a way of relaxing the grip of self-concern.

It's his dying in Johannine love, then, that addresses the disintegrating loss of self that constitutes the stinging threat of death for the Jesus of the Gospels. The incarnate Son is no bright bearer of infrangible glory, able to keep intact the foundations of his own existence. His hour of death becomes the hour of glory because it is the experience, the requiting, and the manifestation of divine love in the midst of a most human contingency and surrender.

Now if, as I've maintained, John is able to appreciate the nature of glory as love in backward glance from Easter Day, then that perspective is also available to those who wish to learn something from John's Jesus about their own dying. What they encounter is a glorified Jesus, one whose experience of resurrection confirms the trust he displayed in the loving surrender of his life to the Father. That he received his life again from God, and was exalted into the fullness of the Father's presence, provides ground for the hope of their own resurrection. Even should they be unable to derive strong comfort from metaphysical reasoning about the nature of human souls—resurrection is not immortality—still they may order their love toward the God of Abraham, Isaac, and Jacob, God of the living, Father of Jesus Christ. Although they may not spin plausible Platonic tales about the life to come (resurrection will transform them with an unimaginable glory), they may faithfully sing hymns of praise and worship to their risen Lord. Prayer and liturgy, love and obedience, will be their remedies against the anxiety of death—if "remedy" can be the right term for disciplined practices which have to engage our very selves.

One more thing. In spite of differences between Jesus' dying and his own, Socrates wasn't wrong to practice his dying before his death. The follower of Jesus, too, must die to live. But that's not a Socratic recognition of one's immortality in the time of this mortal life; it's rather an entering into the meaning of resurrection.

Resurrection: Dying to Live in Love

This talk of dying is, I confess, unsettling. It reminds me of my mortality, but that's the least of it; what disturbs more deeply is its attack on my living in the present. Shouldn't I finish with Jesus and Socrates, put death to bed, and get out to live my own life in the world?

But if I try to ignore this business of dying, I also have to ignore the central sacraments of the Christian faith. The waters of baptism can't speak of cleansing without also speaking of death and burial. Nor can we discern body and blood in bread and wine without also discerning death. In baptism we participate in the death of Jesus; repeatedly in the Eucharist we make our remembrance, incorporating the elements of that death in our own flesh. For all their differences over sacramental theology, Christians believe that these rituals have significance for the relation of their own dying in the present to the death of Jesus in the past.

But isn't it best to expunge the morbidity from this language, to translate it into positive terms? The longstanding criticism that the Christian religion is life-denying and death-glorifying has ample evidence in its favor, much of it available to our own personal experiences. So I draw back from this language of dying-to-live. I can proffer all sorts of reasons why it is unwise and unhealthy to continue in this vein. One: I love my life, as I've said. It's precious to me, and not only for self-regarding interests, so why would I want to dwell on the idea of its loss? Two: it's frightening enough to contemplate the end of my life as the result of natural or accidental physical processes. Why raise the level of anxiety needlessly in a deliberate seeking to die in some spiritual sense? Three: this suspicious talk about spiritual dying must disguise a weird and even sick attitude toward life; only really disturbed people would allow themselves to be preoccupied with quasi-suicidal language. Four: maybe a few saints or mystics have employed vivid metaphors about dying; but surely the extremity of their rhetoric is best explained by their particular psychologies, without implication for my more normal life. Five: resurrection, not death, is the end of the story in the Christian Gospel, so we should be celebrating the mysteries and splendors of life, putting crucifixion firmly in the past. Six: . . . well, there must be yet another good reason to deflate this strange hyperbole of dying to self, to sanitize Christian vocabulary for the sake of my mental health. It'll come to me in a minute.

I do protest too much. When I stop piling up objection upon objection, I have to acknowledge that part of what's going on is that I am attempting to secure my existence against invasion—and further, that some of my defenses are insubstantial Styrofoam blocks. However understandable my desire to grasp the conditions and contents of my life, I don't have the power or the wisdom of a god. There's something fundamentally wrong in permitting my urge and care for life to seduce me with the pretense that I'm immortal. Moreover, if not honesty then my family and friends will press out my acknowledgment that some parts of my life ought not to be nourished or cherished. Of my self's flora some ought to become compost for the more wholesome or attractive; and I know I'd be a better self for the pruning and the dying.

Maybe I should make peace with my present dying in these terms, then. To take up my cross and die to self: that's to put the nails into my prideful self, my slothful self, my attention-seeking or my sulking self, and so on. Admittedly the imagery of putting unhealthy desires to death is too strong for contemporary taste, but at least the process moves toward self-improvement.

Yet it won't do. Of course I'd be a better self if I could lop off some sprouting malformations of will or irradiate the malignancies of desire. The problem lies in the relation between me (whoever I am) and all these negative selves that should be dealt with so severely. There are too many of them, frankly. Further, it's curious that I so readily objectify and externalize these "parts" as different selves or desires or impulses that are only accidentally mine. In fact, they don't always have the independent existence of an extraneous growth: I couldn't kill them off without damaging what I think of as the more truly me. (A small example: my sometimes unfortunate tendency to believe I know what's in other people's best interests isn't accidentally related to my genuine concern for their welfare and my willingness to help them discern their good.) Besides, I can't quite bring myself to believe that my heart will ever run out of resources to fashion new devices for old desires.

I'm becoming less comfortable, then, with the practicality and the very meaning of the idea that the "bad parts" of me should be the candidates for some metaphorical dying. Maybe I should not be surprised. If I'm attempting to find the significance of dying-to-live within the Passion, death, and resurrection of Jesus, then I have to remember the meaning of his death. He didn't negotiate a conditional surrender, or bargain about self-improvement. He emptied out his personal presence, inverted his authority, handed himself over to the will of the Father, obediently and in trusting self-sacrificial love.

Again I draw back: a few may be singled out for that imitation of Christ—a Becket or a More, but not the rest of us, surely? Obviously not: the chances of my dying a martyr's death are small indeed. But then I remember that the witness of Christian martyrs is nothing other than our common witness to God, that their surrender to death mirrors bodily the daily dying of the self.

There's nothing for it. I've got to look this death in the face. If my mind doesn't leap up with more objections, I'll stay still long enough to learn a few small things. First, I must recognize that the meaning of dying lies in letting go, in releasing my clamped-down grip on what is most fundamentally mine. As we saw, mortal anxiety fears that this surrender will cause everything dear to fall away into nothingness. So our hearts and guts shrink from dying-to-live as from an existential void. In fact, we are called not to embrace the void but to surrender the self. The difference may appear subtle, but it is profound: whether the letting go will drop us into the void is in God's hands, not ours. Otherwise, this dying would be the wish for self-destruction and not the expression of a loving trust.

Second, if my objections stay quiet I'll learn that this coming-to-an-end-of-the-self is in fact necessary. Love has already begun to teach me something of this lesson. We made note of the paradoxes of the self when we were faced with the self-surrender required for love's intimacy—the displacing of self-attention in the giving of love, the unguardedness needed to experience being loved, the metaphors of eating and being eaten that belong to *erôs* as well as Eucharist. We also saw, though, that intimacy couldn't survive a complete self-giving in death, for that finality would end the relationship. In what sense, then, can my dying-to-self be necessary? Yet how can it not be so? For think: this coming-to-an-end is what we've kept bumping up against all through these studies. That's particularly so around our deployment of language. Words came to their end in the silence of Jesus, who handed over in obedience his inability to sort out the meaning of the will of the Father and his own motivations. Words reach their limit in prayer, as we take up an elemental relation of address and attention toward God. In our attempts at obedient listening to God, our own words falter and get in the way; we have to quieten our hearts, discern the signs, heed the unconditional call of God even in our suffering. So much of the self is constituted in language that our willingness to hand over all of our scheming and conceptualizing, and to deposit our very beings into the divine care, cannot be better expressed than as a dying. And now I glimpse it: that dying is nothing but prayer, nothing but obedience, nothing but love.

And if it is an act of love, perhaps I could face my dying, and my death, were I to participate in some way in the kind of love we've discovered in John's presentation of Jesus. In handing back his life to his Father, Jesus experienced the creative and sustaining cherishing of God, who would not permit his final loss; he surrendered himself in an answering trust to God and on behalf of his own loved ones. His dying was a dying to live again in the resurrection of love and the fullness of the Father; but he could not know resurrection without death as self-loss.

Nor can I. But if I am given so to understand my dying, then I will be able to say a third thing. My dying-to-self is at the same time a *dying-into-God.* Nothing else will work; nothing else will matter. Disease and destruction lie on my path if I negate interests and desires out of self-loathing, if I seek the void as a dying-*for*-self. I don't have to do that in literal suicide to be destroyed; all those self-appointed martyrs bear witness to the disintegration that follows upon self-hatred, to bad dying without resurrection. Exemplary dying gives over the very conditions of my living to God, *but to God alone.* Just as Christian martyrs do not commit suicide, and thus their dying may be known as an act of obedience to God rather than self, so my dying-to-self must be motivated by a like witness. I do not die in surrender to the demands of lesser gods, of state or institution, or even friends, family, self. That would be to fragment the self and feed it to those who devour without return. On the contrary: those who die into God, we are told on good authority, die into Life and Love. To them it is given to receive their lives back again, not as immortal but in the power and grace of resurrection, even now in the time of this mortal life.

It is now Advent as I bring this chapter to its conclusion. The Christian year begins with the End, in anticipation of a coming Judgment; but it looks forward eagerly also to a Birth and a Beginning. "I had seen birth and death," says T. S. Eliot's magus, "but had thought they were different." He learned otherwise from "the hard and bitter agony" of that Birth; no longer at home with an alien people clutching their gods, he looked to another death to deliver him. We have more privilege than he: knowing how the story unfolds, we see past three trees on the low sky to a vacant tomb, the empty shell of death. For that Resurrection we, too, must die in that Death, however discomforting the paradox. For like birth, resurrection is sheer gift, beyond our ability to initiate or determine. Surrendering the defenses, pretensions, and inadequacies of our language and our very selves to God, we who haltingly follow the obedience of Jesus may share thereby in his resurrection—dying, to live in love in this world and in that world to come which will have no end, because it is the very life of God.

Index